CURRENT ISSUES IN DEVELOPMENTAL PEDIATRICS: THE LEARNING-DISABLED CHILD

CURRENT ISSUES IN DEVELOPMENTAL PEDIATRICS

Series Editors
Marvin I. Gottlieb
Peter W. Zinkus
Larry J. Bradford

CURRENT ISSUES IN DEVELOPMENTAL PEDIATRICS:
THE LEARNING-
DISABLED CHILD

Edited by

Marvin I. Gottlieb, M.D., Ph.D.

Professor of Pediatrics, Chief
Section of Developmental and Behavioral Pediatrics
University of Tennessee Center for the Health Sciences
Le Bonheur Children's Hospital and Medical Center
Memphis, Tennessee

Peter W. Zinkus, Ph.D.

Assistant Professor of Pediatrics, Clinical Psychologist
Section of Developmental and Behavioral Pediatrics
University of Tennessee Center for the Health Sciences
Memphis, Tennessee

Larry J. Bradford, Ph.D.

Director
Center for Communicative Disorders
The Menninger Foundation
Topeka, Kansas

GRUNE & STRATTON, INC.

A Subsidiary of Harcourt Brace Jovanovich, Publishers

New York   London   Toronto   Sydney   San Francisco

Grune & Stratton, Inc.
111 Fifth Avenue
New York, New York 10003

Distributed in the United Kingdom by
Academic Press, Inc. (London) Ltd.
24/28 Oval Road, London NW 1

Library of Congress Catalog Number 79-7709
International Standard Book Number 0-8089-1179-1

Printed in the United States of America

CONTENTS

FOREWORD

Pediatric priorities have been modified dramatically during the past decade to reflect the increasing concern for the child in educational jeopardy. Public and professional interests are evidenced by the Education for All Handicapped Children Act of 1975 (Public Law 94–142), the substantial emphasis in the 1976 recommended curriculum for Education and Assessment for Recertification in Pediatrics by the American Academy of Pediatrics, the growth of the Association for Children with Learning Disabilities, the numerous articles about the learning-disabled not only in professional journals but in the popular press as well, and the frequent dramatizations on television. The child with a learning disability is at high risk as a potential candidate for psychoeducational wastage. Ultimately, the child who is lost in the school system may manifest his frustrations in deviant adolescent behavior and depressed adult social productivity. It is not surprising that the child with impaired learning ability has generated a national anxiety as well as a formidable diagnostic/therapeutic challenge for health care professionals.

The pervasive problems of the learning-disabled child are usually multifaceted, influencing educational, psychological, and social development. Often the effects of the child's learning disability extend beyond the confines of the classroom to influence family and peer relationships. The complex nature of learning disorders necessitates a multidisciplinary intervention. Each member of the interdisciplinary team contributes a particular expertise which must eventually be amalgamated into a holistic diagnostic profile that characterizes the child's strengths and weaknesses.

The physician (particularly the pediatrician) has a significant role and responsibility in contributing to the early detection and management of the learning-disabled child. Frequently it is the physician who is expected to assemble and coordinate the interdisciplinary diagnostic/therapeutic effort. A prerequisite for accomplishing this assignment is a familiarity with the contributions to be furnished by a variety of disciplines: psychology, speech and language, special education, and social work, to name only a few. In addition to providing medical expertise, the physician should be capable of (1) interpreting multidisciplinary findings, (2) counseling with parents, children, and professionals, and (3) monitoring the child's progress. The physician is a most important advocate for the child with a learning disability. This responsibility necessitates keeping informed on relevant and related issues.

Since 1969 the University of Tennessee Center for the Health Sciences, Department of Pediatrics, has sponsored, in Memphis, an Annual Leigh Buring Memorial Conference that focuses on topics related to the learning-disabled child. The Ninth Annual Conference in April 1978 was a forum for the interdisciplinary consideration of *Developmental, Learning and Behavioral Disabilities: Causes, Considerations and Complications.* The major theme was a multidisciplinary exploration of the etiology, diagnosis, management, and complications of learning disorders. This conference was the inspiration to construct a textbook with broad considerations of the subject. The end result is volume one of *Current Issues in Developmental Pediatrics,* called *The Learning-disabled Child.* In this text—which, in time, will be followed by volumes exploring problems of communication, behavioral disorders, adolescent difficulties, and other issues in developmental pediatrics—modified versions of many of the papers presented at the 1978 conference have been included with chapters written especially for the book. The text represents an interdisciplinary effort, with particular relevance for physicians interested in the learning-disabled child.

The editors do *not* intend that this book be used as a definitive textbook on learning disabilities. Hopefully, it will serve to stimulate interest in a subject vital to the quality of life for *all* children—their potentials for learning. Several of the chapters are devoted to reviewing issues and concepts about the mechanisms of learning and the factors that jeopardize this ability.

The first section of the volume is primarily an introduction to the medical, neurological, psychological, and educational bases for learning disorders. In addition, the psychosocial complications of impaired learning, as they affect child and adolescent, are reviewed. The second section is an overview that focuses on the testing materials available for diagnostic intervention: medical, psychological, and educational. Overall, the volume should serve as a vehicle for gaining familiarity with the various specialists interested in the learning-disabled child.

Admittedly, *Current Issues in Developmental Pediatrics: The Learning-disabled Child* is medically oriented. The theme of learning disabilities, however, is universal for all professionals dedicated to the welfare of children. The editors would hope that *all* members of the health care team will find materials of interest within their own area of expertise and gain better insight into the contributions of their colleagues in other disciplines. The problems of the learning-disabled cross professional lines. Learning disabilities are everyone's problem!

Marvin I. Gottlieb
Peter W. Zinkus
Larry J. Bradford

CONTRIBUTORS

DANIEL S. BEASLEY, Ph.D., Professor and Chairman, Department of Speech Pathology and Audiology, Memphis Speech and Hearing Center, Memphis State University, Memphis, Tennessee

GEORGE W. BROWN, M.D., Pediatrician, Lovelace-Bataan Medical Center; Adjunct Associate Professor of Special Education, Albuquerque, New Mexico

JAMES S. BROWN, M.D., Commissioner of Mental Health–Mental Retardation, State of Tennessee; Associate Professor, Department of Pediatrics, University of Tennessee Center for the Health Sciences, Memphis, Tennessee

C. HAL BRUNT, M.D., Associate Professor, Department of Psychiatry and Pediatrics; Director, Division of Child and Adolescent Psychiatry, University of Tennessee Center for the Health Sciences, Memphis, Tennessee

BRENDA M. COLE, M.A., Clinical Instructor, Department of Speech Pathology and Audiology, Memphis Speech and Hearing Center, Memphis State University, Memphis, Tennessee

JAN COVINGTON, M.A., Clinical Instructor, Department of Speech Pathology and Audiology, Memphis Speech and Hearing Center, Memphis State University, Memphis, Tennessee

DIXIE R. CRASE, Ph.D., Associate Professor of Child Development, College of Education, Memphis State University, Memphis, Tennessee

AMY P. DIETRICH, M.Ed., Educational Diagnostician, Child Development Center, University of Tennessee Center for the Health Sciences, Memphis, Tennessee

WILSON L. DIETRICH, Ed.D., Professor and Chairman, Department of Special Education and Rehabilitation, Memphis State University, Memphis, Tennessee

HARRIS C. FAIGEL, M.D., Assistant Clinical Professor of Pediatrics, Boston University School of Medicine; Director, University Health Services, Brandeis University, Waltham, Massachusetts; Director, Adolescent Medicine, Kennedy Memorial Hospital for Children, Boston, Massachusetts

JOHN R. GOFF, Ph.D., Clinical Neuropsychologist and Assistant Member, The Neuropsychology Laboratory, Division of Psychiatry/Psychology/Social Services, St. Jude Children's Research Hospital, Memphis, Tennessee

JOHN F. GRIFFITH, M.D., Professor and Chairman, Department of Pediatrics, University of Tennessee Center for the Health Sciences; Medical Director, Le Bonheur Children's Hospital and Medical Center, Memphis, Tennessee

VIRGINIA I. NUNN, Ed.D., Assistant Dean for Academic Affairs, College of Medicine, Clinical Instructor, Department of Pediatrics, University of Tennessee Center for the Health Sciences, Memphis, Tennessee

DANIEL J. ORCHIK, Ph.D., Associate Professor of Audiology, Memphis Speech and Hearing Center, Memphis State University, Memphis, Tennessee

MARY J. SANDERS, M.A., Psychologist, Clinic for Exceptional Children, Department of Pediatrics, University of Tennessee Center for the Health Sciences, Memphis, Tennessee

JUDITH SCHAPIRO, Ed.D., Associate Professor and Graduate Program Director, Educational Foundations and Special Programs, Old Dominion University, School of Education, Norfolk, Virginia

ANNE THOMPSON, M.A., Speech/Language Pathologist, Clinic for Exceptional Children, Department of Pediatrics, University of Tennessee Center for the Health Sciences, Memphis, Tennessee

ROBERT G. THOMPSON, M.D., Pediatrician, Private Practice 1400 Hatcher Lane, Columbia, Tennessee 38401

Part I
DEVELOPMENTAL AND BEHAVIORAL PERSPECTIVES

1

THE NEUROLOGY OF LEARNING DISABILITIES: AN OVERVIEW

The child with learning difficulty presents a formidable challenge to the neurologist. Most learning-disabled children do not manifest classical signs of nervous system dysfunction, as assessed by standard methods of testing. Often the neurological findings are minimal and of debatable significance since they are sometimes found in children without learning or behavior problems. These include slightly impaired motor coordination, hyperactive reflexes, hyperkinetic behavior, clumsiness, and perceptual difficulties. In the child with learning difficulty the presence of these minor neurological signs assume significance because they are thought to be indicative of an antecedent insult to the developing nervous system. Combinations of findings commonly occur in learning-disabled children. As a result, labels have been assigned and a literature has evolved that unfortunately often lacks precision. Minimal brain dysfunction (MBD), hyperkinetic syndrome, the "clumsy-child" syndrome, and perceptual motor disability (PMD) are now popular terms to describe the learning-disabled. It is important to emphasize that these are descriptive terms *only* and do not convey specific information regarding etiology, pathogenesis, cerebral localization, prognosis, or therapy. Nevertheless, certain clinical factors occur with significant frequency to make this terminology useful, providing the reader is aware of its limitations.

The combination of learning and behavioral difficulties has been categorically referred to as *minimal brain dysfunction* (MBD). This designation implies that the child is normal intellectually but has learning and behavioral problems. MBD is characterized by impaired perception, language, fine motor skills, memory, impulse control, and

3

attention. The clumsy child frequently has perceptual motor disabilities. Hyperkinesis may be a feature of all of the syndromes mentioned.

THE INTERRELATIONSHIP BETWEEN HYPERKINESIS, PERCEPTUAL MOTOR DISABILITY, MINIMAL BRAIN DYSFUNCTION, AND THE CLUMSY-CHILD SYNDROME

The etiology of these conditions is unclear, but, presumably, there are a number of mechanisms which could be accountable. It has been observed that certain pharmacologic agents reduce hyperactivity and improve concentration, suggesting a biochemical basis for the motoric symptomatology. The precise mechanism of this is not understood. Certain of the stimulant drugs are known to effect the central monamines, which may induce altered metabolism of serotonin, dopamine, or norepinephrine. Rapoport, Quinn, and Lamprecht (1974) compared the levels of peripheral dopamine beta hydroxylase with the severity of hyperactivity. They found a correlation, suggesting exaggerated neurotransmitter activity in this condition. A biochemical basis for learning difficulties, however, is still unproven; as a result, classification of these disorders is difficult to formulate. Therapy is frequently empiric and is based on experience rather than sound scientific principles.

Very little is known about the neurology of *hyperkinesis,* and its existence as an entity with a neuroanatomic substrate has been contested (Bax, 1978). Aggressivity and impulsivity are components of certain psychiatric syndromes and certainly are observed in many young patients who are mentally retarded. Hyperkinesis may also be a by-product of environmental stresses in an otherwise normal child. A basic question for the neurologist is whether there is an attention center, or centers, in the brain largely responsible for fixating attention and, if so, is the hyperkinetic state a result of altered brain activity in these focal regions. Admittedly, this is an attractive hypothesis in one sense, since there are often no other signs of neurologic dysfunction to suggest a diffuse cerebral process. A related hypothesis suggests that hyperkinesis results from mild but significant injury to the cerebral cortex in the late prenatal or perinatal period. The injury or insult results in a maturational lag in brain development, either in synaptogenesis or neurotransmitter function. This would impair information processing in the young nervous system and lead to inattention and restless behavior.

Synaptogenic or neurotransmitter dysfunction could explain the *perceptual-motor disabilities* observed among these children, resulting in impaired reception, processing, and storage of sensory information. As a result, the child's nervous system cannot retrieve information efficiently in response to sensory stimuli. Similarly, there are disturbances in correlating sensory inputs with associated motor functions. Consequently there is an array of difficulties involving sensory-motor responses, which normally proceed at a subconscious level and which are critical for the learning process. In the absence of a sophisticated and integrated neural activity, a child would be unable to associate automatically a visual or an auditory stimulus with the appropriate memory in order to activate the expected verbal or motor response. A perceptuomotor handicap of this type would cause academic difficulties in the early grades, particularly in reading and writing. Form design, orientation, and sequencing skills are particularly difficult for these children to master.

Perceptuomotor disabilities may be the predominent or only problem a child has to account for his or her learning difficulty. It may, however, be part of the syndrome of *minimal brain dysfunction,* which encompasses additional features including hyperkinesis and motor incoordination. The latter is frequently demonstrable in the learning-disabled child. It interferes with his ability to perform many routine motor functions. An extreme example of this has been referred to by Gubbay and his associates (1965) as the *clumsy-child syndrome.* These children, predominently males, experience difficulties in coordination and cognition, probably as a result of a maturational lag in parietal lobe function. The poor school performance exhibited by these children is in part due to their lowered self-image, developed as a result of an inability to compete physically. This, in turn, leads to poor peer relationships and subsequently to antisocial behavior. The motor difficulties and cognitive problems have a tendency to improve spontaneously with age. Although the precise neuroanatomic basis for this disorder is unclear, it is important to stress that a good prognosis exists for these children. This is predicated on an assumption that they are not labeled as failures or forced to compete in school at a time when they can easily become discouraged and frustrated by their difficulties. The student with the clumsy-child syndrome requires a carefully designed curriculum and a sensitive and well-qualified instructor.

The conditions discussed thus far share several features: (1) they are often interrelated, (2) they may be expressed in a single patient, and (3) they may improve spontaneously with age. The clinical picture of a 7-year-old with MBD is strikingly similar to what is considered normal for a 2- to 3-year-old. These observations, particularly when noted in children who are intellectually normal, have led many to conclude that the underlying problem is a "maturational lag" rather than a structural brain defect. The mechanism of delayed maturation is speculative, but it is presumably biochemical in origin. This could involve synthesis or metabolism of neurotransmitters, or possibly membrane receptor activity in select areas of the brain. It may be related in part to an anatomic defect involving delayed synaptogenesis or possibly a delay in the maturation of neurofeedback circuits.

Even though this is highly speculative, it is conjectured that the explanation will probably prove to be chemical, since impulse transmission is a neurochemical event. Regardless, the practical importance of these observations is that a significant percentage of young children who present to physicians and other medical therapists have a good prognosis. A favorable prognosis, however, assumes that their difficulties in the early school years are not overstressed to the point of producing excessive frustration, anxiety, or negative attitudes about the learning process. If a patient has been evaluated thoroughly, and no other explanation is found to account for a learning or behavior disorder, the therapy should emphasize measures to minimize parental and patient anxiety. Programs should be avoided that stress overly aggressive efforts to condition a nervous system that is not yet ready to process new information. Children should receive special educational support in a noncompetitive school setting. It is of utmost importance that the children be reassured that they are normal intellectually. They require continued support and encouragement during the difficult period when they are noncompetitive learners. Too much emphasis on therapy only reinforces their feelings of incompetency and may cause frustrations to the point of inducing hostility for the entire learning experience. Unfortunately, this occurs too often and represents a failure that has serious consequences, not only for the patient, but for society in general.

SPECIFIC NEUROLOGIC DISORDERS ASSOCIATED WITH LEARNING AND BEHAVIOR PROBLEMS

Seizures

Although seizures are frequently mentioned, when the subject of learning disorders is discussed, they rarely account for the patient's academic difficulty. Recurrent absence seizures (petit mal attacks), or other brief seizures, result in momentary lapses of consciousness. If these seizures are repetitive, they may resemble daydreaming, disinterest, or lack of attention. If unrecognized and of significant frequency, they could lead to problems both at home and in school. Children who are referred to physicians for evaluation for "staring" or "daydreaming" need to be examined carefully. If the cause for this behavior is unclear, an electroencephalogram is indicated. The child with even very brief seizures usually has other clinical features that, in addition to altered consciousness, help make the diagnosis. There may be sudden postural lapses, such as head nodding or ocular signs, fluttering of the eyelids or eye deviation. It is particularly important for the parents and teachers to note these since seizure activity usually cannot be reproduced at the time of the neurological examination.

Psychomotor seizures may be associated with a significant behavioral component, particularly hyperkinesis in children in all ages (Ounsted, Lindsay, & Norman, 1965). In young children lip smacking and various other automatisms frequently occur during the course of a seizure. Episodes of inappropriate fright or bizarre behavior may also be manifestations of this type of seizure. Although seizures of this type are usually obvious to even the unskilled observer, diagnosis may be delayed for prolonged periods. The basis for delayed diagnosis relates to the fact that the behavioral features are frequently more prominent than the motor signs which most associate with seizures. Whenever episodic bizarre behavior recurs, with or without other seizure manifestations, the child deserves careful neurologic evaluation prior to any consideration for psychiatric intervention or therapeutic attempts in behavior modification programs.

Most children who have seizures, however, experience difficulty learning and behave poorly for other reasons. Excessive anticonvulsant medication or idiosyncratic reactions to certain of these antiepileptic drugs can produce clinical symptoms such as inattention, hyperkinesis, depression, or bizarre behavior at home and in school (Hutt et al., 1968; Livingston, 1972). Children who present with these clinical features will obviously experience difficulty with learning and relating to their peers. Treatment consists of careful modification of the drug regimens under expert medical supervision. Occasionally in children with epilepsy who are on therapy, the underlying brain disorder causes personality changes, but this is the exception and usually behavioral problems are present prior to institution of anticonvulsants.

Hydrocephalus

Another condition that deserves particular attention in a discussion on the neurology of learning disorders is hydrocephalus. Individuals with hydrocephalus frequently have relatively well-preserved verbal skills even though motor performance and other higher cortical functions are significantly impaired (Tew & Laurence, 1975). The reasons for this are not clearly defined, although the pattern of ventricular enlargement in progressive hydrocephalus suggests one mechanism. The inferior or temporal horn is usually the last portion of the lateral ventrical to dilate as the hydrocephalic process evolves (Yakovlev, 1947). It is reasonable to assume that there is relative preservation of memory and language function, early in the course of the disease, in as much as that part of the brain is spared the compressive injury, which occurs as the ventricles progressively enlarge.

Hydrocephalus is a treatable disorder, when recognized early and before irreversible injury to the brain occurs. In the patient with open cranial sutures the diagnosis can be made, or suspected, on the basis of progressive head enlargement. In older children or adults hydrocephalus classically presents with signs of raised intracranial pressure. At times the process can arrest spontaneously before nervous system function is significantly impaired. A child with hydrocephalus may present with only slightly hyperactive lower limb reflexes and a discrepancy between verbal and performance IQs. If this combination is found in a child with a large head, or even in someone with a normal head circumference, it is a valuable diagnostic clue and should prompt additional investigations to exclude hydrocephalus.

Mental Retardation

Mental subnormality is an obvious explanation for learning difficulty. Intellectual subnormality, however, may not be detected early because a child may "look normal" and function reasonably well in some areas. From a practical standpoint, it is only the child with mild or borderline mental retardation that presents diagnostic confusion for the trained teacher or therapist. Typically, these children may progress in the early grades. They often escape detection until mathematical concepts and problem solving are introduced into the curriculum. The etiology of most cases of mild mental subnormality is usually unclear, particularly if the parents are intellectually normal and there is no antecedent history of acquired insults to the nervous system in the perinatal period or following.

Infections or trauma may result in mental subnormality, associated with significant behavioral and learning difficulties (Eichenwald, 1962). In some children hyperkinesis, short attention span, and minor personality changes may be the only residual signs of infection or head injuries. It is speculative whether drugs administered early, and for prolonged periods during infancy, affect subsequent behavioral function and impair learning. This subject requires more intensive and critical study, particularly at this time when very small, ill newborns are being treated with potentially toxic compounds for prolonged periods.

Hearing Loss

A discussion of the neurology of learning disorders would be grossly incomplete without reference to deafness. The cochlea is particularly vulnerable to injury from viral and bacterial infections as well as from toxic drugs and other compounds. The deafness associated with mumps, bacterial meningitis, congenital rubella, and hyperbilirubinemia are well known. These conditions represent only a few among many of the ways that this target organ is irreparably injured.

Advanced hearing loss can usually be detected early. The educational needs of deaf children can generally be managed effectively by competent therapists in special education centers. Lesser insults, those that affect only discrimination of certain sounds, deserve special emphasis. They may result in delayed language development or impairment of other verbal skills that are dependent on proper auditory processing (Zinkus, Gottlieb, & Schapiro, 1978). From the practical standpoint, it is important to emphasize not only prevention but also early detection (during the preschool period) and treatment of all patients with hearing impairment, regardless of degree. The physician rarely encounters this as an original observation in the evaluation of the child with learning problems because impaired hearing is usually discovered by screening audiometry in the school. The role of the physician is to verify the diagnosis, define its etiology, and, where possible, to institute specific therapy.

Other Causes

Although rare as a cause for learning difficulties, degenerative diseases of the nervous system may result in insidiously progressive dementia, which is often misinterpreted, particularly in the beginning before seizures or other motor signs of nervous system dysfunction are apparent. Any child with progressive loss of previously acquired functions, deteriorating school performance, or marked change in personality should be seen by a neurologist early for a thorough evaluation. The picture is sometimes obscured if the patient has seizures and is receiving anticonvulsants, but it is usually possible to separate the drug effect from that due to the basic disease. Before a brain tumor or abscess produces the classical signs of raised intracranical pressure, it may account for failing school performance. The symptomatology may follow a protracted course. Prior to onset of classical symptomatology, there may only be low-grade headache, fatigue, lethargy, and irritability to explain the child's problems at school. These complaints do not always mean a sinister underlying disease, since they can be seen with iron deficiency anemia, hypothyroidism, or may even be symptomatic of a mood disorder. Categorically, symptoms like these always warrant a medical consultation.

The psychiatry of learning disorders is a separate topic that is beyond the scope of this review. Nevertheless, it is an important consideration for the neurologist confronted with a learning-disabled child. Childhood depression is a well-documented cause for school failure, but the classic signs of depression are often masked in children (Weinberg et al, 1973). The environmental factors which influence behavior and, in turn, school performance are also extremely important considerations. Frequently, these are secondary to the basic problem causing the learning difficulty; yet for therapy to be successful it must include strategies to modify environmental stresses, parental attitudes, peer pressure, and related factors.

CONCLUSIONS

The child with learning and behavior problems represents a formidable challenge to the neurologist, not only in terms of diagnosis and etiology, but also from the standpoint of when, how, or whether to recommend therapy. Seizures, mental retardation, deafness, and the other specific neurologic disorders explain relatively few of the cases presenting with learning problems. The majority have either no definable neurologic dysfunction or the neurologic signs are minor and of debatable significance. Many of these children, particularly those with hyperkinesis, clumsiness, or perceptual motor dysfunctions, will improve spontaneously; some do not and may be helped by therapy.

When or whether to recommend therapy for this group of patients is uncertain, but it should become clearer as the science of learning disabilities and behavior disorders becomes better defined. In the interim every effort should be made to help these children achieve their full potential by encouragement and positive reinforcement at a time when they often doubt their own self-worth. This is a challenge requiring the best efforts not only of physicians, but also of teachers, therapists, parents, and all who relate to learning-disabled children.

John F. Griffith

REFERENCES

Bax, M. Who is hyperactive? *Developmental Medicine and Child Neurology,* 1978, *20,* 277–278.

Eichenwald, H. F. (Ed.). *Prevention of mental retardation through control of infectious diseases.* U.S. Public Health Service Publication No. 1962. Washington, D.C.: Government Printing Office, 1962.

Gubbay, S. S., Ellis, E., Walton, J. N., & Court, S. D. M. Clumsy children. *Brain; Journal of Neurology,* 1965, *88,* 295–312.

Hutt, S. J., Jackson, P. M., Belsham, A. & Higgins, G. Perceptual-motor behavior in relation to blood phenobarbitone level: A preliminary report. *Developmental Medicine and Child Neurology,* 1968, *10,* 626–632.

Livingston, S. *Comprehensive management of epilepsy in infancy, childhood, and adolescence.* Springfield, Ill.: Thomas, 1972.

Ounsted, C., Lindsay, J., & Norman, R. *Biological factors in temporal lobe epilepsy. Clinics in Developmental Medicine* No. 22. London: Heinemann, 1965.

Rapoport, J. L., Quinn, P. O., Lamprecht, F. Minor physical anomalies and plasma dopamine-beta-hydroxylase activity in hyperactive boys. *American Journal of Psychiatry,* 1974, *131,* 386–390.

Tew, B., & Laurence, K. M. Effects of hydrocephalus on intelligence, visual perception, and school attainment. *Developmental Medicine and Child Neurology,* 1975, *17,* 129–134.

Weinberg, W. A., Rutman, J., Sullivan, L., et al. Depression in children referred to an educational diagnostic center: Diagnosis and treatment. *Journal of Pediatrics,* 1973, *83,* 1065–1073.

Yakovlev, P. I. Paraplegias of hydrocephalus. *American Journal of Mental Deficiency,* 1947, *50,* 561–576.

Zinkus, P. W., Gottlieb, M. I., & Schapiro, M. Developmental and psychoeducational sequela of chronic otitis media. *American Journal of Diseases of Children,* 1978, *132,* 1100–1104.

2

LEARNING DISABILITIES: A PEDIATRICIAN'S OVERVIEW

Pediatricians take pride in two aspects of their work that seem to set "children's doctors" apart from other physicians. First, they demonstrate an inordinate interest in *prevention* of illness and disability. This concern is evident in the pediatricians' advocacy of immunizations and their concern with prevention of accidents, poisoning, abuse, and deprivation. Second, they are stimulated and renewed by the experience of never seeing the same patient twice; each new encounter with a child is colored by the element of change and development occurring in the interval between contacts. They see a person constantly in a process of maturation, unfolding, and becoming.

With these two features in view, it is easy to see why pediatricians might take an interest in learning and development in childhood. In working with the problems of personal, academic, and social adjustment, the pediatrician confronts the issues of (1) how understanding the child and his situation today can prevent later trouble and (2) how the child's development can be best understood as it relates to growing physique, intelligence, communication skills, and personality.

Physicians, including those in pediatrics, have a compelling allegiance to a "biomedical model" of impairment or deviance. Engel (1977) examined the incomplete nature of the biomedical model and argued for a broader and more comprehensive model of disease, impairment, or dysfunction. He proposed that the medical model be supplanted by one with a wider view of man and the human condition. This new view would incorporate social, psychological, and behavioral contributions to illness and disability. Engel advised that the new model might be a "biopsychosocial" one that could provide a blueprint for research, a framework for teaching, and a design for action in the real world.

One aspect of the biomedical model, the preoccupation with *causation,* has detracted from coordination and communication of physicians with other child-study professions. The physician may be the only member of the "child-study team" who is looking backward in time, searching for an etiology. The educator, psychologist, and language pathologist search for understanding of what the child is like *today* and what will help him *tomorrow.* A communication gap may occur when the "past-oriented" biologists (physician, neurophysiologist, geneticist) adopt a viewpoint contrary to the "future-oriented" members of the team (psychologist, linguist, social worker, and educator). Centering on causation may obstruct understanding of complex child development situations. Disparate "causes" can produce similar impairments, for example, the diverse etiologies of mental retardation. Genetic, gestational, infectious, toxic, and traumatic causes can lead to a final common pathway: intellectual subnormality.

In a particular patient it is a relative rarity to find only one cause for one impairment. The law of parsimony seems to be repealed in child development. Instead of a single cause of a discrete condition, clusters of overlapping "causes" are detected, such as disturbed family relationships, neglect, malnutrition, disturbed relatives, environmental misadventure, and biological disruptions. A discrete injury may produce a range of biological responses in different children. For example, asphyxia at birth may cause cerebral palsy in one infant, mental retardation in another, and language disability in another. Similarly, lead poisoning may cause convulsions in one child and hyperactivity in another. These complexities invite changing concepts from a narrow biomedical model toward a broader view that envisions children as developing in a matrix of hereditary, familial, ecological, physiological, and educational influences. It is not nature *or* nurture; it is nature *with* nurture!

In this chapter the traditional biomedical model for reviewing learning disabilities will not be employed. The causes of impairment will not be listed nor the disabilities cataloged. A classification system is presented that reflects organized observations and data about children with learning disabilities. The organizational format does *not* utilize etiology or pathogenesis as crucial elements. Two topics currently under intense study by child development and other professionals will be reviewed: behavioral genetics and cerebral hemisphere localization.

One additional caveat is necessary. A discussion of learning disabilities must avoid the implication that *all* problems are in the child. Although the child is the focus of attention, it must be recognized that, in reality, there is an intractable triangle—the child, the family, the school.

DEVELOPING A CLASSIFICATION SYSTEM

An Operational Definition

A simple, broad definition of "learning disabilities" is presented which may be acceptable to pediatricians and others who work with learning disorders and problems of development:

> A child with learning disabilities is one who is intelligent enough to achieve more developmental or scholastic progress than he has, who has normal vision and hearing, who has received adequate environmental opportunties and conventional instruction in academic areas, and who had adequate motivation to learn, at least during his early school experiences.

Patient Evaluation

The natural course of events in developing a classification system for the problems seen in a clinical population begins with the collection of information about each of the children of concern. Diagnosis of the child comes before decisions about classifications. As Cantwell (1975a) succinctly stated:

> It should be recognized that a classification system emphasizes what a particular patient has in common with other patients. It is not to be confused with a diagnostic formulation—which emphasizes what a particular patient has that is different from other patients. (p. 203)

In each evaluation information is collected concerning the child's family life, education, temperament, and health. A report from the school, preferably from several observers (teachers, counselors, speech therapists, etc.), is vital. The school report should include test results, grades, and *observations* of behavior and performance rather than diagnostic conclusions.

One or both parents are interviewed, apart from the child, with inquiry about the child's health and school history, personality, home behavior, peer relationships, talents, and interests. The past history of previous pregnancies; the gestation, labor, and delivery of the patient; and the child's early health and developmental milestones are discussed. The family and social history are reviewed. The child is examined, using standard physical measurements and observations, in addition to a careful neurological, language, and behavior evaluation.

After the parents have been interviewed and the child fully

examined, other studies may be ordered. Speech, language, and hearing, psychological development, and other health examinations that are needed (ENT, eye, neurological, laboratory, EEG, etc.) may be included as part of the examination. When the evaluation data have been reviewed, an unhurried, nontechnical, detailed parent conference is conducted with *both parents*. The major issues to be discussed are what the strengths, weaknesses, and problems of this child are at this time, in this family, in this learning situation. Labels are avoided.

The parents are provided reading materials, appropriate to their child's problems, to supplement discussions. Permission is obtained to forward summary reports to the school principal (who should review reports with the teachers). Copies can be sent to the parents and to interested professionals (referring physicians, clinics, tutors, etc.). The parents are informed about parent groups (like ACLD—the Association for Children with Learning Disabilities) that might be of interest and help to them. Parents should be assured of continued availability in the event of later crises, teacher apathy, or other failure of response from the school.

The parent discussion invariably focuses on four elements of child growth: (1) physical development and health, (2) intelligence, (3) language development, and (4) temperament. The emphasis is on understanding the child as he is, *not* in speculations about the *causes* of his developmental problems. The discussion avoids the concept that the child must be "cured," reconstructed, or standardized. Instead, the parents are provided information, understanding, and confidences to enable them to work with the schools as advocates for their child.

The Classification System

To organize and make manageable a collection of clinical information, it is useful to devise a classification system. An investigation of classification problems was published in two volumes by Hobbs (1975). A widely accepted classification system, especially for professionals with psychiatric credentials, was the "multiaxial classification of child psychiatric disorders" proposed by Rutter, Graham, and Yule (1970) under the auspices of the World Health Organization.

More recently, Rutter (1975) has extended the multiaxial system to include a five-item classification scheme, summarized as follows:

> The axes which may be employed are five: (1) clinical psychiatric syndrome, (2) intellectual level, (3) associated or aetiological biological factors, (4) associated or aetiological psychosocial factors, and (5) developmental disorders. A diagnosis on this scheme

would say something about the child's problems on all five axes, even though the information might be negative. (p. 26)

A classification procedure is summarized, one that has proved informative in organizing clinical observations gathered in a pediatric practice. In addition to making the data manageable, this system has helped in explaining developmental difficulties to parents, teachers, counselors, and other interested professionals. After each diagnostic evaluation of the child a judgment is made on the *primary* area of disturbance from among seven categories: temperament, intellectual, language, neurologic, psychiatric, physical, and mixed (Table 2–1).

Table 2-1. Primary Categories of Disturbance.

Category	Description
1. Temperament	Behavioral style, activity, attention, mood
2. Intellectual	General intelligence; IQ 70–85 = borderline, below 70 = retardation
3. Language	Communicative skills, central linguistic processing, speech
4. Neurologic	Neurologic syndromes, seizures, cerebral palsy, hemiparesis
5. Psychiatric	Emotional-adjustment reactions; situational, neurotic, psychotic disorders. Self-esteem, identity disturbances.
6. Physical	Disease or physical handicap: Intern. Classification of Disease (ICDA)
7. Mixed	Combinations of impairment; one category not adequate.

Seven primary categories are used to classify conditions observed in children who are having developmental, behavioral, or learning difficulties. Additional descriptive terms can be added to further characterize the problems or impairments observed in the diagnostic evaluation. The classification is based upon the child's current behavior and performance, not on etiology, sociocultural factors, or pathophysiology.

These primary categories are descriptive of the child and his behavior, with no "etiology" or "pathogenesis" involved. There are also no social, familial, or environmental causes invoked; the classification depends entirely on observations of the child, not on presumed causation or psychodynamics. After the decision on primary category each patient may have additional *secondary* descriptions, which serve to enlarge and clarify the primary classification assignment. For example, if the patient were judged to have a "temperament" problem, the specific behavioral traits could be listed, such as excessive activity, impulsiveness, distractibility, and short attention span. If the child also had a reading disability, this could be indicated as a secondary observation. Any physical impairment, such as strabismus, hearing loss, severe allergies, and others, could also be noted. The primary category classification will be more extensively analyzed by reviewing the seven subclassifications.

Temperament disorders include the disturbances of behavior style. This category includes problems in conduct or personality such that the child deviates significantly from expected behavior for the particular age. For example, temperament includes characteristic tempo, activity level, concentration, mood, motor energy output, and interpersonal style (tact, mutuality, patience, etc.) Temperament is not a constant and measurable characteristic; children vary from time to time and place to place in their behavior style. The conclusion that a child has a disorder of temperament is a subjective one and vulnerable to observer biases. A conclusion about temperament should include observations by more than one good observer and should be based on behaviors in several places, not limited to a classroom, school bus, or a doctor's office.

The foundation work concerning temperament has been described by Thomas, Chess, and Birch (1968) in their classic monograph entitled *Temperament and Behavior Disorder in Children*. They followed a group of families longitudinally for several years, observing systematically the temperament traits of the children. They concluded that temperament could be divided into nine compartments: activity level, rhythmicity, approach/withdrawal, adaptability, intensity of reaction, threshold of responsiveness, quality of mood, distractibility, attention span, and persistence (Thomas & Chess, 1977). Carey (1972) discussed infant temperament and the use of a temperament scale in working with parents of infants and young children. He discussed such behaviors as characteristic mood, eating behavior, sleep, fussing, and other traits of parental concern. Garside and associates (1975) published a statistical analysis of "39 temperamental attributes," attempting to determine if behavior traits tended to clump together in particular children.

The most florid temperament disorder is the hyperactive (hyperkinetic) behavior syndrome. Stewart and Olds (1973) discussed these children as follows:

> A number of characteristics which everyone has, to some degree or other, are more marked in hyperactive children, suggesting that hyperactivity is a normal variant of temperament, rather than an illness or emotional disorder. (p. 25)

The child with the hyperactive behavior syndrome usually exhibits purposeless overactivity, restlessness, distractibility, and short attention span. Such children are labile and variable in mood, giving the impression of overreacting, like much younger children. They are quickly bored, impatient, excitable, and hard to satisfy. They may persistently demand amusements or objects, and then seem unsatisfied when they gain them, a trait called "anhedonia." They can be insatiable in appetite for excitement, noise, motion, and attention.

Among researchers there is a controversy about hyperactivity. One group suggests that hyperactivity is merely a symptom of some basic underlying disturbance; another group agrees that there is a symptom—hyperactivity—but that there is also a discrete hyperactive behavior syndrome.

Quinn and Rapoport (1974) reported that the hyperkinetic syndrome is not entirely behavioral in nature; they found an increased prevalence of minor physical anomalies in a group of carefully studied hyperactive boys. The boys also revealed more abnormal electroencephalographic findings and other neurological disturbances, seen clinically as mild abnormalities of body control and coordination.

Many observers have stressed the striking variability in mood, concentration, and persistence that can be observed with temperament disturbances. This same variability seems to occur in the waxing and waning of neurological "soft" signs in some children. As with other aspects of learning disabilities, the occurrence and significance of equivocal neurological "soft" signs remains controversial. According to McMahon and Greenberg (1977), even if these signs are found, they are likely to vary remarkably from one examination to another, and changes in these signs should not be used as a measure of treatment benefits from medication.

Many articles and books have been written about the hyperkinetic child. Werry (1968) wrote a classic description of the hyperactive behavior syndrome. Wender (1971, 1973) has written two books that are major contributions to our understanding of these children. One of these texts (Wender, 1973) is an excellent book of advice for parents. A recent monograph on this syndrome is the comprehensive book by Cantwell (1975a) entitled, *The Hyperactive Child: Diagnosis, Management, Current Research.*

The term "minimal brain dysfunction" (MBD) has not been used in this chapter, since it has not been necessary to use the term in our diagnostic or classification systems. The scope of this discussion does not permit extensive analysis of the controversy associated with MBD.

Similarly, the subject of stimulant medication and other

therapeutic interventions is not pertinent to the present discussion.

The second category in classifying developmental impairment is *intellectual handicap*. The subject of intelligence and IQ tests is an immense one; the literature on the types and causes of mental retardation is extensive and formidable. The scope of this chapter does not permit an elaboration of the factors influencing intelligence and function. For readers interested in the controversial aspects of intelligence testing, a succinct treatment of these complex issues is presented in a book by Loehlin, Lindzey, and Spuhler (1975). An interesting aspect of intellectual development concerns the relative contribution of genetics and environment to the intelligence of adopted children. A review of research design, statistical issues, and results of IQ testing of adopted children was published by Munsinger (1975). After reviewing all the available publications on this subject, he concluded, "Under existing circumstances heredity is much more important than environment in producing individual differences in IQ" (p. 623).

For details on the complexities of mental retardation, causes and classification, a useful introduction is the book by Grossman (1973) entitled *Manual on Terminology and Classification in Mental Deficiency*.

Language is the third primary category of dysfunction. The most common of the language disorders are difficulties in written language, i.e., reading and writing. Estimates of reading disability indicate that perhaps 15 percent of school children in the United States have a significant problem in learning to read. Studies of each child's communication systems is essential if there is difficulty in school, even if the difficulty is reported as behavioral or emotional. Careful examination of language systems may reveal that the child has difficulty with discrimination of spoken words, transient memory for spoken word sequences, or uneven storage and retrieval of spoken language. When children exhibit delays in development of spoken language, they usually have difficulties with written language. A child may be capable in oral language and in reading but frustrated in the production of written language (writing, spelling, punctuation, and math). Some children do well in reception of language, spoken and written, but are inept in expressing their thoughts in any verbal form. Reception of language (spoken or written) is always better than expression.

Frustration with written work, in an otherwise capable and bright child, may be interpreted by the teacher and family as "poor motivation" or "laziness." Unfair or inappropriate criticism, blame, and pressure may be added to the already grinding academic frustration. If the defeats with language in school go on long enough and are severe enough, the child may develop a defeatist attitude, lose confidence, and further deteriorate in performance of academic tasks.

Under the general heading of language would also appear the disorders of speech, such as articulation disorders and dysfluencies. There are also disorders of voice, such as hoarseness, abnormal pitch, and nasal escape due to palate or pharyngeal disorders. Stuttering is a specific kind of speech dysfluency. Some disturbance of speech may be seen in children with cleft palate, maxillofacial deformities, and cerebral palsy.

In a later section the distinction between language disturbance and visual perception defects will be reviewed. Many children are labeled as having a general visual perception impairment when their problem is more accurately termed a visual language disorder or delay.

Chalfant and Scheffelin (1969) presented an excellent summary of language in a monograph entitled *Central Processing Dysfunctions in Children;* Mattis, French, and Rapin (1975) showed that reading problems in brain-damaged children were indistinguishable from reading problems in children with other kinds of developmental language disorders. Therefore, "brain damage" was *not* a critical issue in understanding or treating language dysfunctions. The literature on reading disorders is extensive. A comprehensive survey of the psychology of reading is found in a book by Gibson and Levin (1975) for readers interested in modern research on reading. An excellent discussion of language disorders, written for pediatricians, is found in a two-part article by Gofman and Allmond (1971). Lerner in the second edition (1976) of *Children with Learning Disabilities,* reviews language development and includes a discussion of teaching strategies for oral language, reading, and written expressive language. Menyuk (1975) discusses the relationship of language to other cognitive development, pointing out that thinking and language are separate, but overlapping, developmental phenomena that tend to be confused and confounded in IQ testing and in some classrooms. Menyuk also discusses some of the confusions between "perceptual motor training" and the remediation more appropriate for language impairment. Two relatively recent articles analyzing the relationship of language to developmental disorders are by Knobeloch (1976) and Striffler (1976).

Neurological disorder is the fourth primary category and includes: organic neurological conditions, such as cerebral palsy, the epilepsies, congenital anomalies of the brain, hemiplegias, and other specific neurological disorders. Neurological disorders range from the catastrophic (therefore, highly visible) to the obscure and subtle. Highly trained professionals with expertise in neurological disorders are relatively scarce or even unavailable. In their absence the diagnosis and clarification of complex neurological syndromes are neglected. Otherwise capable and well-trained child development specialists may conceptualize neurological disorders as major syndromes that can be seen from across the room, such as cerebral palsy, hemiplegia, hydrocephalus, epileptic seizures, and other gross disorders. However, there are clinical reports suggesting that there are common syndromes of the central nervous system with which the child-study team must become familiar, mainly because these syndromes may simulate emotional, intellectual, or motivational disturbances.

In addition to the well-defined neurological syndromes of childhood, there is a more obscure spectrum of neurological impairments that have been grouped together as "organic brain syndromes." The categorization includes neurologic syndromes, of diffuse and variable symptomatology, observed in children with demonstrable neurological abnormalities on examinations and with an antecedent history suggesting insult to the nervous system. Conditions that fall under the rubric of "organic brain syndromes" include children with unequivocal changes of gait, balance, body stability, coordination, sequencing, and fine motor control. The children may be labeled as "mild" cerebral palsy, but they do not exhibit the full-blown syndrome of cerebral palsy. In addition to abnormalities of neurological function and organization, these children exhibit disinhibition of mood, emotion, and temperament controls. Often they are negative, withdrawn, listless, perseverative, or explosive. They are usually socially inept because of (1) uneven affect; (2) unexpected overreactions to stimulation, events, or excitement; (3) emotional lability unrelated to ongoing experience; and (4) inappropriate outburst of aggression, anger, or impulsiveness.

There is usually a convincing history of neurological insult or injury early in life, after which development is changed or impaired. In addition to neurological signs, the patients reveal abnormalities in head size and asymmetry of cranial contours, face, or limbs. Additional signs suggest central neurological impairment, such as strabismus, slurred speech, echolalia, bizarre posturing, lack of eye contact, and mild sensory deficits.

It is well recognized that children with neurological impairment are particularly vulnerable to emotional and adjustment difficulties. Neurophysiologists are concerned about the relationship of behavior and interictal personality in convulsive disorders and the association between temporal lobe function, seizure disorders, and behavior control problems. Investigations are in progress attempting to clarify the electrical and chemical neurophysiology of attention, impulse, sleep, arousal, fear, and emotion in the human brain. It has been established that emotion is related to neurology as well as to experience, see Figure 2–1.

Figure 2–1 is a semidiagrammatic drawing of the relationship of the "old brain" that resides deep in the central nervous system, enfolded by the cerebral cortex. These primitive structures are commonly called the "limbic system" (Isaacson, 1974), a locus for the mediation of important subcortical processes. These structures are involved in activity level, arousal, anxiety, primitive appetites (food, water, sex, touch), goal-directed behavior, mood, aggression, mutuality, recent memory, maternal behavior, reward evaluation, anger, and fear. Lezak (1976) presented details of anatomical structures that relate to behavior control in humans.

The limbic structures have been called the "crocodile brain" because of their primitive origins in the evolutionary epochs when reptiles ruled the world (Crichton, 1972). MacLean (1949) referred to limbic structures as the "visceral brain," to distinguish it from the more recently evolved cerebral cortex, where such elegant functions as thinking, planning, verbalizing, and remembering take place. The newer cortical mantle (neocortex) does *not* have very effective control (especially in children) over the old reptilian circuit. Crichton (1972) noted that there may be an uneasy peace between the logical cortical brain and the illogical, atavistic, impulsive, and self-serving old limbic brain. Sometimes the peace breaks down and the reptile gains ascendency (e.g., witness the drinker who tunes out his cortex with alcohol, allowing the old crocodile brain to take over).

Neurophysiologists emphasize that a major function of the higher cortical centers, especially the frontal lobes, may be to *inhibit* the lower, more primitive system. "Maturation," in neurologic terms, may *not* imply simply an acquisition of more skills and knowledge but may indicate a better control and integration of primitive circuitry by higher intellectual/cognitive circuitry. Growing up neurologically involves the development of "brakes." Parents describe behaviors that suggest that the child's difficulty is *not* in thinking, memory, logic, language, or motivation but in an inability to apply brakes, to inhibit reactions, to control impulses.

Current psychiatric research in violent behavior (Frazier, 1977) suggests that aggressive, uncontrolled, impulsive behavior may be due to organic brain malfunction (as distinguished from "emotional" or

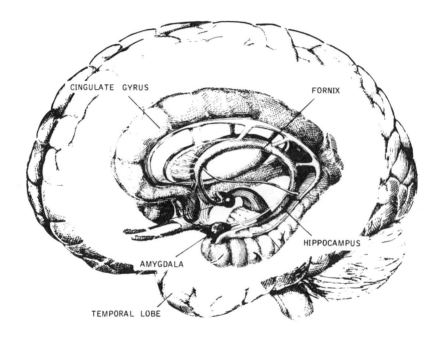

Fig. 2-1. The Limbic System is situated deep in the cranium, enfolded by the cerebral cortex. Several of the component structures are labeled. These structures are old in the evolution of brain systems, sometimes called the paleocortex. The cerebral cortex is new in evolution, i.e. neocortex. The limbic structures process primitive functions like arousal, emotion, sensory input selection, reward evaluation, fear, affection, etc. The neocortex processes the cognitive functions of thinking, planning, language, esthetics, etc.

"acting-out" behavior on a psychodynamic basis). Monroe, a psychoanalyst, has written a book describing sporadic, illogical, primitive outbursts that he has called "episodic disinhibition" or "episodic dyscontrol" (1970). Clinical observations and longitudinal follow-up of patients with episodic outbursts of uncontrolled behavior were described that cannot be classed as psychomotor seizures. Mark and Ervin (1970) wrote on the relationship between brain structure and physiology of violent behavior. Elliott (1977) discussed the neurological aspects of explosive rage and reviewed the medications useful in modulating the disinhibited behavior resulting from brain dyscontrol.

The relationship between seizure disorders, behavioral disinhibition, and episodic behavioral syndromes is of interest. Waxman and Geschwind (1975) discussed interictal behavior in patients with temporal lobe epilepsy, indicating that some changes in ongoing performance may reflect abnormal limbic system function. They pointed out changes in sexual behavior, religiosity, and mood. They particularly noted an exaggerated interest in compulsive drawing and writing behavior in several patients. Disturbed brain physiology with "schizophrenic" behavior was reported by Adebimpe (1977). A case is reported of a patient who had 30 psychiatric hospital admissions for "schizophrenia" before the correct diagnosis of psychomotor epilepsy was made. The patient responded to anticonvulsant medication.

Catastrophic behavior syndromes in adults may be related to neurologic syndromes of children. Organic factors in childhood psychopathology were reviewed by Werry (1972). Werry (1968) had performed extensive research on childhood behavior disorders and had written a classic description of "developmental hyperactivity." A compendium on current research and treatment of childhood psychopathology, including organic brain syndromes, can be found in a monograph by Schopler and Reichler (1976). Thomas and Chess (1975) reported on three children who illustrate behavioral syndromes with organic brain dysfunction. They emphasized that the behavioral component "could *not* be explained only in terms of motor dysfunction, intellectual deficit, patterns of parental management and attitudes, or more general features of environmental demand alone, but also required a consideration of the constellation of temperamental organization" (p. 457). Seidel, Chadwick, and Rutter (1975) investigated psychological disorders in a group of children with "brain lesion," comparing them with controls who were impaired by "peripheral" neurological disorders, such as polio, muscle disturbances, or skeletal defects. It appeared that "psychiatric disorder" was twice as common in children with cerebral impairment than in those with peripheral lesions. The children with brain damage also had a marked increase in reading difficulties and a lowering of intelligence, although still within the "normal" range.

A complete study of these handicapped children must include more than evaluations of intelligence, motor skills, behavior, and temperament controls. A detailed and extensive evaluation of communication systems is required because the majority of children with central neurological impairment will have severe language disabilities. Gottesman, Belmont, and Kaminer (1975) reported on follow-up studies of several children with developmental disabilities, many with neurologic impairments, and found that their progress in language (specifically, reading ability) was discouragingly slow and inefficient. They advised that most of these children would need special educational methods other than those to improve reading skills. This is the group of children in whom the more elaborate neurological diagnostic studies may be informative; that is, these are the children who are most likely to have abnormal EEG, skull Xrays, or computerized axial tomography (CAT scans).

The literature of "standard" neurologic disorders in children is massive, and well beyond the boundaries of this essay. Rutter et al. (1970) published a study of neuro-epileptic disorders in children living on the Isle of Wight. Vining et al. (1976) reviewed cerebral palsy from a developmental point of view. Schain (1977) has published a second edition of his concise monograph on the neurology of childhood learning disorders.

Psychiatric disorders occupy the fifth category of concern in classifying children with learning disabilities. This is a fluid and ever changing area in child development; the literature is extensive, parochial, and polemical. Children with learning disabilities, like children with other chronic disorders, are vulnerable to emotional disturbances. The emotional reaction, however, may be a result of a more basic underlying impairment rather than the fundamental cause of the failure in performance. That is, the learning impairment comes first, probably as some innate developmental delay or difference (Kinsbourne, 1975); the psychiatric component ensues from the defeat and frustration in school.

A classification of psychiatric disturbances was described by Chess (1969) in *An Introduction to Child Psychiatry* and in a recent monograph by Chess and Hassibi (1978). In Chess' system there are a few categories of disturbance, which are understandable by most professionals on the child-study team. The categories proposed for psychiatric impairments (from least handicapping to most severe) are *reactive* (situational) behavior disorders, neurotic *behavioral* disorders, neurotic *character* disorders, *neurosis*, childhood *psychosis*, and *sociopathic* personality. Chess also discussed associated symptoms, generally considered to be of emotional origin, such as fecal soiling, tantrums, school phobia, night terrors, breath holding, and related developmental disturbances. In addition, the organic brain syndromes were reviewed.

Weiner and DelGaudio (1976) summarized current psychiatric concepts of diagnosis and classification of adolescent psychopathology. Adult psychiatric disorders and the relationship of adult psychopathology to problems of childhood development are analyzed by Woodruff, Goodwin, and Guze (1974). Infantile autism has been reviewed by Ornitz and Ritvo (1976), and a more comprehensive discussion is presented in a monograph edited by Ritvo (1976).

Physical disorder, the sixth category, is necessary to accommodate any disease or anomaly that might be discovered, regardless of its impact on intelligence, language, or emotional stability. Some physical illnesses may have little direct effect on the nervous system; nevertheless, they are capable of producing severe disturbances of growth, development, and learning, as, for example, the child with severe, recurrent, and complicated asthma. The code book for diseases is the *International Classification of Disease* (1973) in which most of the illnesses have been cataloged and assigned an ICDA number, e.g. strabismus—ICDA 373.9.

Mixed disorders, the seventh and last category, includes combinations of impairments that could not be accommodated in any other single primary category. A frequent "mixed" disability in our population is a combination of temperament disorder and language disorder. For example, about 85 percent of the children classed in the hyperactive behavior syndrome were found to have significant language problems. Many of the patients in the adolescent age group were found to have language disorders with superimposed psychiatric symptoms, such as poor self-esteem, antisocial behavior, or other maladaptive traits that developed later in childhood than the language impairment.

A mixed category is vulnerable to criticism concerning its validity because different observers stress different components of disturbance or delay in developmental progress. Nevertheless, an "overflow" category is useful for classifying interwoven disabilities that do not show discrete and unitary phenomena.

Clinical Observations in a Pediatric Practice

I have used this classification system in order to organize the diagnostic evaluations of approximately 2000 children. Approximately 80 percent of the subjects were boys and 20 percent girls. About 9 percent were adopted children (by nonrelatives), a larger proportion than expected in a general population (estimated as about 1 percent adopted by nonrelatives). The average age of the patient was slightly less than 9 years. About one-third had temperament disorders; one-third, language disorders; and one-fourth, mixed disorders. The neurologic impairments were seen in about 12 to 15 percent of the patients. Younger patients tended to have higher prevalence of temperament or neurologic disorders, probably because these conditions are more florid and impel parents to seek early diagnostic services. The older patients revealed more language and psychiatric diagnoses. Adopted children had a higher prevalence of temperament disorders than the nonadopted patients.

NEGLECTED AREAS OF CHILD DEVELOPMENT

The remainder of this chapter will focus on two areas of child development that seem to be neglected in conferences and publications concerned with learning disabilities, a neglect especially noticeable in the literature aimed at family physicians and pediatricians. The two areas are (1) behavioral genetics and (2) cerebral hemisphere specialization.

One advantage of the physician, especially the pediatrician, is his freedom to ask about complete family history and personality traits. The physician can inquire in detail, with family acceptance, about educational and behavioral events; maternal health, pregnancy, labor, delivery, and newborn history; and health, development, and learning during infancy, early childhood, and the school years. Of course, such privileges cannot be taken lightly, and the data must be used for the benefit of the patient and family, not simply for curiosity. Nonphysician members of the child-study team may *not* have access to sensitive information about the child and family. The ideas discussed in the next section concern the details of *family* behavior and health if they are available.

Behavioral Genetics

Behavioral genetics is the study of hereditary factors on behavior; in the present context it concerns the potential or "likely" impact of genetic factors on child development, including personality, language, and intelligence.

Variations in the ability to learn to read appear to be related to genetic factors (Gibson & Levin, 1975). Studies of family members have consistently confirmed that reading disabilities run in families in patterns not explained by environment. Studies of twins have indicated that both members of identical twins are much more likely to exhibit reading disabilities (Bakwin, 1973). Intelligence testing, as reflected by IQ testing, seems to have a strong genetic component (Fincher 1976; Loehlin et al., 1975; Munsinger, 1975). Some behaviors are much harder to evaluate (and quantify) than reading performance or IQ test scores, especially subjective behaviors such as personality, temperament, attention control, and mood.

There has been a void in fundamental knowledge in pediatrics about family, twin, and adoption as related to behavioral disturbances, learning disabilities and especially those problems involving temperament and/or psychiatric disturbances. There is sparse discussion in the pediatric and child development literature relating to the possibility of *hereditary* temperament disorders. Morrison and Stewart (1971) were the earliest investigators to report that hyperactive children had a higher prevalence of alcoholism and sociopathic personality in their male relatives and hysteric personality in female relatives. Cantwell (1972) carried out a similar study of 50 hyperactive boys living with their biological parents, contrasting them with 50 nonhyperactive boys also living with both natural parents. He confirmed the increased prevalence of alcoholism and sociopathic personality in the male relatives, especially the fathers, and the higher occurrence of hysteric personality in the female relatives, especially the mothers.

Since these studies, there has been steady acquisition of data suggesting an impact of genetic influences (not just enivironment) on the occurrence of hyperactivity and related psychopathology in some families. Morrison and Stewart (1973a) found that the *adoptive* parents of adopted hyperactive children *did not* have the increased prevalence of alcoholism, sociopathy, and hysteria found in the *biological* relatives of hyperactive children. This suggested that the relationship of the childhood temperament disorder (hyperactivity) to the adult "character" disorders (alcoholism, sociopathy) might be a genetic one rather than just an environmental or "learned" one. Morrison and Stewart (1973b) also studied the possible genetic transmission and concluded that the inheritance profile was polygenetic rather than an autosomal dominant or a sex-linked pattern. They reported further (1974) on more family data, again suggesting that the pattern was probably a polygenetic one.

Cantwell has summarized the genetic data in a book on the hyperactive child (1975a) and in a journal article (1975b). Morrison and Minkoff (1975) reported a relationship between childhood hyperactivity and adult "explosive behavior." There is research to suggest that the adult sociopath, in some cases, was a hyperactive child. Borland and Heckman (1976) reported on the adult adjustment of several men who had been hyperactive children. Many of them (about half) had psychiatric problems as adults, and most had not achieved a socioeconomic status comparable to their biological brothers, who were studied as controls. Safer (1973) reported on a group of patients, all in foster care from an early age, and found that the *full* siblings of hyperactive children had more symptoms of short attention span, antisocial behavior, and other evidence of neurological dysfunction than did the *half*-siblings of the hyperactive children. The half-siblings, of course, would have half the genetic relationship of full siblings; i.e., the fewer shared genes, the fewer symptoms of temperament disorder.

Two issues deserve stressing: (1) the genetic research on behavior has been done almost entirely by psychiatrists, with brief mention in the pediatric and psychologic literature, and (2) there seems to be convincing evidence that there is a biological (genetic) relationship between some childhood temperament disorders and adult character disorders, especially alcoholism, sociopathy, and hysteria (in women).

At the risk of being accused of discarding child rearing as a negligible contribution to "growing up straight," it is of interest to look further at the research on alcoholism and sociopathic personality. Alcoholism is almost certainly related (in some biological way) to the hyperactive behavior syndrome; sociopathy may be one outcome of the childhood hyperactive syndrome. Goodwin and his associates (1975) studied the relationship of alcoholism to hyperactivity in a group of adoptees in Denmark. More of the adult alcoholics had been hyperactive children than had the nonalcoholics. Of the 14 alcoholic adoptees, 10 had alcoholic *biologic* parents, but none of the 199 nonalcoholic adoptees had alcoholic biologic parents.

Alcoholism is almost certainly a hereditary disease in some patients. Schuckit, Goodwin, & Winokur (1972) studied the half-siblings of alcoholics who had been raised either with or apart from an alcoholic parent. The half-sibling who had the alcoholic biologic parent had a greater risk of becoming alcoholic than did the half-sibling who did not have an alcoholic biologic parent. Kaij and Dock (1975) reported on the grandsons of alcoholics. They found that the alcoholic tendency did not follow a sex-linked pattern, i.e., the grandsons through *daughters* of alcoholics had the same risk as the grandsons through *sons* of alcoholics. The grandsons of alcoholics had about three times the risk of becoming alcoholics as the grandsons of nonalcoholics.

Goodwin et al. (1973) studied alcoholism in adoptees raised apart from their alcoholic biologic parents. The children of alcoholics had about three times the prevalence of alcoholism (18 percent versus 5 percent) than the adopted children of nonalcoholic biological parents. Goodwin et al. (1974) compared the drinking problems of adopted and nonadopted sons of alcoholics. The children who *did not* remain in the home with the alcoholic had a slightly *higher prevalence* of alcoholism than the sons who remained in the home, even though the adoptive homes had much less alcoholism, higher socioeconomic status, and less psychiatric illness. Goodwin (1971, 1975) has written extensively on the genetic aspects of alcoholism. Woodruff et al. (1974) discussed the genetic aspects of the psychiatric conditions reviewed here and also adult psychiatric illnesses that are not related to childhood problems, such as depression.

The ominous conclusions from these family studies are that childhood behavior disturbance (especially the hyperactive behavior syndrome) may be genetic in origin, at least in some children; and these children may have biological relatives who also have serious psychopathology: alcoholism, sociopathy, or hysteria. To add to our concern, research suggests that sociopathic men tend to marry (or at least have children with) hysteric women (Guze et al., 1971; Woodruff et al., 1974). If these illnesses are genetic in some degree, the assortative mating of alcoholic or sociopathic men to sociopathic or hysteric women may provide a sociological "time bomb" in regard to childhood behavior problems, since the genetic odds would be tremendously increased and the environmental turmoil, chaos, and disruption would also be superimposed in massive doses.

Research using adoption suggests biological (and genetic) factors in the genesis of serious behavior or character disorders, but the picture may be even darker. Horn, Green, Carney, and Erickson (1975) showed that adoption studies are unfairly against a genetic hypothesis because the "patient" adoptees are compared with "control" adoptees. They stated, "A high risk among the control group of adopted children makes it difficult to find a still higher risk among the children of affected parents."

Professionals interested in longitudinal studies of childhood psychopathology and adult adjustment would find the reports by Robins (1966, 1972, 1973) to be compelling. Among many insights, the research studies revealed that *diagnosis* of childhood and adolescent psychopathology is immensely easier than providing effective therapy.

An important by-product of the review of hereditary aspects of childhood psychopathology is the issue of adoption and the reported higher prevalence of adjustment and behavior problems in adopted children (Bohman, 1972; Taichert & Harvin 1975).

It has been concluded that the behavior and adjustment problems of adopted children are caused by the ineptness, guilt, and rigidities of the adoptive parents (American Academy of Pediatrics, 1973; Schechter & Holter, 1975). Research on the hereditary aspects of some maladaptive behaviors suggests that we should not blame the adoptive parents in the absence of information about the temperament and character of the biological parents.

Dr. Lee Salk, a respected child psychologist, defends adoptive parents (1973, p. 97):

> I have been impressed by the warmth, sincerity, and great skill many of these [adoptive] parents have in raising their children. I could not help but consider some of these [behavior] problems as incompatibility based on temperamental or general constitutional differences that perhaps have a genetic origin. . . . Elimination of the guilt factor made it much easier for the parent to understand the problems and to work out successful methods for dealing with them. . . .

Horn et al. (1975), reviewing adoption studies of behavior disturbance, said, "Misdeeds on the part of the adoptive parents are probably not the factors responsible for the psychopathological disorders in their adopted children" (p. 1367).

The influence of heredity in disturbances like hyperactive behavior, alcoholism, sociopathic personality, and hysteria need not cause pessimism. Many diseases have genetic components (such as allergy) but are treatable. The recognition of hereditary influences reminds child development professionals that behavior, personality, character have innate biological underpinnings. Environment, child rearing, and education are not operating on an "empty slate." The child brings with him propensities, aptitudes, talents, style that then interact with experience and environment. If the interaction is not smooth, development may produce entanglements and crosscurrents that show as rebellion, underachievement, poor motivation, or sickness.

Consideration of the biological underpinnings of behavior should lead us to exercise skepticism about such statements as the following: "the problems of adolescence seem just the last in a mounting progression of behavioral difficulties that originated in parents' earliest misguided encounters with their infants" (Turtle, 1977). Are parents really entirely to blame? Are parents so misguided? Do behavioral difficulties only originate in parent encounter?

Cerebral Hemisphere Specialization

It may seem strange that a pediatrician would be concerned with the influence of cerebral hemisphere specialization on mental function. In defense of the pediatrician, he may actually be the most "biologically" oriented member of the child-study team! Current brain research suggests that cerebral hemisphere organization, especially lateralization of functions, may be one key to the brain physiology that we can observe only as learning and behavior patterns in the child.

The pediatric literature has rare reference to hemispheric specialization (Haywood & Gordon, 1970); therefore, the child development professional must rely on the literature of neurology and neuropsychology. Two relatively recent titles illustrate the engaging "levity with elegance" that characterizes some neuropsychological reports: Nealis, Gascon, Hurwitz, and Holmes (1977) presented data on hemisphere function and learning difficulties with this title: "Right On! or Left Out?" Witelson (1977) used the title. "Developmental Dyslexia: Two Right Hemispheres and None Left."

The research literature on cerebral specialization is already extensive and is growing exponentially. Most of the research to be mentioned here involves direct clinical observations and does not cover the more esoteric research involving unilateral anesthetizing of a cortex, dichotic listening tasks, or split-brain research, each of which has a formidable literature. A review of the research on commissurotomized (split-brain) patients was published by Nebes (1974). Joynt and Goldstein (1975) pointed out that over-enthusiasm about the separate functions of the two hemispheres should be tempered with caution. The specialization is probably a relative preponderance, with one hemisphere overshadowing the other but not totally "dominating" a process.

With the caveat that hemispheric lateralization is much more complex and unsettled than we would like, Table 2–2 shows some of the "tentative preponderance" that the neuropsychologists have been studying. There are many exceptions to these oversimplified assignments, especially in left-handed people, some of whom have their language function in the right hemisphere, or in people who sustained cerebral injury in early life and had some "plastic" rearrangement of cerebral function.

The concept of "field independent" and "field dependent" is related to a person's ability to be analytic, logical, or conceptual without

Table 2-2. Hemisphere Specialization (Tentative Preponderance).

Left	Right
Linguistic	Spatial–gestural
Sequential	Form–pattern
Analytic	Intuitive
Abstract	Concrete–structural
Speech sounds	Noise–music
Familiar	Novel–unfamiliar
Particulate	Holistic
Logical	Emotional
Time distributed	Spatial display
Field independent	Field dependent

Cerebral hemisphere lateralization is not as compact as the table suggests. The functions assigned to the hemispheres seem to be "preponderant" in one or the other hemisphere rather than present or absent. Some of the lateralizations are on firmer research foundations than are others. The "linguistic" verus "spatial-gestural" is better established than the "field independent" versus "field dependent."

regard for the field conditions of the performance, in contrast to persons who are "sensitive" to the field in which the operations are to be performed. Ramirez and Casteneda (1974) commented on the relationships among political, cultural, cognitive, and linguistic characteristics and the hemispheric assignment of field-independent versus field-dependent factors. Their sociocultural concepts were interesting, but they did not coincide well with the neuropsychological assignment of cerebral lateralization and specialization.

For specific reports concerning cerebral specialization and learning disabilities, research findings are summarized by Dimond and Beaumont (1974) and by Knights and Bakker (1975). Guyer and Friedman (1975) also discussed concepts of cerebral lateralization as related to learning disabilities in children.

Some of the specializations tentatively proposed in Table 2–2 are unsubstantiated and philosophical. The issue of "familiar" versus "novel, unfamiliar" was discussed in a psychological essay by Gardner (1974). He indicated that much of the neuropsychological research on hemisphere specialization had confused "familiar" versus "unfamiliar" aspects of the tasks that were being studied.

The relationship of "emotion" to cerebral lateralization has received less attention than some of the more traditional cognitive tasks. Schwartz, Davidson, and Maer (1975) reported some interesting interactions among processing styles for verbal/spatial tasks interwoven with emotion/nonemotion aspects of the tasks. The right hemisphere seemed to predominate in the "emotion-laden" kind of cognitive task. An interesting study of the particulate/holistic dichotomy was performed by Bever and Chiarello (1974), indicating that the left hemisphere seems to be dominant for analytic processing of music but the right hemisphere for esthetic, holistic appreciation of melodies.

An imaginative use of the concepts of hemispheric lateralization was reported by a classroom teacher (van den Honert, 1977) who tried to channel visual language to the left hemisphere while also sending language sounds to that hemisphere. Although her interventions were not controlled, they illustrated a creative application of some theoretical neurophysiological concepts.

Some children with learning disabilities are nonverbal but adept in the functions tentatively assigned to the nonlinguistic hemisphre: they are nonreaders who are quite capable with pictures, maps, cartoons, diagrams, caricatures, and spatial processing. Some of the functions of the "linguistic" type seem to mature on a completely different time scale than some of the nonlinguistic skills. A diagrammatic illustration of these different channels of development is shown in Figure 2–2.

The solid diagonal is a hypothetical "standard progress" through childhood. The other curves are drawn to illustrate one familiar pattern with normal physical growth and superior intellectual development (I.Q.) over time but with delayed rates of development of some "linguistic" skills (e.g., reading and writing) and some irregular and delayed curves for "temperament controls."

The question mark near the upper reaches of the "temperament" curve suggests that some children mature their controls as they enter

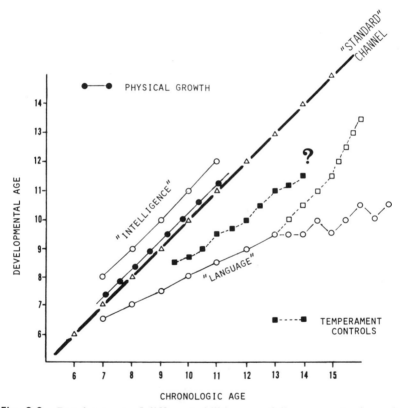

Fig. 2-2. Development of different abilities may follow separate channels, with considerable displacement from an assumed "standard" channel of maturation. The channel for "intelligence" may be separated from, and be well above, the channel for "language" or for "temperament" controls. This illustrates the futility of saying to a child, "As smart as you are, you should be able to sit still, pay attention, and read your lesson!"

adolescence, but others do not. Satterfield and Cantwell (1975) suggested that some children with severe temperament problems develop, as adolescents, antisocial and aggressive behavior. They suggested also, in the absence of effective prevention or therapy, that consideration be given to continuing stimulant medication in hyperactive children who were responding well, in the hope of reducing delinquent or criminal behavior in those at risk.

The splitting of the "language" curve in Figure 2–2 is to suggest that some children experience a "late-bloomer" effect and rapidly mature their language skills; others continue to have more or less handicapping language disabilities into adulthood as a lifelong impairment. Trites and Fiedorowicz (1975) reported on follow-up studies of reading disability suggesting that the "maturing-out" phenomenon may be infrequent; poor readers tend to get poorer rather than turning toward the "standard" performance line for language function. The use of long-term observations of learning-disabled children was an important contribution described in follow-up studies by Koppitz (1971). Rourke (1975) discussed a variety of developmental curves, illustrating how different kinds of learning and language skills might show departures from "standard" or expected time-readiness curves.

Parents and teachers seem to find this kind of multichannel diagram, or developmental map, a useful and reassuring model for understanding variation in learning, behavior, and language.

A final comment may clarify the concept that the pediatrician and other child development professionals would profit from attending to possible cerebral hemisphere specialization. The literature of child development, early childhood education, and learning disability is disrupted by mistaking "language" problems as "perception" problems. The confusion in the professional literature results in errors published in articles designed for distribution to parents and other interested nonprofessionals. For example, an article in the *New York Times Magazine*, by David Milofsky (1977), discussed "perceptual learning disabilities" in a way that equated perceptual systems with ability in language; these are two separate issues. The confusion of perception versus language is a roadblock to classroom teachers, councelors, diagnosticians, and tutors who have not recognized the distinction. Developmental studies clearly demonstrate that some children with central *language* impairments (auditory, visual, or both) may have excellent *perceptual* systems for nonlinguistic processing, such as pictures, maps, diagrams, environmental sounds, music, etc.

Stark (1975) made an excellent case for the linguistic nature of reading failure. He stressed that remedial approaches aimed at revising or standardizing the visual perceptual system (the right hemisphere processes) are doomed to failure if the child has a language disability (a left hemisphere function). He confirmed an observation that reading teachers have noted: the ability to recongize (visually perceive) individual letters on the page, in written words, may have no relationship to the ability to read the words.

Vellutino, Smith, Steger, and Kaman (1975) and others have shown that reading disability is *not* a "visiual spatial" disorder (the right hemisphere), but it is a disorder of language processing (the linguistic left hemisphere). They confirmed that visual word processing in skilled readers is *not* accomplished by a stepwise mechanical process of (1) individual letter identification, (2) serial phonemic analysis of syllables, then (3) comprehension. The process is not that simple, and it is more "linguistic" than it is "perceptual."

A lucid and persuasive discussion of these themes, written in language meaningful to parents, teachers, and other child-study people, appeared in an article by Wallach and Goldsmith (1977) reminding us that "Reading Is Language, Too!" They also presented a brief discussion of some of the components of all human languages: phonology (sounds), lexicon (vocabulary), and semantics (meaning). They noted that the ability to process a string of *geometric forms* (as in the visual sequential memory subtest of the ITPA) may not be related in a meaningful way to the ability to process a string of *letters* in a written word. Forms are right brain; words are left brain.

Language development (auditory and visual) can be considered as a separate maturational phenomenon from spatial-gestural-pictorial processing, perhaps with different developmental schedules. Some children have a right hemisphere preponderance early and should be provided learning experiences that exploit spatial-pictorial-pattern circuits rather than attempting to accelerate the sluggish linguistic-sequential-analytic systems that are not yet ready for efficient processing. The educational systems have been referred to as a half-brained enterprise. I have heard them called worse! Perhaps one of our commitments should be to encourage the schools, "from K through Kollege," to recognize the "minor" right hemisphere and give it a chance to demonstrate its potential.

The blood supply to the right hemisphere in humans tends to be significantly better than to the left hemisphere (Porch, 1977). This would suggest that, through eons of human evolution, the right brain may have been, for survival purposes, the "dominant" hemisphere. In the evolution of man it may have been more "fit" to remember where his cave was and what his enemies looked like than to remember a street address or the enemies' names. Visual-spatial-pattern recognition of the sabre-toothed tiger was more advantageous for survival than remembering his verbal label. Maybe we modern "talking animals" should pay more attention to that educationally despised "minor hemisphere."

CONCLUSIONS

Pediatricians are deeply concerned with (1) prevention of handicap and (2) with the ever changing patterns and schedules of growth and development. The pediatrician never sees the same patient twice!

An overview of a diagnostic evaluation process and the kinds of clinical observations that have resulted from these diagnostic efforts has been presented. The classification system proved useful in organizing clinical data on children examined because of failure to succeed in school.

Departing somewhat from traditional "pediatric" issues, the author reviewed research findings on the genetic aspects of behavioral syndromes. These syndromes are important components in a population of children experiencing defeat or jeopardy in the educational system.

Cerebral hemisphere specialization of function was discussed. The main issues concerned the need to recognize variations in schedules of development of different cognitive, language, and behavior systems, some supposedly preponderant in the left cerebral hemisphere and others in the right. The discussion touched upon the difference between a global "perceptual" impairment versus a more specific "language" disability. Reading is a language-based skill, and the child with reading disability may have excellent perceptual development (the right hempishere is on; the left is lagging?).

It was suggested that the academic establishment abandon its "half-brained" preoccupation with education only through language and instead give attention to the spatial-gestural-pattern processing postulated to be operating in the right hemisphere.

Through the discussion it was emphasized that the pediatrician has advantages over other professionals on the child-study team:

1. He has access to the child's health history, and to the behavioral and health history of family members.
2. He can examine (lay hands on) the body of the child.

3. He can see the child sequentially, over time, in nonstress situations.

4. He can discover, through discussions with the family and children, that the central nervous system mediates more than just sensation, movement, memory, and intelligence; it also manages language processes and temperament controls.

George W. Brown

REFERENCES

Adebimpe, V. R. Complex partial seizures simulating schizophrenia. *JAMA*, 1977, *237*, 1339–1341.

American Academy of Pediatrics. *Adoption of children* (3rd ed.). Evanston, Ill.: the Academy, 1973.

Bakwin, H. Reading disability in twins. *Developmental Medicine and Child Neurology*, 1973, *15*, 184–187.

Bever, T. G., & Chiarello, R. J. Cerebral dominance in musicians and nonmusicians. *Science*, 1974, *185*, 537–538.

Bohman, M. A study of adopted children, their background, environment and adjustment. *Acta Paediatric Scandinavica*, 1972, *61*, 90–97.

Borland, B. L., & Heckman, H. K. Hyperactive boys and their brothers: A 25-year follow-up study. *Archives of General Psychiatry*, 1976, *33*, 669–675.

Cantwell, D. P. Psychiatric illness in families of hyperactive children. *Archives of General Psychiatry*, 1972, *27*, 414–417.

Cantwell, D. P. *The Hyperactive child: Diagnosis, management, current research.* New York: Spectrum, 1975. (a)

Cantwell, D. P. Genetics of hyperactivity. *Journal of Child Psychology and Psychiatry and Allied Disciplines*, 1975, *16*, 261–264. (b)

Carey, W. B. Clinical applications of infant temperament measurements. *Journal of Pediatrics*, 1972, *81*, 823–828.

Chalfant, J. C., & Scheffelin, M. A. *Central processing dysfunctions in children.* NINDS Monograph No. 9. Washington, D.C.: U.S. Department of Health Education and Welfare, 1969.

Chess, S. *An introduction to child psychiatry* (2nd ed.). New York: Grune & Stratton, 1969.

Chess, S. and Hassibir, M. *Principles and practices of child psychiatry.* New York, Plenum Press, 1978.

Crichton, M. *The terminal man.* New York: Bantam, 1972.

Dimond, S. J., & Beaumont, J. G. *Hemispheric function in the human brain.* New York, Halsted, 1974.

Elliott, F. A. Neurological causes and cures of explosive rage. *Medical Opinion,* 1977, *6,* 34–46.

Engel, G. L. The need for a new medical model: A challenge for biomedicine. *Science,* 1977, *196,* 129–136.

Fincher, J. *Human intelligence.* New York: Putnam, 1976.

Frazier, Jr., S. J. *The murderer.* Paper presented at the Conference on Violence and Aggression: A Perspective, El Paso, Texas, 1977.

Gardner, H. A psychological investigation of Nelson Goodman's theory of symbols. *The Monist,* 1974, *58,* 319–326.

Garside, R. F., Birch, G., Scott, D. M., et al. Dimensions of temperament in infant school children. *Journal of Child Psychology and Psychiatry and Allied Disciplines,* 1975, *16,* 219–231.

Gibson, E. J., & Levin, H. *The psychology of reading.* Cambridge: MIT Press, 1975.

Gofman, H., & Allmond, Jr., B. W. Learning and language disorders in children *Current Problems in Pediatrics,* 1971, September–October.

Goodwin, D. W. Is alcoholism hereditary: A review and critique. *Archives of General Psychiatry,* 1971, *25,* 545–549.

Goodwin, D. W. Genetic determinants of alcohol addiction. *Advances in Experimental Medicine and Biology,* 1975, *56,* 339–355.

Goodwin, D. W., Schulsinger, F., Hermansen, L., et al. Alcohol problems in adoptees raised apart from alcoholic biologic parents. *Archives of General Psychiatry,* 1973, *28,* 238–243.

Goodwin, D. W., Schulsinger, F., Hermansen, L., et al. Alcoholism and the hyperactive child syndrome. *Journal of Nervous and Mental Disease,* 1975, *160,* 349–353.

Goodwin, D. W., Schulsinger, F., Moller, N., et al. Drinking problems in adopted and non-adopted sons of alcoholics. *Archives of General Psychiatry,* 1974, *31,* 164–169.

Gottesman, R., Belmont, I., & Kaminer, R. Admission and follow-up of reading-disabled children referred to a medical clinic. *Journal of Learning Disabilities,* 1975, *8,* 642–650.

Grossman, H. J. *Manual of terminology and classification in mental deficiency.* Washington, D.C.: American Association on Mental Deficiency, 1973.

Guyer, B. L., & Friedman, M. P. Hemispheric processing and cognitive styles in learning disabled and normal children. *Child Development,* 1975, *46,* 658–668.

Guze, S. B., Woodruff, R. W., & Clayton, P. Hysteria and antisocial behavior: Further evidence of an association. *American Journal of Psychiatry,* 1971, *127,* 957–960.

Haywood, H. C., & Gordon, J. E. Neuropsychology and learning disorders. *Pediatric Clinics of North America*, 1970, *17*, 337–346.

Hobbs, N. *Issues in the classification of children*, (Vols. 1 & 2). San Francisco: Jossey-Bass, 1975.

Horn, J. M., Green, M., Carney, R., & Erickson, M. T. Bias against genetic hypotheses in adoptive studies. *Archives of General Psychiatry*, 1975, *32*, 1365–1367.

International Classification of Disease. Ann Arbor, Mich.: Commission of Professional and Hospital Activities, 1973.

Isaacson, R. L. *The limbic system*. New York: Plenum, 1974.

Joynt, R. J., & Goldstein, M. N. Minor cerebral hemisphere. In W. J. Friedlander (Ed.), *Advances in neurology*, (Vol. 7). New York: Raven, 1975, pp. 147–183.

Kaij, L., & Dock, J. Grandsons of alcoholics. *Archives of General Psychiatry*, 1975, *32*, 1379–1381.

Kinsbourne, M. Models of learning disability: Their relevance to remediation. *Canadian Medical Association Journal*, 1975, *113*, 1066–1069.

Knights, R. M., & Bakker, D. J. *The neuropsychology of learning disorders*. Baltimore: University Park Press, 1975.

Knobeloch, C. Speech and language. In R. B. Johnson & P. R. Magrab (Eds.), *Developmental disorders: Assessment, treatment, education*. Baltimore: University Park Press, 1976, pp. 295–313.

Koppitz, E. M. *Children with learning disabilities: A five-year follow-up study*. New York: Grune & Stratton, 1971.

Lerner, J. W. *Children with learning disabilities* (2nd ed.). Boston: Houghton Mifflin, 1976.

Lezak, M. D. *Neuropsychological assessment*. New York: Oxford University Press, 1976.

Loehlin, J. D., Lindzey, G., & Spuhler, J. N. *Race differences in intelligence*. San Francisco: W. H. Freeman, 1975.

MacLean, P. D. Psychosomatic disease and the "visceral brain:" Recent developments bearing on the Papez theory of emotion. *Psychosomatic Medicine*, 1949, *11*, 338–353.

Mark, V. H., & Ervin, F. R. *Violence and the brain*. New York: Harper & Row, 1970.

Mattis, S., French, J. H., & Rapin, I. Dyslexia in children and young adults: Three independent neuropsychological syndromes. *Developmental Medicine and Child Neurology*, 1975, *17*, 150–163.

McMahon, S. A., & Greenberg, L. M. Serial neurologic examination of hyperactive children. *Pediatrics*, 1977, *59*, 584–587.

Menyuk, P. The language-impaired child: Linguistic or cognitive impairment? *Annals of the New York Academy of Sciences*, 1975, *263*, 59–69.

Milofsky, D. Schooling the kids no one wants. *New York Times Magazine*, Jan. 2, 1977, pp. 24, 25, 28, 33.

Monroe, R. R. *Episodic behavioral disorders*. Cambridge: Harvard University Press, 1970.

Morrison, J. R., & Minkoff, K. Explosive personality as a sequel to the hyperactive child syndrome. *Comprehensive Psychiatry*, 1975, *16*, 343–348.

Morrison, J. R., & Stewart, M. A. A family study of the hyperactive child syndrome. *Biological Psychiatry*, 1971, *3*, 189–195.

Morrison, J. R., & Stewart, M. A. The psychiatric status of the legal families of adopted hyperactive children. *Archives of General Psychiatry*, 1973, *28*, 888–891. (a)

Morrison, J. R., & Stewart, M. A. Evidence for polygenetic inheritance in the hyperactive child syndrome. *American Journal of Psychiatry*, 1973, *130*, 791–792. (b)

Morrison, J. R., & Stewart, M. A. Bilateral inheritance as evidence for polygenicity in the hyperactive child syndrome. *Journal of Nervous and Mental Disease*, 1974, *158*, 226–228.

Munsinger, H. The adopted child's IQ: A critical review. *Psychological Bulletin*, 1975, *82*, 623–659.

Nealis, J. G. T., Gascon, G. G., Hurwitz, I., & Holmes, J. *Right on! or left out?* Paper presented at the 5th Annual International Neuropsychological Society, Santa Fe, New Mexico, 1977.

Nebes, R. D. Hemispheric specialization on commissurotomized man. *Psychological Bulletin*, 1974, *81*, 1–14.

Ornitz, E. M., & Ritvo, E. R. The syndrome of autism: A critical review. American Journal of Psychiatry, 1976, *133*, 609–621.

Porch, B. Personal communication, 1977.

Quinn, P. O., & Rapoport, J. L. Minor physical anomalies and neurologic status in hyperactive boys. *Pediatrics*, 1974, *53*, 742–747.

Ramirez, M., & Casteneda, A. *Cultural democracy, bicognitive development, and education*. New York: Academic Press, 1974.

Ritvo, E. R. *Autism: Diagnosis, current research and management*. New York: Spectrum, 1976.

Robins, L. N. *Deviant children grown up*. Baltimore: Williams & Wilkins, 1966.

Robins, L. N. Follow-up studies of behavior disorders in children. In H. C. Quay & J. S. Werry (Eds.), *Psychological disorders of childhood*. New York: Wiley, 1972, pp. 414–450.

Robins, L. N. Discussion of genetic studies of criminality and psychopathy. R. R. Fieve, D. Rosenthal, & H. Brill (Eds.), *Genetic research in psychiatry*. Baltimore: Johns Hopkins Press, 1973, pp. 117–122.

Rourke, B. P. Reading retardation in children: Develomental lag or deficit? In R. M. Knights & D. I. Bakker (Eds.), *The neuropsychology of learning disorders*. Baltimore: University Park Press, 1975.

Rutter, M. *Helping troubled children*. New York: Plenum, 1975.

Rutter, M., Graham, P., & Yule, W. *A neuropsychiatric study in childhood. Clinics in Developmental Medicine*, Nos. 35/36. Philadelphia: Lippincott, 1970.

Rutter, M., Shaffer, C., & Shepherd, M. *A multi-axial classification of child psychiatric disorders*. Geneva: World Health Organization, 1975.

Safer, D. J. A familial factor in minimal brain dysfunction. *Behavior Genetics*, 1973, *3*, 175–186.

44 / GEORGE W. BROWN

Salk, L. Emotional factors in pediatric practice. *Pediatric Annals*, 1973, *2*, 96–97.

Satterfield, J. H., & Cantwell, D. P. Psychopharmacology in the prevention of antisocial and delinquent behavior. *International Journal of Mental Health*, 1975, *4*, 227–237.

Schain, R. J. *Neurology of childhood learning disorders* (2nd ed.). Baltimore: Williams & Wilkins, 1977.

Schechter, M. D., & Holter, F. R. Adopted children in their adoptive families. *Pediatric Clinics North America*, 1975, *22*, 653–661.

Schopler, E., & Reichler, R. J. (Eds.). *Psychopathology and child development: Research and treatment*. New York: Plenum, 1976.

Schuckit, M. A., Goodwin, D. W., & Winokur, G. A study of alcoholism in half-siblings. *American Journal of Psychiatry*, 1972, *128*, 1132–1136.

Schwartz, G. E., Davidson, R. J., & Maer, F. Right hemisphere lateralization for emotion in the human brain: Interaction with cognition. *Science*, 1975, *190*, 286–288.

Seidel, U. P., Chadwick, O. F. D., & Rutter, M. Psychological disorders in crippled children. *Developmental Medicine and Child Neurology*, 1975, *17*, 563–573.

Stark, J. Reading failure: A language-based problem. *ASHA*, 1975, *17*, 832–834.

Stewart, M. A., & Olds, S. W. *Raising a hyperactive child*. New York: Harper & Row, 1973.

Striffler, N. Language function: Normal and abnormal development. In R. B. Johnson & P. R. Magrab, (Eds.), *Developmental disorders: Assessment, treatment, education*. Baltimore: University Park Press, 1976, pp. 75–90.

Taichert, L. G., & Harvin, D. D. Adoption and children with learning and behavior problems. *Western Journal of Medicine*, 1975, *122*, 464–470.

Thomas, A., & Chess, S. A longitudinal study of three brain-damaged children. *Archives of General Psychiatry*, 1975, *32*, 457–462.

Thomas, A., & Chess, S. *Temperament and development*. New York: Brunner/Mazel, 1977.

Thomas, A., Chess, S., & Birch, G. G. *Temperament and behavior disorder in children*. New York University Press, 1968.

Trites, R. L., & Fiedorowicz, C. Follow-up study of children with specific (or primary) reading disability. In R. M. Knights & D. J. Bakker (Eds.), *The neuropsychology of learning disorders*. Baltimore: University Park Press, 1975.

Turtle, W. J. Prevention of behavior problems: A clinician's view. *Pediatrics*, 1977, *59*, 489–490.

van den Honert, D. A neuropsychological technique for training dyslexics. *Journal of Learning Disabilities*, 1977, *10*, 15–21.

Vellutino, F. R., Smith, H., Steger, J. A., & Kaman, M. Reading disability: Age differences and the perceptual-deficit hypothesis. *Child Development*, 1975, *46*, 487–493.

Vining, E. P. G., Accardo, P. J., Rubenstein, J. E., et al. Cerebral palsy, a pediatric developmentalist's overview. *American Journal of Diseases of Children,* 1976, *130,* 643–649.

Wallach, G. P., & Goldsmith, S. C. Language-based learning disabilities: Reading is language, too! *Journal of Learning Disabilities,* 1977, *10,* 178–183.

Waxman, S. G., & Geschwind, N. The interictal behavior syndrome of temporal lobe epilepsy. *Archives of General Psychiatry,* 1975, *32,* 1580–1586.

Weiner, I. B., & Delgaudio, A. C. Psychopathology in adolescence. *Archives of General Psychiatry,* 1976, *33,* 187–193.

Wender, P. H. *Minimal brain dysfuction in children.* New York: Wiley-Interscience, 1971.

Wender, R. H. *The hyperactive child—A handbook for parents.* New York: Crown, 1973.

Werry, J. S. Developmental hyperactivity. *Pediatric Clinics of North America,* 1968, *15,* 581–599.

Werry, J. S. Organic factors in childhood psychopathology. In H. C. Quay, J. S. Werry (Eds.), *Psychopathological disorders of childhood.* New York: Wiley, 1972, pp. 83–121.

Witelson, S. F. Developmental dyslexia: Two right hemispheres and none left. *Science,* 1977, *195,* 309–311.

Woodruff, R. A., Goodwin, D. W., & Guze, S. B. *Psychiatric diagnosis.* New York: Oxford University Press, 1974.

3

AN HISTORICAL OVERVIEW OF EDUCATION AND THE LEARNING-DISABLED CHILD

Although learning disabilities involve many facets and require inter-disciplinary interaction, general and special educators are ultimately responsible for providing the major diagnostic inputs and the most significant components of the rehabilitation program. The educational specialist is the key to successful therapy for the learning-disabled child. This responsibility mandates a thorough familiarity with the etiologies, manifestations, and therapeutic approaches to disorders of learning. In addition, the educator must be able to blend the findings of a multidisciplinary evaluation into a meaningful educational prescription.

In this chapter we will review various aspects of the educator's approaches to the learning-disabled child. Terminology, educational approaches, and theoretic implications will be examined. Hopefully, the discussion will stimulate interest and concern for the child who is unable to achieve in a traditional academic environment.

HISTORICAL INFLUENCES

Learning disabilities is a relatively young field. With the exception of investigations by Morgan and Hinshelwood (1896), the advances in the field have taken place within the twentieth century. Morgan described the characteristics of a learning disability in an article on "word blindness" in 1896. The symptoms of learning disabilities were not unknown in children, but they were ignored by medical and educational specialists. Consequently, the prevalence in the population was unrecognized. After World War I, some studies of factors affecting learning were undertaken. The behavior of soldiers who had sustained head wounds during the war was studied by Boldstein (1927, 1936), and Orton, a neurologist, analyzed the problems of children with language difficulties. Orton (1937) explored the possible effect of cerebral dominance on learning-related behaviors. Simultaneously, Fernald (1934) and a few others were exploring methods of remediating the problem that was later to be called "learning disabilities."

At the outbreak of World War II, Werner and Strauss (1939a, b, 1940; Strauss and Werner, 1942) began expanding on Goldstein's post-World War I research. Goldstein had found that soldiers suffering from cerebral wounds exhibited signs of perseveration, concrete behavior, figure-ground confusion, and lack of abstract thinking (Goldstein, 1936, 1939). Werner and Strauss observed that these adult behavioral manifestations could be found in children with similar brain damage. The authors noted that children with "exogenous" brain damage (neurological damage not due to genetic factors) could be differentiated from those with "endogenous" (genetic) problems. In addition, they found disorders of figure-ground perception, behavioral and visual perseveration, inability to organize and deal with abstract concepts, and hyperkinetic behavior (Strauss & Werner, 1942). Hyperkinesis took the form of either hyperactivity or distractibility. The children were described as always being in motion and/or having short attention spans. Frequently, they were found to drift into "dissociation," to fail at selecting the appropriate stimuli from the many present in their environment. A child with exogenous brain damage responded only to a portion of what he should and seldom dealt with the totality of either patterns, configurations, or environmental situations. This behavior was described as a disruption of the child's ability to respond to a Gestalt, or whole. For this and subsequent research, the work of Werner and Strauss became the standard for those working in the same behavioral area.

Werner and Strauss also found deficits at the level of abstract thought and developed tests to distinguish between the exogenous and endogenous brain-damaged child. They found that exogenously damaged children could easily be distracted by the intensity of nonessential distractions in their environment. Strauss then looked at personality characteristics (Strauss & Werner, 1942) and found that exogenously damaged children appeared more erratic, impulsive, socially unacceptable, uncontrolled, and uncoordinated. In studies with similar children Strauss and Lehtinen (1947) associated these symptoms with hyperactivity. They advocated a comprehensive psychological and educational program for children with exogenous brain damage. The plan for educational programming was based on the Werner and Strauss (1940) studies with the mentally retarded at Wayne State (Michigan) Training School. The program recommended the attenuation of nonessential stimuli and the accentuation of essential stimuli in the child's environment.

The general theme throughout is that to understand normal child psychology, as well as mental deficiency, one must go beyond standardized acievement test scores. One must analyze the mental processes underlying the achievements and assess each child "intraindividually" in terms of his own abilities and disabilities (Werner & Strauss, 1939a, b).

Werner and Strauss' terms solved some of the labeling problems, but they were also subject to errors and misinterpretation. Other investigators tried different labels. Doll (1951) used the term "neurophrenia" to describe the behavioral symptoms resulting from central nervous system impairment. His concepts, however, were so inconclusive that they lacked the specific reference to the fact that with a learning disability, it is the neurology of learning that is disturbed. Remedial education of some type is required since the child's capacity is average or even greater. Johnson (1962) used the term "marginal children," but this seemed unusually stigmatizing for both the child and his parents and, therefore, inappropriate or even misleading. Chalfant and Scheffelin (1969) employed "central processing dysfunction," a condition described as exhibiting characteristics similar to brain injury but not always accompanied by evidence of a brain injury. This medical model presented several difficulties since evidence of neurological problems was often difficult to establish, was not particularly enlightening for educational or instructional purposes, and presented a completely foreign vocabulary to educators. Orton (1937) had proposed that "specific dyslexia" or "specific reading disability" be used to refer to these children since many of their neurological problems contributed to a concomitant reading disability. This, however, excluded those children who presented the neurological disturbances and symptomatology but had learning problems other than reading.

Many disagreements arose over what actually constituted

exogenous as opposed to endogenous injury. Inadequate diagnosis and difficulty finding descriptive terminology were encountered. Steven and Birch (1957) noted objections to the term "brain-injured": "(1) the etiological term 'brain-injured child' does not deal in behaviors or actual symptoms yet cases of brain-injured patients invariably describe the situation in terms of behavior; (2) the term too often is generalized to other conditions (such as epilepsy) where the relationship is at best tenuous and in many cases completely unsupported; (3) the term does not aid in the development of good teaching techniques and approaches for children so labeled; and (4) the term encourages oversimplification and is too imprecise to be useful descriptively."

Stevens and Birch (1957) suggested substituting "Strauss syndrome" for the old term "brain-injured." With this definition they assumed the following seven symptoms were present: (1) erratic and inappropriate behavior on mild provocation, (2) increased motor activity disproportionate to the stimulus, (3) poor organization of behavior, (4) distractibility of more than a normal degree under ordinary conditions, (5) persistent faulty perceptions, (6) persistent hyperactivity, and (7) awkwardness and consistently poor motor performance. Not wishing to dilute the valuable contributions of Strauss and Lehtinen, Stevens and Birch further suggested that, by definition, Strauss syndrome would be used to describe any child who displayed many or all of these specific problem behaviors.

The new diagnostic term of Strauss syndrome, however, quickly caught on. Although it solved some of the labeling problems encountered with earlier terms, it was not long before it was also subject to similar errors of misinterpretation and overgeneralization. It soon became apparent that it pertained only to a segment of the total group of children with neurogenic disorders of learning. Many of these children could not be described as disinhibited, perseverative, or distractible—the summary of the Strauss and Lehtinen symptomatology for the Strauss syndrome. Chalfant and Scheffelin's broader concept of central processing dysfunction became more accessible as an umbrella term to generalize over a wider range of behaviors related to learning problems (Chalfant & Scheffelin, 1969).

During this formative period in the field of learning disabilities, roughly 1939 to 1960, Hallahan and Cruickshank (1973) noted that there was "a paucity of research, very limited personnel, and no teacher education" specifically oriented to learning disabilities as a discrete educational field. A dramatic change occurred in the early 1960's. General awareness of the existence of a specific group of children experiencing learning problems began to develop. More attention was given to the educational needs of these children. The lack of delineating of the syndrome became apparent, and badly needed theoretical research was begun as a result. Birch and Belmont (1963) initiated research into lateral dominance and right–left awareness. Empirical investigations in different areas expanded, and a data base of knowledge grew upon which important educational decisions of program planning and remediation for the children who presented learning problems could be made.

From parents' groups came pressure for more educational attention to the learning-disabled child and indirectly for a better definition of learning disabilities. In 1963 a conference to examine and explore the problems of the perceptually handicapped was sponsored by a group of parents. Uppermost in the minds of those attending was the lack of definition, the problems involved, and the resulting difficulty in organizing a homogenous group that was needed to foster support and backing for professional training and treatment programs.

Kirk responded and called attention to the two major classifications of definitions: (1) those dealing with causation and etiology involving labels such as brain injury and minimal brain damage and (2) those dealing primarily with "behavioral manifestations of the child" and involving such terms as perceptual disorders and dyslexia.

Kirk put the issue squarely to the participants of the conference—"the term you select should be dependent on your specific aims." He pointed out two major directions for research into the etiology and "effective methods of diagnosis, management, and training of children" with learning disabilities. He also noted that he did not feel the attempts to correlate closely specific central nervous system etiology and resulting behavioral manifestations had been particularly fruitful and that the behavioral direction offered more tangible and functional rewards (Johnson & Morasky, 1977).

Kirk introduced the term "learning disabilities." The conference participants responded quickly by voting to organize as the Association for Children with Learning Disabilities (ACLD). By 1978 the organization had achieved worldwide recognition. The ACLD's interest and activity has resulted in a publication, *The Journal of Learning Disabilities,* and the appearance of texts on learning disabilities.

Wallace and McLoughlin (1975) noted that most definitions of learning disabilities have four points in common: (1) discrepancy between expected and actual achievement, (2) manifestations, (3) focus, and (4) integration.

The discrepancy between expected and actual achievement is usually evaluated in terms of the child's chronological age, mental age, and actual level of classroom achievement in contrast to expected or chronological peer achievement level. Johnson and Myklebust (1967) suggest that 1 or 2 years below the expected level of achievement has been the most common criteria for determining the significance of this discrepancy. They also pointed out that this practice has "serious limitations because 1 year below expectancy at 8 years of age is not comparable to 1 year below expectancy at 16 years of age, or for that matter, at 3 or 4 years of age."

Most learning disabilities are manifested in the areas of arithmetic, reading, writing, spelling, thinking and listening. By relating these disabilities to specific strengths and weaknesses in psychological processes, an educator can usually arrive at a better understanding and definition of the learning disability (Wallace & McLoughlin, 1975).

Furthermore, the definition of learning disabilities as simply the identification of underachievement or lack of learning readiness is not educationally useful. The older learning-disabled child is often 2 or more years behind in academic abilities, but the primary-grade child might be experiencing severe problems in getting started. Also, underachievement may be produced by factors other than a learning disability (Wallace & Kauffman, 1973), such as lack of motivation on the part of the child or inappropriate educational planning.

Learning-disabled children are not primarily hindered by other handicapping conditions such as visual, hearing, or motor impairments, emotional disturbance, or environmental disadvantage. In other words, it is important to determine that these children can, in fact, see and hear normally, are not severely deficient in motor development, and have had the benefit of a normal home and school environment for learning basic skills. Most definitions of learning disability focus on psychological dysfunctions. Efforts to pinpoint specific physical or neurological factors have not always been successful (Kass & Myklebust, 1969; Myklebust & Boshes, 1969).

CURRENT TERMINOLOGY

While each model of the etiology and treatment of learning disabilities has its own unique flavor, the terminology common to all is quite useful in defining the skills necessary for effective learning (Chalfant & Scheffelin, 1969; Johnson & Myklebust, 1967; Kirk & Kirk, 1971). These skills are the same in each model.

1. Attention—the ability to concentrate on a task for a sufficient period of time to localize and receive the essential features of the stimuli. If a child does not look at the page, he will be unable to read.
2. Perception—the ability to organize stimuli in a useful way (Johnson & Myklebust, 1967). This processs can be thought of as a change of transduction of sensory information into electric or neurological impulses. Perceptual disorders are described as deficient channels of organizing stimuli (visual, auditory, motor, etc.) either separately or together. A child who hears oral directions must perceptually organize the auditory stimuli in the correct order. This function does not necessarily require that the child grasp the meaning or significance of the verbal symbols or sounds but merely that he can organize the stimuli as he hears them.
3. Discrimination—the ability to establish a difference between two stimuli on the basis of certain traits. A child who confuses *m* and *n* is not distinguishing the peculiar traits of each letter as he views them.
4. Sequencing—the ability to arrange stimuli in a correct order. Children without sequencing ability cannot follow directions, write a dictated arithmetic problem, or correctly sound out a word.
5. Memory—the ability to recall newly learned (short-term) or stored (long-term) information. A child may be unable to read a word that he has been recently taught. He may not recall his address, how to write his name, or the product of a multiplication problem.
6. Symbolization or representational types of processing—the ability not only to organize phenomena in a fashion consistent with how you heard or saw it, but also to attach meaning to the stimuli. This ability refers to the processing of symbols in oral and written language. A child might be able to sound out a word on a page, but not be able to tell what it means.
7. Synthesis and Analysis—dual functions that allow an individual to compose the necessary elements of a stimulus and subsequently to analyze that stimulus. A child with a synthesis problem cannot blend the elements of a word nor identify the root part of a word.
8. Conceptualization—the ability to group a number of stimuli on the basis of attributes or significant traits (Bruner, et al., 1956). Instruction in reading often takes the form of teach-

ing a particular word and then associating other similar words with it (at, cat, mat, fat, etc.).

While many investigators search for an operational definition of learning disabilities, they seem to be overlooking some basic facts. First, the notion of "learning-disabilities programming" was initially meant to be a vehicle to obtain education support for academic underachievers in the public schools. The concept of learning-disabilities programming has become unwieldly. It incorporates too many widely diverse criteria and recommendations, which have made it impossible for the public schools to implement a program effectively. The practical considerations and problems of these mounting public programs for children with learning disabilities have resulted in confusion among those who have tried to fund, organize and operate them.

Second, the focus of the concept of learning disabilities upon psychological processes has caused innumerable difficulties. Defining these processes, creating efficient, practical, and accurate assessment techniques for them, and designing educational remediative treatments have remained elusive goals. The focus on psychological functions has been, and continues to be, an alternative strategy to identifying neurological bases for the disorders, a much more difficult and frustrating approach.

An ideal program for the learning disabled would have three components: (1) There should be an effort to increase available remedial programs for learning-disabled children (regular classroom modifications, teacher-aide services, resource rooms, itinerant services, and total support systems should be encouraged); (2) there should be educationally relevant diagnosis and remediation, which would provide more time for educators to focus on the major problems in school; and (3) the research into psychological and/or neurological models should not lead to premature concern of teaching children how to read, write, and calculate.

EDUCATIONAL APPROACHES TO LEARNING DISABILITIES

Myers and Hammill (1969) use a six-part conceptualization of educational approaches to learning disabilities by differentiating the different systems into perceptual motor, multisensory, language development, phonics, test-related, and specially structured types. A similar system, used by Gearhart (1973), includes a diagnostic approach and some environmental control systems. Lerner (1971) directs attention to five major areas of sensory-motor and perceptual motor development, perception and memory, language, cognitive skills and maturational psychological social factors. Kirk (1972) lists neurological, perceptual motor, visual perception, multisensory and remedial reading approaches.

Lerner (1971) focuses on categorization of target problems and is closely allied with the approach of Hammill and Bartel (1975). However, the latter classify target problems according to a particular learning disability or behavior problem in areas closely related to academic subject matter, such as reading and arithmetic. Johnson and Morasky (1977) use developmental status, basic processes, deficit behaviors, assessment, and management. The five areas of developmental problems necessitated different techniques and approaches.

Developmental Approach

The developmental approach focuses on the sequential order of each behavior occurring in a prescribed order according to normal development. Developmental theorists define the specific etiology of a learning problem and the remedial approach is directed more toward the cause than toward the reduction of the problem.

Developmentalists use what Baller and Charles (1968) call the "orderliness and coherent design" of the developmental sequences. Designated "critical stages" become points of attention, and it is assumed that these are the times when the organism is "ready" to learn a certain behavior.

Many different theorists utilize the developmental approach. Some focus more on specific aspects of behavior. Piaget (1952), whose interest involves the individual's progressive adaptive and organizational behaviors, works with the cognitive development of the child. Gesell's extensive research in child development resulted in the preparation of detailed tables of typical sequential developmental behaviors of children (Gesell, 1949). Others approach the subject from the standpoint of changes and stabilities in behavior itself (Ball et al., 1967).

There are pros and cons to the developmental approach. One of its major assets seems to be that it provides some type of normative standard at different ages that may be useful in determining the relative status of a child's functioning in comparison with chronological peers. Another is that critical periods or stages in a child's life can be noted with more accuracy, which can be very helpful in considering remediation strategies. Maximizing the advantages of a remediation therapy is a pervasive goal, and the decision of what step or steps to take in treating the problem is always a difficult one. If developmental models of the learning behaviors are available, the process is greatly simplified. Although most well-trained developmentalists are sensitive to the problem and recognize the need to approach the behaviors systematically and sequentially, the role of maturation is not clearly explained by any relatively simple developmental scheme. The reaction of the developmentalists is to divide their programs' focus between a rigid orientation and a more experientially oriented approach (Johnson & Morasky, 1977).

Basic Process Approach

There is much in common between the basic process approach and the developmental approach because both involve basic, established, healthy, normal sequences of behaviors. The basic process approach and the developmental approach adhere to the concept of a lawful and progressive nature to these sequences. Both assume that the disruption of the "normal" progressive development can lead to problems.

The practitioners who adopt a basic process approach subscribe to the developmental approach. Additional assumptions, however, are made that are not found in all developmental theories. For the theorist who subscribes to the basic process theory, the sequential developmental focus is primarily on a narrow or single process rather than an orientation to all phases of development. The basic approach is aimed essentially at unifying all developmental and learning behaviors under one framework. Etiology is important, although the search for cause is apt to be directed along narrower lines. Remedial activities involve reestablishing a developmental sequence in the child. The underlying philosophy is that a normally developed child will yield normal behavior.

Another common approach is to suggest that a primary sensory function, such as vision (Getman & Kane, 1964), or motor movement (Barsch, 1965) is the prime functional initiator of all other learning behaviors. Still another basic approach concentrates on the process of basic integration between two or more systems as in the interaction of visual and motor behaviors (Kephart, 1971).

Some practitioners rely on central nervous system functions for all explanations of development and behavior, directing all remedial activities toward the primary neural connection pathway level (Delacato, 1966). A similar, but less conservative approach focuses on a particular aspect of central nervous system function such as integrative or reciprocal innervation and functioning (Ayres, 1972). Only Delacato (1966) feels that the basic system is fundamental in an absolute way and there are no exceptions. Frostig and Maslow (1968) focus on what they consider to be a principal underlying process (visual perception), but point out that other systems should not be ignored.

In theories involving central nervous system concepts, remediation activities are directed at building or rebuilding a basic system (Delacato, 1966) or at learning to use the preexisting machinery of a system more effectively (Getman & Kane, 1964). Advocates of this approach argue that it provides better explanations of and means for discerning the status of readiness periods and other similar critical stages since these relate to a single system rather than the entire organism. Like the developmental approach, the basic process approach encourages ongoing sequential research and study.

The research evidence, however, is not strong enough at this point to support either the developmental or basic process theories. The research raises enough questions to suggest that care and caution be used with both approaches. The generalization of results achieved as a result of basic process remediation to day-by-day academic learning activities is not always clearly demonstrated, and a great deal more research that is longitudinal in nature is needed before this limitation can be removed. Finally, there is no simple way to resolve the inherent questions when two programs, each advocating a different basic process or system, seem to obtain equally successful results.

Deficit Behavior Approach

The intent and practice of the deficit behavior approach is to strike directly at the problem behavior itself in an attempt to break a nonproductive pattern and substitute more effective or efficient learning behaviors. Kirk (1962), one of the leading proponents of this approach, which he calls the "learning-disability strategy," has written that "the knowledge of the etiology of the disability in most instances is not helpful to the organization of remedial procedures."

The behavioral deficit approach places emphasis on the planning of individualized programs of remediation rather than on a generalized, predetermined structure or sequence. It emphasizes assessment and observation of a child's actual behavior, comparison of the behavior against the criterion behavior already defined, noting any disparity that exists, and then specific work on removing the disparity.

The concept focuses on accurate assessment of an individual's psychological abilities and disabilities and is largely responsible for the qualifier "specific" being added to the diagnostic label of learning disability (Kirk, 1962). It stresses "normalcy" to general functioning level, sensory functioning, and the overall phsyiological status of the child. The learning-disabled child is assumed to be "normal" with a specific learning problem that can be attacked directly.

The deficit behavior approach encourages shifting from one remedial program or activity to another, utilizing evaluation data to determine the existence of different deficit behaviors.

Because the deficit approach to problem learning behaviors is a fairly straightforward process, one can easily relate remedial activities and goals to curriculum activities and goals. Another asset seems to be that generalization of results does not have to be established, since it is a problem-specific treatment.

There are several concerns, however, about this approach. Since the learning-disabled child is frequently suffering frustration because of failure, in addition to the anxiety generated by the actual problem in learning, additional focus on these issues tends to raise anxiety even further. Furthermore, the teacher often encounters difficulties when a child, in order to redevelop or reshape a deficient behavior, has to return to some earlier grade level. This can cause motivational problems for the child and practical planning problems for the teacher.

Assessment-oriented Approach

Assessment oriented approaches are highly formalized and structured. Since the concept of assessment carries with it the implicit questions, assessment of *what* and *why*, there is a predictable progression through the process. Certain behaviors are observed and appear to fit some pattern or model. A theoretical model is built, and data are needed to evaluate it. Assessment instruments are designed to supply the necessary data. A model is formed for which some type of statistical validity can be demonstrated (Johnson & Morasky, 1977).

The model may be of an overall system, as in the Wepman, Jones, Bock and Van Pelt (1960) description of the levels of function in the central nervous system. On the other hand, the model may be of an assessment instrument that represents and measures behavior within the organism, as Kirk, McCarthy and Kirk (1968) propose for the Illinois Test of Psycholinguistic Abilities. In some cases, the model is less formalized but still results in an evaluative instrument that is designed to reflect behaviors pertinent to important facets of the model. The Developmental Test of Visual Perception is an example of this latter type of model (Frostig, Lefever & Whittlesey, 1964).

Assets of the assessment-oriented approach involve the structure and hard data supplied by the instrument and program together. Most learning-disability programs of this type tend to categorize more in terms of behaviors (as defined by the assessment instrument) than in terms of meaningless categories.

There are, however, many problems with this approach. The main criticism is that too much dependence is placed upon a single assessment instrument, which can easily lead to failure in recognizing and dealing with other problems.

Management Approach

The management approach almost entirely focuses on the problem of how to make what the practitioner does be more effective and efficient. Exactly what is to be remedied, what criteria are to be used, and what techniques are to be involved are important aspects of this approach. The approach organizes and establishes managerial procedures as precisely as possible.

The range of application of these principles is quite wide. Hewett (1968) suggested that the planned engineering of classrooms include curriculum content and teaching techniques, as well as phsycial components, to increase the efficacy of handling special problems. His theoretical orientation is largely developmental. Some years ago, Cruickshank (1961) suggested changes in the management of external stimuli in environmental situations, believing this would aid learning-disabled and hyperactive children.

Moraksy (1973) applies systems theory to the instructional design of programs for the learning-disabled to be used by a paraprofessional team. The advantages of this approach center primarily around its organizational aspects: (1) it aids in decision making; (2) it helps avoid problem behaviors; (3) it aids in communication between individuals of different orientations and disciplines; and (4) it coordinates efforts for a defined activity plan, avoiding loss of focus. Disadvantages of this approach are that it can be time-consuming and that it must be consistent to be effective.

In educating the learning-disabled child, there are three basic educational models: the psychodynamic, the psychoneurological, and the psychoeducational (L'Abate & Curtis, 1975). The psychoeducational approach loosely binds together the theories of Kirk, McCarthy, Frostig, Wepman, and others. The basic treatment model (the psychoeducational model) focuses on compensatory training and remediation, and the concern for identified etiology is minimal. The psychodynamic model views the child's problems as a result of environmental factors, thereby stressing the behavioral anomalies more than the educational learning problems. The psychoneurological model leans heavily toward behavioral, as opposed to learning, problems, but it stresses etiology. Herein lies Strauss' thesis that the externally visible problems are the result of injury or damage to the central nervous system occurring during or shortly after the pregnancy. The treatment model, therefore, focuses on medical therapies: pharmacological treatment, physical therapy and/or physical training processes.

Within the field of learning disabilities, many theorists currently make use of two or more different approaches. There is no particular advantage in trying to fit anyone's theory or program into a single approach.

THEORISTS WITHIN THE FIELD OF LEARNING DISABILITIES

Many observers (such as Hallahan & Cruickshank, 1973; Myers & Hammill, 1969) feel that certain theorists have made outstanding contributions to the field of learning disabilities. Dolphin (1950) supplied the needed link between Strauss and Werner's conception of exogenous mental retardation (1942) and children of normal intelligence. She compared cerebral palsied children of average or above average intelligence to normals, and showed deficits in figure-ground skills, concept formation, visual motor performance, and tactual motor skills (Dolphin & Cruickshank, 1951). This was expanded further by in-depth studies of figure-ground relationships (Cruickshank, Bice & Waller, 1957; Cruickshank, Bice, Waller & Lynch, 1965), which supported the similarities of the psychological characteristics manifested by Werner & Strauss's exogenous children and the cerebral palsied children. These in-depth studies criticized the traditional teaching methodologies.

During the 1950's Cruickshank published numerous papers dealing with cerebral palsy, exogenous mental retardation, and epilepsy that provided the impetus for expansion of the ideas of Werner and Strauss to the intellectually normal child. Using language as the explanatory construct, Kendler and Kendler (1959) studied the performance of very young children and lower organisms to problem-solving tasks. This work provided further support for Kephart's correlation between phylogenetic rank and the abilities for complex behavior.

Haring, a student of Cruickshank, extended the former concept by using behavior modification principles. Haring and his associates, at the University of Washington Experimental Unit at the Child Development and Mental Retardation Center, noted the importance of environmental variables that confront the child. He maintained that the environment could be structured by establishing contingency reinforcement procedures.

Influenced by his exposure to Werner and Strauss, Kephart placed paramount emphasis on perceptual motor development. The "servomechanistic" model of perceptual development proposed by Brown and Campbell (1948) initiated Kephart's concept that perception and motoric response are inseparable. Kephart perceived a child's perceptual progress as an evolution from undifferentiated perception, to the breakdown into parts, to the integration and reconstruction of the parts into a whole figure.

According to Kephart, left-right body awareness (laterality) is a mandatory prerequisite for the differentiation of left-right spatial relationship (directionality). An additional premise for Kephart's work was the perceptual motor match which maintains that motor development precedes perceptual development. Thus, in educational programs for the learning-disabled child, perceptual information must be matched to motor information.

Kephart was influenced by his association with Werner and Strauss. In his book *Slow Learner in the Classroom,* Kephart (1960) discusses children with perceptual motor problems and suggests remedial teaching techniques. He feels a child must learn to adapt to the environment and that there is a positive correlation between complex behavior and rank on the phylogenetic scale.

Getman, a collaborator of Kephart's, also contributed to the field of learning disabilities. Both had developed assessment and remediation techniques based on visual motor modalities, applicable to children with perceptual motor problems. Getman, an optometrist, obtained a strong orientation in experimental and developmental psychology from Renshaw and Gesell. This paved the way for the relationship between Getman and Kephart in the 1950's. In 1956 they coauthored a test that stressed using motor and visual perception exercises in learning-readiness programs for children (Getman & Kephart, 1956).

In *The Psychology of Readiness,* Getman and Kane (1964) advocated many of Getman's specific training activities and those of both Kephart and Strauss. Getman's association with Rappaport and The Pathway School (Pennsylvania) for brain-injured and learning-disabled children in the 1960's were an additional influence on Get-man's theoretical development.

Getman created his own model of visual development. The first three levels of the model include innate response systems, general motor systems, and special motor systems. From the fourth level, in ascending order, Getman diverges from the visual development schemes advocated by developmental psychologists to those he had been optometrically researching. The two uppermost levels of his hierarchy stress ocular motor systems and speech motor systems. According to Getman, the visual system is the most important processing system, and the one most necessary for school-oriented learning tasks. His opponents, however, felt that he had devalued the role of language.

In the area of stimulus reduction, Getman espoused specific ideas for the use and modification of cubicles in order to make them more functional tools in the educative process for the learning-disabled. Perhaps one of Getman's greatest contributions has been that, through his theories and practices, he has demonstrated the value of the interdisciplinary approach to the study of the learning-disabled child.

In the learning-disabilities' movement, Barsch (1960a, b; 1965a, b; 1967; 1969a,b) was also strongly influenced by Strauss. In conjuction with Getman, Barsch instituted the Stevens' Point (Wisconsin) Camp for children with learning disabilities and their parents. Both reached a greater awareness of the problems of a learning-disabled child and his interaction with his parents. Barsch is most noted for this theory of "movigenics," the study of the development of spatial movement patterns that provide the physiological basis for a child's learning. He hypothesized that the development of movement patterns was a necessary prerequitiste for communication abilities and that man's evolutionary search for survival is the basic reason for his motor development. However, whether or not man, modern or ancient, requires movement to survive is a point that has been debated frequently. Barsch has been criticized for his underscoring of the importance of motor development. Barsch's training activities involve muscular strength, balance, spatial and body awareness, visual and auditory dynamics, tactile-kinesthetic dynamics, bilaterality, rhythm, flexibility, and motor planning. Despite the acute emphasis on movement and spatial awareness, Barsch's activities are similar to those of Strauss, Kephart, and Getman.

Frostig pioneered the study of perceptual motor development in the 1960's. The Frostig Developmental Test of Visual Perception

(Frostig, Lefever & Whittlesey, 1964) was designed and remedial training programs were constructed (Frostig & Horne, 1964). The five areas of assessment included: (1) eye-motor coordination, (2) visual figure-ground discrimination, (3) form constancy, (4) position in space, and (5) spatial relations.

Criticism of the test continues to focus on its original standardization on a predominantly white, middle-class population of children. Thus, with use of the instrument on non-white, non-middle class, or even non-American populations, a cultural bias is introduced. In addition, whether or not the five areas designated as being tested are truly independent from one another is a question frequently asked. In spite of this, reliability studies on total scores have been very high, and the test serves as a valuable screening tool in forecasting academic achievement at the early primary grade levels.

Frostig's test departs from usual projective testing long used to assess the psychological functioning in children. The remedial programs, dependent on the five subtest areas, provide clues to programming training activities designed to strengthen deficit areas. Within the program as a whole, visual training and visual motor training are stressed, and for this reason Frostig has most in common with the theories of Barsch, Kephart, and Getman.

All of the learning-disability theorists discussed thus far contend that motor development is a necessary precursor for perceptual development. They stress that an accurate diagnosis of a child's specific problems must be obtained before an effective education program can be implemented.

Doman and Delacato, unlike the previous theorists, designed treatments based on central nervous system etiology (Doman, Delacato, & Doman, 1964) rather than behavioral characteristics. In the 1950's they developed a theory of "neurological organization" and presented treatment methods to remediate weaknesses in this organizational development. They strongly advocated treatment programs by which children are trained in specific motor patterns in order to stimulate specific areas of the brain. In this manner the direct treatment of brain function instead of behavior was undertaken.

The Doman-Delacato theory was a source of unprecedented controversy in the field of learning disabilities. Their neurological organization construct was a catalyst allowing theorists to hypothesize on many critical areas.

Although most of the work within the field of learning disabilities has centered around the study of perceptual motor systems, there have been many important contributors who have dealt primarily with the area of language disabilities. Orton, a neuropathologist, was a strong proponent of the neurological "mixed-dominance" theory, theorizing that mixed (as opposed to lateral dominance) negatively affected the development of reading abilities. He further believed that this mixed dominance state (also referred to as a reading disability) was transmitted genetically. Orton's remedial techniques stressed reading instruction primarily through auditory rather than visual modalities. A phonetic approach to reading was advocated with letter-tracing used as an added kinesthetic cue.

Fernald is recognized for the reading program that she developed for learning-disabled children at the Clinic School of the University of California. Believing that successful experiences are necessary for environmental adjustment, she programmed children to master fundamental academic subjects in which they had experienced little previous success. Fernald (1943) developed a kinesthetic remedial reading approach consisting of four stages: First, the child chooses any word he wishes to learn to read and continually traces a copy of the word with his finger until he can both recognize and reproduce the word without being able to see the original copy. He then uses the word in an original short story, thus demonstrating correct contextual usage. Second, the child learns a new word by saying it over to himself and then writing it without copying (no tracing is needed). Third, the child learns directly from the printed word (tracing and vocalization are not necessary). Fourth, the child is now able to generalize sufficiently to discern new words on the basis of their resemblance to known words.

Based on her background in Gestalt psychology and a degree in speech pathology, deHirsch had a great deal of exposure, both practically and theoretically, to neurological dysfunctions. Like Orton, she felt that children's speech disorders could be placed on a continuum of language dysfunctions. In an article published in 1952, she described the receptive and expressive language deficits of dyslexic children. Influenced by Strauss and Werner, she also investigated the perceptual motor problems of dyslexics and her findings were reported in 1954. DeHirsch's remediation techniques are very eclectic in nature and tailored to meet the individual child's specific needs. Her studies on the prediction of reading failure in children in the early school years are well-recognized.

As a member of the pediatric/psychiatric team and a language consultant at the New York State Psychiatric Institute, deHirsch played a major role in integrating various theoretical positions in the area of children's language disabilities. Her work supports perceptual motor theorists. DeHirsch postulates that formal reading instruction for children predicted to have reading problems should be delayed until success with perceptual motor behavior and oral language has been attained.

Another important theory in the field of children's language disabilities is that postulated by Kirk (1962, 1966, 1970). Kirk believed that in order to remediate children's communication problems, adequate tests had to be developed to isolate the discrete abilities and disabilities found within the language of children. After 15 years of clinical experience and field testing, Kirk, in collaboration with McCarthy and Kirk, produced the Illinois Test of Psycholinguistic Abilities (ITPA) in 1961. Further work on the test and its components resulted in a revised edition published in 1968.

Many consider ITPA the primary test for the identification and evaluation of suspected learning disabilities. Appropriate for children 2 to 10 years of age, the test was designed to assess the psycholinguistic abilities and disabilities of children. The evaluation is based upon assessment of a child's channels of communication (receptive and expressive), psycholinguistic processes, and levels of language organization. The authors identified channels of communication as those systems used for the processing of sensory information, whether expressive (output), or receptive (input). These channels are auditory-vocal and visual-motor. Psycholinguistic processes are those internal functions required to assimilate, evaluate, and prepare a response for the sensory information recieved; i.e., the reception, organization, and expression of language. Organizational levels tested by the ITPA are those levels at which the stimulus materials are processed. Kirk identifies these as either representational or automatic.

A tremendous amount of research has been conducted with the ITPA since its publication. It has been, and continues to be, a popular clinical and research test in the area of learning disabilities. Although the ITPA is purported by its authors to be concerned primarily and exclusively with psycholinguistic functioning, both the ITPA itself and the subsequently evolved remediation strategies (Kirk & Kirk, 1971) employ a wide range of both visual perceptual and perceptual motor items.

Myklebust, who was primarily concerned with disabilities of a linguistic nature, conducted research involving children who were unable to develop receptive language even though their hearing was *not* impaired. As a result of this work, he is noted for the identification and construction of diagnostic and remedial recommendations for six types of learning disabilities: auditory, verbal, arithmetic, reading, writing, and nonverbal communication.

"Psychoneurological learning disability," the terminology coined by Myklebust, incorporates his etiological stance that neurological dysfunction is at the base of all learning disabilities (1964a, b; 1968; Myklebust & Boshes, 1969). In an attempt to quantify the range of a child's learning disability, Myklebust also developed a "learning quotient."

Barry advocates a more eclectic approach in working with children with communication disorders and learning disabilities. Her methodology is presented in *The Young Aphasic Child: Evaluation and Training.* Barry's theory for helping such children is highly structured and blocks out all nonessential stimuli. She suggests six behavioral areas for evaluation: (1) complete case history, carefully evaluated, (2) a complete audiological evaluation, (3) a thorough check of psychomotor functioning, (4) a complete speech/language evaluation, (5) an evaluation of gross and fine motor abilities, and (6) a psychological profile emphasizing social and emotional adjustment skills.

Using these six areas, Barry compiled a list of the behavioral characteristics of speech, language, reading, and writing that are most often associated with aphasics. These are particularly useful for informal professional evaluations (Barry, 1955).

The physical setup, corrective therapy for pyschomotor dysfunctions, and the development of language are important parts of Barry's training programs for language dysfunctions. Corrective therapy incorporates training in impaired body image, impaired perceptions, figure-ground disturbances, spatial disorganization, and/or expressive language is the primary goal for the language and language skills training program. It also includes methods to strengthen reading, writing, and number concepts as communication tools.

Benton is noted for his experimental work concerning the various behavioral characteristics that may be associated with a specific cerebral lesion. In the course of his research he elucidated certain hypothetical psychoneurological syndromes.

In 1951 Benton and his associates criticized the previously accepted special arithemtic ability and disability groupings used by Strauss and Werner as classifiers of neurological problem areas. After noting several discrepancies regarding the ability levels of some students (discrepancies that would significantly alter the grouping processes), Benton, Hutcheon, and Seymour (1951) undertook their own replication of mathematics ability groupings. These experiments paved the way for his investigations of right-left discrimination and various aspects of body schema (Benton, 1959). In the course of the later research, he noticed and proved a significant relationship between finger localization and certain kinds of finger praxes. Many of the behaviors noted in his investigation are attributed to children with learning disabilities. Benton later observed and investigated the incidence of these behaviors among neurologically impaired children and compared these behaviors with those of children with reading disabilities. He eventually rejected Kephart's premise that right-left discrimination was important with respect to academic achievement. The Benton Visual Retention Test, published in 1963, is a diagnostic instrument for brain damage. It utilizes a memory-for-designs format.

Reitan (1964) was concerned with psychological characteristics of brain-injured individuals rather than with the specific diagnosis of the condition of brain injury and tests to ascertain if there was injury. He based his work on the investigations of Halstead, who developed an extensive battery of tests for use with brain-injured adults. Modifying Halstead's battery, Reitan developed the Reitan-Indiana Neuropsychological Test Battery for Children (1951) for use with children between the ages of 9 and 14 years. The Reitan battery incorporates the Category Test, the Tactual Performance Test, the Rhythm Test, the Speech-Sounds Perception Test, the Finger Oscillation Test, the Time Sense Test, the Marching Test, the Color Form Test, the Progressive Figures Test, the Matching Pictures Test. With his battery and other testing devices, Reitan was deeply involved in relating psychological abilities to brain damage.

LEARNING DISABILITIES VS. TEACHING DISABILITIES

"What causes learning disabilities?" is a frequent question. Myers and Hammill (1969) noted that the term, "learning disability is used to describe a specific type of exceptional child: it is not a generic term for all children who have learning problems in school." The "true" learning-disabled children have inherent problems (Fairchild & Henson, 1976).

Children's learning disabilities due to internal factors may be the result of some neurological dysfunctioning attributed to: (1) illness or injuries during development of the central nervous system, (2) circulating, toxic, or metabolic dysfunction which occurred during the prenatal development, (3) biochemical irregularities, (4) toxins and poisoning, (5) nutritional disorders, (6) perinatal brain damage, (7) developmental or maturational lags, and (8) inherited familial traits.

Personal factors that contribute to learning problems may be noted in children who have the capability and despite outstanding teaching, are still not achieving. These are the children who are doing poorly because of unidentified needs, interests, attitudes, and/or motivation. These are the children who appear disinterested and who seem not to care. The academic gap widens and soon these children are in serious educational difficulty. For the child who fails to progress properly in school, we must look at the external environment.

External factors are conditions outside the child and beyond his control. For these factors special education uses the term "teaching disabilities." This term, or the term, "instructional disabilities," is used to imply that the child does *not* have an inherent or "true" learning disability. The problem is environmentally or situationally based. The children have learning problems but not learning disabilities.

The "teaching disability" may be the result of inappropriate teaching methodology, materials, curriculum or lack of individualization. Often parents and other professionals will suggest curriculum and content of instruction. However, the ultimate responsibility for learning in the schools rests with the teachers. They must focus upon the development of basic communication skills. Teachers should consider all suggestions but maintain an educational perspective; otherwise, children may be subjected to inappropriate procedures that do not serve their needs (Wallace & McLoughlin, 1975).

Learning disabilities in some instances has become a "catchall" phrase for educators whose estimates regarding our school-age population with disabilities range from 1 to 20 percent. With such a variation in the figures, it is reasonable to assume special educators and other professionals are emphasizing different factors. The lower figure might realistically reflect the prevalence of children with inherent learning problems (Fairchild & Henson, 1976).

In many school systems the definition of learning disabilities is so general and vague that it has become an easy "out" to label nonconforming or nonachieving children. To avoid inappropriate labeling and services for learning-disabled children, teachers must not stop looking for other possible factors that may be causing or contributing to the problem of nonlearning. The school has a definite responsibility in the identification of the learning disabled child. The teacher and support personnel can provide very useful information to aid in rehabilitating this child. The teacher must note the specific problem areas in terms of academic performance, classroom behavior and peer relations (Barin, Liebel and Smith, 1978). Too often they label a child learning-disabled, designate him for special classes or programs, and then everyone waits for the magical cure.

As we look to things that can produce a learning problem, we can divide the causes into two categories: internal or external factors. Internal factors deal with the child's own make-up while external factors deal with the child's environment.

Ironically, with this mislabeling, many "true" learning-disabled children are not receiving proper help. However, recent legislation, Public Law 94-142, referred to as the Education for All Handicapped Chidren Act, which guarantees each child the right to free public education or its equivalent, provides new guidelines for programming for learning-disabled children. In addition, it delineates both program entrance requirements for special education children and intake and managerial procedures for educational personnel. The program includes the involvement of the parents, teachers and medical personnel in each child's evaluation. To fulfill this challenge, the educator has a critical role in diagnosis and therapy. This ensures that in the future the L.D. child will receive proper programming and placement.

SUMMARY

The learning disabilities field is still searching for identity. This is not an insurmountable problem. As better trained new leaders emerge, the necessary changes will occur. Prospects look bright for the future!

Judith Schapiro

REFERENCES

Ayers, A. *Sensory integration and learning disorders.* Los Angeles: Western Psychological Services, 1972.

Baller. W., and Charles, D. *The psychology of human growth and development.* New York: Holt, Rinehart & Winston, 1968.

Baller, W., Charles, D., and Miller, E. *Midlife attainment of the mentally retarded: A longitudinal study.* Genetic Psychology Monography, 1967, *75*, 238.

Barem, M., Liebl, R., & Smith, L. *Overcoming learning disabilities: a team approach.* Reston, Virginia: Reston Publishing Company, Inc., 1978.

Barry, H. Classes for aphasics. In M. E. Frampton & E. D. Gall, *Special education for the exceptional* (Vol. II). Boston: Sargent, 1955.

Barry, H. Training the young aphasic child. *Volta Review,* 1960, *7,* 328–362.

Barry, H. *The young aphasic child, evaluation and training.* Washington, D.C.: Alexander Graham Bell Association for the Deaf, 1961.

Barsch, R. The concept of regression in the brain-injured child. *Exceptional Children,* 1960, *27,* 84–90. (a)

Barsch, R. Evaluating the organic child: The functional organizational scale. *Journal of Genetic Psychology,* 1960, *100,* 345–354. (b)

Barsch, R. *A movigenic curriculum.* Wisconsin Bureau of Handicapped Children Bulletin. Madison: Wisconsin State Department of Public Instruction, No. 25, 1965. (a)

Barsch, R. Six factors in learning. In J. Hellmuth (Ed.), *Learning disorders* (Vol. 1). Seattle: Special Child Publications, 1965, 329–343. (b)

Barsch, R. *Achieving perceptual-motor efficiency: A space-oriented approach to learning.* Seattle: Special Child Publications, 1967.

Barsch, R. The role of cognition in movement. Optometric Child Vision Care and Guidance, Optometric Extension Program Post-Graduate Courses, Series 8, No. 4. (a)

Barsch, R. Counseling the parent of the brain-injured child. *Journal of Rehabilitation,* 1969, *27,* 26–28. (b)

Bateman, B. Learning disabilities—Yesterday, today and tomorrow. *Exceptional Children,* 1964, *31,* 167–177.

Benton, A. L. *Right-left discrimination and finger localization: Development and pathology.* New York: Harper & Row, 1959.

Benton, A. L. *The revised visual retention test: Clinical and experimental applications* (3rd ed.). New York: Psychological Corporation, 1963.

Benton, A. L., Hutcheon, J. R., & Seymour, I. Arithmetic ability, finger localization capacity and right-left discrimination in normal and defective children. *American Journal of Orthopsychiatry,* 1951, *21,* 756–766.

Birch, H., & Belmont, L. Lateral dominance and right-left awareness in normal children. *Child development,* 1963, *34,* 257–270.

Birch, H., & Leford, A. Two strategies for studing perception in brain-damaged children. In H. Birch (Ed.), *Brain damage in children.* Baltimore: Williams & Wilkins, 1964, pp. 46–60.

Boshes, B., & Myklebust, H. Neurological behavioral study of children with learning disorders. *Neurology,* 1964, *14,* 7–12.

Brown, G. S. , & Campbell, D. P. *Principles of servomechanisms.* New York: Wiley, 1948.

Bruner, J. S., Goodnow, J., & Austin, G. A. *A study of thinking.* New York: Wiley, 1956.

Chalfant, J., & Scheffelin, M. *Central processing dysfunction in children: A review of research.* National Institute of Neurological Diseases and Stroke, Monograph No. 9. Washington, D.C.: Department of Health, Education and Welfare, 1969.

Clements, S. *Minimal brain dysfunction in children: Terminology and identification, phase one of a three-phase project.* Washington, D.C.: U.S. Department of Health, Education and Welfare, 1966.

Cohn, R. The neurological study of children with learning disabilities. *Exceptional Children,* 1964, *31,* 179–186.

Cruickshank, W. M. *A teaching method for brain-injured and hyperactive children.* Special Education and Rehabilitation Monograph Series No. 6, Syracuse, N.Y.: Syracuse University Press, 1961.

Cruickshank, W. M. *The teacher of brain-injured children.* Syracuse: Syracuse University Press, 1966.

Cruickshank, W. M., Bice, H. V. & Wallen, N. E. *Perception and cerebral palsy.* Syracuse: Syracuse University Press, 1965.

DeHirsch, K. Specific dyslexia or strephosymbolia. *Folis Phoniatrica,* 1952, *4,* 231–248.

DeHirsch, K. Gestalt psychology as applied to language disturbances. *Journal of Nervous and Mental Diseases,* 1954, *120,* 257–261.

Delacato, C. H. *The treatment and prevention of reading problems: The neurological approach.* Springfield, Ill.: Thomas, 1959.

Delacato, C. H. *The diagnosis and treatment of speech and reading problems.* Springfield, Ill.: Thomas, 1963.

Delacato, C. H. *Neurological organization and reading.* Springfield, Ill.: Thomas, 1966.

Doll, E. Neurophrenia. *American Journal of Psychiatry,* 1966, *108,* 50–53.

Dolphin, J. E. *A study of certain aspects of the psychopathology of children with cerebral palsy.* Unpublished doctoral dissertation. Syracuse University, 1950.

Dolphin, J. E., & Cruickshank, W. M. Pathology of concept formation in children with cerebral palsy. *American Journal of Mental Deficiency,* 1951, *56,* 386–392. (a)

Dolphin, J. E., & Cruickshank, W. M. Visuo-motor perception of children with cerebral palsy. *Quarterly Journal of Child Behavior,* 1951, *3,* 198–209. (b)

Doman, G., Delacato, C. H., & Doman, R. *The Doman-Delacato Developmental Profile.* Philadelphia, Pa.: Institutes for the Achievement of Human Potential, 1964.

Dunn, L. D. Minimal brain dysfunction: A dilemma for educators. In E. C. Frierson & W. B. Barbe (Eds.), *Educating children with learning disabilities.* New York: Appleton-Century-Crofts, 1967.

Dunsing, J. D., & Kephart, N. C. Motor generalizations in space and time. In J. Hellmuth (Ed.), *Learning disorders* (Vol. 1). Seattle: Special Child Publications, 1965.

Fairchild, T., & Henson, F. O. *Mainstreaming the children with learning disabilities.* Auston, Tex.: Learning Concepts, 1976.

72 / JUDITH SCHAPIRO

Fernald, G. M. *Remedial techniques in basic school subjects.* New York: McGraw-Hill, 1943.

Freidus, E. Methodology for the classroom teacher, In J. Hellmuth (Ed.), *The special child in century 21.* Seattle: Special Child Publications, 1964.

Frostig, M., & Horne, D. *The Frostig program for the development of visual perception:* Teacher's guide. Chicago, Ill.: Follett, 1964.

Frostig, M., Lefever, D. W., & Whittlesey, N. The Developmental Test of Visual Perception for evaluating normal and neurologically handicapped children. *Perceptual and Motor Skills,* 1961, *12,* 383–394.

Frostig, M., Lefever, D. W., & Whittlesey, N. *The Marianne Frostig Developmental Test of Visual Perception.* Palo Alto, Cal.: Consulting Psychology Press, 1964.

Frostig, M., & Maslow, P. Language training: A form of ability training. *Journal of Learning Disabilities,* 1968, *1,* 105–115.

Gearheart, B. *Learning disabilities: Educational strategies.* St. Louis: Mosby, 1973.

Gesell, A. *Gesell Developmental Schedules.* New York: Psychological Corporation, 1949.

Getman, G. The Visuo-motor complex in the acquisition of learning skills. In J. Hellmuth (Ed.), *Learning disorders* (Vol. 1). Seattle: Special Child Pulbications, 1965.

Getman, G., & Kane, E. *The physiology of readiness: An action program for the development of perception for children.* Minneapolis: Programs to Accelerate School Success, 1964.

Getman, G., & Kephart, N. *The perceptual development of retarded children.* Lafayette, Ind.: Purdue University, 1956.

Gillingham, A. B., & Stillman, B. L. *Remedial training for children with specific disability in reading, spelling and penmanship* (7th ed.). Cambridge, Mass.: Educators Publishing Service, 1965.

Goldstein, K. *Die lokakisation in der grosshirnrinde.* Handbook of normal pathology and physiology. Berlin: Springer, 1927.

Goldstein, K. The modification of behavior consequent to cerebral lesions. *Psychiatric Quarterly,* 1936, *10,* 586–610.

Goldstein, K. *The organism.* New York: American Book, 1939.

Hallahan, D., & Cruickshank, W. M. *Psychoeducational foundations for learning disabilities.* Englewood Cliffs, N.J.: Prentice-Hall, 1973.

Hammill, D., & Bartel, N. *Teaching children with learning and behavior problems: A resource book for preschool, elementary and special education teachers.* Boston: Allyn & Bacon, 1975.

Hebb, D. *The organization of behaviors.* New York: Wiley, 1949.

Hewett, F. *The emotionally disturbed child in the classroom.* Boston: Allyn & Bacon, 1968

Johnson, J. D., & Myklebust, H. R. *Learning disabilities: Educational principles and practices.* New York: Grune & Stratton, 1967.

Johnson, S. *The marginal child: Workshop proceedings.* Plattsburgh, N.Y.: State University of New York at Plattsburgh, 1962.

Johnson, S. W., & Morasky, R. L. *Learning disabilities.* Boston: Allyn & Bacon, 1977.

Kass, C. Introduction to learning disabilities. *Seminars in Psychiatry,* 1969, *1,* 240–244.

Kass, C., & Myklebust, H. R. Learning disability: An educational definition. *Journal of Learning Disabilities,* 1969, *2,* 377–379.

Kendler, T. S., & Kendler, H. H. Reversal and non-reversal shifts in kindergarten children. *Journal of Experimental Psychology,* 1959, *58,* 56–60.

Kephart, H. *The slow learner in the classroom.* Columbus, Ohio: Merrill, 1960.

Kephart, N. Perceptual-motor correlates of learning. In S. A. Kirk & W. Becker (Eds.), *Conference on children with minimal brain impairments.* Chicago: National Society for Crippled Children and Adults, 1968, 13–26.

Kephart, N. Perceptual-motor aspects of learning disabilities. *Exceptional Children,* 1964, *31,* 201–206.

Kephart, N. *The slow learner in the classroom* (2nd ed.). Columbus, Ohio: Merrill, 1971.

Kephart, N., & Strauss, A. A. A clinical factor influencing variations in I.Q. *American Journal of Orthopsychiatry,* 1940, *10,* 343–350.

Kirk, S. *Educating exceptional children.* Boston: Houghton Mifflin, 1962.

Kirk, S. *The diagnosis and remediation of psycholinguistic disabilities.* Urbana: University of Illinois Press, 1966.

Kirk, S. Lecture appearing in Final Report, USOE Contract, Advanced Institute for Leadership Personnel in Learning Disabilities, sponsored by Department of Special Education, University of Arizona, 1970.

Kirk, S., & Kirk, W. *Psycholinguistic learning disabilities: Diagnosis and remediation.* Urbana: University of Illinois Press, 1971.

Kirk, S., McCarthy, J., & Kirk, W. *Illinois Test of Psycholinguistic Abilities* (rev. ed.). Urbana: University of Illinois Press, 1968.

L'Abate, L., & Curtis, L. *Teaching the exceptional child.* Philadelphia: Saunders, 1975.

Lerner, J. *Children with learning disabilities: Theories, diagnosis, and teaching strategies.* Boston: Houghton Mifflin, 1971.

Morasky, R. *Learning experiences in educational psychology.* Dubuque: Brown, 1973.

Morgan, W. P. A case of congenital word blindness. *British Medical Journal,* 1896, *2,* 1612.

Myers, P., & Hammill, D. *Methods for learning disorders.* New York: Wiley, 1969.

Myklebust, H. R. Learning disorders: Psychoneurological disturbances in childhood. *Rehabilitation Literature,* 1964, *25,* 354–359. (a)

Myklebust, H. R. *The psychology of deafness: Sensory deprivation, learning and adjustment* (2nd ed.). New York: Grune & Stratton, 1964. (b)

Myklebust, H. R. Learning disabilities: Definition and overview. In H. R. Myklebust (Ed.), *Progress in learning disabilities* (Vol. 1). New York: Grune & Stratton, 1968, pp. 1–16.

Myklebust, H. R., & Boshes, B. *Minimal brain damage in children.* Final Report U.S. Public Health Service Contract 108-65-142. Evanston, Ill.: Northwestern University Publications, 1969.

Orton, S. *Reading, writing and speech problems in children.* New York: Norton, 1937.

Osgood, C. *Method and theory in experimental psychology.* New York: Oxford University Press, 1953.

Osgood, C. Motivational dynamics of language behavior. In M. Jones (Ed.), *Nebraska symposium on motivation.* Lincoln: University of Nebraska Press, 1957, pp. 348–424.

Piaget, J. *The origins of intelligence in children.* Trans., M. Cook. New York: International Universities Press, 1952.

Reitan, R. M. *Reitan-Indiana Neuropsychological Battery For Children,* 1951. In communication with Dr. Reitan, University of Arizona, Phoenix, Arizona.

Reitan, R. M. Relationships between neurological and psychological variables and their implications for reading instruction. In H. A. Robinson (Ed.), *Meeting individual differences in reading.* Chicago: University of Chicago Press, 1964, pp. 100–110.

Strauss, A. A., & Kephart, N. *Psychopathology and education of the brain-injured child.* New York: Grune & Stratton, 1955.

Strauss, A. A., & Lehtinen, L. E. *Psychopathological education of the brain-injured child.* New York: Grune & Stratton, 1947.

Straus, A. A., & Werner, H. Disorders of conceptual thinking in the brain-injured child. *Journal of Nervous and Mental Disease,* 1942, *96,* 153–172.

Stevens, G., & Birch, J. A proposal for clarification of the terminology used to describe brain-injured children. *Exceptional children,* 1957, *23,* 341–349.

Wallace, G., & Kauffman, J. M. *Teaching children with learning problems.* Columbus, Ohio: Merrill, 1973.

Wallace, G., & McLoughlin, J. A. *Learning disabilities: Concepts and characteristics.* Columbus, Ohio: Merrill, 1975.

Wepman, J. M., Jones, L. V., Bock, R. D., & Van Pelt, D. Studies in aphasia: Background and theoretical formulations. *Journal of Speech and Hearing Disorders,* 1960, *235,* 323–332.

Werner, H., & Strauss, A. A. Problems and methods of functional analysis in mentally deficient children. *Journal of Abnormal and Social Psychology,* 1939, *34,* 37–62. (a)

Werner, H., & Strauss, A. A. Causal factors in low performance. *American Journal of Mental Deficiency,* 1939, *44,* 163–168. (b)

Werner, H., & Strauss, A. A. Causal factors in low performance. *American Journal of Mental Deficiency,* 1940, *45,* 213–218.

Werner, H., & Thuma B. D. Critical flicker frequency in children with brain injury. *American Journal of Psychology,* 1942, *55,* 394–399. (a)

Werner, H., & Thuma, B. D. A deficiency in the perception of apparent motion in children with brain injury. *American Journal of Psychology*, 1942, *55*, 58–67. (b)
Wiederholt, J. Historical perspectives on the education of the learning disabled. In L. Mann & D. Sabatino (Eds.), *The second review of special education*. Philadelphia, Pa.: Journal of Special Education Press, 1947.

THE
LEARNING-DISABLED
ADOLESCENT

The perceptually handicapped adolescent is an enigma! First, he is an adolescent; second, he has a perceptual disability. The combination of problems makes matters particularly difficult for the adolescent, his family, friends, teachers, and the others who would like to help. Adolescents as a group, even those without problems, are often not well accepted. Many societies have viewed young people as "disruptive and troublesome"; from the ancient Egyptians, who complained that their young were "immoral, irreverent, disrespectful of their elders and frequent the taverns excessively," to Shakespeare grumbing about youth who "do naught save worrying their elders, drink excessively and get wenches with child," to Will Rogers observing that "the reason the young folk seem to get along so well with their grandparents is that they have a common enemy." Idle teenagers—like Romeo and Juliet of the Renaissance who were wealthy and free, or the many of the 1960s who were unemployed—have always been capable of "disrupting" their society. The Capulets and the Montagues, the Democrats and the Republicans—the numbers and the times are different but the effect of the adolescent may be the same.

THE CHANGING LANDSCAPE OF ADOLESCENCE

In the eighteenth century young people like Benjamin Franklin left formal schooling and became apprentices at 12 years of age. They began to work at being adults at an early age, at a time when puberty did not appear until the mid or even late teens.

Beginning with the Industrial Revolution, food, health and nutrition have improved and the age of onset of puberty began a continuing trend downward. Today, girls experience their first menstrual cycle at approximately age 12, whereas 200 years ago menarche usually began at age 16. Boys develop about 2 years behind their female counterparts.

In the first third of the nineteenth century child labor laws moved children out of factories into schools. In the United States public secondary schools were established in the 1850s, lagging behind the private schools which had begun a century earlier. By the last quarter of the nineteenth century children were required to attend school until 16 years of age. Inasmuch as puberty was between ages 14 and 15, a growing class of people was established who were biological adults *before* they were considered old enough to begin adult work. This was something very different from the human experience of only 100 years earlier, when children became biologically mature *after* beginning adult roles in society.

By the start of this century, vocational training and liberalization of the secondary school curriculum were underway. Today young people reach puberty and then mature physically 5 to 10 years *before* society allows them to function and work as adults. Society institutionalizes and perpetuates an agonizingly slow transition: adult ticket prices and transit fares at age 12, religious responsibility at 13 or 14, driving at 16 or 17, drinking and voting at 18, high school graduation around 19, and then college or apprenticeship until 23 when people are finally able to begin to be adults.

Shortly after World War II there was a "baby boom" which lasted for more than a decade and a half. These young people reached adolescence in the 1960s and early 1970s, with peak numbers between 1965 and 1970. Under ordinary circumstances teenagers make up 11 percent of the population of the United States, but between 1965 and 1970 their numbers had grown to 18 percent of the population. Currently, that population bulge is subsiding in the colleges, leaving gaping enrollment chasms in the elementary schools built less than a decade ago. The sudden increase in teenagers had its effect, suddenly thrusting millions of Romeos and Juliets upon a society that did not take the influx kindly and found itself unable to cope.

One result of this population explosion has been that the problems of adolescence have been studied more and are being understood better. We know that adolescence is not an easy time for many young people and that there are specific pitfalls for everyone. Adolescence is the era of transition from childhood to adulthood, and there are numberous adjustments and changes to be made: physically, socially, emotionally, and economically. The biological child must become a physical adult. The social child must become a sexual adult. The dependent child must become an independent adult. The teenager must do all of these simultaneously!

The Body

The physical changes begin at about age 8 in girls, commencing about 2 years later in boys. Biochemically, the hypothalamus, which heretofore was suppressed by clomiphene, becomes insensitive to the chemical, in preparation for the time 2 to 3 years hence when it will stimulate the hypothalamus to trigger the release of pituitary gonadotropin. This changing activity in the hypothalamus is reflected in cyclic changes in the pituitary and the onset of cyclic stomach cramps in some girls at about 9 years of age. Shortly after this, fat deposition begins. The child who was previously regarded as "average weight" becomes chubby, and the chubbies get fat, storing energy for the growth spurt which comes next. First, the foot and hand sizes increase, and then longitudinal growth accelerates. Just after peak growth rate is reached, and, in fact just as it begins to slow, girls have their first menstrual periods (menarche) and boys begin to produce sperm (spermarche). During this rapid growth young people often become slim, awkward, and gawky as ligaments that normally hold the joints together soften and become more elastic. This allows for very rapid growth to occur at the bone ends; but, it also leaves only the muscles to maintain an erect posture. Since muscles fatigue quickly, this can result in poor posture: the round-shouldered, stooped, and slouched age. As height growth slows, the ligaments tighten and muscles begin to develop adult contours. The arrangement of the bones of the face continues to change into the 20s, even though growth of the long bones is over by mid or late teens.

The age at which all of this growth and body modification begins, the rate at which it progresses, and the age when it ends is hereditary and very individual. Families in which parents developed physically earlier than average have children who develop earlier too. Likewise, when parents were late, so will their children be late. Some young people begin to grow at 8 and are finished with their growth by 13, while other may not start until then and continue until past 20. In general, girls begin to change at 10 years, menstruate at 12, and have finished their growth between 16 and 17 years. Boys tend to be 2 years later. The variation, however, is so great that two 13-year-old girls can share a locker in junior high, one so immature she is still physiologically a child and the other so grown she is ready for childbearing. Two 14-year-old boys can compete in the playground, one no more than a Little Leaguer, the other looking like a candidate for a professional team!

When adults react to these young people according to their individual abilities, there are few problems. During this phase of life, however, the abilities vary so greatly that there is a tendency to ignore the developmental range of variation and to deal with the age or academic class. While that may work with the "average" adolescent, it is certain trouble for the teenagers at either of the extremes.

The Mind

The child thinks in concrete terms. Life is black or white, all or none. Suddenly, just prior to puberty, the young person begins to see the semiabstract and discovers Utopia. As Mark Twain observed, "When I was 14, I was disgusted with how little my father knew." Of course, later in adolescence he develops the ability to think in the abstract, and Twain continues, "But when I was 21, I was amazed to discover how much the old man had learned in 7 short years." The timing of these changes in thinking appears linked to the timing of other events of puberty. A child who is late starting puberty will also be late with semiabstract thought. The 11-year-old girl in the pudgy phase often yearns to be a veterinarian, and animals can suddenly become a passion (in suburban and rural areas National Velvet falls in love with horses again). The little girl who joined the Brownies and hated boys is suddenly interested in them. She will not get close to them, but they are fascinating. The pudgy boy, usually around 12 or 13 starts to build models. Bedrooms overflow with pieces of plastic, paper, and balsa wood. Hands are often coated with flakes of glue and model paints. The Cub Scouts who hated girls are Boy Scouts now, and girls are creatures to be examined and even associated with (a little).

Just before menarche and spermarche, at about the time of peak growth rate, boys and girls begin tentative dating. They check carefully to see if the person they like likes them before they chance an encounter, but they quickly begin to "go together" once they make a match. Most are "30-day wonders" with few dating relationships lasting more than a month at this stage. Later, with more physical and emotional maturity, dating lasts about 3 months. Many pairings break up over the realization that the initial interests are not enough to sustain the relationship. Others end because they are nearing sexual intimacy and one of the partners is not ready for it yet. Only with full physical development and psychological maturity of abstract thought does dating one person last more than 3 months and progress to sexual intimacy. Family pressures and problems, peer pressures, and the desire to be like peers can supervene to change the ordinary flow of these maturational events.

The Emotions

The psychological transition is as striking as is the physical transformation. Every person must handle emotions in his own way, no matter how much help he has. Like Peter Pan and Wendy, each retreats to the Neverland of adolescence in which some adults are simply disinterested or univolved (until some disaster occurs), like Wendy's parents, or are downright dangerous, like Hook and the pirates. There are street gangs—the Lost Children and Tiger Lily's Indians—who sometimes play and sometimes fight, and the world itself is not always safe. In the end Wendy goes home and grows up on her own because she sees value in it and Peter stays in Neverland because he does not.

Like the Alice of an author's imagination, the world can suddenly be Wonderland. There are adults who live only for the clock and punish you for being seconds late. Red Queens who are arbitrary, controlling, and impossible are everywhere. Mad Hatters are truly mad and not involved. Cheshire Cats smile smugly but do not do anything. One's own body is unreliable, and teenagers sometimes feel very small and helpless and sometimes so very big they no longer fit. And Alice finds her own way out of it in the end.

Three Questions about Development

Little children, toddlers, have to answer a very important question about themselves. They must determine an answer to "Who are you?" "Whoness" at 2 years is "my name," "my parents' names," and "our labels." "Whoness" at 2 is an extension of parents and family, a simple cogent answer to a pressing problem answered with only the experience and resources of a child of that age. By age 3 the problem is solved!

At age 4 "What are you?" appears. "Whatness" here is gender, and we are what the parent of the same gender is. We are curious about those other folks of a different sex to see how they are different, and we begin to toy with sexuality, with crushes on the parent of the opposite sex. The same-sex parent is a role model for understanding "whatness," but still only in the concrete terms of a child that age. By age 6 the issue is settled!

At 6 years we ask, "Where am I going?" and answer it concretely with "I am going to be a policeman (fireman, teacher, doctor)" and only rarely as "a daddy" for that is too abstract a concept. "Whereness" is to be like someone already known, to be able to try on adult roles and play at being grown. By age 8 the answer is found for a while!

These three concrete questions and answers, each in sequence, suffice until adolescence. Now all three must be answered again in adult and more abstract terms. Rather than one at a time and in an orderly sequence, they must be done *all* at once—not in a child's words but as an adult. Resolution is expected before there has been time to develop adult experience. With all this going on it is not surprising that there is turmoil. The mind is full of new notions and flights of fancy. There is little space left to remember to do chores or to keep a bedroom neat. The backing, filling, constant experimenting, and recurrent trying on of new roles makes adolescence the bargain basement of the mind.

The Emerging Adult

Independence must be tried and autonomy found. Firm secure boundaries known since childhood dissolve as the mind and body change. Only experimentation can find the new limits. Rules and regulations accepted at face value from parents and other adults during childhood must be incorporated into the emerging person, not from rote but for reason. This, however, means questioning and demanding answers. Responsibilities increase along with expectations, at a time when internal changes distract the mind from the world around it. Rights in childhood can change to privileges in adolescence, sometimes with little warning. Hostility at unwanted limits breeds anger and rebellion.

In the midst of all of this psychosocial change, parents may be unprepared for any of it by virtue of their own experiences. Our society does not have rules for parenting teenagers that differ from those for parenting little children. Parents are still expected to feed, clothe, house, cook, wash, sew, wake, urge, cajole, remind, and control until some magic age of emancipation that suddenly sets both parties free of one another. There are no gradual stages for parents to relax their vigil slowly and turn control over gradually to their young in prepara-tion for adulthood. The result, of course, is high school students caught in a guerrilla war with their parents and (sometimes) teachers over who is in charge and who will run their lives. The conflict creates additional rebellion and turmoil. When friction revolves around school work, academic success may suffer. If school work is the prob-lem, it should be resolved before the end of high school, and the young people given some time to learn to run things themselves. If not, then some very tough lessons in self-discipline and self-control will have to be learned at work or in college in the midst of unaccustomed independence. The failure rate when it reaches this point is very high, and the problems are often much worse than if the lessons had been learned in mid teens.

LEARNING DISABILITIES

Against this background of minute-by-minute change, 5 percent of adolescents still have perceptual handicaps and another 5 percent have the scars of handicaps once present but now resolved. The first medical reports of perceptual disabilities more than 80 years ago de-scribed adults. Later similar problems were found in young adults and later still in children.

At first it was thought that the victims could not see words despite normal vision and the condition was called "word-blindness." Fourscore years and nearly 50 descriptive labels later, we now know that perceptual handicaps are a broad variety of communication dis-orders. These deficits are caused by a dysfunction in the integrative areas of the brain controlling the perception, association, and integra-tion of auditory, visual, and motor performance and which appear most strikingly in school-related tasks. Perceptual handicaps are neither new nor rare, although for a long time the medical and educa-tional professions had trouble recognizing them. Folk literature and children's stories abound with tales, such as *Hansel and Gretel* and *Little Red Riding Hood,* that hinge on a child's misperceptions and the failure to make adequate associations. In the *Wizard of Oz* Dorothy's compan-ion, the Scarecrow, is far from dumb, yet he cannot learn and wishes for a brain—a common plea among perceptually handicapped ado-lescents. Nevertheless, individual teenagers with perceptual dis-abilities often feel as if they are the only one with the problem. In most surveys of school-age children, between 12 and 15 percent in the first three elementary grades have some problem managing academic skills. By fifth grade these children are just under 10 percent of the population and by puberty about 5 percent. Three out of four pubertal-age youngsters with perceptual handicaps are boys, but with only one in twenty still affected, they are not very visible.

In most classrooms there are rarely more than two (and almost never more than three) affected youngsters at any one time. The handicaps are so variable it is hardly likely that those who do have the problem will recognize one another. Furthermore, it is not likely that their parents will meet and recognize their mutual problems. Thus, the entire family may feel alone, lonely, and angry with the repeated failure and the lack of knowledge of others in the same predicament. They may also feel helpless and hopeless about ever being able to remedy the situation.

Learning-disabled Adolescents

Studying adolescents with perceptual handicaps helps to understand them. It also helps clarify the nature of perceptual handicaps at any age. Adolescents are particularly good subjects to study because they are old enough and of sufficient maturity to test reliably. In addition, the adolescent is too young to have developed compensatory or evasive methods of dealing with the world, which would hide or camouflage their problems. Adolescents with perceptual handicaps are extremely variable in the extent and severity of their disability, but they still fall into a few large groups. About 40 percent of perceptually handicapped teenagers have a history of having other family members with learning problems and delayed maturational development. The teenagers themselves were slow to meet their own developmental landmark schedule. Many of these young people have major gaps in their knowledge despite only a few perceptual problems remaining by adolescence. Most have normal neurological function.

The rate of development in 5 to 10 percent of families is significantly faster, and in another 5 to 10 percent it is much slower than the average. These ranges of variation in maturation are seen in infancy, when the child walks, talks, dresses, disrobes, and acquires other specific motor skills. Children who are "quicker" than average are often ready to read and to learn academic skills earlier (often well before the usual school-entry age for first grade, at 5½ or 6 years). These children usually have little trouble learning once they get to school, except for bouts of boredom. Children at the other end of the scale, those who have inherited a slower rate of neurological development, are much later meeting their developmental landmarks. Neuronal interconnections in the brain occur later, and they are still not biologically ready for academic tasks when they enter first grade and may not be ready for several more years. Puberty may be delayed! Often called "late bloomers" or "immature for age," these children experience constant failure and inability to keep up despite normal intelligence. School and academics become frustrating, and the constant failures are humiliating. The end result of this anxiety-evoking environment is often serious emotional problems. Some of these children withdraw quietly into a corner, hoping the world will not notice them (and often it works). They are "nice" children and well behaved. As a result, they are often socially promoted from grade to grade, learning little and falling progressively farther behind. Some feel like outcasts, "black sheep" in a world of good achievers. They become angry and resentful. The child may act out, exhibiting disruptive behavior in the classroom and difficulties at home. They are candidates for delinquent behavior in adolescence, if they cannot overcome the causes of maladaptive behavior in the younger years. They need the reassurances that will permit them to adopt more socially acceptable rules of behavior. Most struggle to learn what they can and be as much like the other children in the class. They are confused by their inability to do what everyone else can do, but they keep on trying. They arrive in adolescence ready to give school one more try, hoping that somewhere a personal Tinker Bell will be able to make a miracle and their wishes for scholastic success can come true. If they do not get help quickly here, they will give up on school, alter their goals towards less success-oriented careers as they figure out "Whereness" and try to deal with their loss of hope for the future.

Another 40 percent or so are the only ones in their family ever to have such a problem. Their parents and brothers and sisters and other relatives are disappointed and do not understand why this child is unable to keep up with the success of the rest of the family. To add confusion, these children, like the rest of their families, were close to average or even faster in reaching their preschool developmental levels. Puberty may have been reached at the usual age as well.

What many of these children may have in common in adolescence is a slightly abnormal neurological examination (usually with a normal electroencephalogram). Often there is a history of the type of event which is capable of injuring or insulting the communication areas of the brain, in the temporal area of the dominant hemisphere. Respiratory distress syndrome in the prematurely born baby, hypoxia due to a nuchal cord, precipitous delivery (especially of a large first baby), encephalitis, hydrocephalus, myelomeningocele, meningitis, subdural effusions, and direct trauma are common threads in the life stories of these children. These injuries affect the communication areas particularly severely, and they may leave a permanent dysfunction. The communication areas of the brain, in the temporal and parietal areas, and their intra- as well as interhemispheric connections lie in the arterial watersheds of the brain between major blood distribution systems. They are not well supplied with blood themselves and are very vulnerable to damage from a decrease in oxygen supply, such as may occur in generalized hypoxia, diminished local circulation, swelling or pressure in or on the brain. It does not matter what reduces the available oxygen supply. The result is the same: damage to nerves and a permanent lifelong communication disorder with residuals into adult life.

Similar to the familially determined group, these children enter first grade looking forward to learning to read, write, cipher, and spell. However, they, too, quickly fail. Children in both groups derive negative conclusions about their abilities and themselves. The children develop similar behavior patterns: some crawl into "a behavioral and emotional corner" and glide quietly by: others become angry and act up and may go on to delinquency. Most slog quietly away, storing up their frustrations and rage, hoping against hope that next year will be better. Finally, when next year never arrives but puberty does, they reach into adolescence and surrender all hope of ever being like everyone else. Some see no benefit in ever growing up and try to be like Peter Pan for the rest of their lives.

The remaining one-fifth do not seem to fit precisely either pattern. Some have both a family history of slow development and perceptual handicaps, but they have also experienced an event that is potentially traumatic to the communication areas of the brain. Others seem to have neither high risk. Of course, there is no reason to expect that children with a family history of learning problems would be immune to injury. In this era of small, highly mobile families it can be very difficult to elicit a family history of troubles in school diagnosed as a learning disability. On occasion, months or years later, a family history will emerge as old contacts are restored and new information arrives about relatives who live in other parts of a large and traveling world. It really makes little difference into which group these children fall. The academic and psychological end points are the same.

Grieving

A visible handicap provokes an immediate reaction. The handicapped with an obvious physical problem, their families, and their world go through a grief reaction, recover, and go on with their lives. On the other hand, young people with perceptual disabilities have "invisible" handicaps that lie dormant like booby traps for the unwary. Every day someone trips over them, and they are activitated. Every day the grief reaction is set off once again. The hurt, anger, and guilt fester and erupt and interfere with the happy parent–child and teacher–pupil relationships. The frustrations are stored and, like money banked, gather interest and grow. In adolescence the rebellion, rage, and turmoil are that much worse. The years of pain are stored up. The inability to speak the unspeakable in childhood and the new search for understanding and mastery of self all contribute to the added anxiety. In adolescence the disappointment and hurt for the parents is that much more. The emerging loss of hope and the dimming expectations become exaggerated for every parent. In adolescence this combination makes the parent–child partnership that much more difficult to develop. Learning difficulties in the adolescent can enhance an adversary relationship between parents, teenagers, and teachers and can produce an atmosphere of tension and turmoil that is hard for the entire family to bear.

COMMUNICATION SYSTEMS

The perceptual disabilities are a group of handicaps that may express themselves mildly, moderately, or severely; singly or in groups. Understanding them as separate systems, each with its own parts which must interrelate to produce integrated communication, clarifies the differences between affected individuals. In addition, it is then possible to realize why each adolescent with a perceptual handicap may look so different from one another. It also clarifies why no one remedial method works for everyone and why an individualized developmental diagnostic approach to teaching usually works best.

The major systems involved are visual perception, auditory perception, audiovisual integration, and visuomotor integration. Subsystems involve short- and long-term memory, sequential memory, figure-ground discrimination, spatial relationships, and native ability. Each of these is important in handling the tasks of communication.

Visual Perception

Describing visual perception in words alone is rather difficult. Sequential visual memory keeps things we see in the right order. It affects the recognition of a sequence of letters arranged as a word or words as a sentence. Without sequential memory it is difficult to read, spell, or apply phonic skills in sounding out a word or understanding a paragraph. Short- and long-term memory work like the storing of valuables in a closet in another room. Information is moved into short-term memory first (the room) and then into long-term memory (the closet) for storage. Retrieval moves data out of the closet and into the room in order to be taken outside and used. When access to short-term visual memory is blocked, storage, retrieval, and use of visual information are hindered. On the other hand, when the block is in the transfer system between short- and long-term memory, the use of visual information is normal, but storage and retrieval are limited. Sequential memory keeps *was* the past tense of *is* instead of *saw* the past tense of *see*.

Spatial relationships and memory affect reading because the lower case printed letters. *b, d, p,* and *q* are identical in shape, yet they differ in meaning according to their orientation in space. Turn one around or backward, and the entire meaning of the word can change. For example, a simple rotation of *b* turns *bat* into *pat*. The letters *t* and *f* are similar in shape and *m* and *w, n* and *u* differ in their position in space, while *o, c,* and *e* differ only by whether the symbol is broken or closed and where the break occurs. Spatial relationship problems also interfere with understanding part–whole relationships in arithmetic, geometric designs and geometry, trigonometry and higher mathematics. These young people may learn simple four-function math, but they are clumsy and inept at it.

Ordinarily, the ability to perceive these differences in symbols is a developmental skill achieved at age 6, plus or minus 2 years. How difficult and frustrating first and second grade (and even third) will be for a child who does not have these skills until 8! Understanding spatial relationships and visual perspective allows a person to realize the difference between a photographic and a mirror image. In a mirror your right hand is on the right side of the mirror; in a snapshot it is on the left side of the photograph. Little children cannot grasp this; adults can. The usual age when this skill develops is between 7 and 8 years. An adolescent who still cannot perform this task has trouble reading and following directions.

Understanding perspective and spatial relationships makes it possible to perceive the incongruities of Dali's art and appreciate the drawings by Escher, in which stairways appear to go both down and up, birds become fish, day becomes night, and angels interlock with devils.

Auditory Perception

There is an apocryphal story about auditory perception that goes like this: One Sunday a young child came home from the church Sunday school and told his mother about this strange sermon that had left him very confused. As he told it, his mother heard about a funny bear whose eyes were crossed and this bear with the strange, silly name of Gladly, could perform miracles. None of it made much sense until later that day, driving past the church she saw written out, the title of the day's lesson "Gladly the Cross I'd Bear."

Superficially, the story may be cute and amusing, but the distress of people who perpetually misunderstand what they hear is real and not "gladly borne." Auditory sequential memory keeps instructions in the right order and lets us accomplish tasks or go from A to B without problems. But auditory sequential memory is also important in remembering the sounds strung together to form a word or the words in order to make a sentence. Auditory short- and long-term memory problems affect reading, for they are at the heart of remembering the sound of each visual symbol. Without auditory memory phonics are impossible to learn and reading will never be acquired.

Auditory figure-ground discrimination involves the ability to pick particular sounds out of the background or to isolate certain sounds within a sequence. Teenagers who have auditory discrimination problems can neither work in a noisy classroom nor study in a noisy den; they are too distractible. A teenager who cannot isolate sounds in a sequence may think that there are bears named Gladly, capable of miracles. The adolescent with this problem needs a quiet place to work. Teenagers who can discriminate sounds against background can be allowed to study with any music they like playing in the background. Tests like the Goldman-Fristoe-Woodcock Test of Auditory Discrimination seem effective in sorting out these two groups and defusing arguments at home and in school over study arrangements.

Auditory closure completes a sequence of sounds to fill in the missing unheard portions of words. Speakers often lose volume at the end of a word, passing traffic can obscure the beginning or the middle, a myriad of exogenous noises can cause auditory closure gaps. Most people are able to fill in the gaps and make sense, but not the person with this particular disability. In ordinary life a whole genre of mystery stories hinge on misconstruing what some witness has seen or more often heard. The real possibility of such happening is what intrigues the reader and keeps the story alive.

Auditory and visual perceptual problems sometimes affect musical performance because they make reading music as difficult as reading print or script. Tone deafness is not a handicap for most people because language is spoken. If everyone had to sing his words (and was discriminated against or made fun of or forced to repeat grades in school until the words were sung with grace), however, the world would be a difficult place for many of us.

Audiovisual Association

In order to read, vision must be adequate to register the image on the eye and the message must be recorded in the visual cortex. Then visual memory must be tapped to recognize the symbol and auditory memory entered next to recall the sound. Auditory sequential memory then puts the sounds together to make words and sentences. Each area must work effectively at its own task, but each set of connections must also work properly. Failures of audiovisual integration make it difficult or even impossible to read, even if all the individual components are working normally, much like a stereo system in which the tuner, amplifier, and speakers all work well, but some of the wires have been cut or damaged.

Audiovisuomotor Integration

Speech demands memory of sounds and their meanings as well as auditory sequential memory. Until this is verbalized and communicated to another, these are only ruminations of a fertile imagination. Associative circuits between auditory and speech areas must monitor the sounds produced, listen to what we say, and provide constant feedback while simultaneously producing the speech itself through integration of auditory memory, auditory sequential memory, speech, and motor tasks. Disturbances here cause word-finding problems and dysfluencies.

Reading demands an integrated scanning of the page in which auditory memory and auditory sequential memory provide both recognition of symbols and feedback data for continued control. Difficulties with these skills may cause organizational and scanning problems and add to other specific disabilities of auditory or visual perception. Visual scanning problems are not the cause of the disability, but the result of confusion that the disability creates, and no amount of eye "training" can correct the neurological dysfunction. Writing is a complex auditory, visual, and motor task in which words we hear in our own minds appear on a page, monitored by visual feedback. Dysfluencies, handwriting abnormalities, and organizational problems (including problems with right–left orientation) and neurologically determined inability to cross the midline may combine to make adolescents with this handicap unwilling to commit anything but a signature to writing. They may even have some doubts about the advisability of signing their own names!

Systems Approach

No two perceptually handicapped teenagers are ever exactly alike. The blind and the deaf are clearly in distinctive categories defined by their physical disability. In many respects the perceptually handicapped are like stroke victims, and everyone is different. Each adolescent, however, can be tested, and each system and subsystem component examined and evaluated. A comprehensive view of the adolescent's strengths and weakness can be established, and an individualized rehabilitation program synthesized. Besides the perceptual systems already outlined, there are other systems both within and outside the person, as well as within society, that also must be considered because they will affect performance and success. These, too, must be part of the holistic approach to any teenager who is having probems with academic performance or success.

ADOLESCENCE AND LEARNING DISORDERS

The entire period of transition is itself a source of stress and turmoil which can distract any adolescent from the academic tasks at hand. The constantly changing body and mind of the teenager and the need to determine adult "whoness," "whatness," and "whereness" with inadequate experience adds to the distress. The need to become autonomous and independent in a world not prepared to grant these is especially hard.

Most of the problems of slow development have disappeared by puberty. The synapses have been formed, and the developmental tasks met. But academic skills taught in elementary grades are no longer part of the curriculum of the junior high, and there may be major residual information gaps. The learning-disabled teenagers may be placed in secondary school classes for students with normal ability, but they may have the emotional effects of years of frustration and failure and only elementary school skills.

Neurological Problems

In adolescence the problems of neurological dysfunction from permanent injury have not vanished. They may affect sports performance and choice of physical activities and will certainly impinge on new learning. Learning will always be slow and laborious. Detours will have to be found around the fallen circuits, and these adolescents, like their undamaged compatriots, will have to continue to contend with the feelings and the emotions their frustrations produce.

Emotional State

Physical handicaps in childhood affect success and that, in turn, affects self-esteem. Invisible handicaps are doubly hard to cope with because there is no visible defect to account for the problem. Perceptual handicaps invariably affect self-confidence and self-esteem, leaving the adolescent with severe self-doubts as he or she moves to handle the normal tasks of the age. Everyone needs success experiences in order to develop confidence in one's ability to master new or difficult situations. The learning-disabled individual lacking adequate confidence in himself finds resolving the issues more arduous, more time consuming, and more frustrating.

Young people who arrive at puberty with severe emotional problems from any cause do poorly in school and life. When the problems are caused by academic failure, the mental disarray makes it more difficult to overcome the disability during rehabilitation. Interlocking emotional and perceptual handicaps make life particularly difficult to bear, and ignoring the emotional state may prevent suitable success in remediation.

Intelligence

When a perceptually disabled child's intelligence is above average, he may be able to compensate and camouflage his problems in the elementary grades. The handicap itself will keep overall performance in the average range, and the child may not attract much attention. High schools, however, accelerate the demand for independent study and increase the academic pace (and especially the reading load). This can provoke sudden failure and academic and emotional decompensation. When intelligence is average, then performance may be lowered into the borderline or even retarded range, and the preadolescent child may attract attention and secure testing and early help during childhood. The child who is brighter than average has a good chance of reaching puberty with his disability undetected. Often the frustration exists because of knowing material but still doing poorly on tests. The learning problems will make him feel "dumb and stupid" (even if he is not), and his peers may call him "retarded."

Intelligence testing can be a help or a hindrance, depending on the test and the sophistication of the person interpreting it. Intelligence testing using machine-scored group tests is often given as part of regular school evaluations of all children. Sometimes these tests are administered as part of diagnostic evaluations of specific children. These tests, however, measure performance better than intellect, and the perceptually disabled do poorly because the disability interferes with performance. The best intellectual tests in learning-disabled adolescents are the Wechsler Intelligence Scale for Children (WISC and WISC-R) and the Wechsler Adult Intelligence Scale (WAIS), which are administered individually. Nevertheless, these tests must be interpreted carefully and with sophistication in order to recognize and help a perceptually handicapped youth. The WISC, WISC-R, and WAIS are reported as verbal, perforance, and full-scale IQs, and each subtest of the verbal and performance scales is reported in standardized scores. Since, the perceptually handicapped are usually more severely affected in auditory than visual areas or vice versa, there is usually a discrepancy between the verbal and the performance scale scores greater than 10 points. When the problems are more significant in auditory perception, the verbal scale scores are usually lower, and when visual perception is affected most, the performance scale scores are lower.

The individual subtest scores are reported in a range from 1 to 20, in which 8. 9. 10, or 11 is within the average range; higher scores are indicative of superior ability and lower scores of problems. Retarded learners usually have uniformly low scores and accelerated learners uniformly high ones, whereas the perceptually handicapped have subtest scores that may scatter from lows of 2 and 3 to highs of 16 and 17. The higher subtest scores in these young people measure real ability and show the areas of strength while the low ones show the handicap and the weaknesses. The full-scale IQ score rates like an achievement test. It tells what the average performance is and is a predictor of future performance in the perceptually handicapped only if there is no intervention.

Age a Factor

It is hoped that no one with a learning disability will escape detection until adolescence. By that time emotional reactions will have already been set in place which are very difficult to overcome. In adolescents whose disability was found in the early elementary grades and remediated successfully, there may be little emotional resistance to continued help and few psychological blocks to learning. However, when a child is bright and only mildly handicapped, or has only isolated disabilities, he may escape detection until the academic load of secondary school prompts descompensation. When a school system or a group of elementary school teachers cannot identify even the clearly affected child, let alone the suspicious child, and are unprepared to provide good rehabilitation, it is certain that the perceptually handicapped will experience more problems during adolescence. The earlier a perceptual handicap is identified and proper rehabilitation begun, the better off the child will be. Initial diagnosis and treatment must never wait until puberty creates a crisis.

Intent

Children go to school in first grade expecting to learn to read and write. All that they have heard for several years is that this is when they will be able to read to themselves just like parents and older siblings. For most children this is true! But how disappointing it is to the developmentally delayed, or the child with cerebral dysfunction, who finds he cannot keep up. In a relatively short time his excitement dies and his interest withers. Hope keeps some motivation alive into puberty, but it can dry up quickly if there is no immediate help.

Motivation can determine success even without treatment, for some highly motivated people have managed to do very well despite mild handicaps and no therapeutic intervention. Motivation is also one of the most important factors in success, when treatment is available. Even the best rehabilitation program will fail if the person receiving treatment has given up trying. Adolescents who are no longer interested in school and have given up hope of ever achieving anything academically have tremendous difficulty making the emotional and intellectual commitment to the work at hand. It is especially difficult to get teenagers who are 4 to 6 years (or more) behind in their school work to the point where they have caught up, if they are not interested in the hard work they face. It takes a tremendous amount of psychological support to restore even a glimmer of desire to "try again" when a teenager has given up. However, an adolescent in the early teens, who is no more than 3 years behind academically, has average or better intelligence and has retained motivation, still has the time left to catch up if desire remains high and the rehabilitation program meets his needs.

Teachers

There are two groups of teachers who are important to a perceptually handicapped adolescent—remedial (special-education) types and the regular (mainstream) classroom teacher. The regular classroom teacher is the first person to deal with a child and has to be the first "line of defense" in identifying high-risk children and requesting evaluation. Elementary school teachers must have (1) extensive training in recognizing the many signs of a handicap (which requires more training than most teacher-preparation programs provide), (2) the support of the principal and school system in requesting evaluations freely (a certain number of "false-positives" have to be accepted), (3) a support and testing program, and (4) a rehabilitation program capable of evaluating those referred and treating those diagnosed. The teacher must also be prepared to have the learning disabled student in the regular class program. She/he must utilize those teaching methods in the regular classroom which have been found most effective by the special-education teacher. All, except for the most severely affected children, spend at least half of their time in the regular classroom. If this is to be productive time, the regular teacher must be flexible enough to use teaching methods that work for that youngster while using other methods with the rest of the class.

Laws like Chapter 766 in Massachusetts and the federal Developmental Disabilities Act of 1973 (P.L. 94–142) are changing the role of the regular classroom teacher. Where these laws are already in effect, a teenager cannot be exiled to the special-education program and the regular teacher "wash his/her hands of the problem." It will still be some time, however, before enough information is taught in college education courses (and those in the profession have had retraining) before school districts become able to provide enough help. Nevertheless, classroom teachers must quickly understand the emotional component and deal with it, even before they are experts in the academics. They must be supportive and find ways to promote both real learning and real nonpatronizing success. They need the active support of their administrators and the provision of enough support services so that they can feel comfortable in tackling the job. Special-education teachers are often overburdened with too many students and not enough time. Still, they have to maintain a diagnostic experimental approach with each student and provide the regular teachers with enough guidance so that regular work moves along.

Prostheses

The learning-disabled adolescent with auditory sequential or short-term memory problems has difficulty taking notes or recording homework assignments. Those with visual perceptual and spatial relationship problems may not be able to copy written or diagrammed material from a blackboard. Visual perceptual and auditory memory problems may make arithmetic impossible or interfere with reading charts, graphs, or maps. All of these deficits may make reading nearly impossible and studying foreign languages a disaster.

Students affected by perceptual disturbances are people with real handicaps; like the polio victims of the past they need braces and props—prosthetic devices—to help them. Typewriters end the messy handwriting and organize the material from left to right and top to bottom automatically. Tape recorders take notes and copy down homework assignments for later transcription at leisure. Calculators can do four-function arithmetic and overcome the memory difficulties of a dyscalculia. Talking books on records and tapes aid adolescents in completing reading assignments and open up whole new avenues for education that are otherwise blocked by reading disabilities.

Extra time on tests in class and school as well as on college board and achievement tests is often as much a help for these young people who must work slowly as a compensation for their handicap as any other prosthetic measure that can be employed. Tape recorders and typewriters make it possible to take tests verbally or without writing anything by hand and still do the work required.

The Public School

Mainstreaming (remaining in the regular class) works well for the mildly affected learning-disabled adolescent who has had effective help in the past; but, *it is not for everyone*. Secondary schools still need special-education programs involving both regular and vocational schools. Many young people are academically far behind by adolescence, and the education in the high school must be adapted to both their skills and their interests. This is obviously difficult when teachers must work with 16-year-old tenth graders whose reading skills are only at a fourth or fifth grade level. It is difficult to find academic material for these teenagers to read or work with which is interesting and attractive to the mind of a 16-year-old and the skills of a 10-year-old.

The problems which these handicapped adolescents bring to secondary school vary greatly and demand complex, flexible remedial programs with which many schools are not prepared to cope. Of course, it is the most complicated or most difficult or most silent ones along with the most permanent ones who arrive in high school still needing a lot of remedial help.

Many perceptually handicapped teenagers want to enter vocational programs because they had so many academic problems in the early grades. Vocational and technical high schools have used entrance exams to sort out the less able, and these tests discriminate against the bright but learning-disabled student. Vocational and technical high schools are particularly important to perceptually handicapped students who may not be college bound and who need all the help they can get in developing marketable economic skills. These schools must reserve a fixed ratio of seats for learning-disabled students and must also exempt these teenagers from the usual entrance exam if they are going to make their programs available fairly.

The Parochial School and Private School

Parochial and private schools, like any other school, may not be able to meet the needs of a learning-disabled student if (1) teachers are uncertified and lack training in recognizing or dealing with learning disabilities, (2) classes are too large, and (3) the school lacks remedial programs. At the secondary level entrance exams for the competitive programs exclude most of the learning-disabled adolescents and thrust them back on the public school setting. Inability to pass the entrance exam is another failure. It may be significant and difficult to bear when a teenager is the *only* one to break the family tradition of parochial high school attendance or attendance at a private facility.

Troublesome children, regardless of the reason, are usually dismissed from private and parochial schools and returned to public schools, while quiet ones remain. The troublesome learning-disabled child sent to public school may be tested and remediation provided, if available. The pleasant quiet child will often be kept in the parochial or private school until adolescence, in the guise of providing religious training, despite academic incompetence. At adolescence these youngsters may be so far behind and so discouraged that they will never be able to compensate academically.

The Private School with Learning-disabled Programs

The severely handicapped may not be able to achieve, even in the best regular public school, partly because there they remain different and separate from the mainstream. A good, well-organized private school in which everyone is learning-disabled (LD), and in which everyone is in the mainstream, may help many of these adolescents find success and acceptance for the first time in their lives. The private school with LD programs can be an excellent alternative or transitional education. Some private schools, hoping to close budgetary gaps, have expanded to accept the learning-disabled. Here the handicapped are not part of the mainstream; if this is the reason for choosing private schooling, the adolescent's needs will not be met. Some private schools in this category, though, do have first-rate programs and do merge these adolescents into the mainstream very quickly and, therefore, may be suitable.

In deciding on private school, the parents should be certain that the youngster has the desire to go before he is sent. Personal and family visits must be made, and the selection done with care. Specific academic and faculty facilities together with a good developmental approach should be the hallmark of any school which is chosen.

Retesting

In any school—public, parochial, or private—a teenager receiving educational treatment must be tested at regular intervals. Adolescents have the distressing facility of filling in gaps in one skill while entirely missing those in another, thereby letting everyone think they have improved across the entire board. Usually, retesting once a year will reveal how well a teenager is progressing.

Religious School

Religious school is a special category of education that meets after the regular school day and functions to prepare for confirmation within a particular religious group. Jewish children preparing for Bar or Bat Mitzvah must learn Hebrew, which is a difficult tongue in its own right, and especially difficult for the perceptually handicapped. Yet these youngsters must learn to read proficiently enough to master a portion of the Torah, the Scroll of Laws.

Greek and Russian, like all foreign languages, are also difficult for learning-disabled teenagers. In fact, it is predictable that adolescents who are handicapped in their own language will also have problems with other languages. In regular school they can be excused from foreign language requirements, but this is not true in religious school where the additional language is part of the ritual.

Furthermore, with as little knowledge of perceptual handicaps as there is among teachers in public schools, there is even less among those in religious schools. Usually part-time teachers (most often without regular teaching credentials) or "after-hour" teachers and Sunday school teachers fail to teach the perceptually handicapped and add to the problems which these teenagers face. It is the rare teacher-training program in religious higher education that is developing programs to teach the teachers of these special boys and girls.

The Family

No one wants to be the "black sheep," yet that is what happens to perceptually handicapped children. Misunderstood by well-meaning but unprepared parents and the goat of the other children, the perceptually handicapped teenager finds it very difficult to accept and adopt the family values. Families which understand and are supportive make life much easier for their teenagers. These families are involved in school and school work, become knowledgeable about learning problems, pariticipate in various organizations that help the learning-disabled, and support their children's needs in the community. Brothers and sisters become better informed, and family life and development is smoother and much more pleasant.

Peers

As adolescents move away from family toward independence and autonomy, they reach out to peers with similar interests or problems. Those who feel badly about themselves may choose friends of whom their parents disapprove. Those who are unable to identify with family values may join delinquents, but most often these young people do not fit in at all. Academically and socially awkward, many of these adolescents seem to become isolated and alone. In a society which puts a high value on popularity, and devalues the individual with only a few friends, these disabled young people may withdraw even more to avoid the assults of people around them criticizing them for their apparent lack of friends. Teachers and families need to know about learning disabilities. Peers need some preparation too so that they can be more supportive of people with invisible handicaps.

OUTCOMES

"Whereness," the need to establish "Where am I going?" makes everyone wonder about the future. The future is particularly important to the physically handicapped and uniquely difficult for the perceptually disabled, whose handicap is invisible. Parents and others who work with the perceptually handicapped need specific information about the outcome of treatment programs.

Adolescents whose handicaps have made them "black sheep" and social outcasts often become angry acting-up teens whose behavior can become delinquent. Several studies of delinquent adolescent boys have shown that 25 to 35 percent have learning disabilities, and studies of male inmates of adult correctional institutions show that three out of four repeaters have a learning disability. These are individuals whose handicap was unrecognized by others, and they were made to feel "dumb," "stupid," and "different." They became angry and hurt and retaliated against society. The overwhelming majority of the learning-disabled never become delinquents; those that did may have been prevented from doing so.

In the United States 76 percent of all children entering public school will graduate. Of this group, 44 percent will go to college, 21 percent will be graduated from college, 6 percent will enter graduate school, and 1 percent will obtain doctoral degrees. The untreated perceptually handicapped children are more likely to leave high school without graduating and less likely to go on to college. In a study of one group of learning-disabled individuals, diagnosed during adolescence as being perceptually handicapped, 45 percent graduated high school, 20 percent went to college, 9 percent were graduated from college, and 3 percent went to graduate school.

In a group of 40 enlisted military personnel with learning disabilities none had a history of behavioral problems in the military. All were doing well in mechanical trades, but all were also delayed in receiving promotions based on passing written proficiency tests.

Mildly affected people with good motivation do best, especially when diagnosed early and given adequate help. However, many are bright enough or mild enough to obscure the necessity of early diagnosis and intervention. On the other hand, severely affected people with poor motivation perform the worst, especially when diagnosed and treated late. They are most likely to be school truants by 14 and dropouts at 16, ending up as dissatisfied laborers who are economically handicapped all of their lives. It is important to tell teenagers that the prospects are not bleak and to help them incorporate this optimism into their search for the future.

Community Agencies

There are many agencies that help families in general and some that help the learning-disabled in particular. Various family and children's services can provide excellent counsel, and many mental health and child guidance centers work well with the public and parochial schools in their catchment areas. State Offices for Children or Offices of Education may have advocacy programs which will serve the special needs of the perceptually handicapped. The Orton Society and the Association for Children with Learning Disabilities (ACLD) are national organizations of parents and professionals that allow families to direct their energies in productive ways and that have been very effective in obtaining needed services in many communities.

The Role of the Physician

Rehabilitation for someone with a perceptual handicap is an educational matter, and many have asked why a physician should be involved at all. The general health and the neurologic status, however, are very important factors in the management of the problem. Psychological issues and developmental needs impinge on progress as do changes in social growth. Someone must interpret the findings, the treatment, and the progress to the youth, the family, and the school. Someone must coordinate the special testing, the treatment program, the psychological support and counseling, the family support and counseling, and the efforts of schools and community agencies as they affect one particular special teenager.

Adolescents with perceptual handicaps need one person to be an advocate who understands the physical, social, and emotional needs of adolescents and adolescence, who knows about learning disabilities, and who will work with families, schools, and community agencies in their interests. A physician with experience and training in all of these areas may be the one individual in a young person's life who is trusted by the teenager and able to fill the role.

CONCLUSIONS

The perceptually handicapped teenager was a perceptually handicapped child. He brings to adolescence the scars and leftovers of his earlier growing-up experiences. In some ways these are the same scars as in any child; in other ways they are very different. The perceptually handicapped teenager is an adolescent and adds to his handicap the needs and demands of one of life's major periods of transition. The confluence of these two broad streams establishes a turmoil and turbidity that can interfere forever with the smooth procession of life. Proper help given early and consistantly available throughout the critical periods can bridge these churning waters and ease the flow into adulthood.

It is essential in helping to understand that 1 teenager in 10 has or has had a learning disability. This person suffers some emotional scars as a result. To help is to understand that adolescence is a difficult era made more difficult by a handicap. To help is to be realistic about the present and reasonably optimistic about therapy and the future. To help is to be able to stand aside from the family and school and act as advocate, counselor, and guide through the maze of growth, diagnosis, development, treatment, maturity, and recovery.

Harris C. Faigel

REFERENCES

American Academy of Pediatrics. *School health: A guide for professionals* (2nd ed). Evanston, Ill.: the Academy, 1977.
Anderson, L. E. *Helping the adolescent with the hidden handicap.* Los Angeles: Academic Therapy Publications, 1970.

Buscaglia, L. *The disabled and their parents.* Thorofare, N.J.: Slack, 1975.
Daniel, W. *The adolescent patient.* St. Louis: Mosby, 1970.
Faigel, H. The adolescent with a learning disability. *Practitioner,* February 1975, *214,* 181–191.
Gallagher, J., Heald, F., & Garrell, D. *Medical care of the adolescent* (3rd ed.). New York: Appleton-Century-Croft, 1976.
Gallagher, J., & Harris, H. *Emotional problems of adolescents* (3rd ed.). New York: Oxford University Press, 1976.
Group for the Advancement of Psychiatry (GAP). *Normal adolescence.* New York: Scribner, 1968.
Money, J. *The disabled reader.* Baltimore: Johns Hopkins Press, 1968.
Morgenthau, J. *Adolescent health care.* Stamford, Conn.: Thrush Press, 1976.
Tanner, J. *Growth at adolescence* (2nd ed.). Oxford, Eng.: Blackwell, 1962.

5

LEARNING DISABILITIES: A CHILD PSYCHIATRIST'S OVERVIEW

Many problems in human development may be expressed as a learning difficulty. Rabinovitch (1959) noted that there is little validity in viewing a learning disability as a discrete diagnostic entity. Learning difficulties may be identified in specific forms with degrees of emotional and behavioral complications varying from little or none to severe. A learning difficulty can be associated with any of the psychiatric syndromes, such as the psychophysiologic disorders, psychotic disorders, personality disorders, or affective, anxiety, or attentional deficit disorders. In this chapter a "learning disability" will be operationally defined as a syndrome that is the result of processes that interfere with the acquiring and use of academic knowledge.

THE DIAGNOSTIC PROCESS

When a learning difficulty is suspected, current practice recommends that a diagnostic evaluation be performed to assess the child and the family in the context of their community. A child psychiatrist is often asked to evaluate children who are having a difficulty. The child psychiatrist brings to the diagnostic process a medical and psychiatric knowledge of the spectrum of human behavior, whereby personality development is viewed as a continuum from infancy through childhood, adolescence, and adulthood. The psychiatric examination assesses the mental status of the child as one of three broad dimensions included in the diagnostic process (Goodman & Sours, 1967). The first dimension includes exploring the presenting problem and studying the child in the context of his family and social milieu. Following the initial contact with the parents, a family interview is often requested by the psychiatrist in order to evaluate the family system as it is currently functioning and the role assumed by the child in the family and social environment. A vulnerable child may become the focus of a "family problem" through such mechanisms as scapegoating or overprotection. A family may become dysfunctional as the members attempt to cope with a child who has a problem such as a learning disability. Further, an initial family interview tends to acknowledge total family concern and suggests a need for family cohesion and support. During this time the child is prepared for an individual evaluation.

The second dimension is the developmental biological profile. This is a synthesis of information from the family's report of the child's physical growth and adaptive development including educational adaptation. Reports from the family physician and teachers as well as results from any previous professional examinations should be obtained. The largely historical data helps build a comprehensive view of the child in longitudinal profile.

The third dimension is based on the psychiatrist's observations of the individual child during a clinical interview. Studies by Rutter and Graham (1968) on the use of the psychiatric interview with children have indicated a high degree of reliability and validity. The interview has both structured and unstructured aspects that are designed to elicit specific information, in an atmosphere of comfort, from the child's or adolescent's point of view. It is designed to bring out strengths and assets as well as maladaptive aspects of development. In the unstructured part of the interview the youth is helped to put into words or play his own thoughts and feelings about himself and the presenting problem, which in this case would be a learning difficulty. His view may be different from that of the parents or other family members. As the child relates to the interviewer in verbal and nonverbal ways, observations are made regarding orientation, mood, verbalization (speech and language), thought processes, relatedness, coping mechanisms, use of fantasy, concept of self, intelligence, and conscience formation. Structured questions or tasks are then directed and intermingled to draw out information about specific aspects of development that need further exploration. Various tasks are given to screen for disabilities in visual and auditory perceptual input, integrative function, memory, language and motor output, hyperactivity, distractibility, and attention (Silver, 1976).

Physical examination and neurological screening are performed as needed, within the context of this clinical interview. In screening for the presence of an abnormality, as distinct from diagnosing a neurological disorder, the main items to include are inspection of the movement of eyes, tongue, and face; testing of hearing and vision; distal limb power, tone, and coordination; posture, gait and balance; deep tendon reflexes; plantar responses; and fundal examination (Rutter, Graham, & Yule, 1970; Touwen & Prechtl, 1970). If any clinical abnormalities are found in the neurodevelopmental features, a full neurological examination should be requested.

When indicated by the psychiatric clinical interview, specific educational, psychological, speech, and biologic studies may be requested from a variety of available sources. As in all medical evaluations, clear indications are necessary before ordering tests because of the negative effects of multiple testing on patients and the need for conserving resources. Consultation or collaboration is obtained as indicated from educational diagnosticians, psychologists, speech pathologists, ophthalmologists, neurologists, and audiologists.

An outline of the scope of the evaluation (Simmons, 1974) may help to summarize the diagnostic process. Following is one of several ways to organize the topics:

    I. Presenting Problem

    II. Family Description

    III. Family History

    IV. Sociocultural Issues

    V. Birth, Development, and Medical History

    VI. Peer Relationships and Activities

    VII. Previous and Present School Experience

    VIII. Educational, Psychological, and Biologic Studies

    IX. Other Professional Evaluations

    X. Mental Status

        1. Appearance

        2. Mood or Affect

        3. Orientation and Perception

        4. Coping Mechanisms

        5. Neuromuscular Organization

        6. Thought Processes and Verbalization

        7. Fantasy (dreams, drawings, wishes, play)

        8. Conscience Formation

9. Concept of Self
10. Awareness of Problems
11. Estimate of Intelligence
XI. Diagnostic Formulation
XII. Diagnostic Impression
XIII. Recommendations

The initial diagnostic formulation should support a sound working diagnosis, leading to a valid prognosis and a practical course of action in dealing with the presenting problem. The specialized training of the child psychiatrist provides the expertise and experience for the responsibility of synthesizing the various diagnostic data into a comprehensive diagnosis of the child in his environment. Comprehensive treatment recommendations evolve directly from the diagnostic formulation, which gives purpose and direction to therapeutic goals and prognosis.

The individual treatment plan, or prescription, may include a variety of direct and indirect methods. Occasionally only one type is indicated, centering primarily on physical, social, or psychological factors. For example, the treatment of one child with a learning problem is the direct medical treatment of his visual defect; for another it is direct work with the child in remedial reading; while for a third it consists of an indirect environmental approach by effecting an appropriate grade placement in school (Group for the Advancement of Psychiatry, 1957). More often the treatment plan involves both indirect and direct procedures and deals with multiple interrelated facets of the child's personality and environment.

Following the diagnostic study and treatment planning, it is essential that the findings be carefully and meaningfully communicated to the child and family and to those who will be responsible for carrying out the treatment. Further, it is important to remember that assessment (evaluation) is an ongoing process that should be continuous and interwoven with the treatment program.

Classification

A commonly used etiologic classification of learning disabilities separates neurological disorders from functional disorders. A neurologic disorder is diagnosed when neurologic dysfunction is identified on physical examination and psychometric or neuropsychological testing. A functional disorder is diagnosed when no structural or organic changes are apparent. Psychological or behavioral changes that occur without apparent organic changes are often classified as functional.

The use of this etiologic model is illustrated in Table 5–1, which is a listing of primary diagnoses of a group of 100 disadvantaged children with learning disorders reported by Kappelman, Luck, and Ganter (1971). The neurological disorders are divided into various perceptual handicaps, mental retardation, neurologic dysfunction, and auditory or visual impairment. The functional disorders include emotional disturbance, emotional or social immaturity, and cultural or environmental deprivation. The most common primary diagnosis in this series is functional disorder, approximately 35 percent of the cases. The next most common disorder is the neurologic perceptual

Table 5-1. Primary Diagnosis of Children in LDC Clinic.

All Diagnoses		Cases 100
Perceptual handicaps		33
Visual motor perceptual disorders	19	
Central communication disorder	2	
Auditory discrimination disorder	2	
Abstract concept formation disorder	2	
Undifferentiated perceptual disorder	8	
Mental retardation		12
With evident neurological dysfunction (diffuse brain injury)	7	
Other	5	
Neurologic dysfunctioning (diffuse brain dysfunctioning		19
With hyperkinetic manifestations	8	
Other	11	
Functional disorders		35
Significant emotional disturbance interfering with learning	15	
Emotional or social immaturity	9	
Cultural or environmental deprivation	11	
Auditory impairment		1

From "Profile of the Disadvantaged Child with Learning Disorders" by M. M. Kappelman, E. Luck, and R. L. Ganter, *American Journal of Diseases of Children,* 1971, *121,* 371–379. Copyright 1971 by the American Medical Association. Reprinted by permission.

handicap, accounting for 33 percent of the cases. Gross neurologic dysfunction was identified as a primary diagnosis in 26 percent of cases. The authors further analyzed their cases in terms of a secondary diagnosis as illustrated in Table 5–2.

Of the 54 children reported with more than one diagnosis, 34 had a functional disorder as the second diagnosis and 13 had neurologic perceptual disorder as the second diagnosis. Thus, approximately 69 percent of the clinic population had a primary or secondary diagnosis of functional disorder and 46 percent had a primary or secondary diagnosis of perceptual handicap. Gross neurologic dysfunction was reported as a primary or secondary diagnosis in 27 percent of the clinic population. Primary functional disorders that were given secondary diagnoses showed 82 percent of the secondary diagnoses as perceptual disorder. Primary perceptual diagnoses that were given secondary diagnoses showed 90 percent of the secondary diagnoses as functional disorder. Although the reported clinic population is small, these figures reflect what is generally reported in many populations.

The data suggest that the diagnoses of functional disorder and neurologic perceptual disorder are sufficiently mixed as to render these diagnoses misleading in reference to etiology. Both functional and perceptual disorders may diminish, disappear, or reappear in children. Both diagnoses ultimately have some structural basis. The authors (Kappelman et al., 1971) found a significant history of organic insult in the prenatal and postnatal history among the children with functional disorders as well as the children with neurologic perceptual disorders. Most longitudinal studies of neurologic dysfunction conclude that perinatal events are most related etiologically to socioeconomic status. In the Isle of Wight studies, dyslexia, which is considered a defect in visual motor processing, did not appear to be a single homogenous entity but was found to be associated with multiple factors, including developmental delays (especially in speech, language, and sequencing), temperamental attributes, family characteristics, and quality of schooling (Rutter, Graham, & Yule, 1970; Rutter & Yule, 1973). Rutter (1976) noted a substantial overlap between reading difficulties and psychiatric disorders. Eisenberg (1966) suggested overlap and multiple causes for reading retardation and suggested a provisional classification as illustrated in Table 5–3.

It is misleading to continue to use the terminology that separates neurologic and functional disorders in describing learning disorders because it implies the absence of physical factors in "functional" disorders, implies their origins are different, and reduces our thinking

Table 5-2. Secondary Diagnosis of Children, According to Primary Diagnosis.

Secondary Diagnosis	Primary Diagnosis					
	All Diagnoses	Perceptual Disorders	Mental Retardation	Diffuse Brain Injury	Functional Disorders (Psychosocial)	Auditory Impairment
Total	100	33	12	19	35	1
Without secondary diagnosis	45	12	4	5	23	1
With secondary diagnosis		21	8	14	11	⋯
Perceptual disorders	13	0	3	8	2	0
Mental retardation	3	0	0	3	0	0
Diffuse brain dysfunctioning (with hyperactivity or autism)	1	0	1	0	0	0
Functional disorders (psychosocial)	34	19	3	3	9	0
Speech or visual program	3	2	1	0	0	0

From "Profile of the Disadvantaged Child with Learning Disorders by M. M. Kappelman, E. Luck, and R. L. Ganter, *American Journal of Diseases of Children*, 1971, 121, 371–379. Copyright 1971 by The American Medical Association. Reprinted by permission.

Table 5-3. Provisional Classification.

A. Sociopsychological factors
  1. Quantitative and qualitative defects in teaching
  2. Deficiencies in cognitive stimulation
  3. Deficiencies in motivation
     (a) associated with social pathology
     (b) associated with psychopathology ("emotional")

B. Psychophysiological factors
  1. General debility
  2. Sensory defects
  3. Intellectual defects
  4. Brain injury
  5. Specific (idiopathic) reading disability

From "Reading Retardation: 1. Psychiatric and Sociologic Aspects," by L. Eisenberg, *Pediatrics*, 1966, *37*, 352–365. Copyright American Academy of Pediatrics 1966. Reprinted by permission.

to an artificial dichotomy which neither helps in understanding the child nor in planning interventions. Such a dichotomy is harmful to many children in that certain programs or interventions may be available only to certain physical or nonphysical (organic versus functional) diagnostic categories although no sound basis for differentiation exists and both may need similar interventions.

The Task Force on Nomenclature and Statistics of the American Psychiatric Association (1978) has published a draft of *The Diagnostic and Statistical Manual*, Third Edition (DSM-III), which outlines a multiaxial scheme of five axes. Each individual is described in terms of all five axes:

Axis I   Clinical Psychiatric Syndrome
Axis II   Specific Developmental Disorders
Axis III Physical Disorder
Axis IV   Severity of Psychosocial Stressors
Axis V   Highest Level of Adaptive Functioning Past Year

Most of the categories are primarily descriptive with no implications regarding known etiology, prognosis, and optimal treatment. The purpose of DSM-III is to provide clearer descriptions of diagnostic categories to enable clinicians and research investigators to diagnose, treat, study, and communicate about the various disorders with specific criteria in mind.

Many of the disorders arising in childhood or adolescence are related to the syndrome of learning disabilities. Recognition of this frequent association between developmental disorders related to biological maturation and the manifestation of psychiatric disorders is made by the inclusion of Axis II. A partial listing of disorders with emphasis on those associated with academic or learning difficulties as the major presenting problem follows. (For a more detailed description and criteria, the DSM-III draft (1978) should be consulted.) All categories refer to Axis I except those listed under Specific Developmental Disorders (Axis II):

> Mental Retardation
> Pervasive Developmental Disorders
>   Infantile Autism
>   Atypical Childhood Psychosis
> Specific Developmental Disorders (Axis II)
>   Specific Reading Disorder
>   Specific Arithmetical Disorder
>   Developmental Language Disorder
>   Expressive Type (Expressive Dysphasia)
>   Receptive Type (Receptive Dysphasia)
>   Developmental Articulation Disorder
>   Mixed Specific Developmental Disorders
>   Other Specific Developmental Disorders
> Attention Deficit Disorder
>   With Hyperactivity
>   Without Hyperactivity
> Conduct Disorders
> Anxiety Disorders
> Affective Disorders
> Schizophrenic Disorders
> Other Disorders of Childhood or Adolescence
>   Introverted Disorder of Childhood
>   Oppositional Disorder
>   Elective Mutism
>   Academic Underachievement Disorder

Disorders Characteristic of Late Adolescence
Emancipation Disorder
Identity Disorder
Specific Academic or Work Inhibition
Eating Disorders
Speech Disorders
Stuttering
Stereotyped Movement Disorders
Transient Tic Disorder
Chronic Tic Disorder
Tourette's Disorder
Atypical Tic Disorder

Specific reading and arithmetic disorders are determined by a performance on a standardized test of reading or arithmetical skills significantly less than predicted on the basis of the child's chronological age and an individually administered full-scale IQ test. The significant impairment in skills cannot be explained on the basis of mental age or inadequate schooling.

In reading, faulty oral reading is characterized by omissions and additions of words or by defective visual discrimination of graphemes. In arithmetic the child has a pronounced difficulty in learning and retaining arithmetic facts such as multiplication tables and other rules of computation. The prevalence is not definitely known, but the reading disorder is more common than the arithmetic disorder.

Reading disorders are commonly associated with spelling and dictation deficits, characterized by numerous and bizarre errors that cannot be explained in phonetic terms and by reversal of letters (such as *b–d*) and reversal of reading direction (such as *god–dog*). Other common associated features include poor language skills, particularly impaired sound discrimination and difficulties with sequencing words properly; lack of firm dominance as seen in difficulties of hand–eye preference and impaired left–right discrimination; motor problems, including awkwardness and dyspraxia; and behavioral problems, including immaturity, impulsivity, and short attention span.

Reading and arithmetic disorders must be differentiated from mental retardation, defects in peripheral visual or auditory acuity, and social factors. Often, these disorders are seen mixed with attention deficit disorders and conduct disorders.

As the authors of DSM–III point out developmental language

disorder is delayed language acquisition of the expressive or receptive types. Delayed language acquisition is different from a failure of any language to appear and an acquired language disability. In the expressive type of developmental language disorder the defect or delay is in the production of language. The child responds normally to sounds and does not appear to have a hearing impairment. Parents report that the child seems to understand language, but "can't get the words out." The presence of "inner language," pretend play, gestures, and warm social relationships rule out a diagnosis of pervasive developmental disorder (infantile autism or atypical childhood psychosis). Early learning may be impaired particularly in tasks involving perceptual or sequencing skills. Learning of reading and spelling are common academic problems in the school years. General retardation, trauma, or seizures are not present to explain the defect in production of language.

The receptive type of developmental language disorder shows a defect in both comprehension and production of language present from the first year of life so that language acquisition is severely impaired. Deficits occur in sensory perception, integration, storage recall, and sequencing. In general, language is usually difficult to acquire, and learning difficulties are inevitable. An IQ within the normal range rules out mental retardation, although testing may be difficult, especially in the early years. The impaired comprehension of language will rule out the expressive type of developmental language disorder, but it may suggest a diagnosis of infantile autism. The child with infantile autism will rarely attempt to communicate, whereas children with receptive dysphasia will watch faces and use gestures to communicate.

The diagnostic criteria for developmental articulation disorder, as outlined in DSM–III, state that consistent and frequent misarticulations of the later acquired speech sounds are necessary to make the diagnosis. Language impairment and physical or intellectual disorders are absent. Developmental language disorder may be ruled out if vocabulary and grammatical structures are normal for age.

All of the above specific developmental disorders may serve as stress factors to influence the development of anxiety, emotional conflicts, social adjustment problems, and many of the described clinical psychiatric syndromes. Attention deficit disorders and conduct disorders coexist with learning disabilities to a greater degree than the other clinical disorders. Attention deficit disorders display developmentally inappropriate short attention and poor concentration. Previously, this disorder has been referred to by many names including

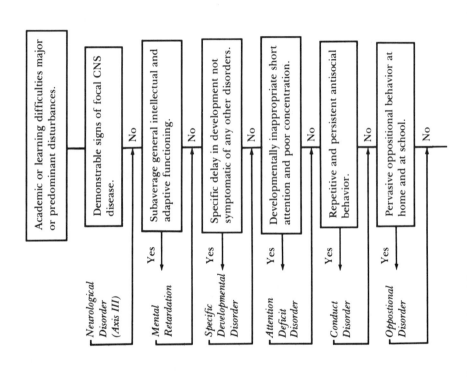

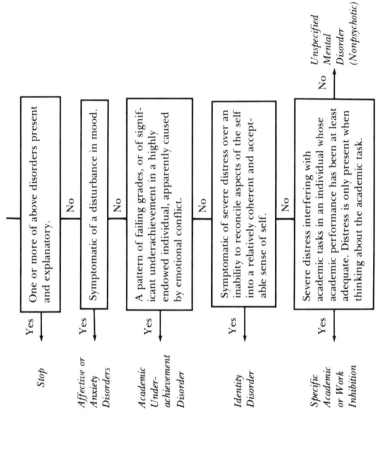

Fig. 5-1. Differential diagnosis of academic or learning difficulties. (From *Diagnostic and Statistical Manual of Mental Disorders*, 3rd ed. Washington, D.C.: American Psychiatric Association, 1978. Copyright 1978 by the American Psychiatric Association. Reprinted by permission.)

minimal brain dysfunction, minimal cerebral dysfunction, hyperactive child syndrome, and hyperkinetic reaction of childhood. The change in terminology stems from the recognition that the central and sustaining feature of those children, adolescents, and adults who may be described in this category is the attentional difficulty. Excessive motor activity (hyperactivity) may or may not be sustained as the child grows older. The child who shows attention deficit with hyperactivity is impulsive in his work and his play, with adults and with peers, at school and at home. A "driven" quality is present in his motor behavior. He has difficulty in completing tasks in school and becomes more disorganized in unstructured situations where supervision is minimal. Attention deficit without hyperactivity is different in that these children are able to sit still and do not show excessive, gross motor movements for their age.

The attention deficit disorders must be distinguished from disorders which are reactive to specifically identified psychosocial stressors and the negative, uncooperative, oppositional behavior of oppositional disorder. Anxiety disorders may influence attention and motor activity, but a source for the anxiety can usually be determined on evaluation; whereas in the attention deficit with hyperactivity the excessive activity seems purposeless and unrelated to emotional conflict.

Conduct disorders show repetitive and persistent patterns of antisocial behavior. Often there is irritability, temper outbursts, and provocative recklessness. Academic achievement and reading performance are often below the expected level, and attentional difficulties are common. Varying degrees of aggression and social bonding may be present in the conduct disorders.

The affective disorders, especially depression, are receiving increased study in children and adolescents. Depression may be a symptom of a learning disability or depression may lead to learning difficulties. The dysphoric mood of depression may lead to a loss of interest or pleasure in most of a child's or adolescent's activities, including school work and social activities. Other symptoms may include changes in appetite or weight, changes in sleep habits, loss of energy, psychomotor retardation or agitation, and feelings of self-reproach or excessive guilt. Some complain of difficulties in concentration with slow thinking and indecisiveness. Some have recurrent thoughts of death or suicide.

To aid in understanding the organization of the classification the authors of DSM–III included samples of "decision trees" that can be used by the clinician to rule in or out various diagnostic categories. It is emphasized that the questions are only approximations of the actual diagnostic criteria. The example for differential diagnosis of academic or learning difficulties is reproduced in Figure 5–1 (see pages 116 and 117).

FACTORS ASSOCIATED WITH LEARNING DISABILITIES

When we carefully evaluate the child, the family, and the community, we see multiple factors in action. These factors relate in an integrated manner through mechanisms yet to be determined that result in the expression of a learning difficulty at some point along a spectrum. A model shown in Table 5–4 will serve to focus on certain influential factors.

Table 5-4. Multifactorial Model for Conceptualizing Etiological Factors Related to Learning Disorders (x = unknown quantity).

x(Genetic factors) + x(Physiological factors) + x(Psychosocial factors) + x(Developmental factors) + x(Cultural factors) → Spectrum of learning-related disorders

Genetic Factors

Critchley (1964) described studies by others which indicated that in 30 to 88 percent of cases of developmental dyslexia other members of the family had reading problems. A series of 12 monozygotic twins have shown a 100 percent concordance rate. Vernon (1957) stated that there is *no* specific inheritance of reading disorder, but there is an inherited predisposition in certain cases toward the occurrence of the related difficulties of reading disabilities, speech impairments, motor incoordination, impulsivity, and attention span. A vulnerability might be inherited in the unknown biological mechanisms that influence the ordering of intentional behavior or the modulation of anxiety, arousal, motility, and attention. Individual variation in these mechanisms would be expected, and the vulnerability alone would not lead to expression unless other factors were added.

Some observers have hypothesized a high incidence of left-handedness among relatives with reading disabilities and suggested this implied a genetic factor. A review of epidemiological studies (Rutter & Hersov, 1977), however, has shown that reading difficulties are not associated with any pattern of handedness, eyedness, or footedness but, rather, can be associated with confusion between right and left. General intelligence is important in learning to read; thus, to the extent that general intelligence is genetically based, this factor is represented. The finding of a consistently higher proportion of males with reading and learning disabilities may suggest a genetic basis; other developmental factors, however, could influence this higher incidence in males. Family studies are influenced by environmental factors and genetic factors. Therefore, no definite conclusions can be drawn from this data.

Physiologic Factors

Perinatal physical factors, (such as toxemia of pregnancy, maternal infection, drugs taken during pregnancy, labor, or delivery, and twinning) stress the physiology of the newborn that may result in changes in brain physiology and subsequent learning disabilities. Brain damage incurred at an early age, as seen in children with cerebral palsy, interferes with the acquisition of reading skills even when IQ is normal (Rutter & Hersov, 1977). In a longitudinal study of 241 children from birth through 7 years of age, subjects with low birth weight (less than 2500 gm) scored lower on all measures of mental development, language development, school readiness, and academic achievement than subjects with full birth weight (Rubin, Rosenblatt, & Barlow, 1973). A greater frequency of pregnancy complications and premature infants was found in a group of subjects with reading disabilities in comparison to a control group by Kawi and Pasamanick (1959). Nutritional factors may influence physiologic mechanisms that interfere with learning; however, no systematic studies to date have offered conclusive evidence. Defects in neurophysiological pathways as measured by visual motor perceptual tests of coordination at age 5 to 6 years in 41 children were followed up 3 years later by Robinson and Schwartz (1973). The children showed no more reading difficulties than did a matched control group without visual motor perceptual difficulties. Others have demonstrated similar findings (Rutter & Hersov, 1977). It may be that the visual motor perceptual difficulties are more important in younger than older children. Adams, Kocsis, and Estes (1974) found that 9- and 10-year-old learning-disabled children cannot be reliably distinguished from normally achieving children on the basis of "soft" neurological signs, which are elicited as indicators of neurophysiological factors. Additional studies in this area are needed.

A neurophysiological hypothesis has been used by Satterfield, Cantwell, and Satterfield (1974) to explain the behavior of children who are labeled "hyperactive" and are characterized by excessive non-goal-directed motor activity, short attention span, easy distractibility, and impulsivity, all of which lead to learning problems. This hypothesis suggests the presence of low central nervous system arousal and insufficient inhibitory controls over motor outflow and sensory input. The physiological phenomena of arousal and cortical inhibition may be influenced by genetic, psychosocial, or developmental factors as well as physical factors surrounding birth.

Psychosocial Factors

The psychological aspects of a person include *cognitive* (comprehension, reasoning), *conative* (volitional behavior and actions), and *emotional* (feelings of fear, anger, grief, joy, love) areas. In an individual all aspects are expressed in relation to the social environment (those persons with whom the individual is associated). Performance on intelligence tests is strongly influenced by environmental experiences, stimulation, and motivation, although part of what we call intelligence is genetically determined. Zigler and his associates (1968, 1973) showed that in tests to measure intelligence given to disadvantaged children lower performance resulted from emotional and motivational deficits.

A child must be sufficiently free of emotional conflicts and be psychologically available to learn. Emotional conflicts may lead to increased anxiety, fear, depression, and increased or decreased aggression, which may lead to learning difficulties. Preoccupation with fantasy and low self-esteem are frequently associated with learning disorders. All of these psychosocial factors are influenced by socioeconomic conditions. Rutter and Hersov (1977) point out that low verbal intelligence and poor reading ability are associated with low socioeconomic status and large family size. Environmental factors are clearly influential under these conditions as well as probable genetic factors.

Developmental Factors

Development progresses or regresses as a result of the interaction of constitutional factors and environment. It is an ongoing and ever changing process with emphasis on the interaction between the innate and the experiential, and not on the one or the other. A useful approach is to look at the phenomenon of temperament, which has been defined at birth and followed in the New York Longitudinal Study.

Chess (1968) and Thomas and Chess (1977) observe, identify, and describe nine categories of temperament. Chess (1968) summarizes them in Table 5-5.

Table 5-5. Categories of Temperament.

1. *Activity level:* The motor component present in a given child's functioning, and the diurnal proportion of active and inactive periods.
2. *Rhythmicity:* The predictability of such functions as hunger, feeding pattern, elimination, and sleep–wake cycle.
3. *Approach or withdrawal:* The nature of the child's response to a new food, object, or person.
4. *Adaptability:* The speed and case with which current behavior can be modified in response to altered environmental structuring.
5. *Intensity of reaction:* The energy level of response, irrespective of its quality or direction.
6. *Threshold of responsiveness:* The intensity level of stimulation required to evoke a discernible response to sensory stimuli, environmental objects, and social contacts.
7. *Quality of mood:* The amount of pleasant, joyful, or friendly behavior as contrasted with unpleasant, unfriendly behavior or crying.
8. *Distractibility:* The effectiveness of extraneous environmental stimuli in interfering with, or in altering the direction of, ongoing behavior.
9. *Attention span and persistence:* These two categories are related. Attention span concerns the length of time a particular activity is pursued by the child. Persistence refers to the continuation of an activity in the face of obstacles to the maintenance of the activity.

From "Temperament and Learning Ability of School Children" by S. Chess, *American Journal of Public Health,* 1968, *58,* 2231-2239. Copyright 1968 by American Public Health Association. Reprinted by permission.

These qualities are viewed as constitutional phenomena which do not imply etiology. Genetic and physiological factors are undoubtedly influential. A child's personality and behavioral characteristics develop as a result of the interaction between temperamental qualities and environment. Certain clusters of temperamental qualities correspond to certain general temperamental or behavioral styles. One general style is the "slow-to-warm-up" style, which refers to an infant who is mildly negative to new stimuli and who adapts slowly. It is important to allow such children to adapt to the new at their own tempo and to allow them to reexperience situations without pressure. Impatience and pressure lead to destructive interaction. The "difficult child," another general style, also gives negative responses to new stimuli and shows slow adaptability but reacts with high intensity. The demands of socialization, the conforming to family, school, and peer groups are stressful. Once such a child learns the rules, he functions easily, consistently, and energetically. It takes special care by parents to be patient, consistent, firm but tolerant.

In a learning situation the interaction between the child and the care-giving adult results in developmental changes in the child that clearly influence learning. If the temperamental style of the child is understood and responded to appropriately, development and learning are facilitated.

Another general style is described as the "easy child" who is "regular, responds positively to new stimuli, adapts quickly to change, and shows a positive mood of mild or moderate intensity." Chess (1968) describes how such infants adapt easily to the family and, as they enter school, adapt easily to the peer group and school expectations. Developmental and learning difficulties, however, may occur in the case of the "easy child" if there is a severe difference between family and school expectations and demands. If so, then conflict results that adversely affects development. Stress resulting from this conflict when added to other predisposing factors might result in a learning-related disorder.

Cultural Factors

Varying cultural traditions place different values on academic learning. Educational philosophies vary between cultures. Also, the prevalence of reading disability varies with the language used. The highest prevalence of reading disability is found in English-speaking countries or in German-speaking countries, next lower in Latin-speaking countries, such as Italy or Spain, and less than 1 percent among Japanese children. Makita (1968) proposes that the "specificity of the used language is the most potent contributing factor in the formation of reading disability." The KANA script in Japanese is "almost a key-to-keyhole" situation in the script-phonetic relationship and thus may account for the low prevalence.

Culturally influenced child-rearing and educational attitudes may account for some variance of reading disabilities among languages. Cultures that follow the child's lead as demonstrated by maturational readiness in implementing individualized instruction in the various academic areas may have fewer learning disabilities. Timing of intervention seems to be crucial in influencing any system. Thus, those cultures that ignore individual characteristics and variability, for whatever reason, may influence the development of disabilities in those individuals who are ready to learn sooner or later.

All of the above factors—genetic, psychophysiologic, psychosocial, developmental, cultural—reflect a constant interaction and reciprocal interplay between several groups of variables that result in the spectrum of learning-related disorders. The following case material illustrates the interaction of the various factors.

CASE ILLUSTRATIONS

An Adolescent

Jane was a 15-year-old eighth-grade girl with a chronic learning difficulty. Her development had proceeded without any observed difficulty until the second grade. At that time her performance in general began to decline. Her lowest grades were in mathematics. A mild perceptual problem was diagnosed at the time, but no definite intervention was undertaken. Jane repeated the second grade and passed each year in a rigorous school until the seventh grade, when failure seemed likely. She had attended summer school for three summers. On achievement tests she was reading a full 2 years above her age. In arithmetic, her grade level was 1 year below the expected. She described herself as someone who had a low frustration tolerance and difficulty expressing anger toward others. She became angry with herself when she could not accomplish something. She had very high aspirations and expectations. She was overweight and depressed. An older, very successful sibling was in college. Jane was provocative to her father, who was an imposing, stern, and judgmental individual. Her father was described as "the wall" and her mother as "the daydreamer." Jane was preoccupied with fantasies of dying or being killed. Psychological testing showed a slightly less than average IQ with evidence of a mild auditory processing deficit involving auditory memory.

Family therapy was initiated while school placement in a more flexible program with specific educational interventions was sought. No medication was indicated. After 6 months of weekly family therapy no residual of depression was evident and she lost 10 pounds of weight. She passed the year, and placement in a more appropriate school was arranged for the following year.

In this case a genetic predisposition for average intelligence was likely. The most striking influences on her performance, however, were the high value placed on academic learning by her family, her strong motivation for overachievement, and the overly rigorous academic environment. Had these factors not been present, the expression of a learning difficulty and the emotional difficulty might never have appeared.

A School-aged Child

Billy was referred at the age of 9 by his school social worker and pediatrician because of failure in school and behavioral difficulties. He had repeated the first grade and now was failing the second grade. His poking and touching children at school was provoking. His attention span was short, and he was easily distracted by external stimuli. His distractability, however, was also related to inner stimuli. He would inappropriately and repeatedly question others about death, birth, and their feelings toward him. Rocking body movements, stomachaches, headaches, and "nervous rashes" were continuing in spite of medication. Autoerotic behavior was present at home and at school. He was secretly dressing in girl's clothing. He had difficulty in going to sleep at night. His mother emphasized that he had two problems. "Trouble going to sleep at night" and "trouble finishing work at school."

Billy was a slim, pale, sandy-haired boy who was tall for his age and resembled his father in physique. His blue eyes had circles under them, and his fingernails were bitten to the quick. His body movements were awkward, and many of his mannerisms were feminine. He was polite and timid but verbalized well, using a good vocabulary. His thought processes demonstrated loosening of associations; however, his reality testing was not defective. He was preoccupied with death and separation.

His scores on the Wechsler Intelligence Scale for Children indicated the dull normal range. On the subtest for similarities (assessing capacity for abstract reasoning), however, he corresponded to the 12-year-old, suggesting an intellectual potential much higher than reflected on full-scale IQ. Other subtest scores, the Bender-Gestalt Test, and lack of hand preference suggested a specific cognitive disability in selected areas of visual perception and visual motor coordination. Other factors that contributed to his low test performance were his low motivation, distractibility, and impulsivity in answering.

Billy's parents had been unhappily married for 12 years. His mother had become depressed shortly after his birth and had remained withdrawn from most social relationships. Billy's father was a business executive who was a friendly outgoing person who spent about half of his time traveling away from home. He recalled being withdrawn, submissive, and fearful in peer relationships as a child. In the extended families of both parents chronic alcoholism and psychiatric hospitalization were present in first-degree relatives.

Billy was characterized as an "easy" baby to care for at birth. At times the mother was overprotective, and at times she withdrew during her depressions. Although Billy was easy to care for, this inconsistency in his parenting environment may have created some dissonance with resulting anxiety and physiologic stress. A genetic predisposition may be present as indicated in the family history. Psychosocial stress factors within the family included parental discord and the father's frequent and lengthy absences.

The treatment program included individual psychotherapy twice weekly, group psychotherapy weekly at his school, educational placement in a regular classroom with supplemental educational therapy, and marital couples therapy for the parents. A trial of stimulant medication prior to this evaluation had resulted in what was described as increased disorganization in Billy's behavior. Thus, another trial was not attempted.

After 2 years of this therapeutic program, Billy had grown to accept his own masculinity and had progressed along the developmental line from egocentricity to companionship. He was slightly above grade level in arithmetic and spelling, while average in reading, language, and social studies. His physical symptoms and anxiety had disappeared. The parents expressed happiness with each other, appeared to have a warm personal relationship and enjoyed life together.

A Preschool Child

Joey, age 4½ years, was referred because of his parents' continuing concern over his speech, fine and gross motor difficulties, loss of toilet training, and excessive autoerotic behavior. Factors at birth indicated that Joey might be at risk for normal development. He was unusually mature for a newborn, showed some asymmetry of face and head, had a slight tremor of the jaw and hands and was somewhat drowsy at 2 days of age. As an infant, he was "difficult," irritable, and overactive. His parents had been unusually inconsistent, using coercive, teasing, and overstimulating techniques of child rearing. Much of the parent's behavior was related to their lack of guidance and help with this difficult first child. The father at times was very proud of the persistently stubborn behavior of Joey when he was a toddler because the father wanted him to develop "a mind of his own." Stimulant medication without parent guidance had been attempted at the age of 2 years. A positive response was obtained but not sustained, and records were not available from the previous city where the parents had lived.

On evaluation, Joey was a fair-haired, neatly groomed boy of average size. Movements of his body were clearly recognized as clumsy. He was apprehensive, cooperative, and often turned to the mother for help during the developmental and play evaluations. Often he seemed preoccupied but was able to make himself available to attend to tasks of the evaluation. Observations in the clinic were quite in contrast to the hyperactive, distractable, and impulsive child that had been described in the history. At the next meeting the mother brought a neighbor who described the same behavior as the parents. Joey's motor, cognitive, and emotional development was immature as measured by developmental schedules, but a certain unevenness on accomplishment was observed. Some aspects of cognitive development were fully age adequate. He appeared to know more than the testing could reveal, but this was obscured by his impaired expressive language and his occasional illogical way of responding. His play was repetitive and unimaginative. Joey was aware of his learning difficulties and would become frustrated and anxious when unable to accomplish a task. He would either withdraw to autoerotic behavior, show outwardly aggressive behavior or purposeless activity. A physiologic predisposition was evident from the history. This resulted in behavior with which these parents had difficulty coping. The interaction between the child's behavior and the parental response resulted in increased behavioral and learning difficulties.

Recommendations included placement in a prekindergarten class for children with learning difficulties, stimulant medication, increased supervised motor activities, parent guidance, and individual play psychotherapy to help him cope with his anxiety by developing more flexible coping mechanisms. With development of more flexible coping mechanisms, it was predicted that he would find more effective and appropriate measures to gain pleasure and be able to approach satisfactory relationships with other children. After 1 year improvement was sufficient to allow placement in a regular kindergarten class with supplemental educational therapy plus stimulant medication provided by the pediatrician. The parents returned periodically to the psychotherapist for guidance in managing Joey's behavior as development progressed.

TREATMENT

As seen in the case illustrations, once the diagnostic process has been completed, comprehensive treatment planning will generally indicate several simultaneous interventions to treat the various components of the syndrome of learning disabilities and associated difficulties. Little or no evidence exists to support the efficacy of any single treatment modality: Supplemental instruction in the form of either perceptual training or remedial education alone have not proved to be significantly helpful in raising the educational level of children studied (Birch & Belmont, 1964; Mann, 1971). In a study reported by Arnold et al. (1977), however, a group of first-grade children identified as vulnerable to academic failure and tutored by perceptual techniques developed by Silver and Hagin (1976) were found to improve in areas of social and emotional behavior and academic achievement significantly more than control groups receiving regular academic tutoring. This study deserves careful analysis and replication.

Programs based on social learning theory alone are not sufficient. The available evidence does not suggest that medication alone or psychotherapy alone will help a child with multiple difficulties associated with learning disabilities. Systematic studies of dietary control have not demonstrated usefulness in treating any of the associated features such as hyperactivity. Although good empirical evidence is not available to indicate how best to treat the specific developmental disorders or learning disabilities, general principles of clinical judgment have been helpful in designing programs.

Remedial education is almost always needed. An individualized approach is necessary in establishing a remedial education program with skilled teachers. Data are lacking on whether to conclude it is better to teach a child through his strengths or weaknesses (Rutter, &

Hersov, 1977). Initially, however, it is most likely better to emphasize the child's assets, reward successes, and provide teaching on an individual basis using specialized techniques to help the child cope with specific difficulties. It is essential to change any emphasis on failure to emphasis on success with systematic rewards for progress and accomplishments. The program needs to be designed so that small increments in progress are evident with early and frequent signs of success (Rutter & Yule, 1975). This process may take several years of uninterrupted work. Children tend to progress at varying rates with some improvements coming in thrusts and others in small increments.

For children with attention deficit disorders, with or without hyperactivity, stimulant medication may help to restore the central nervous system to a more normal state in which the child can be in control of screening out sensory input and controlling motor responses (Satterfield et al., 1974). Only an empirical trial of medication can determine usefulness in the management of the individual child. In considering a trial of medication certain principles of prescribing have been recommended. Werry (1977) has suggested the following:

1. Drug treatment should not be used alone but in combination with other types of treatments.
2. Drug treatment should be viewed as synergistic, not competitive with other treatments.
3. An untreated baseline should be obtained before initiating treatment.
4. Nonspecific improvement should be considered and may be noted by the use of placebo initially or at a later stage.
5. The lowest dose possible should be used initially.
6. A single drug should be introduced and effects carefully measured before adding another drug or changing drugs.
7. Dosage should be increased gradually and adjusted with close monitoring for side effects and clinical response.
8. Children on long-term psychotropic medication should have periodic assessments to check their response and necessity for continuing the medication. This may be done by substituting placebo or discontinuing the medication for a "drug holiday."

The specific medications most widely used are dextroamphetamine, methylphenidate, and caffeine. Others, such as the tricyclic antidepressants, have been used, but adequate systematic studies have not been done to allow current conclusions regarding their effectiveness in treatment. The stimulants have been in use since

1937 and are the best investigated and most useful of psychotropic drugs used with children. A recent study by Arnold and his associates (1978) in which a double-blind crossover comparison of methylphenidate hydrochloride, dextroamphetamine sulfate and caffeine after placebo wash out in children with minimal brain dysfunction showed that methylphenidate and dextroamphetamine were significantly better than placebo and caffeine, but not significantly different from each other. Thus, present studies do not offer specific guidance about whether to choose methylphenidate or dextroamphetamine in a specific case. However, it is significant to note the importance of trying another stimulant if the first one tried is not efficacious. In the Arnold et al. (1978) study a child had almost as good a chance (60 percent) of responding well to the second of these two stimulants after the first one failed as another child had of responding to the first one tried (65 percent chance). Failure with either methylphenidate or dextroamphetamine did not seem to reduce substantially the chance of benefit with the other medication.

Effects are clearly related to dosage. Daily dosage varies over a wide range as seen in Table 5–6. The upper limits of this dosage range are regarded as unusually high by some clinicians, while others have suggested even higher dosages than indicated in Table 5–6 (American Academy of Pediatrics, 1975). Others who have conducted systematic studies (Sprague & Sleator, 1975) have suggested that many children will respond to a dose of methylphenidate as low as 10–15 mg or .3 mg/kg daily and many respond adequately to a single morning dose. Clearly, the goal is to prescribe the smallest dose needed for a maximally therapeutic response.

The general procedure is to begin the medication at a single low dose in the morning and gradually increase the dose in the morning and/or then add a noon dose and alternately increase the morning

Table 5-6. Medication for Children with Attention Deficit Disorder.

Generic Name	Trade Name	Daily Dosage Range (mg)	Number of Divided Doses
Dextroamphetamine	Dexedrine	5 to 30 mg	1 to 2
Methylphenidate	Ritalin	5 to 60 mg	1 to 2
Caffeine	Cafamil Cafecon	80 to 300 mg	1 to 2

and noon dose gradually until the point of maximum therapeutic benefit or the presence of side effects is reached. The measurement of therapeutic benefit requires baseline and later systematic observations by teacher, parent, and physician. Various scales may be helpful in recording these observations and the substitution of placebo without informing the teacher is useful in obtaining an objective measurement.

Doses in excess of 20 mg of methylphenidate or .5 mg/kg may produce anorexia, weight loss, and growth inhibition that may persist as long as the medication is given with possibly a compensatory growth spurt when medication is stopped (Safer & Allen, 1975). Other side effects include irritability, stomachaches, headaches, tearfulness, personality change, toxic psychosis, and insomnia if given too late in the day. No addiction or dependency has been reported in the many years of experience with the use of these stimulants for hyperactivity and/or attention deficit disorders.

In children who have felt repeated failure with subsequent lack of self-confidence and depressive symptoms, individual, family, and/or group psychotherapeutic techniques may be necessary. Psychotherapy helps the child to deal with anxiety, low self-esteem, or reactive depression and helps the child to remain in the total program. As pointed out initially, an individualized treatment program based on the comprehensive evaluation of the child and his family leads to the best management. Generally, however, a child with learning disabilities is best considered to require a treatment program with multiple modalities.

C. Hal Brunt

REFERENCES

Adams, R. M., Kocsis, J. J., & Estes, R. E. Soft neurological signs in learning-disabled children and controls. *American Journal of Diseases of Children,* 1974, *128*, 614–618.

American Academy of Pediatrics, Council on Child Health. Medication for hyperkinetic children. *Pediatrics,* 1975, *55*, 560–561.

American Psychiatric Association, Task Force on Nomenclature and Statistics. *Diagnostic and statistical manual of mental disorders* (3rd ed.). Washington, D.C.: The Association, 1978.

Arnold, L. E., Barnebey, N., McManus, J., et al. Prevention by specific perceptual remediation for vulnerable first graders. *Archives of General Psychiatry*, 1977, *34*, 1279–1294.

Arnold, L. E., Christopher, J., Huestis R., & Smeltzer, D. J. Methylphenidate vs. dextroamphetamine vs. caffeine in minimal brain dysfunction. *Archives of General Psychiatry*, 1978, *35*, 463–473.

Birch, H. B., & Belmont, L. Audiovisual integration in normal and retarded readers. *American Journal of Orthopsychiatry*, 1964, *34*, 852.

Chess, S. Temperament and learning ability of school children. *American Journal of Public Health*, 1968, *58*, 2231–2239.

Critchley, M. *Developmental dyslexia*. London: Heinemann, 1964.

Eisenberg, L. Reading retardation: 1. Psychiatric and sociologic aspects. *Pediatrics*, 1966, *37*, 352–365.

Goodman, J. D., & Sours, J. A. *The child mental status examination*. New York: Basic Books, 1967.

Group for the Advancement of Psychiatry (GAP). *The diagnostic process in child psychiatry*. Report No. 38. New York: GAP, 1957.

Kappelman, M. M., Luck, E., & Ganter, R. L. Profile of the disadvantaged child with learning disorders. *American Journal of Diseases of Children*, 1971, *121*, 371–379.

Kawi, A. A., & Pasamanick, B. Prenatal and paranatal factors in the development of childhood reading disorders. *Monographs of the Society for Research in Child Development*, 1959, *24* (4).

Makita, K. The rarity of reading disability in Japanese children. *American Journal of Orthopsychiatry*, 1968, *38*, 599–614.

Mann, L. Perceptual training doesn't help. *Rehabilitation Literature*, 1971, *32*, 322–327.

Rabinovitch, R. D. Reading and learning disabilities. In S. Arieti (Ed), *American handbook of psychiatry* (Vol. 1). New York: Basic Books, 1959, pp. 857–869.

Robinson, M. W., & Schwartz, L. B. Visuo-motor skills and reading ability: A longitudinal study. *Developmental Medicine and Child Neurology*, 1973, *15*, 281–286.

Rubin, R. A., Rosenblatt, C., & Barlow, B. Psychological and educational sequelae of prematurity. *Pediatrics*, 1973, *52*, 352–363.

Rutter, M. Research report of the Institute of Psychiatry, Department of Child and Adolescent Psychiatry. *Psychological Medicine*, 1976, *6*, 506–516.

Rutter, M., & Graham, P. The reliability and validity of the psychiatric assessment of the child. I: Interview with the child. *British Journal of Psychiatry*, 1968, *114*, 563–579.

Rutter, M., Graham, P., & Yule, W. *A neuropsychiatric study in childhood. Clinics in Developmental Medicine*, Nos. 35/36. London: SIMP/Heineman, 1970.

Rutter, M., & Hersov, I. *Child psychiatry.* London: Blackwell, 1977. pp. 559–575.

Rutter, M., Tizard, J., & Whitmore, K. (Eds.). *Education, health, and behavior.* London: Longmans, 1970.

Rutter, M., Yule, W. Specific reading retardation. In L. Mann & D.A. Sabatino (Eds.): *The first review of special education.* New York: Grune & Stratton, 1973.

Rutter, M., & Yule, W. The concept of specific reading retardation. *Journal of Child Psychology and Psychiatry and Allied Disciplines,* 1975, *16,* 181–197.

Safer, D., & Allen, R. Side effects from long-term use of stimulants in children. *International Journal of Mental Health,* 1975, *4,* 105–118.

Satterfield, J. M., Cantwell, D. P., & Satterfield, B. T. Pathophysiology of the hyperactive child syndrome. *Archives of General Psychiatry,* 1974, *31,* 839–844.

Silver, A. A., & Hagin, R. A. *Search and teach.* New York: Walker Educational Books, 1976.

Silver, L. B. The playroom diagnostic evaluation of children with neurologically based learning disabilities. *Journal of the American Academy of Child Psychiatry,* 1976, *15,* 240–256.

Simmons, J. E. *Psychiatric examination of children.* Philadelphia: Lea & Febiger, 1974.

Sprague, R., & Sleator, E. What is the proper dose of stimulant drugs in children. *International Journal of Mental Health,* 1975, *4,* 75–104.

Thomas, A., & Chess, S. *Temperament and development.* New York: Brunner/Mazel, 1977.

Touwen, B. C. L., & Prechtl, H. F. T. *The neurological examination of the child with minor nervous dysfunction. Clinics in Developmental Medicine,* No. 38.

Vernon, M. D. *Backwardness in reading. A study of its nature and origin.* Cambridge, Eng.: Cambridge University Press, 1957.

Werry, J. S. The use of psychotropic drugs in children. *Journal of the American Academy of Child Psychiatry,* 1977, *16,* 446–468.

Zigler, E., Abelson, W. D., & Seitz, V. Motivational factors in the performance of economically disadvantaged children on the Peabody Picture Vocabulary Test. *Child Development,* 1973, *44,* 294–303.

Zigler, E., & Butterfield, E. C. Motivational aspects of changes in IQ test performance of culturally deprived nursery school children. *Child Development,* 1968, *39,* 1–4.

6

LEARNING DISABILITIES: A PROBLEM IN COMMUNICATION?

In 1969 Chalfant and Scheffelin presented the final report of a three-phase project dealing with central auditory processing problems in children to the National Institute of Neurological Disease and Stroke (NINDS). In the report they discussed several of the neurological, psychological, and educational manifestations of the child who has been described as having learning problems. As their final recommendation, the project directors suggested that one of the most pressing needs was that of providing more systematization to the study of learning disabilities. Related to such systematic study was the necessity for better interdisciplinary cooperation in the research and remediation of learning disorders.

Cruickshank in a 1974 conference report indicated that one of the major problems confronting the learning-disabled child was the lack of a true interdisciplinary approach to the solution of these children's problems. More specifically, the "interdisciplinarians" traditionally have been more concerned with their own discipline's viewpoint of the learning-disabilities field. The result of such narrowness in point of view has been that much of the research and subsequent remediation of learning problems have been limited in scope, with the consequence that many children who need help have received, in fact, very little. Cruickshank (1974), who was an early proponent of the multidisciplinary approach to the study of the learning-disordered child, has begun to question its feasibility.

Thus, it would appear that the major problem confronting the learning-disordered child is indeed that of *communication*, namely, communication between those professionals who claim to be most concerned with solving the dilemma of the learning-disordered child. This contention is supported by simply reviewing the many definitions of learning disabilities, each of which emphasizes a different view, such as the educationally retarded definition (Kirk, 1962), the psychoneurological definition (Johnson & Mykelbust, 1967), the developmental definition (Gallagher, 1967), the intellectual definition (Bateman, 1965), the behavioral definition (Kass, 1966), the psychoeducational definition (Wood, 1975), and the aphasoid definition (Clements, 1966). The federal and state governments, on the other hand, have attempted to include nearly all definitions into their legislative acts. The most direct result of these philosophical issues has bearing upon the language problems in the learning-disabilities field, namely, the problem of adequate recall and recognition (and sometimes articulation) of vocabulary items such as psychoeducational, neuropsychological, dyslexia, perceptual motor (assuming, of course, that a motor perceives), minimal brain dysfunction (as opposed to a maximal brain?), intermodality transposition, behavioral brain dysfunction, and others. In the field of learning disabilities of interest also has been the apparent synonymity of words, such as disability, impairment, problem, disorder, handicap, retardation, deficit, dysfunction, insufficiency, injury, disadvantages, and so on.

Indeed, there is a problem in communication associated with the area of learning disabilities, and the problem has been enhanced and perpetuated, in some instances, by professional self-interests. Nevertheless, this communication problem has begun to be recognized and dealt with. For example, research in the area of auditory perceptual problems has begun to be related to empirically based concepts of auditory processing. The growth and development of such research has required the collaboration of persons in various professional areas in specialities such as education, communication disorders, psychology, and medicine. Of course, there is disagreement among people relative to the conceptual bases upon which to base their data, and even more disagreement on the necessary remedial procedures to employ. (Unfortunately, diagnosis and particularly remediation are too seldom based upon the available research in the area, and perhaps even more serious is the fact that remediation is not often tied to diagnostic profiles.) Such disagreement is professionally healthy, however, when it occurs in a spirit of cooperation and is used to test hypotheses that lead to solutions of problems. Thus, auditory perceptual problems recently have been related to what is known about basic information processing (Barrett, 1975; Brugge, 1975; Masland, 1975), and particularly language processing (Pisoni, 1975).

Further, we have come to realize the importance of including parents in the diagnosis and remediation of learning problems. It might even be argued that it has been the recent action by parents of children with learning problems that has been the impetus for increasing professional cooperation in dealing with the learning-disordered child.

The problem of learning disorders in children is often a subtle one that has led to misdiagnosis, not because of incompetency but rather because of our own professional biases and myopic views. Indeed, it has been several years since Rosenthal and Jacobson (1968) described the Pygmalion effect that occurs in the average classroom, and yet there has been a paucity of research and application of the "experimenter-bias" data in the learning-disorders field. Additionally, audiologists and physicians have known for years that children are prone to middle-ear problems; yet these problems only recently have been studied relative to the learning problems of children, primarily due to the collaboration of physicians, audiologists, and educators. That children with learning problems suffer communication problems is fairly well accepted, but, again, only recently have the communication problems of reading been associated empirically with those of audition. The nature of the interpersonal communication problems experienced by the learning-disordered child is another area that has begun to play a major role in the research and clinical activities in learning disabilities.

We hope that in this chapter the reader will gain both some new information and suggestions for new avenues (and/or reemphasis of old avenues) for the diagnosis and management of children with learning problems. In addition, it should be emphasized that in the areas chosen for discussion, no single individual is likely to be adequately prepared to study the problem independent of other professionals; rather, the areas covered are assumed to demand the cooperation and collaboration of various professionals in medicine, education, and social sciences.

TEMPORAL PROCESSING AND AUDITORY PERCEPTION

Traditionally, a great deal of emphasis has been placed upon the "spatial" aspect of perception, particularly in the recall and recognition of linguistic information. Perception, however, is a process that occurs over time, and there has been increasing interest in recent years in the role that time plays in the perceptual processing of language. For example, sound blending, whereby the child must repeat a word which the examiner says with a temporal delay between sounds (e.g., "c-a-t," repeat "cat") was included in the early edition of the Illinois Test of Psycholinguistic Abilities (ITPA) (McCarthy & Kirk, 1961). However, Shriner and Daniloff (1970) showed that the length of the temporal delay between sounds played a significant role in the child's ability to give the correct response. In more recent editions of the ITPA (Kirk, McCarthy, & Kirk, 1968) the sound-blending task is controlled by presenting it via a recording. This is an example of a situation whereby research data, contributed by professionals from several areas, had a direct result upon the development of an important tool in the diagnostician's armamentarium.

In order to study the temporal nature of auditory processing, it has been necessary to employ stimuli which have been temporally distorted in a controlled and systematic manner. Beasley and Maki (1976) have described several methods of temporal distortion. One of the most frequently employed means of temporally altering linguistic stimuli has been through the use of time compression. Briefly, time compression is a means of systematically deleting segments of a recorded signal and subsequently putting the undeleted segments of the signal back together. Consequently, the resultant signal is time compressed, i.e., is shorter in time than when originally recorded. For example, a signal that is time compressed by 40 percent takes 40 percent less time to play back. (The exact mathematical result of 40 percent time compression is 58 percent of original; for an explanation, see Konkle, Freeman, Riggs, et al., 1976). The most efficient means commonly employed to time compress speech and language has been through the use of electromechanical time compressors (Beasley & Maki, 1976). More specific controls of the deleted and retained linguistic samples, however, normally have employed a manual "cut-and-splice" procedure. The manual sampling technique, however, is extremely tedious and inefficient. Fortunately, computer synthesis of speech has begun to be employed on an experimental basis in the study of the temporal processing of speech (Huggins, 1972).

Jerger (1960), Miller (1956), and, more recently, Noffsinger and Kurdziel (1977) have emphasized that adequate assessment of the integrity of central auditory pathways requires measures of increased complexity. The internal redundancy and complexity of the central auditory processor combined with the external redundancy of normal linguistic messages results in an inability of standard linguistic messages to differentiate subtle neurological processing problems. A reduction in the temporal redundancy of verbal messages through the use of time-compressed speech, however, results in an increase in the complexity of the presented message by taxing the central auditory processor without unduly penalizing a listener because of lack of experience with the language.

The use of temporally altered speech stimuli has been employed primarily with adults (Beasley, Schwimmer, & Rintelman, 1972; Kurdziel, Rintelmann, & Beasley, 1975; Noffsinger & Kurdziel, 1979). Beasley, Maki, and Orchik (1976) time compressed words on two standard intelligibility measures used with children: the four lists of the PB-K 50 Test (Haskins, 1949; Sanderson-Leepa & Rintelmann, 1976; Haskins, 1949) and the three lists of the Word Intelligibility by Picture Identification (WIPI) Test (Lerman, Ross, & McLaughlin, 1965) by 0 percent (i.e., normal), 30 percent, and 60 percent of normal duration using the Lexicon Varispeech I (Lee, 1972) electromechanical time compressor. The listeners in this study were 60 normal children ranging in age from 3½ years to 8½ years. The stimuli were presented to the listeners in controlled listening situations. The results indicated, not surprisingly, that the children's intelligibility increased as a function of increasing age and intensity level of presentation and decreasing percentage of time compression for both the PB-K 50 and the WIPI. In addition, the WIPI, which was originally designed for use with children, resulted in higher scores than comparable conditions of the PB-K 50.

Manning, Johnston, and Beasley (1977) presented the time-compressed versions of the PB-K 50 Test to children who were labeled as learning-disabled by virtue of observed auditory processing problems in school. The results of the Manning et al. study indicated that learning-disordered children had depressed scores at 0 percent and 60 percent time compression but performed essentially normal under the 30 percent condition. The authors contended that the improvement of 30 percent compression for the learning-disordered children was possibly the result of the faster presentation rate permitting the children to overcome the initial rapid decay of stimuli in short-term memory. That is, verbal stimuli decay rapidly in short-term memory, and this rapid decay may not allow children with certain learning disabilities enough time to process the stimuli. The faster presentation rate, however, may permit the child to process larger chunks of information prior to decay. Similar results have been found with adults (Mackworth, 1964). If confirmed in future studies, this could have significant effects on the remediation techniques employed with children who exhibit auditory perceptual problems.

In order to further assess linguistic performance relative to auditory processing, several investigators have used sentential approximations (i.e., word strings that approximate sentences) to study the relationship between duration and the syntactic and semantic characteristics of language processing in adults (Beasley & Shriner, 1973; Speaks & Jerger, 1965). Beasley and Flaherty-Rintelmann (1976) presented normal sentences and first- and third-order sentential approximations to 30 first-grade and 30 third-grade children. In addition , they used sentence lengths of three words and five words and also included three conditions whereby the words of the sentences were either normal or separated by interstimulus intervals of 200 msec or 400 msec of silence. The results of the Beasley and Flaherty-Rintelmann study indicated that recall scores increased as a function of increasing sentential approximation and decreasing sentence length. There were minimal differences between the first- and third-graders when the silent interstimulus interval was 200 msec. Under the 400 msec condition, however, the older children clearly performed better than the younger children. Apparently, for the younger children, the 400 msec interstimulus interval served to create a situation whereby the auditory stimulus decayed in short-term memory before being adequately processed. Children with an adequately developed auditory processing system, however, were better able to retain and use the multiple cues of language (Harris, 1960) during the silent interstimulus interval. This contention also has been supported in the psychological literature by Aaronson (1967) and Mackworth (1964).

Freeman and Beasley (1978) presented the WIPI and three-word and five-word sentential approximations, all compressed to 0 percent and 60 percent of normal duration, to children who were labeled as learning disordered by virtue of their poor reading skills. The results clearly indicated that the children with reading problems were unable to process the auditorally presented stimuli as well as comparably normal children when the duration of the stimulus items were altered. These results were related to theoretical models and empirical findings that indicate a close interrelationship between visual and auditory central processing (LaBerge & Samuels, 1974; Locke, 1968; Marquardt & Saxman, 1972; Mattingly, 1972). More specifically, Beasley and Freeman (1977) presented a case study of an 8-year-old boy who was referred for audiological testing in order to determine if the child had a hearing loss that was contributing to his learning problem in school. The general audiometric results were normal, but the child showed reduced scores on time-compressed sentence-like sequences presented to the right ear. Thus, the time-compressed stimuli suggested that the child had an auditory-processing problem that was likely associated with the ability to accurately sequence temporally distorted stimuli. The major implication of the Freeman and Beasley studies is that we can no longer ignore pragmatic implications of the intermodality nature of learning disabilities, either diagnostically or, perhaps more importantly, therapeutically. The recognition of the intermodality concept, though not new, nevertheless, demands that individuals from several professional molds interact in the management of the learning-disordered child. In the meantime, from these and other studies currently underway, it may be suggested that when a child shows a difference score of greater than 10 percent between ears or a difference of 10 percent between a 0 percent and 60 percent time-compression presentation, that child should be carefully followed and monitored for a possible auditory-processing problem.

The foregoing should serve to familiarize the reader with certain "new" trends in the learning disabilities area as it pertains to auditory processing. Certainly, other equally interesting and crucial directions of study are underway, including the use of binaural fusion and alternating speech with learning-disordered children (Willeford, 1976). In a different vein, there currently exists some evidence that children who exhibit severe articulation problems also have associated auditory processing problems (Orchik & Oelschlager, 1974). A major point to be made, however, is that these recent research directions are being pursued with a common theoretical foundation by a number of various professionals who have chosen to pool their research and clinical expertise and resources. By definition, they require the complete cooperation of the classroom teacher, the special educator, the physician, the audiologist, the speech pathologist, the psychologist, and various others who deal with the child on a routine basis. An interesting outgrowth of such cooperation has been the development of hearing screening programs for peripheral hearing problems as related to learning problems.

PERIPHERAL HEARING LOSS AND HEARING PROBLEMS

The importance of hearing to normal learning has been well documented (Myklebust, 1960). In terms of the impact of hearing loss upon learning, however, much of the concern has focused upon the effects of severe sensorineural deafness upon speech and language development and subsequent academic difficulties (Elliott & Armbruster, 1967; Vernon, 1969).

The effect of mild to moderate sensorineural hearing loss has been given much less consideration in the literature. Available data, however, suggests that even mild sensorineural hearing loss has a detrimental effect upon learning.

Young and McConnell (1957) compared 20 hard-of-hearing children to a matched group of normal-hearing children, using a nonverbal performance measure of intelligence and a vocabulary test. The children ranged in aged from 8 to 14 years and hearing losses for the hearing-impaired group ranged from 32 dB to 75 dB (pure-tone average, ASA-51). Although the hearing-impaired children performed in an equivalent manner to the normal-hearing children on the intelligence test, they demonstrated a significant deficit on the vocabulary measure when compared to the normal controls.

Goetzinger and his associates (1962, 1964) examined the effects of mild sensorineural hearing loss upon factors such as speech and language development, auditory discrimination, reading ability, and classroom adjustment. The results of both investigations suggest that a hearing loss as mild as 40 dB (pure-tone average, ISO-64) can have a significant negative effect upon speech and language development and overall academic achievement. This finding is even more significant in the presence of normal intelligence for the hearing-impaired children studied.

It was this group of children, those with mild to moderate sensorineural hearing loss, that was considered the target of traditional hearing screening programs. Children with severe sensorineural deafness were generally identified much earlier in life because of their dramatic lack of speech and language. Children with mild to moderate sensorineural hearing loss, however, were very often not identified until their initial school hearing screening. Even though a language delay may have been in evidence, a hearing loss had been unsuspected by parents and others.

Traditional screening programs were not designed to identify transitory, mild conductive hearing loss related to diseases such as serous otitis media. As stated by the Committee on Identification Audiometry of the American Speech and Hearing Association (Darley, 1969), the goal of hearing screening programs is not to identify every child who at some time in his life may experience a hearing loss. The general belief was that mild transient conductive hearing loss was of little consequence to the development of auditory skills and subsequent learning.

Serous otitis media, however, presents the most common cause of hearing impairment in preschool and elementary school-age children

(Goin, 1975). The underlying cause of serous otitis media is a malfunctioning eustachian tube. Tubal obstruction produces absorption of air by the middle-ear mucosa and results in negative middle-ear air pressure. Membrane changes occur in the mucosal lining of the middle ear when it is continuously exposed to negative pressure, and increased secretion of fluid results. Middle-ear effusion hinders the action of the middle-ear system, which results in a mild-to-moderate conductive hearing loss. Because serous otitis media is often episodic and because the concomitant hearing loss is of mild degree, this disease has been considered primarily a medical problem in the past (Lewis, 1976). Since the age of onset of serous otitis media occurs during critically formative years, however, the possibility of adverse effects on both cognitive development and language skills exists (Paradise, Smith, & Bluestone, 1976).

Recent research has suggested that children with even slight hearing impairment due to middle-ear disease score lower on vocabulary and reading tests than do normal-hearing children (Schwartz & Redfield, 1976). The problem is further complicated when one considers that many of these same children come from low-socioeconomic backgrounds (Lewis, 1976). For example, the language development of 16 children who experienced fluctuating hearing loss as a result of serous otitis media were evaluated by Holm and Kunze (1969). These children, between the ages of 5 and 9 years, had chronic serous otitis media but no other known medical problems. They all were placed in the regular classroom, according to school attendance records. Serous otitis media had appeared in these children before 2 years of age and continued to be a problem throughout the children's school years. A group of standardized speech and language measures were administered to the 16 children with chronic serous otitis media and to a control group of children. Results revealed that the children suffering from fluctuating hearing loss due to serous otitis media were delayed on all language skills tested as compared to the control group of children. Results also suggested that the difference between these two groups of children was greater on the tests more dependent on auditory and vocal skills than on the tests designed to measure motor and visual skills. These findings indicated that children with chronic serous otitis media had a marked language handicap (Holm & Kunze, 1969).

Two groups of aboriginal children (mean age: 8 years) were selected for study by Lewis (1976). The experimental group of 14 children, diagnosed as having chronic serous otitis media, had consistently failed audiometric, tympanometric, and otoscopic examinations administered every 6 months for 4 years. The control group of 18 children had consistently passed the auditory tests during the 4-year period and were presumed to have normal middle-ear function.

All of the children were administered a battery of seven measures of language processing and cognition. Results showed a general tendency for the control group to perform better than the experimental group. Those aboriginal children who had suffered chronic serous otitis media did not perform as well as aboriginal children of equivalent background who were disease free, as shown by significant differences between groups which were obtained on the Wepman Auditory Discrimination Test and a recorded measure of phonemic synthesis skills. Results of this investigation suggested that middle-ear disease is potentially harmful to a child's educational achievement (Lewis, 1976). Traditionally, it has been generally thought that only a sensorineural hearing loss of significant degree would be sufficient to impair speech and language development.

The data presented here are admittedly limited. The implication, however, is clear that a significant contributor to language and learning problems in early school age may have been routinely overlooked in the past. The need for further research is obvious. It may be that supportive educational services may become a necessary part of the overall treatment regimen for the child with recurrent serous otitis media who exhibits associated problems of learning and communication. Before supportive services can be provided, the child with serous otitis media must first be identified. The efficiency of traditional screening programs in identifying serous otitis media has been questioned (Brooks, 1968; McCandless & Thomas, 1974, Orchik & Herdman, 1974). This has led in recent years to the use of impedance audiometry as a primary tool in hearing screening programs. The audiometric evaluation of children has improved substantially with the use of impedance audiometry, which is quick to administer, requires little patient cooperation, and provides objective results (Jerger, 1975).

Impedance is a measure of a system's ability to transmit or accept energy. Acoustic impedance is used to measure the opposition encountered by an acoustic wave at the lateral surface of the tympanic membrane. In order to accomplish this, electroacoustic bridges measure the sound pressure level of a reflected acoustic wave as air pressure is varied in the external ear canal.

The three basic test components of the impedance audiometry battery are tympanometry, static compliance, and acoustic reflex threshold. Tympanometry is the measurement of compliance changes at the tympanic membrane as air pressure is altered in the external-ear canal. These measurements are graphically plotted on a tympanogram. Jerger (1970) has developed a basic classification system for tympanograms as they relate to middle-ear function. Static compliance provides an estimate of middle-ear volume. Static compliance is estimated by comparing middle-ear compliance with the tympanic membrane at a point of maximum compliance and in a position of poor compliance (Jerger, 1975).

The acoustic reflex threshold is the third portion of the impedance battery. The stapedius muscle contracts bilaterally when one or both ears is stimulated with a sufficiently loud sound. This activity may be observed using the impedance bridge in the form of increased acoustic impedance at the tympanic membrane.

A number of investigations have supported the increased efficiency of impedance audiometry in identifying middle-ear disease in children (Beery, Bluestone & Cantekin, 1975; Bluestone, Beery, & Paradise, 1973; Schwartz & Redfield, 1976). The available data suggest that the judicious use of impedance audiometry in a hearing screening program enhances significantly the ability to detect middle-ear disorders too subtle to influence pure-tone audiometry. This information coupled with the recent suggestion that serous otitis media may have important implications for learning (Holm & Kunze, 1969; Lewis, 1976) should result in increased efforts at developing programs to detect even slight changes in peripheral sensitivity as a means of preventing future learning problems.

SPEECH AND LANGUAGE PATHOLOGY AND THE INTERPERSONAL COMMUNICATIVE NATURE OF LEARNING PROBLEMS

The communication problems encountered by the learning-disordered child may take verbal as well as nonverbal forms. The verbal communication problems will likely include problems of articulation as well as problems of a more general language nature, such as delays in language acquisition and development. The child may exhibit spontaneous and/or inappropriate verbalizations, which may be related to forced responsiveness to internal stimuli. The learning-disordered child also may exhibit frequent outbursts of emotion as a result of frustration and embarrassment associated with inappropriate communicative behavior. He may often indicate that he knows less than he does simply because he fears making a mistake. He may exhibit problems related to time and problems in pretending and general play behavior. Memory problems, including recalling sequential information (e.g., days of the week, store numbers, addresses, months of the year, and counting) are not uncommon with the learning-disordered child. Nonverbal communication problems may include difficulty in attending to the appropriate environmental stimuli. As a result, the child may appear bored, or lazy, or preoccupied and may complete only the first or last task requested of him.

Speech and language pathologists are concerned with a person's communication skills and, as professionals, must determine if there is an interference or barrier to one's communication. If a learning disability is considered as a barrier to communication, then it is the speech pathologist's responsibility to recognize such and to provide the most appropriate means of diagnosing these children's problems and to plan appropriate programs for them. It is paramount that the diagnosis be determined by the combined observations and test results obtained by persons from various disciplines, i.e., a multidisciplinary approach. One person cannot diagnose a learning disability without appropriate input from other sources. The results on any one test or battery of tests should be considered with caution and must be supplemented by appropriately related history information and observations of behavior.

An important factor to consider before making a diagnosis is that children who have a specific learning disability usually perform better in a one-to-one situation than they do when in a group or classroom. Thus, when interpreting test results and noting behaviors, one should consider the fact that this same child might perform differently on the same tasks if he were in a different setting. Additionally, the diagnosis of an auditory processing problem, as a specific type of learning disability, should be based on a group or constellation of various characteristics, all of which occur in varying degrees and differences among children. No child exhibits the same degree of difficulty or necessarily the same group of characteristics. Specifically, each child's learning disability is unique (Rampp, 1972).

Much literature has been devoted to discussing learning disabilities and, more specifically, auditory processing problems. Most professionals, however, agree upon certain basic characteristics which are normally exhibited by the population of children with learning disabilities. While it is difficult to dichotomize each characteristic due to their interrelatedness, nevertheless, a list of some of the most commonly observed characteristics of those children who have a learning disability primarily involving auditory processing skills can be delineated as follows:

Attention or attending behaviors. It is often difficult for such children to attend to pertinent auditory stimuli, particularly when multiple background stimuli are present. Teachers report that they "don't listen" or "don't pay attention" in the classroom. In the testing situation, they might have difficulty attending to the various test items.

Auditory sequential memory and/or serial memory. There is generally difficulty remembering and carrying out verbal instructions, particularly in a group setting. Tests that use a string of digits or words are often difficult for him, as is recalling and sequencing auditory stimuli. Also, learning from rote memory (for example, days of the week, months of the year, nursery rhymes, the alphabet) seems to take longer for this child. Teachers and parents report that "he can't follow instructions" or "he forgets half of what I tell him to do."

Auditory discrimination. A child may experience (exhibit) discrimination problems. He may confuse rhyming words (mat/bat) or cognate sounds *(p/b).* This may be evident in problems with learning phonics and basic reading skills.

Auditory sound blending. Often there is a problem in learning to blend (or synthesize) the sounds of a word into the whole word (for example, "c-a-t" is "cat"). This seems to be related to a child's difficulty with auditory sequential memory in that it involves similar processes of recall.

Spatial and temporal concepts and relationships. The child with a learning problem not only experiences difficulty in learning the sequencing of concepts, such as days of the week or months of year, but also has problems with relationships of these concepts. For example, questions such as "What day comes after Tuesday?" or "What month is before April?" may pose a problem for this child. Concepts involving directions of left and right or even telling time or recalling events of time, such as his birth date, are usually more difficult for this child to learn.

Reading and associated reading skills. Problems with auditory discrimination and auditory sound blending are common. Thus, learning to read is usually a major disability. In fact, the child may not even be suspected of having a problem until he enters an academic setting and exhibits reading difficulties. Myklebust (1965) noted that reading is the ultimate in language achievement. In order to break the code for learning that the written (visual) symbol together with its auditory signal represents the spoken language is a complex set of processes. Thus, a child who is experiencing difficulty with auditory processing skills also often will show difficulty in learning to read.

Inadequate self-concept. As the child with a learning disorder experiences increasing failure and difficulty in school and at home, he may become frustrated and fail to develop a sense of accomplishment. Many times behaviors such as "crying more easily" or demonstrating frustration over even "simple failures" or being "too sensitive" are noted by parents and teachers as descripters for a child with a learning disorder.

When a child is seen by the speech pathologist for a diagnostic evaluation, several sources of information must be considered before a diagnosis can be made. The teacher can supply needed information regarding the child's performance and behavior in the classroom setting. Regarding this, the diagnostician should formulate appropriate questions before consulting with the teacher. Such questions as "How many verbal directions can Johnny follow?"; "Is he easily distracted?"; and so on, need to be raised. In addition, the speech pathologist needs to obtain an accurate assessment of the child's school performance.

The parents are another valuable source of information. They can provide additional information about the child's behavior relative to his attention span, the number of verbal directions he can follow, distractability, rote memory, and so on. Information from other professionals, such as the child's pediatrician, psychologist, and social worker, also should be included in the diagnostic process. Input from these sources might include such reports as medication for hyperactivity, EEG results, performance on intelligence tests, or other pertinent findings.

Ideally, all of the above-mentioned information should be obtained prior to the child's being seen for a diagnostic evaluation, thereby assisting the speech pathologist to make the best possible diagnosis of the child's learning disability. When the child is seen for the diagnostic evaluation, the speech pathologist should administer a variety of appropriate measures as well as make clinical observations of behaviors exhibited by the child. Test measures should include an assessment of receptive language, expressive language, articulation, hearing acuity, auditory sequential memory, auditory discrimination, tasks of spatial and temporal relationships, auditory sound blending, reading, and visual motor skills. Numerous diagnostic measures which assess these areas are available to the diagnostician, who should use clinical discretion in determining which tests are the most appropriate to administer for each child.

After it has been determined that the child does exhibit a specific learning disability, then it is the responsibility of the diagnostician to inform the parents, explaining the child's difficulty to them and answering questions that would help them to deal appropriately with the child's problems. Subsequently, the several persons involved in the diagnosis (speech pathologist, teacher, physician, psychologist, tutor, social worker, and others) meet and design an individualized program that can meet the child's specific needs. As previously discussed, each child's learning disability is unique, and a program should be specifically designed to meet the particular child's needs. The program can be adequately designed only by careful analysis of the areas or skills in which the child is experiencing difficulty. For example, if the child has difficulty with following verbal directions (auditory memory) and with reading skills, then the program should stress remediation of these skills, not only in the classroom setting, but also in the home environment. Therefore, the key to providing an appropriate and effective program for the child would be to have an accurate and descriptive diagnosis of the child's difficulty with specific skills and behaviors as well as an understanding of how to deal with these difficulties.

Many commercial programs and aids to be used with the learning-disordered child are available for the classroom teacher, speech pathologist, and parents. These should be carefully selected and modified for the child's specific needs. The program should be constantly modified as the child makes progress with certain skills and behaviors. Special therapy programs, reading programs, classroom activities, and activities at home should be planned for the child and implemented by both the appropriate professionals and the parents. Equally important, programs should be implemented with due consideration given to the interpersonal nature of communication. That is, recognition of the total child's communicative environment and associated difficulties must be continually monitored.

Learning-disabled children who frequently experience breakdowns in communication between themselves and those in their environment become increasingly angry and tense when their behaviors are misinterpreted or when they do not understand. They often become withdrawn or demonstrate anger or frustration through aggressive behavior. Wyatt (1976) is among those who noted that it is important for parents of learning-disabled children to understand underlying causes of these unacceptable behaviors and then to work to assure the child that he will have help from those in his environment to reduce frustrations in the communication process.

Parents, by their very existence, are in daily communication with their children in all areas of development, including that of speech and language acquisition. For example, Wyatt (1965, 1969) noted that the mother was the primary language teacher, and, therefore, communicative interactions between mother and child played a major role in the child's early development of communication skills. As such, the professionals who deal with children with disorders of communication have begun to realize that parents of these children need more than simply diagnostic information and therapeutic prescriptions. In addition to providing understanding and support for the child and appropriate verbal interaction with the child, parents will need to be guided in establishing clear ground rules with the child regarding behavior. Parents will need to be firm and consistent in their expectations of the child. Parents also need avenues for expressing and clarifying their own attitudes and emotions as these relate to the communication problems experienced by their children (MacDonald, 1962; McWilliams, 1976; Webster, 1977; Wyatt, 1976).

The initial contact between the speech and language pathologist and the parent(s) of a learning-disabled child normally occurs at the time of the dignostic evaluation. In many instances parents of the learning-disordered child are confused and perplexed by the fact that their child appears to be quite normal in many respects and may even perform normally in certain academic areas. Academic performance in other areas, however, may be quite poor, and certain of the child's behavior patterns may not be consistent with other "average" children (Todd & Gottlieb, 1976). As a result, the parents may be experiencing feelings of anxiety and concern regarding the ambiguity of their child's welfare, and this anxiety may be expressed through a number of various emotional patterns, including anger, rationalizations, denial that a problem exists, and so on. The parents may experience a sense of embarrassment and disappointment, in that their child seems to be some sort of social and/or intellectual "deviant." In the extreme, they may very well believe that their child is mentally retarded and must be interred in some form of a hospital or institution.

With all of these possibilities at the outset, the initial meeting of the diagnostician and the parents (or one parent) is crucial, for what follows for the child and the parents will be directly dependent upon, in many instances, the clinician's initial awareness of the parents' anxieties (Buscaglia, 1975; Todd & Gottlieb, 1976). Thus, at the first meeting, which normally occurs concurrent with formal evaluation of the child, the diagnostician, in addition to evaluating the child, must do the following:

1. Obtain the parents' perception of the child's problem (McWilliams, 1976; Webster, 1977)
2. Deal with parents' feelings of confusion by providing appropriate, clear, and accurate information to the parents (Cruickshank, 1967; McDonald, 1962; Webster, 1977)
3. Initiate a positive action toward remediation (Cruickshank, 1967; McDonald, 1962; Todd & Gottlieb, 1976).
4. Reflect an honest concern and understanding for the parents' confusion about their "normal" child who is not so "normal" (Todd & Gottlieb, 1976; Wood, 1975).

By obtaining the parents' perceptions of their child's problem, the diagnostician is better able to determine how much information the parents have about their child and, equally important, the accuracy of such information. The diagnostician also will be able to identify potential feelings of guilt, denial, and other forms of anxiety that the parents may be experiencing and, in turn, prepare to deal with the behaviors associated with these internal emotional states.

Having determined the parents' position with respect to the information needs, the clinician can then better explain the nature of the child's problem and more effectively impart clinical impressions (McWilliams, 1976; Webster, 1977) and evaluations. In discussing the learning-disabled child's problem with parents, Webster (1966, 1977) has cautioned that, although the clinician must avoid talking down to parents, one must also be equally careful to avoid the overuse of professional jargon. For example, a parent could easily become lost if the speech pathologist reported, "Mildred has an auditory processing problem involving memory skills." A more realistically understandable means of expressing the same concept to the parent might be, "Mildred hears what you say to her, but she may have difficulty remembering more than one idea at a time. For example, if you say to Mildred, 'Go upstairs, get your sweater, and turn off the radio,' she may do only the first or last thing she has been asked to do." Through the use of descriptive examples by the speech pathologist, parents of the learning-disabled child will be better able to comprehend how their child's communication is affected by the learning disability. In turn, the parents will discover that they may need to communicate "differently" with their child.

In addition to providing information designed to improve

parent–child interactions, the clinician will also want to discuss educational implications, recommendations for therapy, and possible referrals with the parents. At the end of the initial conference it will be beneficial for the clinician to summarize the information presented and ask the parents to feed back specific instructions or recommendations made during the session (McWilliams, 1976). That is, clinicians can assess parental understanding by making such statements as, "I want to make sure I have explained things clearly; please tell me how you understand what I've said, then we can clear up areas where I might have confused you." Such probes will serve to clarify misconceptions and reduce the possibility of misunderstandings by the parents (Webster, 1977).

Unfortunately, in most cases, the conference time associated with the initial evaluation is insufficient for effectively meeting the needs of parents. Thus, it is recommended to many parents that they participate in a series of follow-up counseling sessions. At the Memphis Speech and Hearing Center these sessions may take the form of individual meetings where appropriate. A more typical pattern entails discussions in sessions with several parents, at least as an adjunct to individual sessions and, more often, in lieu of individual sessions.

The parent group usually consists of a speech pathologist serving as a group leader and includes two to six parents of children currently enrolled for therapy at the Center. Several investigators have indicated that parents of children with various types of handicaps often share similar feelings of concern and confusion (Barsch, 1968; J. B. Beasley, 1956; MacDonald, 1962; Webster, 1972, 1974) and, therefore, it is not necessary that the participants in parent groups have children with the same communicative disability. Rather, it is only necessary that the parents share the need to communicate more effectively with their child. These similarities among parents allow them to share experiences, successes, and failures and to acknowledge that their problems no longer isolate them from other parents (Todd & Gottlieb, 1976). They learn from each others' questions and concerns and serve as resource for each other.

Normally, at the outset of the counseling sessions parents appear more concerned about their child's communication problem and related socialization skills and educational potential (Webster, 1974). As the parent groups progress, the discussions tend to become more parent-oriented than child-oriented. For example, Cole (1975) observed that parental responses to clinician questions more often reflected parental attitudes and feelings about themselves as parents rather than about their children, particularly after the first few sessions. Thus, a major goal of the counseling session should be to provide parents an opportunity in which they are allowed to be themselves, to disclose their own thoughts and feelings, and to speak to their needs, anxieties, fears, and successes. As J. Beasley (1956) stated, "When parents are granted acceptance and respect, it will enable them to show more acceptance to their children." In essence, once parents are able to identify and clarify their own feelings, they can more effectively deal with their child's problems.

In the parent counseling session the therapist can provide the necessary therapeutic support for parents to experience rewarding communicative interactions. The group structure provides an excellent framework for parent training and explaining and clarifying information through role playing, demonstrations, and videotaping. Guest speakers and panel discussions can be incorporated into the group sessions to provide information on topics of specific interest. The primary medium in the parent counseling session, however, is informal discussion (Webster, 1977; Webster & Cole, 1977). Topics may be suggested by the group leader or the parent participants and may range from topics such as ways to discipline children to ways to promote better parent–child communication. Examples of parent–child communication are (1) learning how to "listen" to the child rather than simply "hearing" him, (2) learning how to accept the child's views and concerns while not necessarily accepting his behaviors, (3) learning to verbalize and discuss the child's feelings, and (4) learning to communicate with the child in a child's world rather than an adult world. Recommendations and suggestions that were discussed during the diagnostic conference can be pursued in depth during the parent counseling sessions. For example, parents can be assisted in learning to cope with unusual behaviors on the part of their children as well as to develop means for setting realistic goals for their children. In addition, the group participants can provide positive reinforcement when parents experience success, and, in turn, provide suggestions and support when parents' efforts fail.

A significant portion of the parent counseling sessions will involve aiding the parent in dealing with the child's miscommunication with the many people with whom he must interact. As noted earlier, the learning-disordered child will exhibit verbal and nonverbal behavior that may very well interfere with his interpersonal interactions unless those in his environment understand the child and develop adequate compensatory means to interact and communicate with the child. Thus, an added parental responsibility is to assist those people with whom the child interacts to understand and cope with the child's differences. Specifically, family members and peers will need to understand that the learning-disordered child cannot help being impulsive, loud, forgetful, and clumsy. Indeed, they will need to develop some of the same techniques as the parents in communicating with the learning-disordered child, and the child's parent(s) may very well serve as the "prime mover" in this "educational" process. The parent counseling sessions can serve quite well as a means for parents to learn from each other to develop such understanding on the part of the child's family members and peers.

Because children with communicative handicaps, particularly those with learning disorders, often experience intense frustration and subsequent failure upon entering school, it is imperative that parents be able to communicate effectively about their children with the teacher. Initially, a teacher may question the child's intellectual abilities and react adversely to the inconsistent behaviors or emotional outbursts exhibited by children with learning disabilities. The teacher may feel that such children are "spoiled" or "lazy," and, consequently, the teacher may experience a sense of frustration. With increased understanding of these children, however, teachers may alter expectations for them with accompanying reduction of frustration. Rosenthal (1971) has shown quite conclusively that teacher expectations can be altered in a positive or negative direction by simple biasing cues. This Pygmalion effect is not limited to the field of education. Indeed, research in medicine and communciation is often conducted using the so-called double-blind technique to avoid such biasing influences. Unfortunately, this technique cannot very easily be used by classroom teachers to manipulate 30 children on a day-to-day basis. Thus, it is essential that parents communicate with teachers what they know of their child's problem; in turn, it is incumbent upon parents to make every attempt to understand the teacher's position and problems in a classroom of 30 young, energetic children. Clinicians can help parents to *communicate with* the teacher, not simply to talk *to* the teacher. As a result of the mutual understanding and communication between the parent and teacher, the child's initial experiences with learning may very well prove to be rewarding and exciting rather than simply an exercise in continual frustration and confusion.

The suggestions that follow for use by the parents at home also could be used in school by the teacher:

1. Be certain the child is attending prior to giving verbal instructions.
2. Keep instructions short, precise, and easy to recall.
3. Repeat instructions when the child makes such a request.

4. Ask the child to repeat instructions to assure that he understands.
5. Pair visual cues with verbal instructions when possible, i.e., "Bring your book and your pencil," pointing to each as they are named.
6. Provide structure through the use of routines in the daily schedule.
7. Reduce the number of distractions and competing stimuli in the environment and in communicative situations.
8. Require the child to work for short periods of time to help maintain attention to the task.
9. Provide opportunities for success.

Related to these suggestions, investigators (Beasley, Shriner, Manning, & Beasley, 1974; Zigmond, 1968) have suggested that otherwise normal children who manifest severe articulation problems in the absence of hearing impairments may have deficiencies in auditory processing. Thus, a parent who speaks excessively using long sentences, a rapid speaking rate, and a vocabulary developmentally incongruent with that of the child's may "overload" the capacity of the child's auditory processing channel and, consequently, exacerbate the child's auditory processing problem (Hoerman, 1970). Todd and Gottlieb (1976) have suggested that, when communicating with the learning-disordered child, adults state their wishes in simple single-concept commands using modified rates of speech.

In conclusion, the child who suffers from some form of learning problem indeed will exhibit some form(s) of communication disorder(s). Equally important in the treatment process, is adequate and clear understanding of other communication problems in the child's world—between parent and child, teacher and child, parent and teacher and other professionals, and even parent and parent. Such understandings are particularly significant in the child's early years, for children with learning disorders, as they grow and experience further negative communicative interactions, become increasingly tense and angry and embarrassed. As a result, the older child may become withdrawn; such withdrawal too often results in school dropout and the personal and social consequences associated with this phenomena. Or the older child may release his frustration and anger in socially unacceptable ways. Our nation's penal institutions can attest to the results of such behavior.

Unfortunately, we have spent too little time and effort in empirically evaluating the significant variables in parent–child and other social communicative interactions. Thus, what is too often offered to educators and parents is simply "armchair" theories and ideas, which may or may not have basis in fact. It is imperative that professionals engaged in clinical research, and clinicians engaged in the daily therapeutic process, make every effort to discover and study these variables and subsequently employ them in the therapeutic process. By doing so, we will enhance our perceptions of the child as something more than "an auditory processor," or "a visual processor," or "a learning disability" and consequently better realize our goal of treating the child as though he were a person who must interact in a world of people.

SUMMARY

We have attempted to provide a very cursory overview of areas in the field of communication disorders that may be pertinent to the education and welfare of the learning-disabled child. A great deal more could be written, discussed, reviewed. It seems almost trite to say that many questions remain unanswered about the "different child" in our society. Indeed, we are not even clear on the nature of many of those questions, less able to study them and even less able to deal with them. Thus, it is imperative that we make every effort to work not as physicians, or audiologists, or speech pathologists, or educators or politicians, or parents, but rather simply as people with various skills and knowledge to contribute to the pursuit of understanding these questions and seeking solutions to them. The children we desire to help will be a direct reflection of our own communicative interactions, and if we do not communicate appropriately, we cannot expect the handicapped children to whom we direct our efforts to communicate appropriately. Thus, we must work together if we are to achieve the goal of training children who are together.

Daniel S. Beasley
Brenda M. Cole
Jan Covington
Daniel J. Orchik

REFERENCES

Aaronson, D. Temporal factors in perception and short-term memory. *Psychological Bulletin*, 1967, *67*, 113–114.

Barrett, T. W. The basic nature of information and its relevance to neural systems. *Acta Symbolica*, 1975, *6*, 1–34.

Barsch, R. H. *The parent of the handicapped child: The study of child-rearing practices.* Springfield, Ill.: Thomas, 1968.

Bateman, B. An educator's view of a diagnostic approach to learning disorders. In J. Hellmuth (Ed.), *Learning disorders* (Vol. 1). Seattle: Seattle Sequin School, 1965.

Beasley, D. S., & Flaherty-Rintelmann, A. Children's perception of temporally distorted sentential approximations of varying length. *Audiology*, 1976, 15, 315–325.

Beasley, D. S. and Freeman, B. Time-altered speech as a measure of central auditory processing. In R. Keith (Ed.), *Central auditory dysfunction.* New York: Grune & Stratton, 1977, pp. 129–175.

Beasley, D. S., & Maki, J. Time- and frequency-altered speech. In N. Lass (Ed.), *Contemporary issues in experimental phonetics.* New York: Academic Press, 1976, pp. 419–458.

Beasley, D. S., Maki, J. E., & Orchik, D. Children's perception of time-compressed speech on two measures of speech discrimination. *Journal of Speech and Hearing Disorders*, 1976, *41*, 216–225.

Beasley, D. S., & Orchik, D. Time-altered speech as a measure of central auditory processing. In R. Keith (Ed), *Central auditory dysfunction.* New York: Grune & Stratton, 1977, pp. 129–175.

Beasley, D. S., Schwimmer, S., & Rintelmann, W. F. Intelligibility of time-compressed CNC monosyllables. *Journal of Speech and Hearing Research*, 1972, *15*, 340–350.

Beasley, D. S., & Shriner, T. II. Auditory analysis of temporally distorted sentential approximations. *Audiology*, 1973, *12*, 262–271.

Beasley, D. S., Shriner T., Manning W., & Beasley, D. C. Auditory assembly of CVCs by children with normal and defective articulation. *Journal of Communication Disorders*, 1974, *7*, 127–133.

Beasley, J. Relationship of parental attitudes to development of speech problems. *Journal of Speech and Hearing Disorders*, 1956, *21*, 317–321.

Beery, Q., Bluestone, C., & Cantekin, E. Otologic history, audiometry and tympanometry as a case-finding procedure for school screening. *Laryngoscope*, 1975, *85*, 1976–1985.

Bluestone, C., Beery, Q., & Paradise, J. Audiometry and tympanometry in relation to middle ear effusion. *Laryngoscope*, 1973, *83*, 594–604.

Brooks. D. An objective method of detecting fluid in the middle ear. *Audiology*, 1968, *7*, 280–286.

Brugge, J. F., Mechanisms of coding information in the auditory system. *Acta Symbolica*, 1975, *6*, 35–64.

Buscaglia, L. *The Disabled and their parents: A counseling challenge.* Thorofare, N. J.: Slack, 1975.

Chalfant, J., & Scheffelin, M. *Central processing dysfunction in children: A review of research.* National Institute of Neurological Disease and Stroke (NINDS) Monograph No. 9. Washington, D.C.: U.S. Department of Health, Education, and Welfare, 1969.

Clements, S. D. *Minimal brain dysfunction in children.* Public Health Service Publication No. 1415. Washington, D.C.: U.S. Department of Health, Education and Welfare, 1966.

Cole, B. M. *An analysis of clinician question forms and the type of parent responses elicited by these forms.* Memphis, Tenn.: Department of Audiology and Speech Pathology, Memphis State University, 1975.

Cruickshank, W. M. *The brain-injured child in home, school and community.* Syracuse, N.Y.: Syracuse University Press, 1967.

Cruickshank, W. M. Introduction and overview of the problem of the conference. In M. Krasnoff (Ed.), *Learning disabilities: The decade ahead.* Proceedings of a conference. Ann Arbor: Institute for the Study of Mental Retardation and Related Disabilities, University of Michigan, 1974.

Darley, F. (Ed.). Identification audiometry. *Journal of Speech and Hearing Disorders,* Supplement 9, 1969.

Elliott, L. L., & Armbruster, V. Some possible effects of the early treatment of deafness. *Journal of Speech and Hearing Research,* 1967. *10,* 209–224.

Freeman, B., & Beasley, D. S. Discrimination of time-altered sentential approximations and monosyllables by children with reading problems. *Journal of Speech and Hearing Research,* 1978, *21,* 497–506.

Gallagher, J. Children with developmental imbalances: A psychoeducational definition. In W. M. Cruickshank (Ed.), *The teacher of brain-injured children.* Syracuse, N.Y.: Syracuse Unviersity Press, 1967, pp. 23–43.

Goetzinger, C. Effects of small perceptive hearing losses on language and speech discrimination. *Volta Review,* 1962, *64,* 408–414.

Goetzinger, C. Small perceptive hearing loss: Its effects on school-age children. *Volta Review,* 1964, *66,* 124–131.

Goin, D. W. Acute inflammatory diseases of the middle ear and mastoid. In G. M. English (Ed.), *Otolaryngology.* New York: Harper & Row, 1975.

Harris, J. D. Combinations of distortion in speech: The twenty-five percent safety factor by multiple-cueing. *Archives of Otolaryngology,* 1960, *72,* 227–232.

Haskins, H. A. *A phonetically balanced test of speech discrimination for children.* Unpublished master's thesis, Northwestern University, 1949.

Hoermann, H. *Psychologie der Sprache.* New York: Springer/Verlag, 1970.

Holm, V. A., & Kunze, L. H. Effects of chronic otitis media on language and speech development. *Pediatrics,* 1969, *43,* 833–839.

Huggins, A. W. F. Second experiment in temporally segmented speech. *Quarterly Progress Report, MIT,* 1972, *106,* 137–141.

Jerger, J. Observations on auditory lesions in the central auditory pathways. *Archives of Otolaryngology,* 1960, *71,* 797–806.

Jerger, J. Clinical experience with impedance audiometry. *Archives of Otolaryngology*, 1970, *92*, 311–324.

Jerger, J. (Ed.). *Handbook of clinical impedance audiometry.* Dobbs Ferry, N.Y.: American Electromedics Corporation, 1975.

Johnson, D., & Myklebust, H. Learning disabilities: Educational principles and practices. New York: Grune & Stratton, 1967.

Johnson, W. *People in quandaries.* New York, Harper & Row, 1946.

Kass, C. *Conference on learning disabilities.* Lawrence, Kans.: University of Kansas, 1966.

Kirk, S. *Educating exceptional children.* Boston: Houghton Mifflin, 1962.

Kirk, S., McCarthy, J., & Kirk, W. *Illinois Test of Psycholinguistic Abilities.* (Rev. Ed.). Urbana: University of Illinois Press, 1968.

Konkle, D., Beasley, D. S., & Bess, F. Intelligibility of time-altered speech in relation to chronological aging. *Journal of Speech and Hearing Disorders*, 1977, *20*, 108–115.

Konkle, D., Freeman, B., Riggs, D., et al. Calibration procedures for time-compressed/expanded speech. In E. Foulke (Ed.), *Proceedings of the third Louisville conference on time-compressed speech.* Louisville, Kentucky: Center for Rate-Controlled Recordings, University of Louisville, 1976.

Kurdziel, S., Rintelmann, W., & Beasley, D. S. Performance of noise-induced hearing-impaired listeners on time-compressed CNC monosyllables. *Journal of the American Audiology Society*, 1975, *2*, 54–60.

LaBerge D., & Samuels, S. Toward a theory of automatic information processing in reading. *Cognitive Psychology*, 1974, *6*, 293–323.

Lee, F. F. Time compression and expansion of speech by the sampling method. *Journal of the Audio Engineering Society*, 1972, *20*, 738–742.

Lerman, J., Ross, M., & McLaughlin, R. A picture identification test for hearing-impaired children. *Journal of Auditory Research*, 1965, *5*, 273–278.

Lewis, N. Otitis media and linguistic incompetence. *Archives of Otolaryngology*, 1976, *102*, 387–390.

Locke, J. Discrimination learning in children's acquisition of phonology. *Journal of Speech and Hearing Research*, 1968, *11*, 428–434.

Mackworth, J. F. Auditory short-term memory. *Canadian Journal of Psychology*, 1964, *18*, 292–303.

Manning, W., Johnston, K. L., & Beasley, D. S. The performance of children with auditory perceptual disorders on time-compressed speech discrimination measures. *Journal of Speech and Hearing Disorders*, 1977, *42*, 77–84.

Marquardt, T. F., & Saxman, J. H. Language comprehension and auditory discrimination in articulation deficient kindergarten children. *Journal of Speech and Hearing Research*, 1972, *15*, 382–389.

Masland, R. L. Neurological bases and correlates of language disabilities: Diagnostic implications. *Acta Symbolica*, 1975, *6*, 1–34.

Mattingly, I. G. Reading, the linguistic process, and linguistic awareness. In J. F. Kavanaugh & I. G. Mattingly (Eds.), *Language by ear and by eye.* Boston: MIT Press, 1972, pp. 133–148.

McCandless, G., & Thomas, G. Impedance audiometry as a screening procedure for middle ear disease. *Transactions; American Academy of Opthamology and Otolaryngology,* 1974, *78,* 98–102.

McCarthy, J., & Kirck, S. *The Illinois Test of Psycholinguistic Abilities* (Experimental Ed.). Urbana: University of Illinois Press, 1961.

McDonald, E. T. (1962): *Understand those feelings.* Pittsburgh, Pa.: Stanwix House, 1962.

McWilliams, B. J. Various aspects of parent counseling. In E. J. Webster (Ed.), *Professional approaches with parents.* Springfield, Ill.: Thomas, 1976, pp. 27–63.

Miller, G. The magical number seven, plus or minus two: Some limits on our capacity for processing information. *Psychology Review,* 1956, *63,* 81–97

Myklebust, H. *The psychology of deafness.* New York: Grune & Stratton, 1960.

Myklebust, H. *Development and disorders of written language.* New York: Grune & Stratton, 1965.

Noffsinger, D., & Kurdziel, S. Assessment of central auditory lesions. In W. Rintelmann (Ed.), *Measurement of hearing disorders.* Baltimore: University Park Press, 1979.

Orchik, D., & Herdman, S. Impedance audiometry as a screening device with school-age children. *Journal of Auditory Research,* 1974, *14,* 283–286.

Orchik, D., & Oeschlager, M. *Time-compressed speech discrimination in children: Its relationship to articulation ability.* Paper presented before the American Speech and Hearing Association, Las Vegas, 1974.

Paradise, J. L., Smith, G. C., & Bluestone, C. D. Tympanometric detection of middle ear effusion in infants and young children. *Pediatrics,* 1976, *58,* 198–210.

Pisoni, D. B. Mechanisms of auditory discrimination and coding of linguistic information. *Acta Symbolica,* 1975, *6,* 65–112.

Rampp, D. L. Auditory perceptual disturbances. In A. Weston (Ed.), *Communicative disorders: An appraisal.* Springfield, Ill.: Thomas, 1972.

Rosenthal, R., & Jacobson, L. *Pygmalion in the classroom.* New York: Holt, Rinehart & Winston, 1968.

Rosenthal, R. Teacher expectation and pupil learning. In R. D. Strom (Ed.), *Teachers and the learning process.* Englewood Cliffs, N.J.: Prentice-Hall, 1971.

Sanderson-Leepa, M., & Rintelmann, W. Articulation functions and test–retest performance of normal-hearing children on three speech discrimination tests: WIPI, PB-K 50, and NU Auditory Test No. 6. *Journal of Speech and Hearing Disorders,* 1976, *41,* 503–519.

Schwartz, D., & Redfield, N. Evaluation of automatic screening tympanometry in the identification of middle ear pathology. *Journal of the American Audiology Society,* 1976, *1,* 276–279.

Shriner, T. H., & Daniloff, R. G. Reassembly of segmented CVC syllables by children. *Journal of Speech and Hearing Research,* 1970, *13,* 537–547.

Speaks, C., & Jerger, J. Method for measurement of speech identification. *Journal of Speech and Hearing Research,* 1965, *8,* 185–194.

Todd, M., & Gottlieb, M. I. Interdisciplinary counseling in a medical setting. In E. J. Webster (Ed.), *Professional approaches with parents.* Springfield, Ill.: Thomas, 1976, pp. 191–229.

Vernon, M. Sociological and psychological factors associated with hearing loss. *Journal of Speech and Hearing Research,* 1969, *12,* 541–563.

Webster, E. J. Parent counseling by speech pathologist and audiologist. *Journal of Speech and Hearing Disorders,* 1966, *31,* 331–340.

Webster, E. J. Procedures for group parent counseling in speech pathology and audiology. *Journal of Speech and Hearing Disorders,* 1968, *33,* 127–131.

Webster, E. J. Parents of children with communication disorders. In A. Weston (Ed.), *Communication disorders: An appraisal.* Springfield, Ill.: Thomas, 1972.

Webster, E. J. Studies involving parents of children with communication handicaps. *Acta Symbolica,* 1974, *5,* 25–37.

Webster, E. J. *Counseling with parents of handicapped children: Guidelines for improving communication.* New York: Grune & Stratton, 1977.

Webster, E. J., & Cole, B. M. *Improving discussion in parent groups.* Paper presented before the Tennessee Speech and Hearing Association Conference, Memphis, 1977.

Willeford, J. Central auditory function in children with learning disabilities. *Audiology and Hearing Education,* 1976, *2,* 12–30.

Wood, N. Assessment of auditory processing dysfunctions. *Acta Symbolica* 1975, *6,* 113–124.

Wyatt, G. L. Speech and language disorders in preschool children: A preventive approach. *Pediatrics,* 1965, *36,* 637–647.

Wyatt, G. L. *Language learning and communication disorders in children.* New York: Free Press, 1969.

Wyatt, G. L. Parents and siblings as co-therapists. In E. J. Webster (Ed.), *Professional approaches with parents.* Springfield, Ill.: Thomas, 1976, pp. 115–145.

Young E., & McConnell, F. Retardation of vocabulary development in hard of hearing children. *Exceptional Children,* 1957, *23,* 368–370.

Zigmond, N., & Cicci, R. *Auditory learning.* San Rafael, Calif.: Dimensions Publishing Company, 1968.

7

A NEUROPSYCHOLOGICAL APPROACH TO THE LEARNING-DISABLED CHILD

The study of learning disabilities is a unique endeavor in that, by its very nature, it forces together a widely disparate group of professionals. Educators, physicians, audiologists, speech pathologists, and social workers all have contributions to make. While there are numerous positive aspects of such interactions, the diversity of emphasis inherent in the various disciplines often leads to confusion, redundancy, and disagreement. The traditional role of the psychologist has been largely limited to diagnosis. As will be discussed, the diagnostic evaluation often neither asks nor answers questions that are regarded as appropriate by other professional personnel. The neuropsychological approach to learning disability has the potential for providing an expansion of communication in two directions. Aspects of learning disability which have typically been the purview of psychologists represent a middle ground between physical and educational issues. Cognition, perception, memory, attention, and other elements of the learning process have been explored on a parallel course with attempts at physicalistic (neurological) explanations for deficits and educational programs which attempt to alleviate them. The neuropsychological approach to learning disability provides an expansion of the middle ground between these endeavors by attempting to establish behavior–central nervous system (CNS) correlates—and by providing a framework for the building of hypotheses for remediation. This endeavor is fraught with difficulties, and there are those who would prefer a continuation of an emphasis on parallel study (Escalono, 1974). The nature of the subject will force a continuation of correlational study, but the gap is already being bridged to some extent.

A NEUROPSYCHOLOGICAL DEFINITION

No essay on the subject of learning disability would be complete without a discussion of the "definition problem." Proposed definitions abound, and they will not be comprehensively reviewed here. In order for a neuropsychological model to be of utility, however, some delineations are necessary. The definition which may be most appropriate is provided by Kirk and Bateman (1962). They define the term "learning disability" as describing "a retardation, disorder, or delayed development in one or more of the processes of speech, language, reading, writing, arithmetic, or other school subjects resulting from a psychological handicap caused by a possible cerebral dysfunction and/or emotional or behavioral disturbance." Kirk and Bateman specifically exclude disturbances resulting from mental retardation, sensory deprivation, cultural or educational factors. When these exclusions are added to the definition, it tends to limit the discussion to children with presumed cerebral dysfunction. This is not to say that factors such as mental retardation and cultural deprivation do not influence learning; they certainly do, but for the purposes of this discussion they are assumed not to fall under the rubric of "learning disability."

An alternative term, "minimal brain dysfunction," (MBD) is often suggested as being more descriptive (Clements, 1973). This well might be the case except for the nebulous meanings of the words "minimal" and "dysfunction." Despite the fears of some investigators that use of the word "brain" is threatening to parents (Silver, 1975), it must be accepted that we are speaking of the brain. The word "dysfunction" is used to negate the necessity of demonstrating actual anatomical damage when the diagnosis is made. The use of the MBD label actually has the effect of excluding children with documented lesions who should be regarded as learning-disabled for the research effort. The neuropsychological model for learning disability, therefore, attempts to exclude children who do poorly in school because they are mentally retarded, culturally deprived, or unmotivated. It includes children with demonstrable CNS damage, such as children with seizures, head injuries, etc., and also includes children who appear to be experiencing some dysfunction of the CNS whether or not the dysfunction can be attributed to the actual presence of an anatomical lesion.

THE NEUROPSYCHOLOGICAL APPROACH

Human or clinical neuropsychology is a subspecialty of clinical psychology, which interests itself in brain-behavior relationships. Experimental work in the field usually involves explorations of the behavioral concommitants of various brain lesions. When applied to the clinical endeavor, neuropsychological investigation attempts to use an inferential method to draw conclusions concerning the status of the central nervous system of an individual. The conclusions are drawn on the basis of psychological test data, but the methods of inference may vary greatly from those typical to clinical psychology. The focal point for neuropsychological investigation is the CNS. While clinical psychology has always viewed concepts such as intelligence and personality as complex multifaceted systems necessitating detailed and intricate description, the status of the CNS has usually been relegated to a simplistic, often unitary concept. The clinical psychologist might determine whether a patient is "organic" or not on the basis of a single measure. The neuropsychological approach recognizes that simplistic methods cannot be descriptive of complex systems. Hence, multiple methods of inference have become an integral part of neuropsychological investigation.

The term "organicity," much like the neurological term "dementia," actually tells us very little about the individual to whom it is applied. Terms such as "borderline organicity" and even "minimal brain dysfunction," as typically used, are of little or no help to anyone in either describing a problem or in assisting in the development of remediation strategies. There are a number of psychometric tests, discussed elsewhere in this chapter, that provide alleged indices of "organicity." By and large, they are drawing tests that seek to provide cutoff scores of one type or another. The very nature of such spatial tests suggests that they will be poor identifiers of learning-disabled children. Many children who can draw quite well cannot read or spell and vice versa. Visual motor performance has been found to be a very poor predictor of reading achievement (Giebink & Birch, 1970; Wetzel, Welcher, & Mellits, 1971). The same can probably be said for any unitary test of "organicity." For this reason most neuropsychologists have attempted to develop and use batteries of tests which seek to describe fully the behavioral repetoires of children. In so doing, it is recognized that the examination must effectively assess a broad range of abilities represented in the brain (Benton, 1975; Golden, 1978). Just as no single unitary test can adequately describe the overall status of a child's CNS, no single method of inference can be effectively applied. One of the principle points of departure between traditional clinical approaches and modern neuropsychological techniques is the application of a multiple method of inference in neuropsychological investigation (Reitan, 1974), some aspects of which will be described.

METHODS OF INFERENCE IN NEUROPSYCHOLOGICAL INVESTIGATION

Level of Performance

It is, of course, important to know how a particular child "stacks up" against his peers of the same age. This has been the principle approach of traditional clinical psychological descriptions of learning problems. The level-of-performance approach usually results in the application of such terms as "slow learner," "exceptional child," and "mentally retarded." In applying a level-of-performance criterion, the psychologist merely compares the score obtained by a child on a given measure to the mean score obtained by a standardization group or normative sample. Most tests of intelligence and academic achievement, and some unitary tests of organicity, are based on a level-of-performance approach. This method of inference provides some very important information. There are, however, limitations to its use in isolation. Strict application rarely provides information as to the reasons for low scores or, perhaps more importantly, concerning the location, chronicity, or extent of brain lesions.

Right-Left Differences

There are two types of right-left differences that are important to neuropsychological investigation. They are right-left body differences and right-left hemisphere differences (Golden, 1978). Right-left body difference analysis is based upon the well-known premise, derived from neurology, that sensory-motor functions are mediated by the contralateral hemisphere. Hence, a marked deficit in the sensory or motor function of the right extremity on any number of tasks impli- cates the inferiority of the contralateral (left, in this case) hemisphere. As a child matures, relationships between right- and left-hand per- formance also change (Finlayson, 1976), and assessment of the rela- tionships is sometimes important to diagnosis (McBurney & Dunn, 1976).

The analysis of right-left hemisphere differences is based on another well-recognized principle, i.e., that the two cerebral hemi- spheres are asymmetrical in function. The dominant hemisphere (al- most always the left hemisphere) is primarily responsible for language functions (Luria, 1966). The nondominant hemisphere is largely re- sponsible for nonlanguage or spatial functions including spatial orien- tation (Benton, 1967; Kohn, & Dennis, 1974), depth perception (Ben- ton & Fogel, 1962), and such specialized spatial skills as the ability to recognize faces (Benton & Van Allen, 1972). Wide disparities between verbal and spatial skills will, therefore, implicate the appropriate hemisphere as a site of dysfunction.

Pathognomonic Signs

The method of pathognomic signs is borrowed from clinical neurology and is the principle type of diagnosis used by European neuropsychologists (Christensen, 1975). These signs are usually dis- crete behavioral events that rarely occur in normal individuals. The inability to reproduce correctly a simple geometric figure is a common pathognomonic sign, as is the inability to name a common object.

An example of a pathognomonic sign is presented in Figure 7–1. The top row of geometric designs are stimulus figures which children are asked to reproduce as part of the Reitan-Indiana Aphasia Screen- ing Test. The reproductions below the stimulus figures were pro- duced by two children, a set of twins, 8 years of age who had experi- enced strokes associated with sickle cell hemoglobin disease. The inability to reproduce the Greek cross, in particular, is associated with lesions of the right cerebral hemisphere in adults. Both of the chil- dren whose efforts are presented in Figure 7–1 had documented strokes of the right cerebral hemisphere. Hence, in this case the rela- tionship between the sign and the site of the lesion held true.

Although the analysis of pathognomonic signs is a very produc- tive method of inference, it is difficult to deal with from a quantita- tive standpoint and some neuropsychologists have attempted to de-

Fig. 7-1. Geometric forms from the Reitan-Indiana Aphasia Screening Test. Top row—stimuli; middle row—Twin 1; bottom row—Twin 2.

velop scoring systems allowing for the summation of signs allowing for a level-of-performance application (Russell, Neuringer, & Goldstein, 1970).

Pattern Analysis or "Score Scatter"

Pattern analysis is a method of inference which assumes that discrete abilities are more or less evenly distributed within normal individuals. If on a level-of-performance measure, a child obtains a very high score on a test of verbal facility, he should not obtain a very low score on a test of spatial facility. It is also assumed that certain skills are more likely to be affected by certain types of CNS insults, environmental deprivation, educational deficiencies, etc. This method is particularly useful for the diagnosis of learning disabilities since by definition such children have specific deficits in skill areas along with normal functioning in other areas (Ackerman, Dykman, & Peters, 1977). Pattern analysis is very difficult in children primarily because the relationships between performance on tests and subtests often do not correspond to specific types of CNS dysfunction in the same fashion as is exhibited by adults.

THE TEST BATTERY

Since all of the methods of inference noted are based upon psychometric test scores, the battery of tests used to make the inference is of primary importance. Literally thousands of tests, both published and unpublished, are available for use by the psychologist. In actual practice relatively few (not more than 20) are routinely used. An exhaustive review of the standard instrument is beyond the scope of this chapter. The following are brief descriptions of the most commonly used tests with some comments as to their utility in the diagnosis of a learning disability.

Tests of Intelligence

Although there are many tests of general intelligence for use with children, only four or five are likely to be encountered. The most widely used series of tests is the Wechsler examinations. This series consists of three tests, all similar in structure, designed for use with different age groups.

The Wechsler Adult Intelligence Scale (WAIS) has the advantage of extensive standardization and validation (Wechsler, 1958). Unlike several other measures of general intellect, it also has the capability of providing a broader range of information. The WAIS consists of 11 subtests, which are divided into two subgroups, one purporting to evaluate verbal skills, the other seeking to assess "performance" or "visuopractic" aspects of intelligence. Because of the construction of the test it is possible to compare verbal and visuopractic scores and to make comparisons among the various subtests. Unfortunately, the WAIS does not, by itself, meet the criteria for a test battery (Golden, 1978). The test was not developed in correspondence with actual brain-behavior relationships. Analysis of the test reveals that it actually measures four independent factors: verbal comprehension; visual motor organization; memory or freedom from distractibility; and in some studies, a "g" or general intelligence factor (Wechsler, 1958).

The WAIS was standardized on adults aged 16 and over. The Wechsler Intelligence Scale for Children (WISC) is a downward extension of the WAIS, standardized for children between the ages of 5 years and 15 years, 11 months. Its construction is similar to the WAIS in that it provides both verbal and visuopractic scores and allows a pattern analysis of various subtests. The factor structure of the WISC is similar to that of the WAIS at the upper age ranges (Cohen, 1959) and scores of 15-year-olds on the WISC are highly correlated with WAIS scores obtained from the same subjects at age 16 (Ross & Morledge, 1967). The WISC and the WAIS are less comparable as wider age ranges are considered and the comparability of factorial composition disappears at the lower age ranges (Cohen, 1959). The WISC is perhaps the most sensitive test available for the diagnosis of brain dysfunction (Reitan, 1974) and the subtests in particular have proved to be quite useful in diagnosis (Reed, Reitan, & Klove, 1965).

Wechsler (1974) has recently introduced a revision of the WISC (the WISC-R). It has the same subtests as the WISC. Some of the items have been made simpler, and some cultural biases inherent in the WISC have been responded to. The interpretation of test scores has remained the same although the WISC-R tends to yield lower IQ scores, perhaps because today's children have stronger skills than their 1949 counterparts (Golden, 1978).

The Wechsler Preschool and Primary Intelligence Scale (WPPSI), introduced in 1966, is an attempt at a downward extension of the WISC for children between the ages of 4 years and 5 years 11 months. The utility of the WPPSI as an indicator of learning disability or brain damage remains to be thoroughly demonstrated.

There are several other tests of intelligence that may be encountered. Chief among them is the Stanford-Binet Scale of Intelligence (Terman & Merrill, 1973). The Binet, as it is usually referred to, has the advantage of being appropriate for patients of very high or very low intelligence. It has the disadvantage of providing less information than the Wechsler series. Scores are reported only in terms of IQ and mental age (M.A.). There is no breakdown of separate abilities or components.

The Peabody Picture Vocabulary Test (PPVT) is sometimes presented as a test of intelligence, probably because the test is constructed in such a way as to allow for the computation of a standard score ferred to as an IQ score (Dunn, 1965). In actuality, the test measures receptive or "hearing" vocabulary. It will tend to yield higher scores than either the WISC or the Stanford-Binet when administered to learning-disabled or brain-damaged children.

The Halstead Neuropsychological Test Battery for Children and the Reitan-Indiana Neuropsychological Test Battery

Both of these test batteries consist of downward extensions of a neuropsychological battery referred to as the Halstead-Reitan Neuropsychological Test Battery, which is used with adults. The

Halstead Neuropsychological Test Battery for Children is generally appropriate for children 9 to 15 years of age and is sometimes referred to as the Mid-Range or Intermediate Battery. The Reitan-Indiana Battery is used for children 5 through 8 years of age and is also called the Young Children's Battery. Certain portions of the test batteries can be administered to children younger than 5 years of age. Both of these test batteries seek to sample a broad range of CNS functions. Different tests are used to facilitate inferences concerning differing types of CNS dysfunction. The tests included in the Mid-Range Battery are primarily revisions of tests used in the adult battery. They include the following:

1. *The Category Test*—a series of slides divided into subsets, each one necessitating the understanding of a central concept for solution of the problem.
2. *The Tactual Performance Test*—a modification of the Sequin-Goddard Form Board which the subject must perform blindfolded. Scores are obtained for the right hand, left hand, and both hands and for the ability to remember the shapes of the forms and their locations on the board.
3. *The Trail-Making Test*—a visual motor problem-solving task which requires the subject to connect a series of numbered circles. The second part of the test, Trails B, requires an alternation between numbers and letters.
4. *The Rhythm Test*—a test of nonverbal auditory discrimination which requires the subject to compare two sets of rhythmic tones, determining whether they are the same or different.
5. *The Halstead Speech Sounds Perception Test*—a test of verbal auditory discrimination requiring the subject to listen to a word tape and select the correct written representations of nonsense words presented from sets of three choices on a printed page.
6. *The Halstead-Wepman Aphasia Screening Test*—a test that essentially screens for pathognomonic signs. It covers tasks such as drawing, naming, spelling, reading, arithmetic, speaking, and gesturing.
7. *The Finger Oscillation Test*—a test of motor speed requiring the subject to depress a lever as rapidly as possible over several 10-second trials. It is primarily used as a test of right-left body differences.
8. *The Reitan-Klöve Sensory Perceptual Examination*—consists of a number of procedures for evaluating tactile, auditory and visual perception, astereognosis, and suppression of sensation.

The Reitan-Indiana Neuropsychological Test Battery consists of a number of modifications of tests in the Halstead Children's Battery. In addition, there are several tests developed specifically for inclusion with consideration of the special needs of young children. The modified tests include simplified forms of the Category Test, Tactual Performance Test, Aphasia Exam, and the Finger Oscillation Test. Additional tests include the Marching Test, a test of gross motor coordination; the Color Form Test and Progressive Figures Test, which are roughly comparable to the Trail-Making Test; the Matching Pictures Test, a visual matching task; the Target Test, a test of visual memory; and the Individual Performance tests, which include a number of tests of visual spatial skills. Complete descriptions of these tests are available elsewhere (Reitan & Davison, 1974).

The Halstead Children's Battery and the Reitan Indiana Battery are the most widely used and most successful neuropsychological techniques available for use with children (Boll, 1974; Klonoff & Low, 1974). Among their many advantages are the norms available for the various tests (Reitan & Davison, 1974). In addition, the batteries have been thoroughly factor analyzed (Crockett, Klonoff & Bjerring, 1969). Various investigators have provided supplements to the batteries that are useful in general and with specific types of patients. One of the most useful additions to the typical batteries is the Klöve-Matthews Motor Steadiness Battery (Matthews & Klöve, 1976), which includes a group of tests designed to assess motor coordination and tremor. It is particularly useful for the evaluation of children with motor disorders such as cerebral palsy.

The batteries of tests described have largely replaced unitary measures of brain dysfunction such as the Bender-Gestalt Test and the Memory for Designs Test. Though these tests are still used by some clinicians, they do not provide sufficient information upon which to base a diagnosis of learning disability or brain dysfunction. Several unitary tests have proved more useful than the Bender or the Memory for Designs Test, though they still are not comparable to a comprehensive battery approach. These tests, which may be added to comprehensive batteries, include the Benton Visual Retention Test (Benton, 1962), the Perceptual Maze Test (Elithorn, 1955), and Raven's Progressive Matrices (Raven, 1960).

Academic Achievement

Neuropsychological assessment of both children and adults usually includes a test of academic achievement. For the most part, this portion of the evaluation represents a mere screening and does not approach the detail or intricacy available from educational evaluations done by reading or educational specialists. The Wide-Range Achievement Test (Jastak & Jastak, 1965) provides measures of word recognition (listed as "reading"), arithmetic skills, and spelling skills. Scores are reported in grade-level equivalency scores, standard scores, and percentiles.

More comprehensive tests of academic achievement are sometimes included in neuropsychological evaluations of children. The Peabody Individual Achievement Test (Dunn & Markwardt, 1970) provides measures of mathematical skill, word recognition, reading comprehension, spelling, and general information. It is particularly useful for patients with motor dysfunctions involving speech or motor praxis since no written or verbal responses are necessary (Golden, 1978).

There are numerous other neuropsychological tests of considerable value that may be used. The important point, which should be reemphasized, is that no *single* test or procedure is adequate for the assessment of a learning disability. The physician, teacher, or parent should be wary of diagnoses made on the basis of one or two tests. By necessity then, the neuropsychological evaluation is an exhaustive, time-consuming endeavor.

A "quick look" will not provide sufficient information for diagnosis and for the generation of recommendations. Parents frequently complain about the time factor. Other diagnostic procedures such as EEGs, brain scans, standard psychological evaluations, social histories, and physical examinations can be done in relatively brief periods of time when compared to the time necessary for the completion of a comprehensive neuropsychological evaluation. It is not unusual for an evaluation to require 4 to 8 hours of the patient's time. This seems like a long period until it is compared to the length of the child's life which may be considerably influenced by the results. A brief evaluation that misses important characteristics of a child's performance can actually be detrimental in that it may prove a false negative. On occasion, very subtle deficits can have serious effects upon a child's classroom performance. Brief evaluations may result in "sins of omission" creating situations in which other factors are implicated as contributing to the child's problem by exclusion. Unfortunately, the ascription of deficits in learning to emotional factors is still a fairly common practice, probably because of the frequent psychological concomitants of learning disability, i.e. hyperactivity, emotional lability, and impulsivity (Clements, 1973). Most of us have had an episode of psychological trauma residing in the dim mist of our childhood which skillful interviewing can uncover. Hence, deficits which go undiagnosed in the neuropsychological evaluation may launch a child on a lengthy course of treatment which is not directed toward the basic problem.

ASSESSING THE ASSESSMENT

When a physician, educator, or other professional requests an evaluation, the psychologist should submit a written report in narrative form. A mere listing of test results is of little value either in providing an understanding of the problem or in the development of remediational suggestions. Since most professionals outside of the field of psychology receive little training in the interpretation of test findings or the meanings of test scores, it becomes the psychologist's task to interpret those results in a meaningful and useful manner.

There are many acceptable formats for psychological reports, and psychologists will vary as to their presentations. There are, however, certain common elements which should always appear.

Patient identification. Identification of the patient is a rather simple matter. Its importance lies in the fact that mistakes, particularly in date of birth recording, can result in serious alterations in test interpretation.

History and statement of the problem. Neuropsychological examinations do not occur in a vacuum. The report should reflect a good understanding of the referral question and a history relevant to the problem. There is an important exception to this point. Reitan (1974) prefers to interpret neuropsychological test data "blindly." In this way he assures that his interpretations are not biased in any way by other information available on the patient. There are a number of positive aspects to this approach, but ideally historical information should accompany the report separately. Both the physical and educational history may have been obtained by the referring agent. Regardless of the information already available, the psychologist must take the historical, physical, and educational data into important consideration. For this reason it should be clearly presented in the psychological evaluation.

Behavioral observations. While variables such as anxiety, motivation, attention, and familiarity with testing procedures are difficult to measure objectively, they do exert an influence on test results (Glassner & Zimmerman, 1967). The report should include a description of the patient's behavior during the evaluation and answer questions concerning the potential effects of extraneous factors on the test results. If the evaluation succeeds in providing a valid estimate of the patient's neuropsychological functioning, this fact should be clearly stated. If there are doubts about validity due to any extraneous variable, this fact should be clearly stated and explained.

Neuropsychological evaluation assumes relatively intact functioning of peripheral systems, i.e. vision, audition, tactile sense, etc. If there is any reason to believe that the child cannot see well, hear accurately, feel or move because of peripheral injury, this fact must be clearly recognized and stated at some point in the report. An old finger fracture, for instance, can seriously affect tactile sense in that finger. If this fact is not taken into account serious misdiagnosis may occur.

Test results. While most sections of the neuropsychological evaluation should be written for nonpsychologists, the reporting of test results should be accomplished in such a way as to facilitate communication between psychologists. Common names of the tests and procedures performed should be given and the results outlined. The neuropsychological report should include a review of systems, i.e., provide information concerning vision, audition, tactile sense, motor functioning, memory, and cognition as well as the typical IQ scores and academic achievement test scores usually reported in psychometric evaluations.

Impressions. A summary of the examiner's findings and the application of the methods of inference cited earlier in this chapter may appear in the "test results" section of the report or under a separate heading. At this point test results should, if possible, be tied in with the referral questions and historical information. If ascertainable, the manner and extent to which any neuropsychological dysfunction has exerted an influence upon the child's learning should be explored. This discussion should be relatively free of jargon (Huber, 1960) or overqualification. Since the nature of impediments to learning may directly relate to suggestions for remediation, recommendations may also appear in the impressions section or under a separate heading.

Recommendations. Specific recommendations represent one of the most neglected aspects of neuropsychological investigation. Many reports provide information concerning specific areas of dysfunction but fail to provide any information concerning remediation techniques. To some extent this failure relates to lack of knowledge. It is much easier, of course, to describe diagnostic features than it is to provide meaningful suggestions for dealing with the diagnostic findings. Problems in nomenclature exert more of an influence in this area than perhaps any other. Neuropsychological research in the area of learning disabilities is vast, but the task of weaving research findings into networks with specific heuristic value for individual children is sometimes passed over (Knights & Bakker, 1976). As has been mentioned, it is the task of the neuropsychologist to provide a meaningful presentation and interpretation of test findings. Of late, it is increasingly apparent that an extension of this principle necessitates an application of the principles of remediation techniques.

The identification of specific areas of dysfunction usually implies that these areas need special attention via drill, multimodal presentation, relearning of basic skills necessary for mastery of more complex applications, etc. This is usually the case. If a child cannot read the word "cat," he must be taught to read the word "cat." Hence, many of the neuropsychologists' recommendations will be rather simplistic formulations of a child's area of weakness with suggestions that concentration in these areas is necessary. As the complex nature of learning and brain function become more clearly understood, a principle of avoidance of problem areas is suggested more and more frequently. Research by both psychologists and educators makes it apparent that learning to read, for instance, is a very complex task which can be interefered with at a very basic "prereading" level. In such instances strategies can sometimes be suggested which will avoid or bypass the interfering factor.

Mattis, French, and Rapin (1977) have applied the principle of avoidance of interfering factors to the study of dyslexia. Using some very intricate statistical procedures Mattis and his associates have "clustered" dyslexics into several groups on the basis of test findings. They identified three specific dyslexic syndromes each with identifiable characteristics. In their study they found children who could not read because of:

1. A language disorder typified by anomia, disorders of comprehension, disorders of imitative speech, and poor speech sound distribution.
2. Articulatory or graph-motor dyscoordination.
3. Visuospatial perceptual disorders.

These three groups represented fairly independent syndromes of dyslexia, and Mattis suggests very different approaches to remedial education. Mattis and his co-workers suggest methods that bypass the troublesome area for the first two groups. Simply stated, the anomic group had difficulty with letter names, suggesting that a method of reading which avoids naming letters or grounding the letter phoneme in the letter name should be successful. The group with an articulation deficit also had a poor phonic attack. Hence, phonics should be avoided in teaching these children to read in favor of a "look-say" or "root word" approach.

NEUROPSYCHOLOGY IN THE MEDICAL SETTING

Historically, most work in pediatric neuropsychology has been done with patients with specific learning disabilities not associated with medical conditions. Within recent years clinical neuropsychologists have begun to apply their skills in the medical setting to children with conditions which may result in disorders of learning. The expansion of neuropsychology into a cooperative effort with pediatricians and neurologists is an important development both in the areas of clinical services and research leading to a fuller understanding of the developing nervous system. The emergence of cooperative efforts between pediatrics, neurology, and neuropsychology is a natural phenomenon that would seem to follow from similarities of interest. Neurological deficits and neuropsychological dysfunctions tend to co-occur (Kinsbourne & Warrington, 1963; Rourke, Deitrich, & Younge, 1973). Available research strongly suggests that various neurological diseases among children and adults result in fairly consistent patterns of neuropsychological deficit. Research with adults is more extensive than with children and includes studies of multiple sclerosis (Beatty & Gange, 1977), various forms of epilepsy (Klöve & Matthews, 1976), and degenerative diseases (Miller, 1973). Research with children has sought to evaluate the neuropsychological ramifications of birth trauma (Reed & Fitzhugh, 1966). As yet, however, the effects of numerous other childhood illnesses have not been explored. Ongoing research at St. Jude Children's Research Hospital (Memphis, Tenn.) is seeking to establish the neuropsychological correlate of a number of diseases which may result in acquired learning disabilities, including childhood leukemia, histiocytosis X, and stroke associated with sickle cell anemia.

The case studies that follow provide examples of the utility of neuropsychological evaluation in defining the behavior of the child with acquired learning disability.

CASE MATERIAL

The two children upon whom this report is based are identical twin girls who were 8 years, 0 months old at the time that the evaluations were performed. Both children were enrolled in the third grade and were doing poorly, according to the mother's report. They were evaluated simultaneously (Goff & Anderson, 1977).

Case 1

Approximately 9 months prior to the evaluation, Twin 1 experienced what appeared to her mother to be a stroke. It began with a twisting of her mouth. She eventually developed paralysis of the left arm and leg. An EEG performed 2 days following the incident resulted in an abnormal recording by virtue of central temporal slowing on the right; a brain scan done 10 days after the stroke was normal, as was a four-vessel arteriogram done 15 days after the stroke.

The patient was seen for a neuropsychological evaluation approximately 9 months following the stroke. No paralysis was noted, but the patient exhibited a stumbling gait. Her speech was slurred, giving the impression of mild dysarthria. Test results are presented in Table 7-1, with the exception of the Reitan-Indiana Aphasia Screening Test figures, which are presented in Figure 7-1 (see page 166). On the WISC, the patient obtained a full-scale IQ of 67, which falls within the mildly retarded range of psychometric intelligence. The Verbal IQ was 77, while the Performance IQ was 62. Subscale analysis revealed widespread low levels of performance with particularly low scores on the types of tasks which, in adults, have been ascribed to lesions of the right temporal-pareital area, i.e. block design and picture arrangement (Reitan, 1974). Subscale scores do not reflect the actual level of this child's performance. In actuality, no items were passed on the block design subtest, while only one item was successfully completed on the picture arrangement subscale. The patient's receptive vocabulary as assessed by the Peabody Picture Vocabulary Test (PPVT) was within the dull normal range (PPVT IQ = 83), suggesting that her receptive skills had not been affected to the extent that expressive vocabulary skills had been compromised.

The patient's scores were quite low on the category test, a measure of nonverbal concept formation and utilization. In each case where right–left comparisons were made, the right extremity was found to be superior, while left extremity fucntion was minimal or nonexistent. In some cases muscular weakness played a significant role in failure to complete the required task.

The patient's visuopractic skills were noted to be severely affected as evi-

Table 7-1. Neuropsychological Test Performance of Identical Twins following Sickle Cell-associated Cerebral Vascular Accidents.

Test		Twin 1	Twin 2
Wechsler Intelligence	Full-scale IQ	67	67
Scale for Children	Verbal IQ	77	71
	Performance IQ	62	69
	Information	8	8
	Comprehension	6	3
	Arithmetic	7	7
	Similarities	5	6
	Digit span	6	4
	Vocabulary	6	4
	Picture completion	6	5
	Picture arrangement	2	5
	Block design	2	4
	Object assembly	4	3
	Coding	9	11
Wide Range Achieve-	Reading	1.9 (85)*	2.1 (87)
ment Test	Spelling	1.5 (80)	1.8 (83)
	Arithmetic	1.2 (77)	2.6 (92)
Peabody Picture	Mental Age	6 yr/1 mo	5 yr/7 mo
Vocabulary Test	IQ	83	78
Category Test		37 (13)**	32 (20)
Tactual Performance	Dominant time	4.2 (50)	7.00 (36)†
Test (TPT)	Nondominant time	—	3.12 (51)
	Both hands time	1.26 (55)	2.18 (47)
	Total time	—	12.50 (42)
	Memory	0 (21)	0 (21)
	Location	0 (35)	0 (35)
Finger Tapping	Right	33 (49)	44 (70)
	Left	9 (6)	34 (59)
Foot Tapping	Right	11.3	42.8
	Left	7.3	36.2
Grip Strength	Right	10.25 (45)***	10 (45)
	Left	5 (15)	8 (35)
Progressive Holes (total	Right	13	5
count for first 5 holes)	Left	69	34
Maze Steadiness (mean	Right	35	43.5
of two trials)	Left	45.5	49

*Standard scores; **t scores calculated according to norms provided by Klonoff and Low (1974). ***t scores calculated according to norms provided by Spreen and Gaddis (1969); †Test not completed.

denced by her performance on the Aphasia Screening Test figures (see Figure 7–1, p. 166) and the memory localization task of the Tactual Performance Test, which resulted in a series of squares with *X* marks in them.

The patient was approximately halfway through the second grade at the time of the stroke. Though she was in the third grade at the time of the evaluation, all academic grade-level equivalency scores fell within the second-grade level. Her academic achievement test scores were among her best performances, however, which probably confirms her mother's observation that she was a good student prior to the stroke.

Case 2

According to the patient's mother Twin 2 had a cerebral vascular accident approximately 3 weeks prior to the evaluation. The patient reportedly became weak on the left side of her body. No other symptoms were observed. The patient's mother noted that Twin 2's stroke was less severe than was Twin 1's. Immediately after the stroke she was described as having left facial and extremity weakness. By the time that the evaluation was done, this was noted to be a questionable finding.

An EEG done 2 days after the stroke included frontocentral slow waves. A repeat EEG done 11 days later reported centroparietal slowing. Computerized coaxial tomography done 2 weeks poststroke was normal, as was four vessel arteriography 1 month post-CVA.

Psychological test results are again presented in Table 7–1. As with Twin 1, a Full Scale IQ of 67 was obtained. Twin 2 obtained more consistent test scores, with a Verbal IQ of 71, and a performance IQ of 69. Subscale scatter was quite similar to Twin 1's performance, but Twin 2 was able to produce minimal scores on the block design and picture arrangement subscales. Peabody scores were almost identical with Twin 1's, as was performance on the category test.

Examination of motor test scores points out rather graphically that Twin 2 did not exhibit motor dysfunction to the extent noted in her sister. With the exception of an inability to complete the TPT board with her right hand, which is difficult to explain, and a poor performance on the progressive holes task, with the left hand, her motor performance was essentially normal. Visuopractic skills did appear to be rather significantly affected as evidenced by her reproduction of the Aphasia Screening Test figures (see Figure 7–1, page 166), and her reproduction of the TPT, which was quite poor. The patient's academic achievement, though poor in spelling, did not appear to be nearly so affected as Twin 1's.

These two cases serve to demonstrate that widely differing problems can exist in children with very similar presenting problems. Both children had strokes affecting the right hemisphere caused by the same underlying condition. They are also identical twins, and it is tempting, though erroneous, to assume that their problems are the same. There are certain similarities between the two since they have similar radiologic results (all negative), similar electroencephalographic results, and similar neurological findings. In addition, the results of standard psychological tests (WISC, PPVT, WRAT) are quite similar. In light of several factors, however, Twin 1's future appears to be much more frought with difficulty. Though Twin 2's stroke has had a negative effect upon her, its recency, the minimal effect upon motor functions, and the fact that low but significant scores were obtained on right hemisphere indicators are a positive sign. Twin 1 may have recovered some function since her stroke. Regardless of the passage of time, however, she still exhibits more widespread and severe dysfunctions than does her sister. Motor functions on the left side of her body, sensory functions, and perceptual functions are all obviously poor.

The differences between these two children are such that, provided that no strokes occur in the immediate future, plans for remediation and rehabilitation will of necessity be quite different. Expectations for Twin 1 will have to be somewhat reduced in relation to her sister to the extent that while special-education placement must be considered for Twin 1, it may be possible to defer such a placement for Twin 2.

These cases also point out the utility of neuropsychological investigation in describing and understanding the behavioral concomitant to disorders of this kind. While abnormalities were determined to exist by means of conventional procedures, particularly EEG in these cases, neuropsychological examination was shown to produce a further refinement and definition of the problems experienced by these two children.

While most children with learning disabilities do not exhibit discrete etiological features as did our set of twins, the cases do serve to demonstrate the fact that children with brain dysfunction, even though they may be identical twins, do not exhibit identical problems. Neuropsychological evaluation is a very powerful technique for expanding knowledge of individual children, groups of children, and the developing CNS in general. Review of the massive literature of the past three decades makes it quite clear that learning-disabled children and/or brain dysfunctional children differ widely among themselves. They cannot be described on the basis of a unitary construct or test instrument. Comprehensive neuropsychological evaluation in concert with other approaches provides a potential for more heuristic descriptions and definitions which may lead to enhanced techniques of remediation and rehabilitation.

John R. Goff

REFERENCES

Ackerman, P. T., Dykman, R. A., & Peters, J. E. Learning disabled boys as adolescents. *Journal of the American Academy of Child Psychiatry*, 1977, *16*, 296–313.

Beatty, P. A., & Gange, J. J. Neuropsychological aspects of multiple sclerosis. *Journal of Nervous and Mental Disease*, 1977, *164*, 42–50.

Benton, A. L. The Visual Retention Test as a constructional praxis test. *Confinia Neurologica*, 1962, 22, 141–155.

Benton, A. L. Constructional apraxia and the minor hemisphere. *Confinia Neurologica*, 1967, *29*, 1–16.

Benton, A. L. Psychological tests for brain damage. In H. I. Freeman, H. Kaplan, & B. J. Sadock (Eds.), *Comprehensive textbook of psychiatry* (Vol. I). Baltimore: Williams & Wilkins, 1975, pp. 757–768.

Benton, A. L., & Fogel, M. L. Three dimensional constructional praxis. *Archives of Neurology*, 1962, 1, 347–354.

Benton, A. L., & Van Allen, M. W. Prospagnosia and focial discrimination. *Journal of Neurological Science*, 1972, *15*, 167–172.

Boll, T. J. Behavioral correlates of cerebral damage in children ages 9 through 14. In R. M. Reitan & L. A. Davison, *Clinical neuropsychology: Current status and applications.* New York: Halsted, 1974, pp. 91–120.

Boller, F. Destruction of Wernickes areas without language disturbance. *Neuropsychologia*, 1973, *11*, 243–246.

Christensen, A. L. *Luria's neuropsychological investigation.* New York, Spectrum, 1975.

Clements, S. D. Minimal brain dysfunction. In S. G. Sapir & A. C. Nitzburg, (Eds.), *Children with learning problems.* New York: Bruner/Mazel, 1973, pp. 159–172.

Cohen, J. The factorial structure of the WISC at ages 7/6, 10/6, and 13/6. *Journal of Consulting Psychology*, 1959, *12*, 285–299.

Crockett, D., Klonoff, H., & Bjerring, J. Factor analysis of neuropsychological tests. *Perceptual and Motor Skills*, 1969, *29*, 791–801.

Dunn, L. M. *Peabody Picture Vocabulary Test manual.* Circle Pines, Minn.: American Guidance Service, 1965.

Dunn, L. M., & Markwardt, F. C. *Manual, Peabody Individual Achievement Test.* Circle Pines, Minn.: American Guidance Service, 1970.

Escalona, J. The present state of knowledge and available techniques in the area of cognition. In D. P. Purpura & G. P. Reason (Eds.), *Methodological approaches to the study of brain maturation and its abnormalities.* Baltimore: University Park Press, 1974, pp. 135–140.

Elithorn, A. A preliminary report on perceptual maze test sensitivity to brain damage. *Journal of Neurology, Neurosurgery, and Psychiatry,* 1955, *18,* 287–292.

Finlayson, M. A. J. A behavioral manifestation of the development of interhemispheric transfer of learning in children. *Cortex,* 1976, 12, 290–295.

Goff, J. R., & Anderson, H. R. *Neuropsychological status of identical twins following sickle cell associated cerebral vascular accident.* Unpublished manuscript, St. Jude Children's Research Hospital, Memphis, Tenn., 1977.

Giebink, J. W., & Birch, R. The Bender-Gestalt Test as an ineffective predictor of reading achievement. *Journal of Clinical Psychology,* 1970, *26,* 484–485.

Glasser, A. J., & Zimmerman, I. L. *Clinical interpretations of the Wechsler Intelligence Scale for Children.* New York: Grune & Stratton, 1967.

Golden, C. J. *Diagnosis and rehabilitation in clinical neuropsychology.* Springfield, Ill.: Thomas, 1978.

Huber, J. C. *Report writing in psychology and psychiatry.* New York: Harper & row, 1960.

Jastak, J. F., & Jastak, S. R. *The Wide-Range Achievement Test.* Wilmington, Del.: Guidance Associates, 1965.

Kirk, S. A., & Bateman, B. Diagnosis and remediation of learning disabilities. *Exceptional Children,* 1962, *29,* 73–78.

Kinsbourne, M., & Warrington, E. K. The development of Gerstmann syndrome. *Archives of Neurology,* 1963, *8,* 490–501.

Klonoff, H., & Low, M. Disordered brain function in young children and early adolescents: Neuropsychological and EEG correlates. In R. M. Reitan & L. A. Davison (Eds.), *Clinical neuropsychology: Current status and application.* New York: Halsted, 1974, pp. 121–165.

Klöve, H., & Matthews, C. C. Neuropsychological evaluation of the epileptic patient. *Wisconsin Medical Journal,* 1976, *68,* 296–301.

Knights, R. M., & Bakker, D. J. (Eds.). *The neuropsychology of learning disorders.* Baltimore: University Park Press, 1976.

Kohn, B., & Dennis, M. Selective impairment of visuo-spatial abilities in infantile hemiplegia after right hemidecortication. *Neuropsychologia,* 1974, *12,* 505–512.

Luria, A. R. *Higher cortical functions in man.* New York: Basic Books, 1966.

Mattis, S., French, J. H., & Rapin, I. Dyslexia in children and young adults: Three independent neuropsychological syndromes. In S. Chess & A. Thomas (Eds.), *Annual progress in child psychiatry and child development.* New York: Brunner/Mazel, 1976, pp. 281–300.

Matthews, C. G., & Klöve, H. Differential psychological performances in major motor, psychomotor and mixed seizure classification of known and unknown etiology. *Epilepsia,* 1976, *8,* 117–128.

McBurney, A. K., & Dunn, H. E. Handedness, footedness, eyedness: A prospective study with special reference to the development of speech and language skills. In R. M. Knights & D. W. Bakker (Eds.), *The neuropsychology of learning disorders.* Baltimore: University Park Press, 1976, pp. 139–147.

Miller, E. Short- and long-term memory in patients with presenile dementia. *Psychological Medicine,* 1973, *3,* 221–224.

Raven, J. C. *Guide to the standard progressive matrices.* London: Lewis, 1960.

Reed, H. B. C., & Fitzhugh, K. B. Patterns of deficit in relation to severity of cerebral dysfunction in children and adults. *Journal of Consulting and Clinical Psychology,* 1966, *30,* 98–102.

Reed, H. R., Reitan, R. M., & Klove, H. Influence of cerebral lesions on psychological test performance in older children. *Journal of Consulting Psychology,* 1965, *29,* 247–251.

Reitan, R. M. Methodological problems in clinical neuropsychology. In. R. M. Reitan & L. A. Davison (Eds.), *Clinical neuropsychology: Current status and application.* New York: Halsted, 1974.

Reitan, R. M., & Davison, L. A. *Clinical neuropsychology: Current status and applications.* New York: Halsted, 1974.

Ross, R. T., & Morledge, J. Comparisons of the WISC and WAIS at chronological age sixteen. *Journal of Consulting and Clinical Psychology,* 1967, *32,* 331–332.

Rourke, B. P., Deitrich, D. M., & Younge, G. C. Significance of WISC verbal/performance discrepancies for younger children with learning disabilities. *Perceptual and Motor Skills,* 1973, *36,* 275–282.

Russell, E. W., Neuringer, C., & Goldstein, G. *Assessment of brain damage: A neuropsychological key approach.* New York: Wiley, 1970.

Silver, L. B. Acceptable and controversial approaches to treating the child with learning disabilities. *Pediatrics,* 1975, *55,* 406–445.

Spreen, O., & Geddes, W. H. Developmental norms for 15 neuropsychological tests ages 6 to 15. *Cortex,* 1969, *5,* 171–191.

Terman, L. M., & Merrill, M. A. *The Stanford-Binet Intelligence Scale.* Boston: Houghton-Mifflin, 1973.

Wechsler, D. *The measurement and appraisal of adult intelligence.* Baltimore: Williams & Wilkins, 1958.

Wechsler, D. *WISC–R manual.* New York: Psychological Corporation, 1969.

Wetzel, K. H., Welcher, D. W., & Mellits, E. D. The possibility of overdiagnosing brain dysfunction from a single administration of the Bender-Gestalt Test. *Johns Hopkins Medical Journal,* 1971, *129,* 6–9.

8

BEHAVIORAL AND EMOTIONAL SEQUELAE OF LEARNING DISORDERS

Learning disabilities represent a multifaceted problem which has been intensively studied by numerous disciplines. Professionals involved in the diagnosis and treatment of the learning-disabled child can appreciate the chaotic array of terminologies and classifications used to describe this enigmatic disorder. The numerous descriptive labels reflect etiological concepts based on neurological deficits, perceptual handicaps, delayed maturation, dyslexia, emotional disorders, and teacher disability. In addition, there are other widely divergent terms that describe essentially the same set of behaviors in the child. Diagnostic labels such as minimal brain dysfunction, hyperkinetic behavior disorder, perceptual deficit, and "clumsy-child" syndrome are examples of the 30 or so terms which are often used interchangeably. Despite confusions in terminology, one fact remains clear: the child in educational jeopardy is at an extreme disadvantage in a culture which places a high value on achievement and rewards those who are successful in that endeavor.

The value of educational achievement is understood by children at a very early age, and by the time that the child enters the educational system he is well aware of the premiums placed upon good grades and overall academic achievement. Children who cannot succeed in the traditional school environment are confronted by numerous problems. In essence, the child beginning school is under a spotlight and watched carefully by parents, teachers, relatives, siblings, and peers. Deviations from the normal pathways of academic achievement are sources of parental anxiety and often dealt with in harsh and inconsistent ways, always stressing that the child must live up to his expected role as an academic achiever.

Estimates of the incidence of learning disabilities in the United States range from 5 percent to 20 percent. Although these estimates vary in terms of the criteria used to identify the learning-disabled child, there is general agreement that literally millions of children are in educational jeopardy due to problems in learning. Of even greater significance is the fact that educational problems often begin at a very critical point in the child's emotional development. At approximately 5 years of age the child begins to achieve a level of independent functioning and role definition that enables him to formulate the basic structure of his personality. The stresses of this age have been well documented by numerous personality theorists, who caution that considerable emotional damage and turmoil can be precipitated by overly stressful conflicts.

The child in educational jeopardy is, in many ways, "a victim of the times." The accelerated technological world in which we live is reflected in the educational process to the point where many parents are baffled by the concepts and techniques being taught. Parental confusion is apparent when they attempt to assist their child with homework or when they are asked by their child to explain academic materials. Often a parent will comment, "I didn't have this until the sixth grade," with a developing awareness of the pressures for academic excellence which exist in our technologically oriented society. Lesson plans are usually programmed and must be followed. The child who falls behind must play the incredibly difficult game "keep up and catch up." Parental responses to the underachieving child are often harsh, even though done with the best of intentions. First, reasoning, encouragement, or "structured study time" are attempted, but, failing to achieve the desired goals, parents often resort to punishment techniques. The child is threatened with loss of privileges (or given other types of punishments) if he does not perform in the school situation. Bribery may also be utilized, but the end result is that the child becomes aware of his lack of achievement and inability to please parents and teachers in his quest for success.

Rarely will a child receive diagnostic and therapeutic intervention before some degree of emotional damage and loss of self-concept has occurred. The results of emotional stress make these children easily identified at the time of their professional evaluation for learning difficulties. Typically, they enter the room with their head down, and their eyes to the floor, realizing that they are going to have to perform for one more individual who will observe their lack of success. Characteristically, the child reveals a series of defensive behaviors in the examining room attempting to excuse what he already anticipates to be a poor performance. The child assumes that he will do poorly, even though the examination has not yet begun and despite considerable reassurance from the examiner. As the child performs in the examination, one can observe avoidance of areas in which he feels he will have difficulty. He may become thoroughly frustrated with his inability to perform a task and may become aggressive toward the examiner or the test materials. He frequently asks, "Is the test over yet?" or "When are we going to be finished?" It is not unusual for this child to approach the testing situation by attempting to impress the examiner with the facade of lack of concern for his performance rather than that he is afraid he is going ot fail. The striking aspect of these defensive maneuvers is that they are relatively uncommon in the normal, well-adjusted child who is succeeding in the classroom. The learning-disabled child does not eagerly accept a challenge and is not able to "fail gracefully." In contrast with the child who is achieving academic and social success, this child lives in a state of anxiety, frustration, and fear.

It is easy to appreciate how emotional factors can rapidly become more serious than the learning disability itself. During these very formative years a number of defensive or inappropriate behaviors utilized to cope with the anxiety and frustration become habitual and ingrained as part of the child's personality. Lack of success generates more failure until the child anticipates defeat in almost every situation. It is difficult, even with the best remediation program, to convince this child that he should "take a chance" and accept the challenge of improving his academic status. Too often parents tend to interpret the child's behavior from their adult frame of reference and longer periods of study or other "work harder" techniques are encouraged with very little understanding of his dilemma. The child is a captive in the classroom situation and has no chance to escape. Adults, finding themselves in frustrating situations on the job or in the family, have a considerable number of options available to them, even to the point of leaving that situation and finding another less frustrating environment. The learning-disabled child, on the other hand, is compelled to attend school daily. The child in educational jeopardy who is not achieving in school cannot leave physically but may attempt to leave the classroom situation mentally. The mental escape is manifested by daydreaming or looking out the window, thinking happier thoughts of enjoyable times, and avoiding what he considers to be the aversive stimulus—the teacher and the blackboard.

The child who is overactive in the classroom is another child whose emotional well-being may be compromised. Too often, we assume that this child is hyperkinetic or suffering from an organic condition termed "minimal brain dysfunction." The child, however, may also be reacting to the effects of anxiety, tension, and frustration, which cause an increase in activity level. This type of *situational hyperactivity* may or may not be observed in the home situation or during a professional testing situation.

It is often assumed that the etiology of the hyperactivity is a form of cerebral dysfunction. As a result, medication may be prescribed with little understanding of the emotional and behavioral components unrelated to a malfunctioning nervous system. The fact that overactivity can also be induced by anxiety is often overlooked in the haste to resolve the problem. Manipulation of the diet or the use of medications may be attacking only one facet of the overactivity. If the overactive child is performing poorly academically and as a result experiencing increasing levels of frustration and anxiety, attention must be focused on problems of emotionality and personality. The child who reacts aggressively to the teacher is often attempting to gain attention and desires a good relationship with her. As the child's educational program continues to deteriorate and successes are lacking, the teacher is blamed and anger is generated. The emotional overlay, secondary to absence of academic success, may, in fact, present more serious problems than the learning disability itself.

EMOTIONAL DEVELOPMENT IN CHILDREN

In general, theories of childhood development encompass two major areas: (1) organic growth and development involving the various organ systems, especially the central nervous system, and (2) the personality and emotional development of the child. The latter includes a myriad of factors such as emotional, temperament, social, and behavioral characteristics of the child. These personality factors emerge, reach a level of sophistication, and then progress to more complicated stages in the future. Physical growth cannot be separated from emotional development, for both are intimately associated and mutually dependent. The efficiency of the central nervous system influences the course of behavioral development.

A "building-block" concept is hypothesized in both organic and personality development. At birth the child has a complement of reflexes which are necessary for survival. Temperament, which also becomes apparent shortly after birth, appears to be genetically based. As the child's age increases, various learned behaviors become more pervasive. Initially the child responds to various external signals in his environment, especially the mother's voice as well as visual, auditory, and tactile stimuli. With time the child develops increasing sophistication in integrating these impulses in the central nervous system. As speech and motor development progress, the child is capable of independently responding to his environment. Capacities are then established which enable the child to alter behavior and adapt to the environment. During this interval the child develops a personality or behavioral pattern for interacting with his environment. The child must learn to control frustrations, stress, and his insatiable egocentric demands. The parents are the major influence in establishing and modifying the child's infantile responses, preparing the child for increasing maturity. As one set of learned behavior is superimposed upon another, the sophistication of the child's ability to respond to his environment improves greatly. The child learns methods of coping with the stresses in his environment and eventually achieves greater independence.

At the chronological point called "school age" the child is expected to have sufficient maturity to engage successfully in the formal process of learning. In general, maturity implies that the child is capable of responding appropriately to the teacher's instructions and acquiring the academic skills necessary for advancement. Inability to deal effectively with school pressures can impair the child's overall emotional growth. In the traditional classroom the learning-disabled child is only *one* of twenty or thirty other children whose needs must also be met. It is difficult for a teacher to devote her entire attention to the child who cannot cooperate in the learning process. The child is often faced, for the first time, with an anxiety-provoking situation he cannot resolve. Debilitating stress may ensue, causing emotional and behavioral immaturities to surface. Hyperactivity, poor attention span, distractibility, and other symptoms of the minimal brain dysfunction syndrome may be exaggerated due to psychological stress. These manifestations may be based in organic dysfunctions, but it should be noted that organic and personality factors are too closely related to give sole priority to either. Due to stress, school becomes traumatic for the learning-disabled child and, therefore, affects his emotional development, producing a wide range of inappropriate behaviors both at home and in the school.

Numerous investigators have noted the effects of stress on the learning-disabled child. Bender (1956) has stated, "It has long been recognized that reading disabilities are accompanied by special behavior disorders." Bryant (1966) reported, "Few cases of learning disabilities are without emotional disabilities," and Griffin (1968) noted, "Insofar as children with learning disabilities have poor perceptual or other organic problems, the child, by definition, has an ego defect." Harris (1970) pointed out that among the reading-disabled children whom he has studied, "close to 100 percent showed maladjustment of some kind." It is often the case that a learning-disabled child exhibits behavioral disturbances and emotional problems are suspected. There is, however, a paucity of research regarding the personality and behavioral development of learning-disabled children.

In addition to organic factors, the child's development is based upon what is learned from the environment. A learning disability is *not* confined to the classroom. Interaction with the environment requires intact learning capabilities and is a critical area of emotional development. The child who is handicapped by misperceiving or misinterpreting parental, teacher, or peer demands may often be punished for reasons that are misunderstood. For example, the child with an auditory processing disturbance may be told to "go upstairs, change your socks, make your bed, and brush your teeth." This child may walk to the staircase, pause, remember one element of the multiple commands, and return triumphantly only to find that he has *not* followed the directions correctly. At this point he may receive disapproval for his actions. A thoroughly bewildering situation is created and causes anxiety and tension which will often cause the child to be more defensive and less likely to listen to his parents the next time. It is *not* unusual for parents seeking help at a child guidance clinic to report that "Johnny never listens to me." The child may be "tuning out" his parents, or he may be manifesting an auditory processing deficit which renders him incapable of performing the series of directions that the parents give. Simply reducing the number of directions given may cause a remarkable change in the child's behavior.

The child with visual processing deficits or motor coordination problems may be extremely clumsy when dealing with the physical aspects of his environment. Often he is punished for clumsy behaviors which he could not avoid. "Normal" and expected activities, such as throwing a ball, coloring in a coloring book, and dressing without supervision, may be beyond the child's abilities. The ensuing parental frustration with the child's motor difficulty soon becomes apparent. Fear, anxiety, and tension develop, which further inhibit the child's performance. Praise and recognition, which are extremely necessary for healthy adjustment, are not forthcoming, and the child is placed in emotional jeopardy.

The learning-disabled child may also experience a handicap in his social development, as a result of delayed or disturbed visual perceptual and visual motor development. Much of the interaction between children involves motor activity and an integration of visual stimuli. The child with a visual perceptual problem may be unable to keep pace with his peers and unable to participate in their games. The child is singled out as being "different," and he may feel compelled to "fight his way back" into the good graces of his peer group. The child with an auditory processing problem similarly finds it difficult to adjust to peer activities. For example, he may find it impossible to memorize football plays in the junior football league. Again his peers may give him considerable negative feedback due to his inability to perform the play correctly. Since he cannot remember the sequence of directions given, an emotional conflict is an indirect sequela of the learning disability.

Behavioral difficulties are not always related to disturbances of personality or emotionality. Often an organic etiology may underlie the hyperactivity, impulsiveness, distractibility, and aggressiveness that is characteristic of the learning-disabled child. Organic disturbances can cause inappropriate behavior and may be improved in numerous ways, such as the use of medication. Uncontrollable or disinhibited behavior, however, may generate an emotional overlay in the child. Seldom does he receive the positive feedback so necessary for healthy development.

The hyperkinetic child is extremely difficult to live with at home and at school, a fact which is not too surprising. Even a one hour office evaluation with a hyperactive child can be frustrating for the patient and the examiner. The child's behavior also creates innumerable stresses on the family constellation. The parents develop strategies in an attempt to cope with the behavior, but most are illogical and few are applied consistently. The parents of a hyperkinetic child, like parents of a child with any chronic handicap, are extremely vulnerable to stresses, strains, frustrations, and anxieties. Often they need support and assistance to help the child as well as themselves (Todd & Gottlieb, 1976). Verbal and/or physical restraints, spankings, and other types of short term behavioral controls provide only marginal results. Frequently, the child's behavior disrupts normal family life (Gottlieb, 1975). Attempts to control the child's behavior may also create profound effects on developing personality. The hyperkinetic child receives a great deal of negative feedback as compared to the "normal" child. The continued exposure to a negative environment takes its toll in terms of the developing self-concept. The child often becomes the "black sheep" of the family. Since he is too difficult to control, he is usually not invited to play with neighborhood children. Frequently the marginally hyperkinetic child engages in inappropriate behaviors in order to gain attention upon recognizing that he is being isolated by classmates, peers, and family members. Attention, even in the form of punishment, is acceptable to the child. Hostility and aggression can become a way of life for the hyperactive child. This child will inevitably be poorly socialized when he enters the classroom situation. In addition to physical hyperactivity, the child may exhibit verbal hyperactivity. The verbally aggressive child may also be reflecting a neurological deficit. The child becomes aversive to others, and often his attempts to express himself are met with negative feedback. The profound effects on the child's personality and development cannot be overestimated.

In summary, a complex relationship exists between the physical, cognitive, and emotional aspects of a child's development. No single component can be viewed in isolation; the child must be appreciated in total. Children are a potpourri of constant changes, and organic, cognitive, or emotional components are influential factors in this change. Dealing with only a single facet of the total child may create considerably more jeopardy. Frustration, tension, and anxiety are a part of the everyday life for children as well as for adults. Anxiety can be a motivator for change and many times can result in productive behavior. The learning-disabled child, however, faces many obstacles in relieving himself of the tense or anxious state. Difficulty in resolving frustrations plays a larger role in his social adaptation. There are no medications for improving a poor self-concept, which develops as a result of unresolvable frustrations. In the same sense, there are no behavior modification programs or special-education techniques which can exist independently from knowledge of the child's organic limitations. Approaches to the behavioral problems of learning-disabled children are numerous. It is disheartening when physicians or other professionals advise special diets, medications, or exercise programs without a thorough evaluation of the child's psychosocial status. It is similarly discouraging when mental health professionals view counseling or behavioral techniques as the *only* approach to modifying a child's behavior. Inadequate funds of knowledge, communication gaps, and professional biases permeate the field. Personality and emotional well-being are integrally related problems. Left untreated, they may develop into the more serious complications of emotional disability, behavior disorders, and juvenile delinquency.

CASE HISTORIES

John

John is a 13-year-old child who is incarcerated in the detention center at juvenile court for the fourth time in 4 months. His present difficulty stems from having stolen a car and money. John ran away from home for 48 hours prior to his arrest. When he returned home, John was taken by his probation officer to juvenile court for disposition. The child will probably be placed in an institution, either a private school or correctional institution, in an attempt to deter his delinquent activity. John's problems, however, did not begin at the point of his introduction to the juvenile court system but rather can be traced back to earlier periods in his life. John was diagnosed in the sixth grade as having a learning disability which involved both auditory and visual processing deficits. Even as a preschooler, John was described as hyperkinetic, showing all the manifestations of poor attention span, overactivity, difficulty following directions, and other behavioral problems. John received a thorough diagnostic workup in the sixth grade, and special education was attempted. For the most part, things went smoothly for approximately two years, but considerable damage had already been done prior to this time. John was an extremely difficult child to manage. Teachers and parents found him very frustrating, not necessarily in his inability to learn, but in his difficulty in remaining in his seat and paying attention in the classroom. He frequently would come into conflict wiht his peers, and over time developed considerable resentment toward society. During his first six years in school poor report cards were met with considerable disfavor on the part of his parents. While not showing open aggression toward the child because of their disappointment, the parents' overall attitude induced considerable guilt in John. The guilt led to significant amounts of anger, which were then translated into rebellion and antisocial acts. While minor at first, these acts rapidly grew to the point where the child was brought to the attention of the juvenile court.

Examination of John's past history reveals many factors that appear to have compromised his emotional development. Considerable difficulty was encountered in his relationships with authority figures as well as with peers. The child was in many instances "an outcast," and his needs for recognition could not be met through normal channels. Considerable hostility and aggression were built up due to the constant negative feedback from those attempting to help him control his behavior. John was disruptive in the classroom and certainly distracting to other students. His negative attitudes toward school increased over the years. In this case, diagnostic evaluation and placement in special education in the sixth grade was too late to forestall further emotional conflicts. At the time of evaluation it was apparent that John viewed the world as a hostile and threatening place, against which he must defend himself. The impulsiveness of his acts, the "driven" quality of his behavior, and the inability to gain acceptance represent a link between organic problems and the personality difficulties which stemmed from these problems.

John's case history illustrates a loss of human potential and a cost to society, which will continue over the years. It is important to recognize that the learning-disabled child suffers significant emotional trauma from his lack of ability to learn. John's case is *not* unusual. Early identification and diagnosis of John's learning disorder may have prevented many of these problems from developing. Therapeutic measures should have been instituted early in order to help the child as well as to prevent the behavioral difficulties which complicated the learning problem.

Jamie

Jamie, 4 years of age, has been attending preschool for 3 months. Problems were encountered immediately upon his entering the preschool situation. Jamie is hyperactive and does not respond well to discipline or controls. Jamie had a normal birth history; no other significant factors present which could compromise his central nervous system. His developmental history was within normal limits and precocious in many areas, especially the motor area. Problems started almost immediately when the child began to walk. He would "get into everything" and was a constant source of frustration for his mother and father. Numerous types of discipline were tried, such as ignoring the behavior or attempting to punish the child whenever negative behavior occurred. The mother was spending an inordinate amount of time punishing the child. Each day she could see the child becoming more unhappy and more reluctant to abide by her disciplinary approaches. It seemed to the mother that the more she punished, the more the child behaved inappropriately. Jamie was controlling the home situation with his inappropriate behavior.

With the birth of a new sibling, his behavior worsened considerably. His mother now had to spend time protecting the young baby from Jamie, who would take any opportunity he could to poke the baby with his finger or do things to make the infant cry. It was apparent in listening to this history that this child was extremely hyperactive and that normal types of discipline had essentially proven useless. Jamie would respond to the parents' shouting by shouting back, and his "undisciplined" behavior was a source of frustration not only to the parents and relatives but to other children in the neighborhood. Jamie was seldom invited to children's homes because his behavior was so "obnoxious." No one could give Jamie instructions and achieve much in the way of success in stopping his inappropriate behavior.

Jamie had a comprehensive evaluation which revealed he had average intelligence but significant auditory processing deficits. It was virtually impossible for Jamie to follow more than one direction at a time. In the classroom or at home, this child was unable to follow multiple directions. In addition, he would many times be baffled by parental insistence upon correct responses to their directions. Jamie responded physically rather than verbally since the verbal modality betrayed and confused him on so many occasions. The child was extremely hyperactive, and a neurological examination demonstrated the presence of organic difficulties. The child was placed on appropriate medication, and his behavior improved to some degree. He was less hyperactive but remained very resistant to change because of the resentment and hostility which were so much a factor in this child's personality. In school the other children began to view him as "different." He was shunned and isolated by his peer group. The negative peer pressures increased Jamie's sense of resentment provoking numerous fights in order to gain recognition. Frequently Jamie was sent home from school because of his aggressive behaviors.

The similarities between the two case histories is obvious. Both children have encountered roadblocks to normal emotional development. It is readily apparent that due to his unrewarding interactions with his environment, Jamie could very well follow John's path to delinquent behavior. Jamie's first four years of life were rather confused. The obvious hostility and resentment which he exhibits reflect the deficiencies in affection, nurturance, and warm relationships that a child of this age needs so badly. Jamie discovered at an early age that the world can be a hostile and threatening place. Thorough analysis of this case indicates that many of the behavioral problems could be prevented through early diagnosis and therapeutic intervention. Jamie's auditory processing deficits rendered him incapable of following multiple directions. Organic deficits in part accounted for his hyperactive behavior, poor attention span, and other annoying behavioral characteristics.

The most significant aspect of these case histories is the interaction between personality development and organic deficit. The presence of a learning disability, as well as hyperkinetic behavior related to neurological conditions, set the stage for faulty interactions with the environment. Jamie did not conform to the acceptable pattern of a child 4 years of age. Therefore he received considerable censure from parents, teachers, and peers and began to develop defensive attitudes toward what he perceived as hostility and aggression from others. A vicious cycle develops. Self-image develops out of the interactions between a child and his environment. If the child receives negative feedback over lengthy periods of time, the self-image becomes negative. In this sense, the child views himself as a "bad person" and behaves consistently with this image. The cycle continues as the bad self-image promotes more negative behavior, which eventually elicits more negative feedback from the environment. The behavior problems which develop are then the product of multiple etiologies. Behavior, which was initially the product of central nervous system dysfunction, becomes self-perpetuating as a result of a negative self-image. This process illustrates the need for viewing the child as a total entity when performing diagnostic and therapeutic studies. The interaction between organic, emotional and behavioral factors, as well as the learning capabilities of the child, must be integrated into a consistent and appropriate plan of therapy.

DIAGNOSIS AND TREATMENT OF EMOTIONAL AND BEHAVIORAL PROBLEMS IN THE LEARNING-DISABLED CHILD

Zinkus (1977) reviewed various methods of assessing the learning-disabled child, with basic techniques used to estimate intelligence, perceptual abilities, reading skills, and developmental progress. In order to evaluate properly the "total child," his intelligence as well as capabilities and potentials are evaluated. Determinations are made of the child's central visual and auditory processing abilities, since these are the major channels of interaction between the child and his environment. Thorough medical and neurological evaluation is mandatory in order to appreciate the child's organic capabilities and to determine his limitations resulting from a faulty central nervous system (Thompson & Gottlieb, 1973). Assessing personality is somewhat more difficult. Numerous techniques are available for the older child, adolescent, and adult. For the very young child behavioral observations are most informative. Care must be taken to obtain as much information as possible from various sources in the child's environment.

Standardized behavior observation checklists are useful for parents, teachers, and others familiar with the child. In this way a profile of the child's behavior in many situations can be obtained. It is critical to understand how the child's behavior in school compares with behavior at home and how the child interacts with significant people in his enviornment, such as parents or teachers. In addition, differences in the child's relationship between his mother and father may also be of significance. If the child responds better to discipline from the father, then care is taken to understand the techniques utilized by the father which can possibly be incorporated into a behavior modification program.

Direct observations of the child are also very valuable. The child should be observed in the classroom and in the home situation as well as in the examining room. In this way information can be collected concerning the degree of the child's hyperactivity. It would be important to know if behavior can be controlled during the examination. The child's response to success and failure in the examination situation is noted. It would also be significant to learn if the consistent use of praise improves the child's behavior. Does the child avoid difficult tasks by using inappropriate behavior to distract the examiner? If this is the case, it may well be that the child is aware of his difficulties and is sensitive to failure, thereby setting up a situation where he attempts to avoid failure by behaving inappropriately.

The child should be observed in the classroom situation. As a rule, most examinations occur in a one-to-one setting in a quiet room. When the child moves out into a school environment with 30 other children, his behavior may change radically as the number of distractions increases. The child should also be observed in the home situation to determine the pattern of interactions with parents and siblings, as well as other behavioral characteristics.

Many tests to assess personality and behavioral characteristics are available for children. Interviewing is perhaps the most effective means. If sufficient rapport is developed, a good interviewer can elicit considerable information. The interview situation should be such that the child perceives himself in a warm and friendly environment, with the examiner presenting no major threat to his psychological integrity. Often, in this environment, the child responds honestly and enumerates the probelms *as they appear to him*. It is always important to solicit the child's opinion, whether or not this appears valid to the interviewer. The interviewer can assess the degree of defensiveness and insight that this child may have.

Psychological tests for personality disturbances consists of two major varieties: the personality inventory and projective tests. Personality inventories are structured evaluations in which the child usually performs by answering a series of questions. His responses generate a profile indicating strengths and weaknesses in his emotional life. Self-concept may be evaluated with a personality inventory. Projective tests are a more unstructured type of test situation. The child is given an ambiguous stimulus, such as an inkblot or a picture of a situation, and is encouraged to make up a story or to tell the examiner what he sees in the picture. Responses are characteristically indicative of the child's conflicts and difficulties in various situations. The examiner may then gain insight into the child's feelings and view of his environment and thereby arrive at a better understanding of the most effective means of therapeutic intervention.

Psychological tests and inventories can provide a better understanding of the child's behavioral and emotional strengths and weaknesses. In addition to pathology, areas of strength must be determined, since they offer avenues of assistance for the child who is suffering from behavioral, emotional, and learning problems. It is important to note that *no* single test, in and of itself, is completely adequate. Interviews and observations of the child as well as information obtained from other reliable sources in the environment provide a more comprehensive picture. Tests alone tell us very little without the competent observations of those who administer the tests. A child may perform poorly on a test for a number of reasons, such as poor motivation, lack of rapport, anxiety, or depression. His responses, while not offering much insight into his true abilities, may reveal a pattern adjustment which precludes effective educational remediation until the emotional problems are solved. Many excellent therapeutic programs are doomed to failure because of interpretation of test performances "by the book." Properly administered, an IQ test can be an excellent assessment of not only intelligence, but also personality, self-image, and behavioral characteristics crucial to effective therapy.

THERAPEUTIC APPROACHES TO BEHAVIOR PROBLEMS

Therapeutic approaches to behavioral and emotional problems vary widely. In spite of numerous theoretical orientations, most therapeutic approaches conceptualize the final goal as being a change in the individual's behavior patterns. This change may be viewed as arising out of improvement of some internal state of affairs such as self-concept or personality or, as with the behavioral approaches, resulting from environmental manipulations utilized to change the behavior itself. Therapeutic approaches with children must of necessity involve more people than the child. Parents, teachers, and others in the child's immediate environment must assist in creating a "therapeutic milieu" in order to foster the desired change in behavior. It is difficult for a young child of 6 or 7 years to sit in a therapist's office and relate life experiences, with the therapist assisting in the child's gaining insight. With older children insight therapy is possible, but with younger children, problems with attention span as well as immature conceptual skills may be detrimental to this type of approach. For the younger child numerous techniques are utilized, such as play therapy or other less formal techniques.

Even though the direct emphasis of therapy may be focused on the child's personality, parents must be incorporated into the therapeutic plan. For example, parents who are overindulgent, thereby compounding the difficulties in discipline, may require counseling to work through their own reasons and feelings for approaching the child's behavior in this manner. Often a sense of guilt or problems in their own childhood foster parental overindulgence. With the help of the therapist the parents may gain insight into their mismanagement of the child's behavior. A similar problem is noted with the overly strict parent who attempts to overcontrol the child. The therapist must be alert to parental styles in relating to their children. Marital problems or other significant aspects of the relationship between the parents often manifest themselves in subtle ways. No therapeutic program will meet with much success unless these problems are identified and resolved in the therapeutic situation.

Psychotherapy may be used with the older child. In psychotherapy the child's problems are discussed in a warm and accepting environment, enabling the child to feel free to express his feelings. Although the feelings may sound unrealistic and inappropriate, the therapist presents an accepting attitude and listens to the child in order to gain an understanding of the problems. As time progresses, the child may develop new insights into his feelings. Critical elements of the child's personality are examined, and change fostered through insight techniques.

Psychotherapy sessions may involve only the child or, in some cases, the entire family. Often a myriad of problems develops, not only in the child's ability to understand his feelings, but also parental reactions to the child. Counseling must involve significant people in the child's environment. Although they may not attend counseling sessions, they are involved in providing a more "therapeutic" environment for the child. A very significant source of assistance are the teachers, with whom the therapist may keep contact over a period of time. The rapport with teacher is important not only to obtain information about the child's behavior, but also to provide directions for dealing with the child. Properly guided, the teacher can become as much an agent of change as parents and therapist.

Behavior modification techniques utilize different approaches in obtaining behavior change. Problems are defined as specific problem areas, and through manipulation of environmental rewards and punishments the behavior is changed. Behavior modification approaches assume a basic principle that all behavior is maintained by environmental consequences. Rewarding any behavior tends to increase the likelihood of that behavior occurring. Nonreward tends to make the behavior decrease in frequency. It should also be noted that some behavior is maintained by punishment and that children who are seeking attention will often accept any kind of attention, even though it is punishing. In this sense, attention itself is rewarding.

The emphasis of behavioral approaches is on environmental responses to the child's behavior. Consistency is stressed, and very specific reactions to specific behaviors of the child are made. It is often easier for parents to understand behavior modification approaches since the parents are given simple actions used to respond to the child's behavior. Toilet-training techniques, control of hyperactivity, and even such catastrophic conditions as infantile autism are a few examples of problems which have been managed successfully with behavior modification approaches.

In order for behavioral approaches to be effective, continued contact with the therapist is maintained until the desired behaviors are well ingrained. Behavior modification approaches involve combinations of rewards and punishments. The major emphasis, however, is always on rewarding good behavior since this, in the long run, leads to more permanent behavior changes. Behavior modification approaches have been extremely valuable with the hyperactive child. The results obtained in behavioral improvement, with or without medications, are often dramatic. The child who is poorly motivated in the classroom because of a learning disability may show a dramatic increase in his level of motivation as a result of a system of rewards being attached to his "studying" behavior. Shaping procedures are often utilized. Rather than expecting a high level of performance immediately, graduated steps approximating the final goal are taken. For example, if the child is poorly motivated to complete his arithmetic homework, initial steps involve choosing only a portion of that homework to be completed in order for the necessary reward to be obtained. As the child improves in his ability to perform, the amount of completed work necessary to obtain reward is gradually increased. In this way a change in the child's environment occurs, and parents and teachers rapidly gain insight into the fact that they may have been spending more time punishing nonsuccess rather than praising appropriate behavior. Frequently a learning-disabled child requires more tangible types of rewards. The child is often given a chart or some other concrete method of recording rewards. In this way constantly giving the child candy, for example, or other types of immediate reinforcement can be avoided.

Most therapeutic techniques dealing with the emotional problems of the learning-disabled child have a similarity in that the emphasis is on *changing behavior,* with ensuing improvement of some internal state of affairs such as self-concept. Children are amazingly flexible in their ability to change. Most therapeutic approaches are very successful if applied in a patient and understanding manner. In most cases there is no quick way to obtain improvement. A therapist is only as effective as his empathy for the child and his creativity. Parents of learning-disabled children are extremely vulnerable to fads and approaches that conceptualize the child in a very narrow manner. Dietary manipulations to control hyperactivity, megavitamins, hypoglycemic diets, and other techniques have many ardent followers who claim dramatic changes. Yet, many of the techniques are unproven and often applied at the expense of missing the complex interrelationship of problems facing the child. As mentioned previously, a child may well be hyperactive as a result of a dietary problem, but the years of hyperactive behavior and resulting negative environment have taken their toll on the child's emotional well-being. The negative response to the child's hyperactivity may have left indelible marks on the self-concept and personality. Simply treating the hyperactivity fails to acknowledge the complexity of variables which produced the behavior. The child is not an entity which can be fragmented into many parts, thereby risking the professional "perceptual problem" of tunnel vision.

Illustrations of Therapeutic Techniques

As mentioned previously, behavior modification involves manipulation of the child's environment so that desired behavior is reinforced and undesirable behavior is not. Ideally, and with a good deal of patience on the part of the parents, rapid changes in a child's behavior can be accomplished in a relatively short period of time. Many behavior problems, however, are manifested with such intensity that parents are frustrated by approaches that require them to wait for a good behavior to occur so that they can reward it. Various techniques of behavioral control must be implemented in addition to positive reinforcement plans. Often both are used simultaneously in order to effect more rapid change.

As an example, we will explore a behavior modification program utilized for a hyperactive preschooler. It will be assumed that this child also has an auditory processing problem. This makes it difficult for him to follow multiple directions. In addition, the child is hyperactive, distractible, and has a poor attention span, thereby reducing further his ability to respond appropriately to verbal commands. On examination of this child's history, it is noted that many aspects of his behavior have progressively deteriorated. Due to the frequent punishments administered by his parents, the child has developed a habit of striking back aggressively when corrected for his behavior. Scoldings by the parents, deprivation techniques, and spankings have proven to be of little value.

The frequent use of the word "no" without consistent follow-up encourages children to regard this and other behavior-control words as meaningless. The parents frequently express frustration with the fact that the child "tunes them out" and that they must yell in order to get his attention. This behavior of "tuning out" parents is, however, nothing more than a conditioning process that has taken place over a period of years teaching the child not to respond to the word "no" unless emitted by a parent at 90 decibels 3 inches from the child's ear.

Most human behavior is a response to signals. These signals can be internal, that is, from within the organism, or external, from outside the organism. For example, radical changes in behavior occur when approaching a signal such as a stop light. Immediately, many reflexes go into action, and the individual, if driving a car, gradually stops the automobile. The process of conditioning has built in these reflexes. We have learned that failure to heed certain signals may bring dire consequences. At birth a red or green light has no significance, but over a period of time these signals have grown in significance to the point where they can elicit significant changes in behavior. Internal cues may also occur, such as feelings of anxiety over a misdeed, fear reactions from the signal of a certain type of animal or situation, or the sense of satisfaction after accomplishing a difficult task. These internal cues also function as signals to encourage or discourage continuing a certain course of behavior.

Children also respond to signals. The word "no" has been utilized as a signal to effect some change in a child's behavior. Through the process of conditioning, however, the child was taught to respond only when the word was spoken very loudly. By yelling at the child, we induce a fear response in the child which only further activates reactions of anger and aggressiveness. Therefore, increasing the intensity of the verbal signal to a child by yelling at him does not often effect the desired change. With the hyperactive child in the example, we require a new signal which will then be followed by specific consequences. Care must be taken not to reinforce negative behavior with attention. In many cases even negative attention reinforces a behavior to the point where we are actually encouraging rather than discouraging it.

The behavior modification program to be described has been attempted by the author in approximately 65 cases. These cases cover the full range of children with overly aggressive behaviors, hyperactivity, perceptual handicaps, low intelligence, brain injury, and mild emotional disturbances. The program has effected rapid and dramatic changes in behavior in every case. Up to the time of this printing, there has not been one failure in this program, and no harmful side effects or factors detrimental to a child's emotional well-being have been encountered. This success has been documented not only by parents, but also by teachers and other professionals working with the children who observed the dramatic changes in behavior and further documented the absence of harmful side effects. In some cases these behavior programs were utilized with medication, although in the majority of cases medication was not utilized as an adjunct. Results were similar in all cases.

Following the complete evaluation of both medical and psychological factors in our hypothetical case of the hyperactive preschooler, the parents are given a brief course in behavior modification techniques and terminology. Aspects of positive and negative reinforcement are discussed. Stress is placed upon long-term behavioral changes occurring through positive reinforcement of appropriate behavior. This aspect is stressed due to the tendency to observe some change by the use of punishment techniques. Long-term behavioral changes, however, seldom occur through punishment techniques alone. After the session on behavior modification, aspects of signals and the mistakes frequently made by parents in using verbal signals with children are discussed. The program is stated very simply. A new signal is chosen, and for ease of application the word "check" rather than "no" is utilized. The parents are instructed to purchase two blackboards—one to be set up in a conspicuous location in the house and the other to be carried with the parent to various parts of the house. Since children are very mobile, the portable blackboard allows application of the check-mark system throughout the house. The fixed board is utilized in a place (e.g., the den) where the family is typically together as a unit.

The parents are asked to choose no more than *three specific* categories of behavior that they desire to change. The category of "bad behavior" is avoided because of its generality and the fact that it can be too contingent on the parents' state of mind on that particular day, the degree of frustration which they are feeling, or other factors inherent in the parents' personality. Therefore, in our example of the hyperactive child, the behavioral categories may include (1) argumentative verbal behavior, (2) aggressive behavior toward siblings, and (3) destructive behavior. Each time a behavior in any of these categories occurs, the parent says "check" in a firm but modulated tone of voice and also places a check mark on one of the blackboards. With a perceptually handicapped child, a dual sensory modality approach is most appropriate. These children often miss a unimodal signal, but if presented in dual sensory modalities, the signal tends to have more impact. In addition, a check mark written on a blackboard can be observed by the child over a period of time. If the behavior does not cease, the parent again says the word "check." The child is then given an appropriate period of time, usually dependent upon the type of behavior emitted, to obtain the third check mark.

Following the third check mark, the parent states "time-out," and the child is placed in his room for no more than 10 minutes of quiet. This is a very critical period of time of the program since the removal of the child from the situation to the time-out room is accomplished with a "matter-of-fact" attitude. The parents during this time-out period do not respond to the child with verbal signals. Parents frequently use a common oven timer in order to signal the child that time-out has been completed and that the child is allowed to leave the room. On initial attempts to place the child in the room, opposition frequently occurs. The child may verbally or physically fight the parent or may be destructive in the room. The parents are encouraged not to respond to the child during this period of time. The child rapidly learns that acting-out behavior will not gain him added attention from the parent. If after the first or second check mark the child ceases the undesirable behavior, he is allowed to erase the check marks and starts over again. The parents are encouraged to remember that after a few minutes of good behavior all check marks should be removed.

The child immediately begins responding to the word "check." The parents, utilizing a "matter-of-fact" attitude and tone of voice will notice that the child is happier with the parents feeling less guilty and more comfortable in dealing with the child's behavior. This initial improvement offers encouragement to the parents, and they are anxious to proceed with all aspects of the program with considerable enthusiasm. As an exercise, the parents are also encouraged to write down all aspects of the child's behavior to which they previously responded with negative feedback. They are often surprised to see how lengthy this list becomes. The parents are then encouraged to respond to no more than half of these. They immediately discover that they either responded impulsively with the word "no" many times without thinking or the behavior really was not as significant as they thought.

As the program continues, the number of times-out decreases dramatically, and it is not usual that after the third or fourth day no times-out are received by the child.

As mentioned previously, no program of negative behavioral control will work consistently to increase positive behavior. The child is placed, therefore, on an additional program of positive reinforcement. Frequently the categories involve three major areas of desirable behavior, one of which the child already performs consistently and two other behavior categories that are listed in terms of problem areas. These behavior categories are chosen and stated in positive terms. For example, a behavior category chosen for positive reinforcement related to mealtime should not be stated in negative terms such as "not yelling, not arguing during dinnertime." The behavior should be stated in positive terms such as "talking quitely during mealtime." Another frequently used behavior for positive reinforcement is not exceeding a certain number of times-out. In each case the child receives a star if he fulfills the behavioral goal. Children are very rapidly intrigued by this "behavior game." Immediate reinforcement is utilized. Often a tray is constructed with three parts to it. The first section would be a one-star tray for such desirable yet not "overwhelming" rewards or presents such as a half of a stick of gum or a half a candy bar. The second or two-star section may involve a whole candy bar, a whole pack of gum, and other reinforcements which in comparison to the one-star tray appear more desirable to the child. The third category, the three-star tray, involves something rather special, for example, certain desirable toys. Based upon his performance on a given day, the child may earn up to three stars which are linked to rewards.

The effects of the program are often dramatic. Not only does the child begin to organize and plan his behavior more appropriately, but the parents find they are spending less time monitoring the child's behavior. The positive feelings permeating the household are often contagious with family life improving as a result.

A modification of this program can also be utilized in a classroom. The teacher who encounters a child with behavioral difficulties can devote a section of a blackboard to check marks. The school program is always complemented with a similar program at home so the child is quite familiar with check marks. Each time inappropriate behavior occurs in the classroom, the teacher simply walks over to that section of the board and places a check mark. If the child accumulates a certain number of check marks in a half-hour period of time, the child must go to a "time-out" either in the classroom or in another room in the building. In order to leave the time-out, the child must complete some aspect of school work, such as 10 math problems or other similar tasks which involve 5 to 10 minutes of time. Removing the child from the classroom situation eliminates reinforcement by classmates. Again the teacher is encouraged to act "matter-of-factly."

Teachers often spend considerable amounts of their time controlling the child's behavior. Institution of this program, while it seems complicated initially, reduces considerably the period of time spent controlling the child. It should be noted that a positive reinforcement program is instituted. The child is rewarded each day he reduces or maintains a low number of times-out. The teacher may reinforce with special attention to the child. Often a hyperactive child may be rewarded by being allowed to earn the privilege of running around on the playground for a 5-minute period of time every hour. While this does involve some change in procedure on the part of the teacher, it is generally useful since the child is able to rid himself of a great deal of excess energy during this 5-minute period and also will work hard to obtain this reward.

There are many variations of the program that may be utilized by parents and professionals dealing with the learning-disabled child. There is abundant literature pertaining to behavior modification techniques. These behavior modification approaches, however, if not controlled carefully with thorough understanding of all possible contingencies, are doomed to failure. The approaches are deceptively simple, yet errors can occur which will destroy the effectiveness of the program and increase parental frustration through lack of success. It is recommended that a therapist have (1) a continued familiarity with the literature of behavior modification and (2) at least some degree of supervised experience. These requirements should be necessary prerequisites for instituting effective behavior modification programs.

LEARNING DISABILITIES AND JUVENILE DELINQUENCY

In recent years there has been an alarming growth in the rate of juvenile crime. Public awareness and a national anxiety, born in terms of staggering financial losses as well as an enormous waste of human potential, has been generated. Kessler (1966) has noted the marked increase in the incidence of juvenile crime since the late 1940s in relation to adult arrests. The dramatic rise in reported juvenile offenses in part reflects the growth in the population of persons under 18 years of age, improved reporting methods, changes in public attitude, and modifications of social attitudes and values. These factors, however, appear to be of minor significance since the increase in the numbers of youthful offenders far surpasses the increase in the general population. Weiner (1975), citing official juvenile court statistics, found that approximately 3 percent of American children age 10 to 17 years appears in juvenile court each year for offenses other than traffic violations. In an average year this percentage included hundreds of thousands of children. Mangel (1974) has addressed the issue of juvenile crime with some poignant comments:

> . . . about six of every ten juveniles in jail—and I mean jail with locks and bars and guards—have committed no criminal acts.
>
> . . . eight out of these same ten *do* commit crimes after they leave jail.
>
> . . . some three out of four juveniles who are put in jail as juveniles are convicted of crime as adults.
>
> . . . more than 1 million boys and girls are caught up in American's juvenile justice system each year. . . . On any day, today, more than 100,000 juveniles are behind bars.

Mangel expresses much concern about our priorities in seeking to prevent delinquency, noting that in 1973 the federal government spent approximately *$14 million* for delinquency prevention and about *$5 billion* for highway construction. As many researchers point out, the statistics reflect only a small sampling of the total picture for "only a small portion of youngsters who commit illegal acts are detected, of those detected only a portion are arrested, and of those arrested only a portion come to trial in a juvenile court" (Weiner, 1975).

Poremba (1974) estimated that juvenile crime costs approximately $8,000 for each delinquent each year and for each adult criminal it costs about $27,000 a year. The "criminal career" costs "one-half million dollars—$250,000 in terms of property loss, etc." (Poremba, 1974). Poremba emphasizes that the loss of dignity and human potential cannot be measured in dollars and cents.

At the 1974 International Conference of the Association for Children with Learning Disabilities, Mauser (1974) presented a profile of the typical juvenile delinquent. The average age for the adolescent offender was 13.5 years. The peak years for arrest of the juvenile lawbreaker occurred between ages 13 and 14 years. The delinquent as described by Mauser was *not* retarded, having an average IQ of 95. The type of crimes committed appear to have a cultural influence. Mauser (1974) further noted that the juvenile delinquent of today is "a tougher, meaner and sicker individual than his counterpart of 10 to 15 years ago." The exact nature of this difference is unknown but may be reflecting the influence of the drug culture.

In the spring of 1974 a conference was held in Dallas to discuss "Youth in Trouble." Those attending included educators, physicians, psychologists, and legal advocates of the juvenile justice system. What emerged from this conference was the need to focus on education and delinquency. Kratoville (1974) succinctly summarized the issue:

> [A] concensus of opinion quickly emerged, that is, adolescents are not properly nor humanely served in our educational and judicial systems. Education seems determined to push problem youngsters out rather than to keep them in as potentially productive citizens. Justice seems determined to keep them in rather than to push them out as potentially productive citizens. The net result, in terms of recidivism, is that more problem youngsters return to correctional institutions each year than return to school! (p. 7)

It is readily acknowledged that juvenile delinquency is a multifactorial problem and represents an ill-defined syndrome of behaviors fashioned by a complex amalgam of cultural, social, psychological, neurological, and educational influences. The author (Zinkus & Gottlieb, 1978) has been investigating various problems of the learning-disabled child, especially the influence of education (or lack of academic achievement) on developing antisocial, delinquent behaviors. The review to follow focuses on academic achievement, reading skills, perceptual development, learning disorders, and self-esteem as crucial ingredients in this multifactorial synthesis generating juvenile delinquency.

The juvenile delinquent has generally been regarded as a non-learner, an academic underachiever, an educational dropout—the generalization often proposed that the delinquent behaviors have interfered with learning and academic progress. Inasmuch as it was recognized that as a group youthful offenders were *not* mentally retarded, it was quickly assumed that behaviors and attitudes adversely influenced learning skills and academic achievement. In the 1930s Monroe (1932) fashioned "academic delinquency" as a typical characteristic of the juvenile delinquent and postulated that "the inability to read may be one of the prolonged school problems until the child drifts into truancy and incorrigibility." During this period Harrington (1936) added supporting evidence to the claims that lack of success in school could serve as an important cause of juvenile delinquency. This hypothesis, which is now generally recognized as a plausible explanation of the delinquent's poor school performance, adds the significant role of learning disabilities as an etiological agent in aberrant behaviors and juvenile deliquency.

Fendrick and Bond (1936) observed that 90 percent of the delinquent children in their studies were school failures. Their survey further revealed that reading performance, in a selected group of delinquents with average intelligence, was significantly below a normal control group of the same age and intelligence. The reading deficits were *not* related to mental deficiency, which accounted for only a small segment of the delinquent population. Woodward (1955) and Kessler (1966) reported that there was little or no correlation between intelligence and juvenile delinquency. They did observe, however, a strong relationship between academic retardation, especially in the area of reading. Similar reports from Great Britain, by Scott (1971), confirm the lack of correlation between intelligence and delinquency. The substance of these investigations was to arouse interest in reading deficiencies and academic underachievement, unrelated to intelligence, as a cause of juvenile delinquency. Delinquency, in part, was viewed as a by-product of anxieties, frustrations, and anger generated by the lack of success in school.

Kvaraceus (1944), in his article "Delinquency—A Byproduct of the Schools," presented data indicating that 60 percent of the delinquents in his study expressed a marked dislike for school. An equally high percentage repeated one or more grades early in their school career. Although these children had intelligence in the average range, they were unable to develop adequate competency in academics. As a result of continual failure, these children developed frustrations and aggressive behaviors. In addition, school failure seemed to promote antisocial behavior in the form of juvenile delinquency, toward social institutions.

It must be recalled that prior to the early 1960s specific learning disabilities and the learning-disabled child were not prominent national concerns. Indeed, prior to the early 1960s the learning-disabled child was a relatively unrecognized entity. In retrospect many of the early writings (Aichorn, 1935; Gluek & Gluek, 1950) on the relationship between juvenile delinquency and academic underachievement may have been describing a population of children with perceptual disturbances, dyslexia, minimal brain dysfunction, and motor coordination deficits. These reports may have represented a description of children who were unable to learn in the traditional academic environment because of specific learning disabilities.

During the 1974 Dallas conference a variety of comments were offered closely binding learning disabilities and juvenile crime. At this conference pediatricians stressed that failure in school may be one of the most devastating experiences that can affect the personality of the developing child. The blow to self-esteem after years of failure and nonacceptance may cause permanent damage to the personality. Child psychologists and speech pathologists noted that some learning-disabled children did not surface until they were adolescents because they failed in junior and senior high school. Identification of these disabled adolescents and providing meaningful therapy could prevent the need for them to vent their fury at the humiliations they have experienced all through their lives in antisocial behavior. Berman (1974) presented results of some of his research indicating that 70 percent of the youngsters imprisoned in the Rhode Island Training School for Boys had measurable disabilities significant enough to warrant professional attention. Berman further noted that these disabilities were chronic handicaps. Many of his subjects revealed visual perceptual or visual motor disability, impaired nonverbal concept formation, auditory discrimination or memory disability, and impaired kinesthetic feedback. Compton (1974) reviewed a series of behavior patterns exhitibted by delinquents with learning disabilities as they passed through the educational system. He noted that "the average delinquent simply avoids coping with reality. Beginning failure leads to continuing failure which leads to boredom and/or frustration which, in turn, leads to truancy, dropout, and possible delinquency."

A strong case can be made for the fact that learning disabilities, academic underachievement, school failure, lack of successes, deterioration of self-esteem, frustrations, and anxiety can be a contributing factor to deviant behavior—to juvenile delinquency.

From a historical perspective, most investigators exploring the academic capabilities of delinquent youth are immediately aware of the extremely poor reading skills of the youthful offenders. In the initial investigation of delinquents and academics it has been assumed that the reading difficulty was one manifestation of a wide range of psychosocial deficiencies. The reading retardation was often regarded as a complication of the overall rebellious attitude of delinquent youth. The youthful offender was envisioned as a psychopathic personality, and the lack of motivation in the academic setting was presumed to be a component of this antisocial personality factor. In essence, it was *not* that the child could not learn to read, but, rather, he was *not interested* in reading! Subsequent investigations offered a counterargument, suggesting that the reading deficits were manifestations of specific learning disabilities, such as dyslexia, and that aberrant behaviors were secondary to these underlying disturbances in reading and learning.

In 1926 McCready reported on the relationship between dyslexic children and their high-risk status as potential delinquents. He described "the behavior of word-blind children." They develop a "paranoid reaction toward the teacher and develop a sense of inferiority." The child's reaction is to "respond with behavior disorders in school, truancy and depredation upon school property" (McCready, 1926). Fendrick and Bond (1936) described reading problems among delinquent youths with average intelligence. In their group 83 delinquent males, ages 16 to 19 years, had an average reading level of 12 years 11 months as compared to a matched control group of nondelinquents with an average reading level of 17 years 11 months. Margolin, Roman, and Haruri (1955) found that 84 percent of the children examined at a juvenile detention center were reading retarded by 2 or more years. Over half of the children were deficient in reading by 5 years or more! Critchley (1968) surveyed a delinquent population and found that 60 percent were deficient in reading by 2 or more years. Mulligan (1969) found that in his sample of juvenile delinquents only 10 percent were reading at grade level and 80 percent were significantly below their grade level. Tarnopol (1970) confirmed these observations in his sampling of delinquent males, ages 16 to 23 years. The average reading level of 64 percent of his subjects were below the sixth-grade level. All of these analyses confirm and emphasize that juvenile delinquents read poorly.

Many of the studies of reading skills in delinquent populations did not explore the expected level which children of varying intellectual capacities should attain. For example, children with lower than average intellectual capacity could *not* be expected to read as well as children with average or above average intelligence. Using Mulligan's 1969 survey, results indicated that delinquents with IQs in the average range were reading 5.2 grades below their actual grade placement. In addition, most surveys did not explore the basis for the reading disability in the youthful offender. In Mulligan's study some of the children showed classical signs of dyslexia, in the form of word and letter reversals and missequencing of letters in a word. Weinschenk (1967) supported the concept that many of the children in delinquent populations showed symptoms of congenital dyslexia and dysgraphia. Unfortunately, there is a paucity of information concerning the nature and etiology of the delinquent's limited reading skills.

Professionals working with learning-disabled children have been aware of the association between perceptual disturbances and reading disabilities. Clements (1966), Myklebust (1971), and others described children who were unable to process effectively sensory information in the central nervous system. Rampp and Plummer (1977) reviewed auditory processing and learning abilities. Chalfant and Scheffelin (1966) reviewed research information on CNS processing dysfunctions. Although the peripheral sense organs are intact, the decoding of transmitted sensory impulses is impaired, presumably at the cortical level. The child with perceptual lags or dysfunctions may exhibit reversal and rotation of letters and numbers, missequencing auditory directions, difficulty in integrating auditory and visual symbols, and other deficits. The majority of children with significant perceptual disturbances, despite average or above average intelligence, are generally extremely deficient in academic skills, particularly in reading. The children with these particular handicaps are categorized as having "specific learning disabilities."

The association between perceptual disturbances, reading disorders, academic failure, poor self-esteem, and juvenile delinquency can be easily constructed on an empirical basis. Is there, however, a substance or foundation for constructing this hypothetical "syndrome"?

Mauser (1974) reported that 50 to 75 percent of juvenile delinquents in his study exhibited evidence of specific learning disabilities. These statistics corroborated the earlier observations of Poremba (1974), who found that 50 percent of the juvenile delinquents referred to courts revealed a specific learning disability. Berman's (1974) neuropsychological study of specific disabilities in juvenile delinquents revealed that 55 percent of the subjects exhibited visual perceptual or visual motor disability; 31 percent, impaired nonverbal concept formation; 30 percent, auditory discrimination or memory disability; and 28 percent, impaired kinesthetic feedback. Compton (1974) similarly demonstrated perceptual abnormalities in a delinquent population. Of the 444 youthful offenders that comprised his study, approximately 46 percent manifested a significant visual perceptual deficit and 25 percent were deficient in language processing skills. The perceptual disorders were of sufficient severity to compromise academic progress, although overall intellectual abilities were good. It is readily apparent that significant numbers of delinquent children reveal auditory and/or visual processing disturbances. The association between perceptual deficits, resulting reading disorders and subsequent academic failure has been recognized as a hallmark of many learning-disabled children.

Adequate auditory processing skills are essential in developing good educational and social competence. Disturbances in the ability to use properly auditory stimuli may be manifested as deficits in auditory, association, closure, discrimination, memory and sequential memory, blending, and other tasks. These deficits may be subtle but may, nevertheless, adversely influence receptive and expressive language skills, educational development, and social adaptation. The more obvious deficits may be manifested as articulation disorders or aphasic-like symptoms. Disturbances either along the peripheral pathways (such as the middle ear and the eighth cranial nerve, the auditory nerve) or dysfunctions in the temporal lobes of the cerebral cortex may cause abnormalities in auditory processing. The more severe central auditory processing disturbances have been referred to as aphasia. Aphasia basically represents a marked deficiency in symbolic functioning. Less obvious disturbances may be manifested as disturbances in auditory processing or perceptual deficits. The need for intact auditory processing skills is recognized as a fundamental requirement for the development of adequate language and academic skills.

Critchley (1968) reported a higher incidence of articulation deficits in reading-deficient juvenile delinquents. Youthful offenders who manifested severe reading disabilities, however, evidenced articulation disorders to a much greater degree than delinquents with adequate reading skills. Critchley further noted that all children with difficulty in learning to read develop neurotic reactions at an early age. Tarnopol (1969) measured the verbal skills of a delinquent group of adolescents and provided insights into the relationship between juvenile delinquency, learning disorders, and language function. Poor readers performed poorly on psychological tests measuring the function of the left cerebral hemisphere, such as speech, language, and auditory processing skills. In addition, delinquents with lower verbal skills tended to commit more crimes and were arrested more often than subjects with adequate verbal skills.

Jacobson (1974) indicated that a primary characteristic of many delinquents is the capability of learning more efficiently by the visual modality. This observation suggested that there is a higher incidence of disturbed language function among delinquents, that is, a disturbance of skills requiring auditory processing abilities. Faigel (1969) noted the relationship between dyslexia and language and reported that "dyslexia is the defective language achievement in an individual who has normal intelligence." Language in this definition implied "talking, reading, writing, spelling, and speech." The observed high incidence of language-related deficits among delinquent youth suggests an etiology for the associated reading deficiencies in this group.

It must be stressed that learning disorders are not confined to classrooms. The child with a learning disability has a problem that is pervasive in character, a disorder that influences his social adaptation as well as his educational progress. Faulty language and faulty auditory processing skills in general tend to influence the child's social learning as well as his academic achievements. The poor classroom learner is potentially the poor social learner.

Visual processing deficits have also been found in high frequency among juvenile offenders. Visual perceptual disturbances may be manifested as a variety of deficits in visual attention, memory, closure, spatial orientation, motor coordination, and others. Disorders in the central processing of visual stimuli may involve multiple areas along the pathways through temporal and occipital lobes.

Numerous studies have confirmed the high incidence of visual processing disturbances among juvenile delinquents. Petrie, McCullock and Kaydin (1962) and Dzik (1966) reported on the atypical visual perceptual performances in behaviorally disturbed delinquents. A more precise analysis of these visual perceptual deficits were presented by Rubin and Braun (1968). They found that the major deficits in juvenile delinquents appeared to be visual spatial orientation and visual motor coordination disturbances. Critchley (1968), Tarnopol (1969), and Wikler, Dixon, and Parker (1970) demonstrated that visual spatial orientation disturbances, as detected on examinations such as the Bender-Gestalt test, were frequent among youthful offenders. Mulligan (1969) noted that problems in visual discrimination and visual perceptual skills are characteristically found in dyslexic children and among juvenile delinquents. Rubin and Braun (1968) suggested that the visual processing disturbances caused considerable stress for the child as he attempted to cope with the standards established by school and society. The sequence of events begins with pressures in school due to academic underachievement; the resultant anxieties, frustrations, and tensions take the form of behavioral disturbances and finally culminate as antisocial behaviors such as juvenile delinquency.

In a 1978 survey of delinquent youth (Zinkus & Gottlieb, 1978) findings suggest that visual and auditory perceptual disturbances are relatively common causes of the academic underachievement within this group. The results indicate that over 46 percent of the youthful offenders had combinations of both visual and auditory processing deficits. The major areas of weakness involved auditory sequential memory, visual memory, and visual motor coordination. The combination of disturbances, within this group, was associated with more severe deficits in reading, spelling, and arithmetic than delinquents having only single visual or auditory processing disorders. The combination of perceptual deficits appears to affect more acutely language and educational development.

There is a paucity of conclusive neurological data relating to central nervous system dysfunction in juvenile delinquents. Sporadic observations have been reported, but definitive studies are lacking that relate neurological dysfunction to reading and perceptual skills. Investigations of youthful offenders have indicated the presence of subtle neurological signs (Zinkus & Gottlieb, 1978). For example, over 68 percent of the subjects in the delinquent population in the 1978 study exhibited mixed eye-hand dominance. Additional analysis revealed that these subjects were also the poorest readers (Zinkus & Gottlieb, 1978).

Clements (1966) presented data linking neurological dysfunctions with academic and behavioral difficulties in children. Wikler and his co-workers (1970) analyzed psychometric, neurological, and electroencephalographic data in a group of children referred for scholastic and behavioral disorders. When this group was compared with a normal population of children, these children revealed lower scores on psychometric examinations testing perceptual motor skills. In addition, these children manifested a greater number of neurological signs and electroencephalographic abnormalities. Quitkin and Klein (1969) similarly reported a higher frequency of neurological soft signs, EEG abnormalities, and psychological test deficits among children prone to impulsive and destructive behaviors. Many of the children had a history of hyperkinetic behavior during early childhood.

Keldgord (1968) reported that many of the juvenile offenders committed to correctional centers may have subtle neurological damage. The neurological dysfunctions in these children do not cause gross or obvious abnormalities, but they may impair learning and social adaptation. Of particular interest were the behavioral disturbances associated with the minimal brain dysfunction syndrome (MBD), which can also be applied to many delinquent children. Among the more prominent behavioral signs are hyperkinesis, impulsivity, short attention span, aggressive behaviors, emotional lability, and learning disorders. Barcai and Rabkin (1974) hypothesized that the hyperkinetic child was particularly vulnerable and that his behavior and performance "leads to his extrusion from the classroom or his rejection within it." These difficulties eventually lead to school aversion, truancy, and dropping out. The blocking of normal outlets is finally manifested as deviant behaviors or delinquent acts.

Critchley (1968) evaluated a group of male juvenile delinquents with a series of neurological examinations, including (1) laterality preference, (2) right-left orientation, (3) finger agnosia, (4) clumsiness, and (5) graphic and spatial tests. The delinquent children were found to have an increased incidence of disturbances in the performance of these neurological tasks as compared to a matched control series. Of the delinquents, 33 percent showed a cross preference between hand and foot. In reading 70 percent of the delinquents were significantly retarded. Among the retarded readers within the delinquent group, graphic and spatial orientation deficits were significantly greater than expected in the normal population. Left-right orientation confusion was a common problem among the delinquents. These neurological observations were interpreted by Critchley as a neurological immaturity hypothesis to explain dyslexia. The same neurological immaturity may be responsible for impaired learning and poor social adaptation. In Denhoff's 1965 series of studies of children with school adjustment problems and delinquent behaviors, 53 percent were found to have organic brain dysfunction. Most of the subjects with neurological deficits manifested poor learning skills, delayed motor and/or speech development. Once again neurological immaturity was blamed for the child's academic and social problems.

The final common pathway for undiagnosed and untreated learning disabilities is academic underachievement, lack of success experiences, erosion of self-esteem, and, in many children, antisocial behaviors and delinquent behaviors. Adequate feelings of self-worth, self-confidence, self-esteem are important psychosocial elements in maintaining stable character and personality. Disturbed learning abilities threaten behavioral development by endangering the growth of a healthy self-concept.

Kvaraceus (1944) was one of the first to suggest that impaired learning caused delinquent behaviors as a result of the frustrations and anxieties the child experienced. Menkes and Williams in 1976 independently reported on the profound effects on self-esteem generated by school failure. Williams speaks of the academic crippling of the child as an end result of the disease called learning disabilities. Elliot (1966) hypothesized that frustration in school may cause children to attack the system which is causing their discomfort, the school and society. Academic underachievement can evoke pressures from parents and teachers who fail to recognize the child's underlying disorder in learning. Jacobson (1974) and Mulligan (1969) noted that teacher–child relationships are compromised as the child fails to achieve the rewards of success. Often the child is erroneously branded with cruel labels such as "lazy" and/or "retarded." Hyperactive children may become more aggressive as they attempt to gain recognition, as suggested by Wagner (1970).

It is not suggested that learning disorders are the sole cause of juvenile delinquency. The suggestion is offered, however, that juvenile delinquency is a complex syndrome and that learning disabilities is a significant factor contributing to this aberrant behavior. This implies, in a sense, an optimistic approach. If learning disabilities can be identified early and meaningful therapy programs initiated, delinquent behaviors can perhaps be prevented. If teachers, parents, and children have insights and awareness of the complications of impaired learning, they can perhaps be more effective in preserving self-concept and self-confidence of the victimized child.

Peter W. Zinkus

REFERENCES

Aichorn, A. *Wayward youth.* New York: Viking Press, 1935.
Barcai, A., & Rabkin, L. A precursor of delinquency: The hyperkinetic disorder of childhood. *Psychiatry Quarterly,* 1974, *48,* 387–399.
Bender, L. *Psychopathology of children with organic brain disorders.* Springfield, Ill.: Thomas, 1956.
Berman, A. Delinquents are disabled. In B. Kratoville (Ed.), *Youth in trouble.* San Rafael, Calif. Academic Therapy Publications, 1974, pp. 39–43.
Bryant, N. Clinic inadequacies with learning disorders: The missing clinical educator. In J. Hellmuth (Ed.), *Learning disorders* (Vol. 2). Seattle: Special Child Publications, 1966, pp. 265–279.
Chalfant, J. C., & Scheffelin, M. A. *Central processing dysfunctions in children: A review of research.* NINDS Monograph No. 9. Washington, D.C.: U.S. Department of Health, Education and Welfare, 1969.
Clements, S. *Minimal brain dysfunction in children.* NINDS Monograph No. 3, Washington, D.C.: U.S. Government Printing Office, 1966.
Compton, R. The learning-disabled adolescent. In B. Kratoville (Ed.), *Youth in trouble.* San Rafael: Academic Therapy Publications, 1974, pp. 44–56.
Congressional Record, Vol. 23, No. 4, Jan. 11, 1974, U.S. Government Printing Office.
Connally, C. Social and emotional factors in learning disabilities. In H. Myklebust, *Progress in learning disabilities* (Vol. 2). New York: Grune & Stratton, 1971.
Critchley, E. M. R. Reading retardation, dyslexia and delinquency. *British Journal of Psychiatry,* 1968, *114,* 1537–1547.
Denhoff, E. *Bridges to burn and to build. Developmental Medicine and Child Neurology,* 1965, *7,* 3–8.
Dollard, J., Doob, L., Miller, N., & Sears, R. *Frustration and aggression.* New Haven: Yale University Press, 1939.
Dzik, D. Vision and the juvenile delinquent. *Journal of the American Optometric Association,* 1966, *37,* 461–468.
Elliot, D. Delinquency, school attendance and drop-out. *Social Problems,* 1966, *13,* 307–314.
Faigel, H. C. The origin of primary dyslexia. *General Practitioner,* 1969, *36,* 364.
Fendrick, P., & Bond, G. L. Delinquency and reading. *Journal of Genetic Psychology,* 1936, *48,* 236–243.
Glueck, S., & Glueck, E. *Unraveling juvenile delinquency.* New York: Commonwealth Fund, 1950.
Gottlieb, M. I. Pills: Pros and cons on medications for school problems. *Acta Symbolica,* 1975, *6,* 35–64.
Griffin, M. The role of child psychiatry in learning disabilities. In H. Myklebust, *Progress in learning disabilities* (Vol. 1). New York: Grune & Stratton, 1968, pp. 75–97.

Harrington, M. The problem of the defective delinquent. *Mental Hygiene,* 1936, *19,* 429–438.

Harris, A. *How to increase reading ability: A guide to developmental and remedial methods* (5th ed.). New York: McKay, 1970.

Herskovitz, H., Levine, M., & Spivack, G. Antisocial behavior of adolescents from higher socioeconomic groups. *Journal of Nervous and Mental Disease,* 1954, *129,* 467–476.

Hurwitz, I., Bibace, R., Woff, P., & Rowbotham, B. Neuropsychological function of normal boys, delinquent boys and boys with learning problems. *Perceptual and Motor Skills,* 1972, *35,* 387–394.

Jacobson, F. Learning disabilities and juvenile delinquency: A demonstrated relationship. In R. Weber (Ed.), *Handbook on learning disabilities.* Englewood Cliffs, N.J.: Prentice-Hall, 1974, pp. 189–216.

Kappleman, M., Luck, N. J., & Ganter, R. Profile of the disadvantaged child with learning disorders. *American Journal of Disabled Children,* 1971, *121,* 371–379.

Keldgord, R. Brain damage and delinquency: A question and a challenge. *Academic Therapy,* 1968, *4,* 93–99.

Kessler, J. *Psychopathology of childhood.* Englewood Cliffs, N.J.: Prentice-Hall, 1966.

Kvaraceus, W. C. Delinquency—A byproduct of the schools. *School and Society,* 1944, *59,* 350–351.

Mangel, C. The current state of the art. In B. Kratoville (Ed.), *Youth in trouble.* San Rafael, Calif.: Academic Therapy Publications, 1974, pp. 19–23.

Margolin, J., Riman, M. and Harurir, C. Reading disability in the delinquent child. *American Journal of Orthopsychiatry,* 1955, *25,* 25–112.

Mauser, A. J. Learning disabilities and delinquent youth. In B. Kratoville (Ed.), *Youth in trouble.* San Rafael Academic Therapy Publications, 1974, pp. 44–56.

McCready, E. Defects in the zone of language. *American Journal of Psychiatry,* 1926, *6,* 267–277.

Menkes, S. H. On failing in school. *Pediatrics,* 1976, *58,* 392–393.

Monroe, M. Children who cannot read. Chicago: University of Chicago Press, 1932.

Mulligan, W. A study of dyslexia and delinquency. *Academic Therapy,* 1969, *4,* 177–187.

Myklebust, H. *Progress in learning disabilities* (Vol. 2). New York: Grune & Stratton, 1971.

Paremba, C. What are we about? Come, let's counsel together. In B. Kratoville (Ed.), *Youth in trouble.* San Rafael: Academic Therapy Publications, 1974, pp. 9–10.

Petrie, A., McCulloch, R., & Kaydin, P. The perceptual characteristics of juvenile delinquents. *Journal of Nervous and Mental Disease,* 1962, *134,* 415–421.

Quay, H. R., Peterson, D. Personality factors in the study of juvenile delinquency. *Exceptional Children* 1960, *26,* 472–476.

Quitkin, F., & Klein, D. Two behavioral syndromes in young adults related to possible minimal brain damage. *Journal of Psychiatric Research,* 1969, *7,* 131–142.

Rampp, D. L., & Plummer, B. A. Auditory processing dysfunctions and impaired learning. *Learning Disabilities: An Audio Journal for Continuing Education,* 1977, *1*(No. 7).

Rubin, E., & Braun, J. Behavioral and learning disabilities associated with cognitive-motor dysfunction. *Perceptual and Motor Skills,* 1968, *26,* 171–180.

Scott, P. Delinquency. In J. Howells (Ed.), *Modern perspectives in child psychiatry.* New York: Bruner/Mazel, 1971, pp. 370–402.

Tarnopol, L. Delinquency and learning disabilities. In L. Tarnopol (Ed.), *Learning disabilities: Introduction to educational and medical management.* Springfield, Ill.: Thomas, 1969, pp. 305–330.

Thompson, R., & Gottlieb, M. I. Educational jeopardy, an interdisciplinary problem: The physician's contribution. *Acta Symbolica,* 1973, *4,* 46–72.

Todd, M., & Gottlieb, M. I. Interdisciplinary counseling in a medical setting. In E. Webster (Ed.), *Professional approaches with parents of handicapped children.* Springfield, Ill.: Thomas, 1976, pp. 191–216.

Wagner, R. Secondary emotional reactions in children with learning disabilities. Mental Hygiene, 1970, *54,* 577–590.

Weiner, I. Juvenile delinquency. *Pediatric Clinics of North America,* 1975, *22,* 673–684.

Weinschenk, C. The significance of the diagnosis and treatment of congenital dyslexia and dysgraphia in the prevention of juvenile delinquency. *World Medical Journal,* 1967, *14,* 54–56.

Wikler, A., Dixon, J., & Parker, J. Brain function in problem children and controls: Psychometric, neurological and electroencephalographic comparisons. *American Journal of Psychiatry,* 1970, *127,* 634–645.

Williams, J. Learning disabilities: A multifaceted health problem. *Journal of School Health,* 1976, *46,* 515–521.

Woodward, M. The role of low intelligence in delinquency. *British Journal of Delinquency,* 1955, *5,* 281–296.

Zinkus, P. W. Understanding psychological evaluations. *Learning Disabilities: An Audio Journal for Continuing Education,* 1977, *1*(No. 3).

Zinkus, P. W., & Gottlieb, M. I. Disorders of learning and delinquent youth: An overview. *Learning Disabilities: An Audio Journal of Continuing Education,* 1978, *1*(No. 4).

THE LEARNING-DISABLED CHILD: CONTROVERSIAL ISSUES REVISITED

Curiosity often stimulates and enhances thought processes which culminate in the acquisition of knowledge. Man is a curious creature with a passion to explore the unknown. *Concern* implies interest, dedication, and compassion. In a therapeutic setting it symbolizes the foundation of a meaningful professional–patient relationship and often prompts curiosity, initiating efforts to find better methods for serving the diagnostic/therapeutic needs of the client. Concern and curiosity are the driving forces generating creative thinking, from which a basic fund of medical wisdom is eventually accumulated for utilization by the therapist. It is not uncommon for *confusion* to develop during the exploratory phases of concern and curiosity. Confusion may understandably erupt in the interval between theorization and documentation. Confusion, however, may be magnified out of proportion by professional apathy, popularization of undocumented claims, variations in client compliance, exaggeration of patient testimonials, and a research design which does not adhere to the principles of the scientific method.

Controversy in turn may be spawned as a by-product of curiosity, concern, and confusion, precipitated by differences of opinion regarding the methods of gathering or interpreting data. Controversial issues are best resolved professionally, at scientific conferences and in peer-review journals. The more emotionally charged concerns have a tendency to evoke controversies which extend beyond the professional community and involve the public.

During the past decade *the learning-disabled child* has become a center of a galaxy of curiosities, concerns, confusions, and controversies, reflecting the magnitude of a psychosocial problem that has reached alarming epidemic proportions.

Medical controversy is more apt to occur as a consequence of hypotheses formulated solely on case reports or patient testimonials. Frequently these claims are prematurely announced in the popular media (TV, radio, newspapers, and magazines) and capture public awareness, despite a lack of scientific verification. Paradoxically, discordant issues may eventually become the subjects of well-constructed scientific investigations. Thus a medical disagreement often serves to initiate sophisticated research, designed in an effort to resolve the dilemma. The ensuing research may provide a more in-depth understanding of principles, stimulate new curiosities, and enhance the quality of care for the patient. Of paramount importance is that controversy can function as a scientific conscience, periodically reminding professionals of their fundamental responsibility in safeguarding the public. Medical controversy however, has its disadvantages by (1) popularizing and possibly augmenting professional and public confusions, (2) imposing burdensome financial obligations in attempts to resolve the scientific debate, (3) offering premature and unsubstantiated (false) hopes to desperate victims, and (4) delaying the utilization of established avenues of diagnostic and therapeutic intervention.

Controversies in medicine flourish luxuriantly in a milieu characterized by exaggerated public anxiety in combination with a relative professional apathy. Perpetuation of polemics often reflects the conflict between the patient's desire for "a quick cure" and possibly the more protracted conventional therapeutic regimen offered by professionals. "Failures," with standard methods of intervention, similarly prompt anxious patients to explore less conventional and more controversial approaches to their problem. Patients and families with catastrophic disorders are generally more vulnerable because of associated emotional traumas and economic pressures. These patients in their desperation are apt to be less cautious and critical in accepting and utilizing poorly documented approaches. The emotionally distraught susceptible patient may be unwittingly victimized by diagnostic and therapeutic interventions that have little or no scientific substance, despite popular claims and testimonials.

Currently, the child in "educational jeopardy" is the focus of great national interest. The growing anxiety for the learning-disabled child has been intensified by documentation of the devastating psychosocial repercussions of impaired learning. The physician, particularly the pediatrician, has a unique responsibility and contribution to offer in safeguarding the educational development of the child. Menkes (1976) underscored the severity of this issue:

> For the school-aged child, success or failure in mastering educational basics usually determines his future career, his role in society, and, all too often, his personal esteem. It is little wonder, therefore, that school failure represents a major catastrophe affecting both the child and his family. (p. 392)

The learning-disabled child is at high risk for developing deviant and antisocial behaviors (Zinkus & Gottlieb, 1978 a & b). Educational and psychological traumas ensuing in the classroom may be ultimately expressed as aberrant social functioning in the community. Williams (1976) characterized the psychosocial paradigm of the learning-disabled child:

> The basic end results of the "disease" learning disability, is the academic crippling of the child, thus preventing him from taking advantage of subsequent life opportunities. Such a state of unrealized potential is equivalent to "death," not in a physical sense, but in a mental and social sense. (p. 515)

Recently the United States House of Representatives (at a congressional hearing) addressed the issues which suggest a reciprocal relationship between learning disabilities and juvenile delinquency (*Congressional Record,* 1977). Understandably the public has become concerned and alarmed by the increasing frequency of disturbed adolescent behaviors and loss of adult productivity, which have been attributed to impaired learning in school-age children. It is not surprising that within this tense atmosphere a myriad of contestable claims have erupted, controversies that are magnified by an urgency to classify and "cure" the learning deficit. The family of the learning-disabled child is uniquely vulnerable. They recognize that as time passes without successful educational rehabilitation, the developing complications become ominous prognostic considerations. Unfortunately, public and professional confusion has become increasingly magnified as basic facts and issues have been clouded in a quagmire of semantics.

It is often diagnostically and therapeutically convenient for professionals to designate some issues in learning disabilities as "acceptable" and others as "controversial" (Silver, 1975). There are, however, relatively few facets of the learning-disabled child that can be viewed with a unanimity of opinion. The child in educational jeopardy is in part a controversial subject because of the numerous vagueries that constitute the learning-disabled prototype. The text to follow will reflect on some of the controversial topics, recognizing that a comprehensive and in-depth analysis is beyond the scope of the discussion. The intent of the presentation is *not* to "choose sides" but hopefully to stimulate curiosity and concern about various controversial issues as they relate to the learning-disabled child.

THE LEARNING-DISABLED CHILD: A TYPICAL PROFILE?

One of the major dilemmas to be resolved originates from delegating "syndrome" status to the child with a learning impairment. Although each child must be considered on an individual basis, certain characteristics common to the learning-disabled child have been identified. The child often presents a relatively uneventful preschool history, by parental and professional observations. Occasionally, when parents suspect subtle delays in the child's maturational timetable, the apprehensions may be suppressed or completely disregarded. The child is usually enrolled in the first grade with no preconceived suspicions of impending educational disaster. Parents are "shocked" when first advised that their child is experiencing difficulty in school. The disruption of projected parental aspirations for their child often fosters initial reactions of disbelief and hostility, followed by inappropriate feelings of guilt, anxiety, and frustration (Todd & Gottlieb, 1976). The child, in turn, may be unwittingly penalized by well-meaning parents who attempt to bolster the faltering educational experience by unrealistic tutorial supports, deprivation of privileges, threats, bribes and punishments. Frustrations are augmented as pressures from parents and teachers prove ineffectual in enhancing the child's educational progress. The child's academic performance is often further suppressed by a variety of superimposed psychological stresses. The seeds of this vicious *learning-disability cycle* are germinated and nurtured in an atmosphere of emotional pressures, misconceptions, confusions, and controversies.

As a rule, parental orientations for the child, during the preschool period, tend to encourage the formation of a positive attitude about school and teachers. The child usually approaches the academic experience with only minor anxieties, apprehensions which are short-lived. Eventually, for most children, the educational process becomes a pleasant and stimulating experience. For the child with a learning disability, however, academic life is much less enjoyable and exciting. Initially, the child may be an integral part of the social and educational milieu. As problems surface and impaired learning skills become more obvious, the learning-disabled child tends to drift away from "traditional" school routines and normal peer interactions. The affected child may exhibit numerous acting-out behaviors as a psychological defense mechanism. These disturbing behaviors serve to compound the child's academic difficulties. The learning-disabled child is soon perceived as being "different" because of poor academic progress, disruptive behaviors and the necessity for special attention from the teacher, guidance counselor, or resource personnel. Classmates become increasingly annoyed with the learning-disabled child, and normal peer relationships are seriously endangered. The degree of negative (and often antagonistic) attitudes of teachers and classmates are often fashioned by the severity of the child's aberrant behavioral patterns. A self-defeating cycle is rapidly established: the child experiences learning problems, the school and home environments become increasingly tense and pressured, frustrations and anxieties are exaggerated, acting-out aggressive and disruptive behaviors become more pronounced, which, in turn, suppresses the child's abilities to learn. Relationships with classmates may alternate between "passive acceptance" and "active avoidance." The learning-disabled child is frequently isolated by peers and taunted with caustic labels: "weirdo," "retardo," and "bad boy," cruelties that are verbalized openly with increasing frequency.

As the educational environment becomes more oppressive and threatening, the child may experience a myriad of uncomfortable feelings: anxiety, rejection, depression, inadequacy, confusion, and hostility. Self-confidence and self-concept may deteriorate precipitously. The learning-disabled child is often discouraged and fearful, attitudes are defensive and negativistic, and motivation may be lost. Acting-out behaviors such as hyperactivity, disrupting maneuvers, and daydreaming, in order to divert the focus from educational performance and to attract attention, and unconsciously reinforced by the family, teachers, and classmates. The child's disturbed behavior and impaired learning usually generates a state of perpetual anxiety for the entire family constellation. Poorly planned and inconsistent modifications at home and at school contribute significantly to increasing the pressures on an already confused child.

The child with adequate intelligence but learning deficits, behavioral problems, and subtle deviations of the central nervous system is often classified as having "minimal brain dysfunction" (MBD) (Clements, 1973; Haller & Axelrod, 1975; Paine, 1968). The classical clinical picture of MBD is usually envisioned as a complex of manifestations including average intelligence, hyperactivity, short attention span, distractibility, impulsivity, emotional lability, perceptual disorders, speech and language deficits, and disorders of memory and concept formation. Millichap (1977) estimated that approximately 4 percent of children under 12 years of age are hyperactive and manifest behaviors considered to be signs of MBD. Rie (1975), however, noted that definitions of hyperactivity are not only variable, but also lack a base of normative values, provide inadequate tools for measurement, and reflect the influences of subjective impressions.

Of singular importance for physicians is the reference to "soft" or "subtle" neurological signs that are believed to be associated with MBD, (see Table 9–1). Controversy concerning the significance of "equivocal" neurological findings is reflected in the scientific literature (Adams, Kocsis, & Estes, 1974; Hart, Rennick, Klinge, & Schwartz, 1974; Millichap, 1977). McMahon and Greenberg (1977) noted that no single definition of soft neurological signs has received universal acceptance. Their observations raise doubts regarding the value of soft signs as diagnostic and prognostic measurements of hyperactive children. There are no hard evidences to support the belief that drugs improve soft neurological signs. Basic neurodynamic mechanisms have not been clearly elucidated and diverse etiological origins have been postulated (Millichap & Johnson 1974). Grossman (1978) notes that the soft neurological signs focus on neurological findings that are considered to be normal for very young children but imply a dysfunction if found in an older child. He suggests that the concepts of "soft signs" is ambiguous and does not have any well-defined association with specific central nervous system abnormalities. He recommended that the neurologic examination concern itself with the total child, emphasizing behavior. Grossman further stresses the need for evaluation of eye movements, facial apraxia, eye-head coordination, choreiform movements, double simultaneous stimulation testing, finger-to-nose and heel-to-knee tests, rapidly alternating movements, synkinesis, finger agnosia, and right-left orientation. He points out that the evidences from neurologic assessment do not correlate spe-

Table 9-1. "Soft" Neurological Signs
Often Assigned to Minimal Brain
Dysfunction.

Articulation defects
Asymmetry of deep tendon reflexes
Babinski responses
Confused laterality
Crossed cerebral dominance
Dysdiadochokinesia
Dysgraphia
Dyspraxia
Excessive synkinesis
General awkwardness or clumsiness
Graphesthesia
Hyperreflexia
Inability to perform tandem gait
Incoordination and tremors
Poor coordination of fingers
Transient strabismus

cifically with any behavioral manifestations. Similarly, he emphasizes that there is a poor correlation between electroencephalographic changes and learning and behavioral disorders. Grossman concisely indicates that "the neurologic and electroencephalographic findings do not specifically relate to educational or behavioral diagnosis or remediation and are not substitute for adequate psychosocial and educational assessment and intervention" (p. 66). Schmitt (1975) proposes that the obviously confused and conflicting evidences suggest that MBD is a medically constructed myth.

Although certain characteristics appear to dominate the profile of the more severely learning-disabled child, the "syndrome status" remains controversial. The spectrum of biological characters associated with learning disabilities is extremely diverse and none of the features are pathognomonic. The child in educational jeopardy is extremely difficult to characterize, inasmuch as there appears to be nothing "typical" about the complex of neurological, educational, or psychological manifestations. A wide range of biological uniqueness, differences in family psychodynamics, personality factors, attitudinal biases of teachers and parents, differing etiologies, and variations in the severity of the learning disorders *all* discourage the formulation of a "learning disability syndrome." The myriad of descriptive characteristics and attributes related to the learning-disabled child strongly imply a heterogeneous group of disorders with a broad spectrum of signs and symptoms, (see Table 9–2). Although a few universal features can be recognized, the general manifestations of learning disorders are protean. Unlike the child with more clearly defined disorders, such as leukemia, chickenpox or Down's syndrome, the learning-disabled child is a much more complex amalgamation of vaguely defined biological, social, emotional, and educational components. It is not surprising that controversial diagnostic and therapeutic claims have blossomed in this fertile medium of confused identities.

Table 9-2. Neurological, Behavioral, and Educational Characteristics Assigned to Learning-disabled Children: A Partial List.

Aggressive behavior	Disinhibition
Hyperactivity	Perseveration
Hypoactivity	Fidgety
Daydreamer	Antisocial
Short attention span	Awkwardness
Impulsiveness	Poor motivation
Incoordination	Negative attitude
Perceptual impairments	Disruptive
Speech problems	Inconsistent
Language problems	Erratic performance
Dyslexia	Passive, shy, withdrawn
Dysgraphia	Depressed
Dyscalculia	Anxious
Hyperdistractibility	Lack of self-confidence
Clumsiness	Poor self-concept
Labile emotions	Hostile
Left-right confusion	Driven
Synkinesis	Moody
Reflex asymmetry	Acting-out behaviors
Academic deficiencies	
Low frustration threshold	

DIAGNOSTIC CONTROVERSIES

Definitions, Incidence, and Etiology

There is seldom any consistency in reporting the incidence of learning disabilities in school-age children due in part to the difficulty in formulating an acceptable *definition* of "learning disabilities." Lerner (1976) reviewed a variety of definitions which reflect concepts of neurological dysfunction, maturational lags, uneven growth patterns, specific educational deficits, discrepancy between achievement and potential, as well as legal formulations. The learning-disabled child has been variously categorized as (1) exhibiting organic brain damage, which interferes with the learning process, (2) having an irregular maturation of mental abilities, which causes a developmental imbalance, (3) exhibiting specific deficits in speech, reading, spelling, or arithmetic from specific cerebral dysfunctions and/or behavioral disturbances, (4) reflecting a discrepancy between potentials for learning and actual level of learning, and others. The definition as stated in the Special Education for All Handicapped Children Act of 1975 (Public Law 94–142) proposed the following:

> Children with specific learning disabilities exhibit a disorder in one or more of the basic psychological processes involved in understanding or using spoken or written languages. These may be manifested in disorders of listening, thinking, talking, reading, writing, spelling or arithmetic. They include conditions which have been referred to as perceptual handicaps, brain injury, minimal brain dysfunction, dyslexia, developmental aphasia, etc. They do not include learning problems which are due primarily to visual, hearing, or motor handicaps, to mental retardation, emotional disturbances, or to environmental disadvantages.

Gearheart (1977) commented on the confusion in semantics that clouds the identity of learning disabilities. He noted that the federal definitions proposed in 1968 were criticized and modified by 1976. The changes culminated in Public Law 94-142. Gearheart further stated, "A national effort to find a more acceptable definition continues and may well reach some conclusion by the time [his] text is published. The one fact which seems most predictable is that whatever is decided will be under attack in a very few years" (p. 15).

A dilemma in terminology exists in that precise descriptions of learning disability are often too constricting, whereas nonspecific definitions tend to encompass the overwhelming majority of school-age children.

The *etiology* of learning disabilities is similarly an ill-defined area in our fund of basic knowledge. Learning disabilities have been attributed to a variety of prenatal, perinatal, and postnatal insults that produce varying degrees of central nervous system damage (Knobloch, Rider, Harper, & Pasaminck, 1956; Pasamanick & Knobloch, 1973; Strauss & Lehtinen, 1947). Advocates of the "brain-injured" hypothesis often rely on retrospective analyses that link nervous system injuries with impaired learning skills (Sell, Webb, & Pate, 1972, Wiener, Rider, Oppell, et al., 1965). Geschwind (1976) suggested that all learning involves the brain, requiring an integration of multiple areas and functions. Different areas of the brain are associated with different kinds of learning. Successful learning involves attention, processing ability, imprinting, and retrieval. Failures in any of these areas, either due to anatomical variations or disease processes, can impair learning. Mykelbust (1973) proposed that children with neurogenic learning disabilities exhibit a failure in the capacity to convert one type of neurosensory information into another.

It has been conjectured that a specific learning disability may be the result of an injury (biological, physical, or chemical) to a particular neurological locus. Stores and Hart (1976) reported, however, that recurrent bursts of generalized seizure discharge, including subclinical seizure discharge, were *not* associated with impaired attention, learning disorders, or reading difficulties. On the other hand, focal spike discharges, particularly if there is a localization in the hemisphere dominant for speech, appeared to create a greater risk for reading problems. Millichap (1977, pp. 7–8) reported the frequency of abnormal EEGs in 100 consecutive patients with minimal brain dysfunction shown in Table 9–3.

The concept which etiologically relates brain injury to a specific learning disability has *not* gained wide acceptance. Arguments and counterarguments have been presented debating whether or not brain injury or minimal brain dysfunction is actually the basis for impaired learning. Controversies concerning the origins of learning disorders are perpetuated because of (1) a lack of specific neuropathological findings in postmortem specimens, (2) a failure to demonstrate pathognomonic neurological signs, (3) the debatable diagnostic value of soft or equivocal neurological signs, (4) the inabil-

Table 9-3. Frequency of Abnormal EEGs in 100 Consecutive Patients with Minimal Brain Dysfunction (MBD).

Grade 1 dysrhythmias	62%
Minimal irregularities (slow-wave transients and excess theta activity)	
Occipital regions (areas that govern visual processing and eye–hand coordination)	
Grade 2 dysrhythmias	19%
Moderate irregularities	
Indicates abnormal susceptibility to seizures or increased neuronal excitability	
Grade 3 dysrhythmias	7%
Severe irregularities, generalized or focal	
Abnormality in temporal area may be associated with auditory processing disorders	
Normal	12%

Adapted from Millichap, J. G. (Ed.). *Learning disabilities and related disorders: Facts and current issues.* (Chicago: Year Book Medical Publishers, Inc., 1977).

ity to define characteristic electroencephalographic changes, (5) the alleged high incidence of brain damage, (6) the preponderant male sex predilection, and (7) the absence of learning disabilities among many children known to have major brain damage, as for example, those suffering from epilepsy and cerebral palsy (Hart et al., 1974; Minde, Webb, & Sykes, 1968; Schmitt, 1976; Wender & Wender, 1976). Attempts to organize an etiological classification system of learning disorders, utilizing a neurological basis as the sole criteria, have been unsuccessful. Walzer and Richmond (1973) proposed that the epidemiology of learning disorders is more "global" than a single origin in central nervous system dysfunction. The "learning disabilities" represent a heterogeneous group of disorders and no single etiological origin can be incriminated.

Controversy concerning the etiology of learning disabilities is further complicated by the changing nature of education. The educational system per se, has been criticized as a cause of impaired learning, recognizing that learning difficulty may result from a "teacher's disability," "rigid educational environments," and "academically accelerated programs" rather than from inherent weaknesses of the child. Larsen (1975) demonstrated that children, especially girls, may benefit from increased teacher support in learning a motor skill, but, apparently, children gain from learning experiences in the cognitive area without increased teacher support. Children who formerly were capable of being promoted are now being singled out as educationally deficient. Silver (1975) noted that "academic demands for the first six years of school have increased. These increasing demands on grade-school children have created difficulties for some. Children who a generation ago might have been promoted grade by grade through school by showing up every day and behaving were now doing poorly or failing" (p. 406). Perhaps the "educational shift," reflecting changes in perspectives and academic demands, may be as significant a cause of impaired learning as that generated by neurological damage.

Documentation and interpretation of the *incidence* of learning disorders is another controversial issue. The reported occurrence rate varies considerably as a result of the biases of definition, a particular school system's interest in learning disabilities, and the variability of reporting mechanisms. The prevalence of learning and reading disabilities among all school-age children has been variously reported from 1 to 40 percent (Goldberg & Schiffman, 1972; Walzer & Richmond, 1973). Dodge (1976) surveyed a select population of children followed at the Developmental Disabilities Unit of St. Louis Children's Hospital and demonstrated the relatively common occurrence of learning disorders within a group of 3,495 patients (see Table 9–4).

Table 9-4. The Occurrence of Learning Disorders in a Developmental Disabilities Unit.

Disorder	% of Group
Mental retardation	14
Mental retardation + epilepsy	14
Mental retardation + cerebral palsy	9
Mental retardation + cerebral palsy + epilepsy	3
Epilepsy	36
Epilepsy + cerebral palsy	1
Cerebral palsy	4
Learning disorders	18

Adapted from Dodge, P. F. Neurological disorders of school-age children. *Journal of School Health,* 1976, *46,* 338–343.

The criteria utilized for defining "learning disorders" are extremely critical variables that can profoundly influence the reported incidence of the disorder. Gaddes (1975) has noted that epidemiological surveys are particularly valuable for some physical and behavioral syndromes (e.g., congenital malformations, epilepsy, suicide) because of their "all-or-none" nature. These disorders, unlike learning disabilities, have discrete parameters for identification and "hence may be relatively easily isolated, observed and counted." He further commented that etiological studies of academic underachievers suggested three causal areas: constitutional, psychological, and social. Gaddes noted that most abnormal psychological and behavioral disorders lack defined criteria for diagnostic classification, and he stated that, "At present, the learning-disabled child is diagnostically almost faceless, until his symptoms are so extreme or his abilities to learn so refractory that there is a general and immediate agreement on his condition" (p. 6). Cruickshank (1977) reaffirmed this view, noting that the true incidence of learning disabilities is unknown because there are *no* adequate epidemiological or demographical data.

Labeling

Classifying and labeling are traditional scientific exercises, necessary for the precise conceptualization of data. Attempts to categorize the learning-disabled child have been difficult. Part of the confusion is related to the particular labels assigned, designations which are often used synonymously, e.g., learning-disabled, clumsy-child syndrome, perceptual problem child, hyperactive behavior disorders, dyslexia, minimal brain dysfunction, and many others. Schain (1977) noted that although the terminology is used interchangeably from a clinical point of view, the terms are *not* so from a theoretical point of view. Labels can either assist learning-disabled children or serve inappropriately to stereotype their potentials. In some instances the needs of the child are ignored while the "label" is glorified. Children may be denied special services until the "proper label" has been determined and assigned. At times, efforts to locate or construct the diagnostic categorization becomes the major professional challenge rather than developing more effective methods of therapeutic intervention. Far too often, completion of a classification designation may be the end point for professional concern and intervention. Realistically, however, this should represent the beginning of professional involvement. Unfortunately there is a popular misconception that the label automatically insures avenues of remediation and rehabilitation.

Labels are often liberally (and erroneously) assigned, but modifying or removing stigmatizing classifications may be a painstaking endeavor.

A commentary from the president of the American Academy of Pediatrics (Low, 1976) reflects on "labeling":

> [Where once] adolescent sluggishness, indolence and moderate obesity "required" a metabolism test and then thyroid or pituitary medication. . . . the areas of concern [now] are more for tranquilizers or "hyperactivity" medication. Labeling has become fashionable at the same time that schools are asked both to avoid it and, in the next breath, to list the numbers and percentages in different categories. (p. 8)

It cannot be denied that a meaningful classification of the child is of critical importance when designing educational remediation programs and for funding purposes. On the other hand, labels are a sensitive controversial professional issue because they may (1) prematurely terminate additional investigations, (2) focus on only one isolated area of a multifaceted problem, (3) represent an incomplete diagnosis, (4) provide no clues for remediation, (5) mean different things to different specialists, (6) brand the child as being defective, and (7) be erroneously regarded as irreversible. Confusion in organizing a specific terminology is readily apparent. The myriad of available nomenclatures used to categorize the learning-disabled child attest to this semantic chaos, (see Table 9–5). Unfortunately, the label, per se, reveals very little about the strengths or weaknesses of the child, limits the scope of the total problem, and may not provide direction for the therapeutic approach.

Probably no single label has generated as much controversy as the term "dyslexia." White, Dwyer, and Lintz (1973) pointed out that dyslexia is probably *not* a meaningful categorization if used for remediation, but it is of value for labeling a specific syndrome. Dyslexia has been used liberally and interchangeably (thereby creating much confusion) with minimal brain dysfunction, perceptual handicap, word blindness, strephosymbolia, congenital aphasia, and hyperkinetic syndrome, to name only a few.

Controversies in terminology and classification may be the resultant manifestation of professional communication gaps which often characterize ineffectual multidisciplinary interactions. Confusions tend to proliferate as a consequence of multiple classifications, overlapping designations, and vague labels. However, the necessity for "proper" labeling cannot be underestimated. Public Law 94–142 mandates free public education for all children requiring special ser-

Table 9-5. Nomenclature of Learning Disabilities: A Partial Listing.

Attention disorder	Minimal brain damage
Auditory perceptual handicap	Minimal brain dysfunction
Brain-damaged child	Minimal cerebral dysfunction
Brain-injured child	Minimal cerebral palsy
Cerebral dysfunction	Neurophrenia
Chronic brain syndrome	Neurological handicap
Clumsy-child syndrome	Organic behavior disorder
Conceptually handicapped	Organic brain damage
Congenital word blindness	Organic brain disease
Developmental dyslexia	Organic driveness
Developmental imbalance	Perceptual cripple
Disorders of concept formation	Perceptual handicap
Disorders of motor coordination	Perseverative
Distractibility	Psychoneurological learning disorder
Dyslexia	Shadow children
Gerstman syndrome	Specific dyslexia
Hyperactive child	Specific learning disability
Hyperkinetic behavior disorder	Strauss syndrome
Hyperkinetic child	Strephosymbolia
Hypokinetic syndrome	Subtle brain damage
Learning disability	Visual motor perceptual lag
Maturational lag	Specific reading disability

vices, but justifiably calls for definitions and labeling in order to determine eligibility for special education. Warren (1978) cautions that the dilemma may cause an "overidentification of children as having learning problems." She further emphasizes this issue by stating that the controversy in part stems from efforts to decrease the practice of classifying (and possibly stigmatizing) children, on the one hand, with the recognition that labels may buy services, on the other. "However, it seems to be becoming a practice to find a child to be learning disabled, by whatever name the state requires, if that student does not fit well into what may be an educational Procrustean bed of curriculum" (Warren, 1978, p. 26).

Professional 'Perceptual' Problems

An obvious diagnostic dilemma can result when there is a professionally biased approach to the learning-disabled child. The client may be inadvertently stereotyped by professional "tunnel vision," that is, diagnostic impressions and therapy plans that reflect only the priorities of the particular discipline involved. The speech pathologist, psychologist, physician, and special educator may each focus on the child through the lenses of their own relatively limited area of skills. Subsequently, diagnostic labels are assigned, and therapy programs constructed, based on the observations and interpretations of the one particular examining professional.

As a rule, however, the child with problems in learning represents multiple areas of strengths and weaknesses. Assessment of a learning disability demands a comprehensive and coordinated multidisciplinary intervention in order to assure an appreciation for the totality of the problem (Boder, 1966). In as much as academically underachieving children usually represent an amalgamation of several learning deficits and behavioral factors, the resolution of the differential diagnosis necessitates multiple fields of expertise. Thompson and Gottlieb (1973) suggested that ensuing professional controversy may occur when (1) selecting the representatives to constitute the interdisciplinary team, (2) integrating professional findings and assigning their priorities, (3) establishing lines of responsibility for coordination of diagnostic and therapeutic recommendations, and (4) determining channels of communication and lines of responsibility between professionals and the family.

Undoubtedly, there is an element of chauvinism, wherein each profession generally regards its contribution as having "top priority." When conceptualizing a holistic profile of the client, however, a lesser value may be assigned to a particular professional observation. If the diagnostic and therapeutic atmosphere is charged with insecurity and rigidity, the intervention may be less than meaningful. Ineffective multidisciplinary interaction generates professional friction, controversy, and confusion that ultimately hinders understanding and assisting children with disorders of learning.

A Role for Physicians?

At first glance, questioning the role for physicians would appear to be rhetorical in nature. However, secreted within the recesses of the letters and words is a possible suggestion that physicians need *not* be involved with the learning-disabled child. Many professionals, including physicians, have indeed questioned the role of the doctor of medicine in this area of pediatric concern.

Historically, physicians were among the research pioneers investigating disorders of learning. The contributions of outstanding physicians such as Kussmaul, Hinshelwood, Morgan, Orton, and others, are legend (Goldberg & Schiffman, 1972). Medical interest in the learning-disabled child, however, has been relatively sporadic since these pioneer efforts. Recently, physicians have demonstrated a renewed concern for children in educational jeopardy. During the past decade many physicians have become active participants in the interdisciplinary team, their professional interest enhanced by a variety of facts:

1. Physicians are the first professionals to have contact with children, thereby defining a responsibility in the early detection of learning disabilities among preschool children.
2. Physicians are usually the first to be consulted regarding academically underachieving children and must meaningfully counsel anxious parents and teachers.
3. Physicians offer a unique area of expertise necessary to successfully resolve the differential diagnosis of academic underachievement, as well as defining and treating underlying organic and emotional deficits.
4. Physicians offer special skills in appreciating, clarifying, and assessing the neurological basis of learning problems.
5. Physicians have a unique responsibility in the decision to prescribe medications, often used as an adjunct in assisting learning-disabled children.
6. Physicians are frequently called upon to coordinate the efforts of an interdisciplinary team, to provide monitoring and follow-up services.
7. Physicians are often asked to determine what is fact, fad, or fiction.

The American Academy of Pediatrics in two issues of *Statement* (1973a, b) reaffirmed the need for early medical intervention in learning disabilities. Expanded roles for physicians in detecting and assisting children in educational jeopardy have been periodically advocated (de la Cruz & La Veck, 1965; Gofman, 1966; Thompson & Gottlieb, 1973). Proponents for medical involvement stress at least three major functions of the physician in dealing with the complex problems of learning-disabled children: (1) assisting in the clarification of the differential diagnosis, (2) parent counseling, and (3) administration and monitoring of medications (Schain 1977).

Arguments undermining medical participation and attacking the so-called "medical model" have included the following: (1) Physicians are usually poorly trained (didactically and clinically) in learning disabilities; (2) physicians are "busy people" and learning disorders are time-consuming problems; (3) physicians may not be knowledgeable about contributions of members of the interdisciplinary team; and (4) physicians cannot (and should not) design educational programs.

Cruickshank (1977) stated that the problem of perceptual processing in children, which leads to specific learning disabilities, is a psychoeducational responsibility and *not* a medical problem. He emphasized that the physician is ill-prepared, by virtue of training, to assume the responsibility for organizing an educational plan for learning-disabled children. Cruickshank allows for some medical involvement in the interdisciplinary "attack" on the problem but stresses a limited intervention. Cruickshank suggests that the problem is basically the concern for educators and psychologists "who are skilled and experienced with the problem" (p. 56).

Philosophically, the basis for a professional controversy is readily apparent. Most will agree with Cruickshank's proposal that the educator "in the long run must be the implementer" (p. 56). The effectiveness of "implementers" (who are often less qualified than pediatricians and neurologists), be they educators, psychologists, or other professionals, are essentially dependent upon the combined skills and contributions of interdisciplinary interactions, *including input by physicians.* For children in whom a learning disability is etiologically couched in neurological delays, dysfunctions and disturbances, the diagnostic and therapeutic expertise of pediatricians and neurologists is mandated.

The medical model has been categorically criticized by some professionals who may possibly have a limited experience with the physician's potentials and contributions. An anxiety state, sometimes bordering on panic, is festered by the fear that the physician will prescribe the educational plan! Although this is *not* the intent of the physician, an educational prescription may indeed require the credibility of prior medical intervention, as well as some meaningful medical ingredients. Comprehensive professional interaction is essential for designing a well constructed rehabilitation program for the learning-disabled child. The physician can contribute significantly to the diagnostic process by providing a detailed history, physical and neurological examinations, developmental inventories, evaluation of hearing, speech, and language, assessment of perceptual skills, and behavioral observations (Bax, 1976; Gottlieb 1975). The comprehensive resolution of the differential diagnosis of impaired learning (and minimal brain dysfunction) frequently requires the expertise of medically oriented personnel. Included in the complex medical differential diagnosis of learning disabilities are children exhibiting autistic behaviors, depressive reactions, juvenile schizophrenia, absence seizures, psychomotor seizures, spinal cord lesions, sensory losses (depressed visual acuity and auditory sensitivity), mental retardation, cerebral palsy, tics, and habit spasms, to mention only a few. Failure by nonmedical professionals to recognize underlying organic or functional impairments may seriously undermine the effectiveness of the most expertly designed educational program. A classical example is the child with chronic otitis media (one of the more common problems in pediatrics) who may be learning impaired as a result of middle-ear pathology possibly causing auditory processing disturbances, and learning disabilities (Katz 1978; Zinkus, Gottlieb, & Schapiro, 1978). Physicians often initiate the interdisciplinary diagnostic team evaluation and frequently serve as the team coordinator in this effort (Boder, 1976). Needless to say, the quality of an individual physician's intervention is based on his competence, degree of commitment, interest, concerns, background experiences, and levels of specific expertise. These basic requirements apply to *all* professionals regardless of their area of interest and training.

Bryan (1978) strikes at the heart of the controversy, noting that in efforts to profile and classify learning-disabled children two philosophies have emerged: the *conceptual* and the *practical* emphasis. The medically oriented approach (the "medical model") suggests that the child with intelligence in the average range but who has learning difficulties is manifesting evidences of a neurological dysfunction. The disturbance in the central nervous system processing mechanism is the etiological basis for impaired learning skills. The areas of the nervous system involved are generally believed to be the left cerebral hemisphere and the reticular activating system. On the other hand, the "educational model" focuses primarily on the child's academic strengths and weaknesses and attempts to define specific academic needs. The emphasis centers on the specific educational problems of the learning-disabled child, stressing needs in oral and written communication, reading-spelling-mathematic skills, and discrepancies between intelligence and achievement.

The controversy regarding the role of the physician in learning disabilities must be resolved with dignity. A relatively uncomplicated approach is recommended: (1) graciously accept the contributions to be made by knowledgeable professionals, including physicians, (2) encourage the training of medical students by including learning disabilities in their didactic and clinical curricula, (3) enhance the interdisciplinary concept by embracing medicine rather than rejecting it, and (4) abandon professional chauvinism, remembering that learning disabilities is a complex problem requiring input from multiple areas of expertise.

THERAPEUTIC CONTROVERSIES

Although technological advances during the past half century have surpassed the most speculative of imaginations, programs and funds for educating children have not appeared to maintain an equal pace. Literacy still remains a national concern; illiteracy is a national crisis. Particular difficulties exist in the provision of educational experiences for the learning-disabled child and "exceptional" children. Many of the educational methods currently in use are *not* universally accepted, some are controversial, and others have little or no value.

Special Education

It is generally accepted that the major method of active intervention for learning-disabled children is a meaningful, "tailor-made," special-education program. Ideally, a well-constructed educational curriculum will be designed, administered, and monitored by professionals trained in special-education techniques. A meaningful comprehensive rehabilitation program, however, utilizes data obtained from an interdisciplinary diagnostic evaluation. Currently, controversy prevails in "education circles" concerning the type of program most profitable for the learning-disabled child, the issue of *mainstreaming vs. self-contained classroom* to serve the child in need of special attention.

For several decades the prescribed setting for the learning-disabled child has been the self-contained special-education classroom. In this educational environment children with similar problems in learning, usually close in age, are assembled together for instruction and remediation with a special educator. Self-contained classrooms were utilized as "educational pressure valves," relieving the general educator of the burden of behaviorally disturbed and severely learning-disabled children. The format is based on an assumption that children with similar difficulties can be more effectively educated in small groups, and thereby provided opportunities for specialized instructions as well as greater chances for success experiences. Recently, controversy has been rekindled regarding this educational approach. The self-contained special classroom has been increasingly criticized because it educationally and socially isolates the child. Opponents stress that the program labels and stigmatizes the child. In the wake of public and professional criticism there has been a rejuvenation of the mainstreaming concept for the developmentally disabled child: "Central to the mainstreaming movement is the theme that given the desire, facilities, and reasonable professional preparation, the average teacher can learn to educate exceptional youngsters in the regular classroom with the support and consultative services of special-education personnel" (Birch, 1974, cited in Lerner, 1976, p. 36). Advocates of mainstreaming suggest that children with special needs are best served by being integrated into regular educational settings, thereby encouraging "broad peer relationships and the concept of self as normal" (Ensher 1976). Tempering the philosophical and emotional aspects of this educational controversy are the legal issues involved.

The philosophical reasons for mainstreaming appear at times to be outweighed by more realistic issues, such as the inordinate demands placed on general educators. Hensley (1972) noted that the special-class concept "was in trouble from the beginning", a program doomed for failure at its inception because of the rapidly expanding school population and simultaneous increase in identifiable "exceptional" children. It could have been predicted that an available manpower source and physical facility growth would not be available to accommodate the children identified. Reflecting on the dichotomy between special education and general education, Hensley suggested that special education has reached the saturation point and commented, on special classes: "Worst of all, there is the haunting idea that there may be better ways of teaching and caring for children, particularly when one considers that the majority of handicapped children are now, have always been, and will continue to be found in regular elementary and secondary classes taught by regular classroom teachers" (p. 49). He argued that most handicapped children can be best educated in regular classrooms, "providing their teachers have the necessary skills and appropriate attitudes."

The controversy is fired by advocates of self-contained classrooms who tend to regard mainstreaming as an educational fad that will eventually be abandoned (Winschel 1976). Cruickshank (1977) stated:

> Unless general elementary educators understand the nature and needs of the problems of processing deficits and know how to adapt the learning situation and teaching materials to the child's needs, the potential for continued failure on the part of the child is present. (p. 58)

Many professionals, including educators, express confusions over these controversial issues: Does mainstreaming in reality represent a financial maneuver to avoid the high cost of self-contained special-education classrooms? Does mainstreaming perpetuate and enhance the social complications of disturbed peer relationships? Does mainstreaming really remove the yoke of being "different," or does it exaggerate it? Does mainstreaming invoke the unfair penalty of forced educational competition for those who cannot compete? Does mainstreaming tax the teaching capacities of general educators and compromise their function?

The dilemma of mainstreaming is a compilation of social, economic, educational, and legal issues. Sarason and Doris (1977) have capsulized the problem by stressing that mainstreaming is a moral issue. They raise the question of "How far does the majority want to go in accommodating to the needs of the minority? The emergence of mainstreaming as an issue raises but does not directly confront these questions" (p. 24).

Resource classrooms have been recommended as a compromise, functioning as a buffer between mainstreaming and the self-contained classroom. For varying periods during the day the resource teacher assists the child with impaired learning as well as provides guidance for the child's regular classroom teacher. Cogent arguments have been offered criticizing and defending the existing types of special-education programs. Unfortunately, these empirical arguments persist because of a lack of data from scientifically controlled studies designed to compare the educational values of various programs.

Educational teaching methods that stress perceptual training as *the* most effective remedial approach for the learning-disabled child have similarly stimulated professional dispute. It has been hypothesized that visual perceptual exercises enhance a child's development in the areas of language, sensory-motor function, higher thought processes, integrative abilities as well as social and emotional growth (Frostig 1972). The concept has been questioned. Those who do not adhere to this approach ask questions such as: Is there really a need to teach visual and/or auditory processing skills per se? Would the child benefit more from the one-to-one relationship which stresses academic rather than perceptual tutoring? Does perceptual training directly or indirectly improve academic skills? Scientific studies do not clearly delineate that current programs of visual perceptual training have a positive effect on either reading or visual perception (Hammill, 1974; Mann, 1972; Sullivan, 1972). Hard facts are unavailable; as a result, controversy flourishes.

Finally, a few words about "educational gimmicks" (more elaborate discussion would lend credibility to this issue). Professionals must maintain an awareness of obviously fraudulent "quick cures," masqueraded as learning aids and reading devices. In this instance controversy should be replaced with caution; many of these useless items are sold under the disguise that it will "help the child learn" (Issues, 1973).

Controversies encountered over educational methods of rehabilitation are not unexpected. Differences of opinion and resulting debate are anticipated because of the broad scope of educational disorders and variations in suggested therapies. Controversy has been perpetuated because of several factors: (1) too few scientifically designed studies to test the hypothesis or claim, (2) too much emphasis and reliance on empirical claims, (3) too little input from multidisciplinary teams, and (4) too much professional chauvinism. Discordant claims about the learning-disabled child, however, are much more pervasive, extending beyond classrooms and involving the use of medications, special diets, neurological organization, and others. Once again, the spectrum of apparent confusions gives testimony to the complexity and the magnitude of the problem of the child in educational jeopardy.

Psychostimulant Medications

The use of psychostimulant drugs in treating the learning-disabled child is (or should be) a major medical concern. Controversy stems from a paucity of fundamental neurological data concerning the pharmacodynamics of psychotropic medications. In addition, there are inadequate objective measures for assessing the effectiveness of these medications. Since reliable tests to determine drug efficacy are unavailable, there is confusion as to proper methods of administration and dosage. Physicians responsible for prescribing and monitoring medications are eventually trapped in a web of controversial issues: What is considered a good drug response? How long should drugs be administered? Should "drug vacations" be employed? What is drug effect and what is placebo effect? (Alta Conference, 1975).

Several psychotropic drugs are regarded as "acceptable" adjuncts to treating the learning-disabled child. Millichap and Fowler (1967) reviewed the numerous medications employed in treating hyperactive, learning-disabled children, including amphetamine (Dexedrine), methylphenidate (Ritalin), chlordiazepoxide (Librium), chlorpromazine (Thorazine), and deaner (Deanol). The utilization of drugs as the *sole* mechanism for modifying behavior has caused concern among physicians, educators and psychologists (Gottlieb, 1975; Lesser, 1970). On the other hand, the judicious use of medications, as an adjunct in assisting the child in educational jeopardy, is unquestioned. Controversy, however, arises from the difficulty in interpreting the chemotherapeutic effects of medications because of (1) nonuniformity of terminology, (2) variations in methods of evaluation, (3) absence of diagnostic criteria and (4) lack of adequate follow-up controlled studies (American Academy of Pediatrics, Committee on Drugs, 1970). To this can be added the confusing results stemming from failures in client compliance. One of the major areas of debate relates to the diagnostic indications for prescribing psychotropic drugs. Well-defined criteria for the use of these medications are unavailable (American Academy of Pediatrics, Council on Child Health, 1975). Pressures to provide a "quick cure" have unfortunately given "panacea status" to the use of psychostimulant medications.

Several drug abuses and misuses are readily recognized: (1) the use of medications in leiu of special-education programs, (2) prescribing medications in the absence of comprehensive diagnostic evaluations, (3) using drugs as a "therapeutic trial" to establish a diagnosis, (4) complications of prolonged use of psychotropic drugs, (5) anticipating that drugs will cause learning, and (6) public concerns regarding drug dependency and drug abuse.

Muir (1975) stressed that complete reliance on medications to improve performances of the learning-disabled child may delay or ignore other avenues of therapy that are critical in resolving underlying psychosocial factors. The efficacy of combined therapeutic approaches, in contrast to the "simple cure" philosophy, has been suggested and needs further exploration (Yang, Risch, & Lamm, 1973). The child with learning and behavior problems is often a pawn in the struggles between parents, teachers, and physicians: "Doctor can't you give him something—the school will not keep him if his behavior doesn't improve." "Mother there is nothing wrong with your child, he's all boy and will outgrow his problem." "I have a responsibility for 25 other children and if you can't slow him down, I can't teach him." The physician must be able to answer, in good conscience, the question, "Am I prescribing the pill for the child, for his parent, or for his teacher?"

Neuropsychological Retraining

A relatively popular neuroeducational concept links defective or delayed perceptual motor development and learning abilities. Gearheart (1977), in summarizing this concept, reviewed the historical contributions of several investigators: Kephart, Getman, Barsch, Cratty and Ayers. He noted that Kephart suggested that all behavior is basically related to muscular and motor responses. Kephart's construct of a motor basis for learning, includes such key factors as posture, laterality, directionality, and body image. After developing these skills the child is capable of interacting with the environment in a meaningful way. Kephart regarded visual motor skills as the critical component for developing foundations for learning abilities. Gearheart noted that Getman, who worked with Kephart, presented a visually oriented model of the perceptual motor therapy. He stressed that visual perception can be developed through training. Getman postulated stages of sequential development, including general motor patterns, special movement patterns, eye movement patterns, visual language patterns, and visualization patterns. Gearheart reviewed the contributions of Barsch and Cratty. Barsch, another advocate of perceptual motor therapy, similarly proposes that movement is the foundation of learning, i.e., slow development of motor abilities affects development of cognitive abilities. Barsch also stressed the importance of the visual component in this relationship. Cratty offered some practical suggestions for educators in utilizing movement to improve learning capacities. Finally, Gearheart comments on Ayers' hypothesis. Ayers developed the concept of "sensory integration and its relationship to learning disorders." Presumably the stimulation of specific sensory pathways and/or activation of specific motor pathways can improve functioning of the central nervous system by retraining or recruiting neuronal integrations. Within the framework of neuropsychological retraining several controversial concepts evolved: (1) ocular training, (2) motor patterning, and (3) sensory integration.

Ocular training. It is well known that ocular problems may be associated with blurred vision, visual fatigue, and inability to read for long periods of time. Dispute, however, is engendered by theorizations that ocular deficits are the primary cause of neurological learning disabilities or reading disorders. The medical (ophthalmological) concepts in this debate have been put forth by van Noorden (1976), who noted that ocular problems themselves do not cause dyslexia. He stated that:

> The teaching of dyslexic children belongs in the realm of educational sciences, it is appropriate also to have the eyes of the dyslexic child examined in order to exclude all possible causes of visual discomfort, and to create conditions of optimal visual functioning by appropriate therapy, in the case of underlying ocular pathology. (p. 336)

Conversely, the optometric hypothesis links visual perceptual skills, sensory-motor coordination, and learning (particularly reading skills). The visuomotor complex model of Getman (1965) is a visual development and learning concept, which stresses the role of visual perception. It is postulated that visual perception is based on developmental sequences of physiological actions of the child and is learned. A variety of sensory-motor-perceptual exercises are employed as the basis for correcting learning problems. Money (1967) commented on the controversial aspects of this viewpoint, taking issue with Getman's hypothesis, and stating that this therapy was basically derived by interrelating motor, auditory, linguistic, and visual maturation. Money further noted that the hypothesis emphasized the association between visuomotor or visuopostural interrelationships. The hypothesis was, he concluded, incompletely tested and could not, therefore, be accepted without question.

The American Academy of Pediatrics, the American Academy of Ophthalmology and Otolaryngology, and the American Association of Ophthalmology issued a Joint Organizational Statement (1972) criticizing the value of eye exercises. In essence, the statement stressed that (1) learning disabilities and dyslexia require a multidisciplinary approach and eye care should never be instituted in isolation, (2) there is no peripheral eye defect which is associated with a learning disorder, (3) evidence is lacking to support improvement in learning as a result of visual training, (4) eyeglasses (other than for correctable ocular defects) have no value in treating problems of learning, and (5) learning disorders are basically the therapeutic responsibility of the educational sciences. Advocates of the multidisciplinary approach argue that an ocular evaluation performed in isolation, may not reveal all of the multifaceted problems of the learning-disabled child. Various arguments and counterarguments have been proposed in this active controversy between physicians and optometrists (Benton, 1973; Flax, 1973). As is the case with most controversial issues, resolution will rest in results to be obtained from experiments designed by principles of the scientific method.

Patterning. The "patterning" theory of neurological organization, the Doman-Delacato method utilized at the Institutes for the Achievement of Human Potential (Philadelphia) has generated active scientific debate among professionals. The theory developed by Delacato, in part, is based on the principal that ontogeny recapitulates phylogeny, recognizing that a human being during embryonic and fetal development proceeds through the evolutionary stages, patterned after the phylogenetic template of the species. It is hypothesized that the development of the human neurological system is a recapitulation of phylogenetic development. Final cortical hemispheric dominance cannot be achieved until all stages of phylogenetic development have been successfully completed; stressing that children must achieve full development at *each* level without skipping or partially completing any level. Cortical hemispheric dominance is the end product of a continuum of neurological organization, i.e., functions such as reading and language disorders represent incomplete or inadequate neurological organizations.

The theory further proposes that since language and reading disorders are faults in neurological organization, treatment must be designed to give the child an opportunity to finalize or complete neurological organization. For example, if a child were identified to be deficient at a spinal cord and medulla level, exercises would be provided that simulate primitive movements associated with these levels of development. A planned program of movements, either active or passive, would be expected to stimulate the brain centers that are functioning inefficiently. The program would take into consideration, for therapeutic intervention, a variety of mobility skills, sleep positions, visual pursuits, feeding procedures, creeping and crawling (cited from Gearheart, 1977, pp. 68–75).

In essence, it is stressed that the development of the brain is the result of the interaction of the organism with its environment. Increased interaction produces increased development, and decreased interaction results in decreased development. This interaction, which is a prerequisite to development, is a requirement for learning (Le Winn et al., 1966). The concept involves the role of hemispheric dominance and the relation of individual sequential development or phylogenesis whereby a failure to pass sequentially through developmental stages may indicate brain damage or poor neurological organization. Mental retardation, behavior problems, and learning disabilities are attributed to poor neurological organization. The recommended therapy program would include a combination of passive movements, sensory stimulation, rebreathing expired air, and dietary restrictions of fluid, salt and sugar.

Sparrow and Zigler (1978) note that a variety of problems have been the focus of patterning treatment: reading disability, hyperactivity, mental retardation, and cerebral palsy, among others. The authors point out that a variety of motor and sensory experiences (e.g., visual and auditory competence, mobility, language) are directed toward the facilitation of "neurological organization," and that the assumption had been made that lower brain structures must be fully developed before the higher cortical structures can become functional. In Sparrow and Zigler's study of seriously retarded children they were unable to demonstrate a value in the patterning treatment.

A Newsletter Supplement in 1968 challenged the "Doman-Delacato Treatment of Neurologically Handicapped Children," and was sponsored jointly by the American Academy of Cerebral Palsy, American Academy of Physical Medicine and Rehabilitation, American Academy of Neurology, American Association of Mental Deficiency, and the American Academy of Pediatrics (American Academy of Pediatrics, Committee on Handicapped Children, 1968). The statement disallows claims made by the Institutes for the Achievement of Human Potential, and their affiliates, focusing on the inconclusive, questionable theories of Doman and Delacato. The statement further stressed the following:

1. Promotional methods put parents into the position of not being able to refuse such treatment without questioning their adequacy of motivation.
2. The program is so rigid that it can cause neglect of other family members.
3. The therapy is made so rigid that if not followed 100 percent, the effort is regarded as useless.
4. Restrictions are placed on age-appropriate behavior.
5. A developmental profile that has been employed by the institute has not been validated.
6. Undocumented claims for cures have been made.
7. The Doman-Delacato philosophy contraindicates a number of typical child-rearing practices, which thereby increases parental anxieties.

Robbins and Glass (1969) concluded that (1) the fundamental tenets of the Doman-Delacato theory are refuted by internal inconsistencies, lack of supporting evidence, and direct contradiction by established knowledge; (2) the cited studies supporting the relationship between neurological organization and reading lack sophistication and proper controls; and (3) there is no empirical evidence to substantiate the values of theory or practice of neurological organization.

Sensory integrative therapy. Interest has been generated regarding the relationship between tactile perceptual development and its relationship to learning skills. Finlayson and Reitan (1976) demonstrated an association between sensorimotor impairment and high-level cognitive functioning, a relationship that appears to be stronger in older than in younger children. Probably the major controversial issues stem from the application of tactile perceptual training (sensorimotor training) to improving cognitive and intellectual abilities.

Ayers (1968, 1972) proposed that perception and learning are dependent upon the ability of the brain stem to organize visual and auditory processes. Normal development of visual perception is believed to require intersensory integration from other sources, especially somatosensory and vestibular sources. In the event that sensory integration is impaired, the child experiences learning disabilities resulting from immature postural reactions, poor eye muscle control, disturbed orientation, and distractibility. Ayers suggested that the child with motor defects, and underlying brain deficits, can be treated by influencing neurophysiological integration through controlling sensorimotor behavior. Activities involving vestibular, postural, and tactile stimulation are utilized to normalize behaviors. She reports that "the emphasis placed on sensorimotor function as a foundation for the development of perception and learning needs to be kept in proper focus. While sensory integrative processes serve an important role, the influence is limited. Where there is dysfunction in these integrative processes, remedial treatment can make a considerable difference in the maturational process, but in a child with normal sensorimotor development, the same procedures will probably not result in substantial gain in cognitive development" (Ayers, 1968, p. 55). Treatment models employing these types of stimulation are presumed to improve auditory and visual processing function. The theoretical models, however, appear to be inconclusive, requiring further exploration and verification.

Nutrition and Orthomolecular Medicine

A variety of biochemical etiologies and dietary management plans have been proposed to treat and understand learning disabilities and behavioral disorders. Speculations on dietary-linked etiologies span the spectrum from nutritional deficiencies to food allergies. Once again, confusions and controversies currently follow in the wake of incomplete scientific documentation.

Megavitamins. Pauling (1968) supported a hypothesis of orthomolecular medicine which postulated that "the functioning of the brain is affected by the molecular concentrations of many substances that are normally present in the brain. The optimum concentrations of these substances for a person may differ greatly from the concentrations provided by his normal diet and genetic machinery. Biochemical and genetic arguments support the idea that orthomolecular therapy, the provision for the individual of the optimum concentrations of important normal constituents of the brain, may be the preferred treatment for many mentally ill patients" (pp. 270–271).

In essence orthomolecular psychiatry attempts to treat mental disease by providing the optimum molecular environment. In the early 1950s, it was suggested that schizophrenia represented a failure in metabolism, resulting from an accumulation of adrenochrome, a toxin oxidation product of epinephrine. Initially, nicotinic acid, ascorbic acid, and pyridoxine were employed in the therapeutic management of schizophrenia. It was presumed that high doses of nicotinic acid would prevent the formation of epinephrine from norepinephrine and, thereby, reduce the production of adrenochrome.

Ross (1974) reported on a successful therapy program for a 11-year-old schizophrenic boy. The regimen consisted of "a high-protein, low-carbohydrate diet, with small meals and frequent in-between-meal protein snacks." The meals were supplemented with a variety of vitamins: pyridoxine (vitamin B-3), ascorbic acid (vitamin C), pyridoxine (vitamin B-6), pantothenic acid (vitamin B-2), vitamin E, and a multiple vitamin B tablet. The author described a dramatic response for this patient within the first week of therapy. Preliminary laboratory investigations revealed only "hypoglycemia"; all other analyses were apparently within normal limits. Ross recognized the controversial attitudes regarding orthomolecular psychiatry, as generated by members of the medical profession, and defended his findings with "let the clinical evidence speak for itself."

Cott originally (1969) reported on the use of megavitamins to treat schizophrenic children and later (1971) extended its use to the management of learning-disabled children. Case reports were cited "to illustrate the confusion in diagnosis and treatment of schizophrenia." Cott reported on the "encouraging results" he observed with escalating doses of numerous vitamins and other medications. In addition Cott utilized "a hypoglycemic diet, with exclusion of sugar and other adrenal stimulants" (Cott, 1969, pp. 47–48). Cott (1971) subsequently reported that "I have seen very few cases of childhood schizophrenia, autism or brain injury in whom seizure activity did not respond to the megavitamins" (p. 98).

With the extension of the orthomolecular medicine approach to treat such disorders of childhood as hyperactivity, academic under-achievement, and perceptual disturbances, its effectiveness has become more debatable. Although this dietary modification has received some public support, to Silver (1975), such treatment is grounded upon the state of the art instead of science. Silver also wrote the following:

> To date there is no objective evidence for the treatment of children with learning disabilities with megavitamins. These studies were based on the earlier literature relating to megavitamins with schizophrenia—all not proven. The claims are based on subjective reporting with a questionable research design. (p. 412)

In 1976 The American Academy of Pediatrics Committee on Nutrition reviewed the issue of megavitamin therapy for childhood psychoses and learning disabilities. Their report concluded that the use of megavitamin therapy as a method of treatment of learning-disabled children and children with psychoses (including autism) was *not* justified on the basis of scientifically documented clinical investigations.

Minerals and trace elements. A variety of deficiencies in trace elements have been postulated as the etiology of disordered learning: copper, chromium, magnesium, manganese, and zinc. In addition, calcium, potassium, iron, and sodium have been incriminated. Although some children have been treated empirically with replacement diets, there is a paucity of scientific documentation defining a cause-and-effect relationship.

Hypoglycemia. A diet-related theory suggests that hypoglycemia is a contributing etiological factor in learning disabilities. The hypothesis maintains that efficient function of the central nervous system depends upon an adequate supply of blood glucose. Glucose deprivation, regardless of etiology, may effect neurological function and possibly learning skills. Hypoglycemia can influence attention, attitude, and organic preparedness for learning. Consequently, therapy is directed toward dietary modifications to improve the hypoglycemic state. This philosophy was supported by Cott (1971), who reportedly observed an abnormally high incidence of hypoglycemia and dysinsulinism in learning-disabled children. He stated that "the universal observations on the dietary habits of brain-injured children, hyperactive children, learning-disabled children and psychotic children have been that these children eat a diet which is high in cereals, in carbohydrate foods, and those foods prepared with sugar" (p. 103). The untreated child presumably exhibits a fall in blood sugar approximately 1 hour after eating. The low blood sugar, in turn, adversely effects the learning process. Once again, well-constructed double-blind and provocative studies are needed to validate hypotheses; reporting and interpolating solely from case observations without scientific design elicits confusion and results in controversy.

Food additives. Feingold (1973, 1975a, b) has advocated that various food additives, artificial food flavors and colors, are potential factors in hyperkinesis and learning disabilities (H-LD). It has been hypothesized that the increasing incidence of hyperkinesis and learning disabilities parallels the rapid increase in the use of synthetic colors and flavors in the food supply (Feingold, 1976), asserting that there is more than a casual correlation between the two. A link is suggested between H-LD and the artificial colors and flavors in our food. Feingold proposes that synthetic flavors and colors can produce a wide variety of adverse reactions, including rhinitis, cough, asthma, pruritis, urticaria, flatulence, buccal chancres, arthralgia with edema, headaches, and behavioral disturbances. It is proposed that artificial food colors and flavors can induce adverse reactions involving every organ system and that involvement of the nervous system is manifested as learning and behavioral disorders.

The Feingold (KP) diet, which is designed to eliminate these offending agents, was reported to control behavioral disturbances in 30 to 50 percent of both normal and neurologically damaged children. Feingold has observed a rapid improvement in behavior and scholastic achievement in children following dietary management that eliminated artificial food colors, flavors, and naturally occurring salicylates from the children's diets. Levine and Liden (1976) pointed out that the Feingold diet coincided with a national enthusiasm for "physiophilia" or naturalism in the life style and diet. The "food-additive villain" received national publicity and was prematurely accepted by many parents and professionals as a definitive method of assisting the learning-disabled child.

The initial publication of the Feingold hypothesis suggested the need for more comprehensive scientific analyses, which have been initiated in several laboratories. Conners and his co-workers (1976) reported on 15 children in a double-blind crossover trial involving a control diet and an additive-free diet as recommended by Feingold. The reported results strongly suggested that a diet free of natural salicylates, artificial flavors, and artificial colors reduced perceived hyperactivity in some children. Teachers, unaware of children placed on the special diet, rated the children less hyperactive, whereas parents did *not* detect a significant behavioral change. The teacher rating scales had a chance probability of only 5 in 1,000 times. The researchers concluded that the Feingold diet may reduce hyperkinetic symptoms but add a word of caution regarding "objective measures of change, manipulation of the independent variable, and reducing the independent variable to more specific components" (Connors, et al., 1976).

The National Advisory Committee on Hyperkinesis and Food Additives, concluded that "data from critically designed and executed studies, free of the deficiencies of designs noted, must be available before firm conclusions can be reached on the Feingold hypothesis" (Lipton, 1975). Spring and Sandoval (1976) argued that food additives may contribute to hyperactivity in some children and that perhaps the Feingold diet may help some of these children, but they suggested "a moratorium on further public advocacy is recommended until the efficacy of the diet for a defined population is firmly established by controlled research." They challenged the hypothesis that claimed a parallel increase in the incidence of hyperkinesis and the use of chemical additives in our food inasmuch as there are no reliable data bases to interpret the incidence of hyperactivity. The measurements of hyperactivity are very unreliable and vague. They also questioned the nature of Feingold's uncontrolled studies and placebo effects. Wender (1977) reviewed the cummulative research findings relative to food additives and concluded that "the studies completed so far refute the general claim that 40 percent or more of the children with hyperkinetic behavior disorder demonstrate global improvement in behavior and/or learning when fed a diet free of artificial food colorings." Harley and his associates (1978) evaluated 36 school-age, hyperactive boys utilizing experimental and control diets. Based on teacher ratings, psychological measures, laboratory observational data and other parameters, the authors could not support the Feingold hypothesis. Williams and his colleagues (1978), however, reported that a diet free of artificial flavors and colors apparently resulted in some reduction of symptoms. The authors note that stimulant medications were more effective than diet changes in modifying hyperactivity.

Food allergies. It has been proposed that food allergy is an important factor in causing behavior and learning problems. Crook (1975) suggested that although learning problems and behavioral disorders have many etiologies, "allergy is the most important factor contributing to such disorders in many—and perhaps most—children." His conclusions were based on case history reviews of 41 children with hyperactivity and/or learning problems who exhibited nervous system flare-ups after consuming foods to which they were sensitive. In most cases allergies were incriminated. Others cite cases to support the concept of a relationship between food allergies and disorders of learning (Havard, 1973). Kittler and Baldwin (1970) suggested that allergy of the "tension-fatigue syndrome" is present in a significant percentage of children with minimal brain dysfunction. Rapaport and Flint (1976) stressed that an allergy may interfere with a child's ability to function at optimum levels. They noted that one out of every five school children has a major allergic disease and that allergic physical symptoms can interfere with learning. It was suggested that a number of children who have been placed in the category of the "learning-disabled" actually are the allergy-disabled.

In essence, an allergic basis is postulated for learning disorders, implying that benefits will be derived by certain food-elimination diets. The hypothesis is again based primarily on case observations. Psychological factors and observer bias, however, may play dominant roles in reporting the influences of food allergy (May, 1975).

Probably no issue in current pediatric medicine has received as much attention and generated as much question and debate as the role of nutrition in learning disabilities. Public and professional zeal in experimenting with modifications of the child's diet has been unique. Understandably, the desire for a panacea to resolve problems of learning has prompted an exaggerated search for a common denominator for these disabled children. Dietary influences have served this need and has become the popular scientific "villain." Double-blind, provocative, crossover studies were not utilized in the initial investigations, thereby casting doubts on the role of diet in learning disorders. Theories generated from case studies, without experimentation, formed the foundations for many of the nutritionally based claims. It was anticipated that controversy would result, and scientific protocols would need to be established in order to test these hypotheses.

Biofeedback conditioning. Alpha waves at 8 to 14 cycles per second are believed to be associated with mental alertness. A high incidence of poorly organized alpha-wave activity in the occipital leads presumably indicates an association with hyperkinesis and learning disabilities. It has been proposed that alpha-wave conditioning by biofeedback techniques might minimize hyperactivity and thereby improve learning abilities. Experimental investigations suggest that individuals can control their alpha-wave activity, but the techniques are still investigational.

SUMMARY

Controversies in medicine are usually spawned from diagnostic and therapeutic claims that have *not* fulfilled the rigid criteria of the scientific method. Often undocumented hypotheses generated solely from case histories and patient testimonials may receive public attention and approval before they acquire the necessary verification based on scientific documentation. Although a controversial issue may ultimately be resolved by proper experimental design, perhaps to support the issue in question, it is the initial responsibility of the proponent to have utilized studies fulfilling the requirements of scientific investigation. Indeed these issues should be reported first to the scientific community for peer-review, before releasing materials to the mass media.

Since disorders of learning are the "most prevalent affliction of childhood," a vulnerable audience is instantly available (Yahraes & Prestwich, 1976). The profound psychosocial and educational sequelae of delayed intervention exaggerates the emotional traumas experienced by client and family. Families of learning-disabled children often seek a foolproof diagnostic analysis and a guaranteed "quick cure." Physicians may be similarly trapped in this "anxiety state," particularly when traditional approaches appear slow and nonproductive. Therefore, it is not surprising that curiosities, concerns, confusions, and controversies are germinated in the environment of the learning-disabled child.

In the interest of patient and public protection, it is essential that all professionals be knowledgeable of established, as well as the controversial issues pertaining to the learning-disabled child. Quality comprehensive medical care is founded on utilization of scientifically acceptable methods; controversial approaches should be questioned and approached with caution.

Marvin I. Gottlieb

REFERENCES

Adams, R. M., Kocsis, J. J., & Estes, R. E. Soft neurological signs in learning-disabled children and controls *American Journal of Disease of Children*, 1974, *128*, 614–618.

Alta Conference on MBD. Stopping medication. *Current Issues in Minimal Brain Dysfunction* (Abbott Laboratories), 1975, *1*, 4–12.

American Academy of Pediatrics, Committee on Drugs. An evaluation of the pharmacological approaches to learning impediments. *Pediatrics*, 1970, *46*, 142–144.

American Academy of Pediatrics, Committee on Nutrition. Megavitamin therapy for childhood psychoses and learning disabilities. *Pediatrics*, 1976, *58*, 910–912.

American Academy of Pediatrics, Council on Child Health. *Statement:* Children with learning disabilities. Evanston, Ill.: The Academy, 1973. (a)

American Academy of Pediatrics, Council on Child Health. *Statement:* Early identification of children with learning disabilities: The Preschool child. Evanston, Ill.: The Academy, 1973. (b)

American Academy of Pediatrics, Committee on the Handicapped Child. The Doman-Delacato treatment of neurologically handicapped children. Announcements. *Journal of Pediatrics*, 1968, *72*, 750–752.

American Academy of Pediatrics, Council on Child Health. *Pediatrics*, 1975, *55*, 560–562.

Ayers, A. J. Sensory integrative processes and neuropsychological learning disabilities. In J. Hellmuth (Ed.), *Learning disorders* (Vol. 3). Seattle: Special Child Publications, 1968, pp. 43–58.

Ayers, A. J. Improving academic scores through sensory integration. *Journal of Learning Disabilities*, 1972, *5*, 339–343.

Bax, M. C. O. The assessment of the child at school entry. *Pediatrics*, 1976, *58*, 403–407.

Benton, C. D., Jr. Comment: The eye and learning disabilities. *Journal of Learning Disabilities*, 1973, *6*, 334–336.

Birch, J. W. Mainstreaming: Educable mentally retarded classes. In J. W. Lerner (Ed.), *Children with learning disabilities: Theories, diagnosis and teaching strategies* (2nd ed.). Boston: Houghton Mifflin, 1976.

Boder, E. A neuropediatric approach to the diagnosis and management of school behavioral and learning disorders. In J. Hellmuth (Ed.), *Learning disorders* (Vol. 2). Seattle: Special Child Publications, 1966, pp. 15–44.

Boder, E. School failure—Evaluation and treatment. *Pediatrics*, 1976, *58*, 394–403.

Bryan, T. H. Learning disabilities. *Pediatric Annals*, 1978, *7*, 31–44.

Clements, S. D. Minimal brain dysfunction in children. In S. G. Sapir & A. C. Nitzburg (Eds.), *Children with learning problems*. New York: Brunner/Mazel, 1973, pp. 159–186.

Congressional Record, 1977, *123*, (4), p. H4712.

Conners, C. K., Goyette, C. H., Southwick, D. A., et al. Food additives and hyperkinesis, a controlled double-blind study. *Pediatrics,* 1976, *58,* 154–166.

Cott, A. Treating schizophrenic children. *Schizophrenia,* 1969, *1,* 44–60.

Cott, A. Orthomolecular approach to the treatment of learning disabilities. *Schizophrenia,* 1971, *3,* 95–105.

Crook, W. G. Food allergy—The great masquerader. *Pediatric Clinics of North America,* 1975, *22,* 227–228.

Cruickshank, W. M. Myths and realities in learning disabilities. *Journal of Learning Disabilities,* 1977, *10,* 51–58.

de la Cruz, F., & La Veck, G. D. The pediatrician's view of learning disorders. In J. Hellmuth (Ed.), *Learning disorders* (Vol. 1). Seattle: Special Child Publications, 1965, pp. 31–47.

Dodge, P. F. Neurological disorders of school-age children. *Journal of School Health,* 1976, *46,* 338–343.

Ensher, G. L. Mainstreaming: Yes. *Exceptional Parents,* 1976, *6,* 7–8.

Feingold, B. F. Editorial: Food additives and child development. *Hospital Practice,* 1973, *8,* 11–21.

Feingold, B. F. Hyperkinesis and learning disabilities linked to artificial food flavors and colors. *American Journal of Nursing,* 1975, *75,* 797–803. (a)

Feingold, B. F. *Why your child is hyperactive.* New York: Random House, 1975. (b)

Feingold, B. F. Hyperkinesis and learning disabilities linked to the ingestion of artificial food colors and flavors. *Journal of Learning Disabilities,* 1976, *9,* 19–27.

Finlayson, M. A. J., & Reitan, R. M. Tactile-perceptual functioning in relation to intellectual, cognitive and learning skills in younger and older normal children. *Developmental Medicine and Child Neurology,* 1976, *18,* 442–446.

Flax, N. The eye and learning disabilities. *Journal of Learning Disabilities,* 1973, *6,* 328–333.

Frostig, M. Visual perception, integrative functions and academic learning. *Journal of Learning Disabilities,* 1972, *5,* 1–15.

Gaddes, W. H. Prevalence estimates and the need for definition of learning disabilities. In R. M. Knights & D. J. Baker (Eds.), *Neuropsychology of learning disorders.* Baltimore: University Park Press, 1975, pp. 3–24.

Gearheart, B. R. *Learning disabilities, educational strategies* (2nd Ed.) St. Louis: Mosby, 1977.

Geschwind, N. The role of the brain in normal and disordered learning. Paper presented at a Conference on Educational Jeopardy: A Multidisciplinary Approach to the Learning-Disabled Child, at the Boston University Medical Center, Boston, 1976.

Getman, G. N. The visuomotor complex in the acquisition of learning skills. In J. Hellmuth (Ed.), *Learning disorders* (Vol. 1). Seattle: Special Child Publications, 1965, pp. 49–76.

Gofman, H. The training of the physician in evaluation and management of the educationally handicapped child. In J. Hellmuth (Ed.), *Educational therapy* (Vol. 1). Seattle: Special Child Publications, 1966, pp. 51–108.

Goldberg, H. K., & Schiffman, G. B. *Dyslexia problems of reading disabilities.* New York: Grune & Stratton, 1972.

Gottlieb, M. I. Pills, pros and cons: Medications for school problems. *Acta Symbolica*, 1975, *6*, 35–65 (a)

Gottlieb, M. I. Educational health and development. In J. Hughes (Ed.), *Synopsis of pediatrics* (4th ed.). St. Louis: Mosby, 1975, pp. 24–48. (b)

Grossman, H. J. Neurologic assessment and management of learning disorders. *Pediatric Annals*, 1978, *7*, 63–67.

Haller, J. S., & Axelrod, P. Minimal brain dysfunction syndrome. *American Journal of Disease of Children*, 1975, *129*, 1319–1323.

Hammill, D. Training visual perceptual processes. *Journal of Learning Disabilities*, 1972, *5*, 552–559.

Harley, J. P., Ray, R. S., Tomasi, L., Eichman, P. L., Mathews, C. G., Chun, R., Cleeland, C. S., & Traisman, E. Hyperkinesis and food additives: testing the Feingold hypothesis. *Pediatrics*, 1978, 61, 818–828.

Hart, Z., Rennick, P. M., Klinge, V., & Schwartz, M. L. A pediatric neurologist's contribution to evaluation of school underachievers. *American Journal of Diseases of Children*, 1974, *128*, 319–323.

Havard, J. School problems and allergies. *Journal of Learning Disabilities*, 1973, *6*, 492–494.

Hensley, H. G. The special education/general education interface, and the integration of professional training. In J. A. Bradshaw, P. G. Langton, & V. W. Patterson (Eds.), *Contiguity and continuity in general and special education.* Boulder, Col.: Western Interstate Commission for Higher Education, 1972, pp. 47–52.

Issues: Early warning preschool fraud. *Journal of Learning Disabilities*, 1973, *6*, 528.

Joint organizational statement: The eye and learning disabilities. *Pediatrics*, 1972, *49*, 454–455.

Katz, J. The effects of conductive hearing loss on auditory function. *Journal of the American Speech and Hearing Association*, 1978, *20*, 10, 879–886.

Kittler, F. J., & Baldwin, D. G. The role of allergic factors in the child with minimal brain dysfunction. *Annals of Allergy*, 1970, *28*, 204–206.

Knobloch, H., Rider, R., Harper, P., & Pasamanick, B. Neuropsychiatric sequelae of prematurity. *JAMA*, 1956, *161*, 581–585.

Larsen, J. M. Effects of teacher support in young children's learning. *Child Development*, 1975, *46*, 631–637.

Lerner, J. W. *Children with learning disabilities: Theories, diagnosis and teaching strategies* (2nd ed.). Boston: Houghton Mifflin, 1976, pp. 8–10.

Lesser, L. L. Hyperkinesis in children. Operational approach to management. *Clinical Pediatrics* (Philadelphia), 1970, *9*, 548–552.

Levine, M. D., & Liden, G. B. Commentaries: Food for inefficient thought. *Pediatrics*, 1976, *58*, 145–148.

Le Winn, E. B., Doman, G. J., Delacato, C., et al. Neurological organization: The basis for learning. In J. Hellmuth (Ed), *Learning disorders* (Vol. 2). Seattle: Special Child Publications, 1966, pp. 51–63.

Lipton, M. Statement issued by the National Advisory Committee on Hyperkinesis and Food Additives, Glen Cove, N.Y., January 1975.

Low, M. B. The pediatrician and the school. The President's Column, *News and Comments* (American Academy of Pediatrics), 1976, *27*, 8.

Mann, L. Perceptual training revisited. The training of nothing at all. In S. Chess & A. Thomas (Eds.), *Annual progress in child psychiatry and child development.* New York: Brunner/Mazel, 1972, pp. 178–190.

May, C. D. Food allergy: A commentary. *Pediatric Clinics of North America,* 1975, *22,* 217–220.

McMahon, S. A., & Greenberg, L. M. Serial neurological evaluation of hyperactive children. *Pediatrics,* 1977, *59,* 584–587.

Menkes, J. H. On failing in school. *Pediatrics,* 1976, *58,* 392–393.

Millichap, J. G. *The hyperactive child with minimal brain dysfunction.* Chicago: Yearbook Medical Publishers, 1975.

Millichap, J. G. (Ed.). *Learning disabilities and related disorders; Facts and current issues.* Chicago: Year Book Medical Publishers, 1977.

Millichap, J. G., & Fowler, G. W. Treatment of minimal brain dysfunction: Syndromes. Section on drugs for children with hyperactivity and learning disabilities. *Pediatric Clinics of North America,* 1967, *14,* 767–778.

Millichap, J. G., & Johnson, F. H. Methylphenidate in hyperkinetic behavior: Relation of response to degree of activity and brain damage. In C. K. Conners (Ed.), *Clinical use of stimulant drugs.* The Hague: Excerpta Medica, 1974, pp. 130–139.

Minde, K., Webb, G., & Sykes, D. Studies on the hyperactive child. VI. Prenatal and paranatal factors associated with hyperactivity. *Developmental Medicine and Child Neurology,* 1968, *10,* 355–363.

Money, J. *Reading disability. Progress and research needs in dyslexia.* Baltimore: The Johns Hopkins Press, 1967.

Muir, M. The consideration of emotional factors in the diagnosis and treatment of learning-disabled children. *Pediatric Psychology,* 1975, *3,* 6–9.

Myklebust, H. R. Learning disorders: Psychoneurological disturbances. In S. G. Sapir & A. C. Nitzburg, (Eds.), *Children with learning problems.* New York: Brunner/Mazel, 1973, pp. 257–269.

National Advisory Committee on Handicapped Children. *Special education for handicapped children–First annual report.* Washington, D.C.: U.S. Department of Health, Education, and Welfare, 1968.

Paine, R. S. Syndrome of minimal cerebral damage. *Pediatric Clinics of North America,* 1968, *15,* 799–801

Pasamanick, B., & Knobloch, H. The epidemiology of reproductive casualty. In S. G. Sapir & A. C. Nitzburg (Eds.), *Children with learning problems.* New York: Brunner/Mazel, 1973, pp. 193–199.

Pauling, L. Orthomolecular psychiatry. *Science,* 1968, *160,* 265–271.

Rapaport, H. G., & Flint, S. H. Is there a relationship between allergy and learning disabilities? *Journal of School Health*, 1976, *46*, 139–141.

Rie, H. E. Hyperactivity in children. *American Journal of Diseases of Children*, 1975, *129*, 783–789.

Robbins, M. P., & Glass, G. V. The Doman-Delacato rationale: A critical analysis. In J. Hellmuth (Ed.), *Educational jeopardy* (Vol. 2). Seattle: Special Child Publications, 1969, pp. 323–377.

Ross, H. M. Vitamin pills for schizophrenics. *Psychology Today*, 1974, *7*, 83–88.

Sarason, S., & Doris, J. Dilemmas, opposition, opportunities. *Exceptional Parents*, 1977, *1*, 21–24.

Schain, R. J. Etiology and early manifestations of MBD. In J. C. Millichap (Ed.), *Learning disabilities and related disorders: Facts and current issues.* Chicago: Year Book Medical Publishers, 1977, pp. 25–31.

Schmitt, B. D. The minimal brain dysfunction myth. *American Journal of Diseases of Children*, 1975, *129*, 1313–1318.

Schmitt, B. D. Letters to the editor: Minimal brain dysfunction myth. *American Journal of Diseases of Children*, 1976, *130*, 901–902.

Sell, S. H. W., Webb, W. W., & Pate, J. E Psychological sequelae to bacterial meningitis: Two controlled studies. *Pediatrics*, 1972, *49, 212*–217.

Silver, L. B. Acceptable and controversial approaches to treating the child with learning disabilities. *Pediatrics*, 1975, *55*, 406–415.

Sparrow, S., & Zigler, E. Evaluation of a patterning treatment for retarded children. *Pediatrics*, 1978, *62*, 137–150.

Spring, C., & Sandoval, J. Food additives and hyperkinesis: A critical evaluation of the evidence. *Journal of Learning Disabilities*, 1976, *9*, 28–37.

Stores, G., & Hart, J. Reading skills of children with generalized or focal epilepsy attending ordinary school. *Developmental Medicine and Child Neurology*, 1976, *18*, 705–716.

Strauss, A. A., & Lehtinen, L. E. *Psychopathology and education of the brain-injured child.* New York: Grune & Stratton, 1947.

Sullivan, J. The effects of Kephart's perceptual motor-training on a reading clinic sample. *Journal of Learning Disabilities*, 1972, *5*, 545–551.

Thompson, R. G., & Gottlieb, M. I. Educational jeopardy, an interdisciplinary problem: The physician's contribution. *Acta Symbolica*, 1973, *4*, 47–72.

Todd, M., & Gottlieb, M. I. Interdisciplinary counseling in a medical setting. In E. J. Webster (Ed.), *Professional approaches with parents of handicapped children.* Springfield, Ill.: Thomas, 1976, pp. 191–216.

van Noorden, G. K. Chronic vision problems of school-age children. *Journal of School Health*, 1976, *46*, 334–337.

Walzer, S., & Richmond, J. B. The epidemiology of learning disorders. *Pediatric Clinics of North America*, 1973, *20*, 549–555.

Warren, S. A. Problems encountered with learning disabilities. *Pediatric Annals*, 1978, *7*, 12–30.

Wender, E. H. Food additives and hyperkinesis. *American Journal of Diseases of Children*, 1977, *131*, 1204–1206.

Wender, P. H., & Wender, E. H. Letters to the editor, minimal brain dysfunction myth. *American Journal of Diseases of Children,* 1976, *130,* 900–901.

White, C. S., Dwyer, W. O., & Lintz, E. Dyslexia: Is the term of value? *Acta Symbolica,* 1973, *4,* 6–28.

Wiener, G., Rider, R. V., Oppel, W. C., et al. Correlates of low birth weight: Psychological status at six or seven years of age. *Pediatrics,* 1965, *35,* 434–444.

Williams, J. F. Learning disabilities: A multifaceted health problem. *Journal of School Health,* 1976, *46,* 515–517.

Williams, J. I., Cram, D. M., Tausig, F. T., & Webster, E. Relative effects of drugs on hyperactive behaviors: An experimental study. *Pediatrics,* 1978, 61, 811–817.

Winschel, J. F. Mainstreaming: No. *Exceptional Parents* 1976, *6,* 9–10.

Yahraes, H., & Prestwich, S. *Detection and prevention of learning disorders.* Bethesda, Md.: National Institute of Mental Health, 1976, p. iii.

Yang, D. C., Risch, M. L., & Lamm, S. S. Rehabilitation of learning in a hospital class using psychoactive drugs. *Journal of Learning Disabilities,* 1973, *6,* 488–491.

Zinkus, P. W., & Gottlieb, M. I. Disorders of learning and delinquent youth: An overview. *Learning disabilities: An Audio Journal for Continuing Education,* 1978, *2*(4).

Zinkus, P. W., & Gottlieb, M. I. Learning disabilities and juvenile delinquency. *Clinical Pediatrics,* 1978, *17*(10), 775–780.

Zinkus, P. W., Gottlieb, M. I., & Schapiro, M. Developmental and psychoeducational sequelae of chronic otitis media. *American Journal of Diseases of Children,* 1978, 132, 1100–1104.

Part II
DIAGNOSTIC AND THERAPEUTIC PERSPECTIVES

10

MEDICAL EVALUATION AND INTERVENTION WITH THE LEARNING-DISABLED CHILD

The practice of pediatric medicine traditionally maintains a strong orientation toward prevention of disease and disability. The preventive approach employs both the techniques of screening a population at risk, as, for example, testing all newborns for pheynlketonuria and active prophylaxis, best exemplified in the immunization of children against common "childhood" infectious diseases. These measures have as their principle goal the protection of the child from disease complications that can produce chronic disabilities. Often the sequelae of these problems jeopardize the child's intellectual and educational development and compromise the ultimate potential of the individual. During the past decade there has been an increasing emphasis on school health and the need for interaction between medicine and the school. Similarly, there has been an increasing emphasis on teaching medical students about children with developmental disabilities and behavioral disorders (Gottlieb, 1978). The American Academy of Pediatrics (1973a, b) has recognized the role of pediatricians in this field of child development.

Unfortunately, the model of preventive medicine as applied to problems of development and learning is not stressed in traditional training programs for physicians. In no area of medicine is the active screening of children (and the benefits derived from early detection, evaluation and intervention) more productive and rewarding than in dealing with developmental disabilities and learning disorders. The complex and multifaceted nature of development disabilities does not lend itself to an impersonal and mechanistic approach, which often may be effective in dealing with biochemical disorders or communicable diseases. Nevertheless, developmental disorders, behavioral problems, and learning disabilities are major medical concerns that are frequently encountered in a pediatric or family practice. Intervention by physicians, particularly in the early detection of children with learning disabilities is essential. The contributions of medicine to the effectiveness of interdisciplinary management of developmentally disabled children cannot be overemphasized (Thompson & Gottlieb, 1973).

GENERAL CONSIDERATIONS

The physician for children must incorporate "mass screening" for problems of development and learning into his standard child care procedures. During his patient's infancy the pediatrician is directed principally toward monitoring the maturationally programmed phenomena of psychomotor development. Later, in the preschool and school years, attention is focused on the child's ability to progress in the graded cognitive and perceptual demands of learning in the academic sphere. The examination and continual reexamination of the phenomena of early development and learning require a constant commitment. At times this commitment is in danger of being diffused as the physician attempts to deal with the sometimes overwhelming "conventional" demands of acute illnesses and medical emergencies of the young patient.

Often the pediatrician is able to monitor the child's psychomotor development from the time of birth. Among all of the professionals, the pediatrician has a unique advantage by being in the best position to be the first to detect developmental problems. Screening the pediatric population requires a knowledge of the many high-risk factors that may affect normal development (see Table 10-1) as well as an appreciation for the variations in normal development. Assessment and discussion of development must be as much a part of a well-infant examination as the traditional auscultation of the heart. Discussions with parents that emphasize the importance of early stimulation and parenting techniques may favorably influence the developmental process. Physicians responsible for the comprehensive health care of

Table 10-1. Possible High-Risk Factors Associated with Developmental Disabilities and Learning Disorders.

Prenatal and Perinatal Factors

Abnormalities of the placenta	Gestational trauma
Birth defects	Low birth weight
Complicated delivery	Maternal anoxia
Complicated pregnancy	Maternal intoxications
Fetal malnutrition	Maternal malnutrition
Genetic factors	Metabolic disorders
Gestational infections	Prematurity
	Radiation exposture

Neonatal Factors

Cyanotic episodes	Metabolic and endocrine disorders
Infections	Seizures
Intoxications	Subdural hematoma
Kernicterus	Trauma
Malnutrition	Vascular disorders

Postnatal Factors

Accidental poisoning	Infections of the nervous system
Cerebral anoxia	Malnutrition
Cerebrovascular accidents	Metabolic and endocrine problems
Cultural deprivation	Pseudoretardation
Drug ingestion	Severe dehydration
Encephalopathies	Severe head injury

children are obligated to be aware of the possible associations between neurological dysfunctions in the newborn period and subsequent learning disorders (Francis-Williams, 1976). Detection of problems during the preschool period may allow for early educational intervention and rehabilitation.

When examining a preschooler, it is very helpful to engage the child in simple conversation. Many early problems in speech and language can be detected in the routine office visit. During the examination of school-age children an attempt should be made to introduce the subject of school work and perhaps incorporate some "on-the-spot" testing as well. Kindergarten and first-grade children are usually delighted to demonstrate writing their name or the alphabet. Older children usually enjoy making a game of questions in geography, spelling, or history, which can be performed during the course of the examination. Although this approach does *not* serve as a valid indicator of a child's academic progress, it is a painless way to introduce the subject of school progress as a legitimate area of the physician's concern. Occasionally, the introduction of questions and discussion about school, in the context of the examination, will serve as the means to identify a multitude of unsuspected child and parental problems regarding academic progress or school behavior.

In addition to learning-disabled children initially identified by the physician, there are increasing numbers of children referred to pediatricians by parents, guidance counselors, teachers, and other medical specialists. The basis for referral is often for delayed development or poor school performance.

At one time the traditional role of the pediatrician was limited to diagnosing and treating those organic, or purely physical, disabilities that could impede developmental and/or learning. The pediatrician's involvement with the identification of specific learning disabilities was a rarity! Medical intervention in this respect, however, has been dramatically expanded. As a child advocate, the physician must be concerned about learning disabilities. Physicians must be equipped to play an active role in the comprehensive initial evaluation, in coordinating an interdisciplinary evaluation, and in serving to insure that the best possible comprehensive treatment plan emerges from the findings and recommendations of the evaluation (Bax, 1976; Boder, 1976; Olson, 1975). The physician who serves as a member of the school health team has increasing responsibilities in dealing with learning and behavior disorders in children (Kappelman, Roberts, Rinaldi, & Cornblath, 1975).

THE MEDICAL EVALUATION

The physician's evaluation of the child with developmental or educational problems initially follows the basic format utilized in the investigation of any traditional medical complaint: (1) history, (2) physical, (3) laborabory and consultation information, and (4) treatment. The evaluation of "exceptional problems" generally requires of the physician, child, and parents more than the usual amount of time and effort. In the framework of a busy office practice, the pediatrician may find that the time necessary to explore these complex problems adequately requires scheduling for an otherwise free Saturday morning or Sunday afternoon. If performed during regular office hours, the evaluation must be allotted sufficient time to do justice to the complexity and subtlety of the problem. Ideally, the evaluation time should be free of interruptions and conducted in a relaxed, unhurried atmosphere.

The History

The initial steps and probably the most important, in the evaluation of a problem in development or learning is the comprehensive history, such as the one presented in Table 10–2 It is often helpful to interview the parents first in order to outline the presenting problem in chronological detail. It is particularly important to get an accurate impression of the *nature* and *source* of the presenting complaint. Difficulties in development and learning, as perceived by parents or teachers, may be accurately identified. Some presenting complaints, however, may reflect unrealistic demands and expectations of parents and teachers or inadequate knowledge of what is a proper level of achievement. The parents' concept of the child's problem may really be the "tip of the iceberg" which suggests serious difficulties in family relationships. Frequently the child is the most valuable source of information! Often the child's perspectives are considerably more accurate than the observations of parents, teachers, and other professionals. It behooves the physician to adhere constantly to the role of being an *advocate for the child* and *not* an agent of the parents.

In assessing developmental problems in young children, it is important to "start at the beginning" with a complete review of the prenatal and perinatal periods. Attention is focused on prematurity, neonatal respiratory distress, hyperbilirubinemia, meningitis, and a variety of other conditions that constitute some of the high-risk factors of the newborn period. A variety of dysfunctions of the central nervous system, ranging from the very subtle to the catastrophic, may be associated wtih injury sustained during the prenatal and perinatal periods. The more subtle injuries may not be manifested until the school years as cognitive dysfunctions. On the other hand, the physician may allay an unfounded parental fear and anxiety concerning many of the events of the prenatal period which clearly do *not* bear on the problem at hand. Despite increasing medical sophistication of the public, numerous misconceptions and "folklore," centering around gestation and childbirth, remain a part of our culture.

A discussion of the child's psychomotor development is one of the most important parts of the history. Though a wide range of normal variation in development exists, the maturational skills of early childhood may give important diagnostic and prognostic clues. An overview of the major sequences in development is in Table 10–3.

Table 10-2. Comprehensive History Form.

Name of patient
Date of examination
Personal statistics (Birth date, Parents, etc.)
Chief complaint
Course of presenting problem

Obstetrical History

Number of pregnancies
Number of living children
Number of miscarriages (cause if known)
Birth order
High-risk factors
    Infections
    Toxemia
    Diabetes
    Bleeding
    Trauma
    Excessive nausea and vomiting
    Other
Weight gain (or loss) during pregnancy
Medications during pregnancy
Excessive use of tobacco, alcohol, or drugs
Exposure to toxins or X-radiation
Length of gestation
Mother's age at conception
Father's age at conception
Mother's past medical history
Father's past medical history
Prenatal care (by)
Hospital for delivery

Perinatal History

Labor
    Induced or spontaneous
    Duration
    Complications
Delivery
    Presentation
    Forceps
    Complications
Condition at Birth
Apgar score
Onset of cry and respiration

Table 10-2. (continued)

Perinatal History (continued)

    Birth weight   Discharge weight
    Head circumference, chest circumference, length
    Sleepy, irritable, lazy
    Jaundice
    Cyanosis
    Convulsions
    Tremors
    Vomiting
    Feeding difficulties
    Other problems
    Attending physician
    Breast or bottle fed
    Number of days in nursery
    Discharged with mother

Developmental History (Documented from "Baby Book?")

    Smiled
    Followed objects
    Laughed
    Held head up
    Rolled over
    First tooth
    Sat alone
    Pulled up
    Crawled
    Walked
    Ran
    Talked, words
    Talked, sentences
    Regression of speech abilities
    Toilet trained
    Enuresis and/or Encopresis
    Rode tricycle
    Rode bicycle
    Comparison with siblings

Past Medical History

    Estimate of general rate of growth (compared with sibs)
    Serious illnesses
    Serious injuries
    Hospitalizations and operations

Table 10-2. (continued)

Past Medical History (continued)

High fevers
Convulsions or neurological problems
Staring spells or "blackout spells"
Head trauma with loss of consciousness
Anorexia, vomiting, diarrhea causing dehydration
Medications taken at this time and dosage
Childhood diseases or vaccines (age and complications)

Measles	Scarlet fever
German measles	Roseola
Mumps	Other
Chickenpox	

Immunizations and severe reactions
Estimate of general health
Attending physicians

Is child being followed for any disorder?

Review of Systems

General health
Allergies
Head
Eyes
Ears
Nose
Throat
Lungs
Heart
GI
GU
Skin
Lymph nodes
Bones and joints
Muscular
CNS Review
Parents' appraisal of intellectual status
Eye blinking or strabismus
Dysphagia or drooling
Spasticity or hypotonia
Coordination problems
Ataxia
Coordination   Gross   Fine

Table 10-2. (continued)

Review of Systems (continued)

Speech problems
　Delays
　Articulation
　Stuttering

Educational History

Nursery (age started, performance)
Kindergarten (age started, performance)
List of schools attended
Current grade, teacher
Problems reported by teacher
Grades completed
Grades repeated
Previous psychological testing and results
Results of achievement tests
Previous evaluations (where, why, when, results if known)
Tutoring (by whom) or special programs
Parents' observations of:
　Word or letter reversals
　Reading approximations
　Handwriting difficulties
　Difficulty following multiple directions
Child's school attitude

Social History

Household members
Father's occupation
Mother's occupation
Marital history
Problems or crises in family continuity
Discipline
　By whom
　Type
　Frequency
　Response
Relationship with siblings
Problems with siblings
Passive or aggressive with other children
Sleep away from home
Close friends (ages)
Living quarters (indoor plumbing, own room)

Table 10-2. (continued)

Family History

Mental retardation
Neurological problems
Emotional disorders
Learning disabilities
Diabetes
Cancer
Cardiovascular
Renal
Sickle cell
Metabolic
Hearing or speech problems

(Construct family tree—record ages, sex of all family members)

Behavioral History

Evaluation of motor activity
Attention span
Distractibility
Temper tantrums
Impulsiveness
Destructiveness
Emotional lability (mood swings)
Reactions when frustrated
Cruelty to animals
Cruelty to children
Hobbies
Favorite TV programs
Favorite school subjects   Worst school subjects
Favorite sports
Additional organized activities (Boy Scourts, etc.)
Plays with younger, older, same-age children
Sleep habits
   Hours/24 hours   Colic
   Night light   Bruxism
   Security objects   Sleepwalking
   Bedroom shared   Sleeptalking
   Nightmares and night terrors   Resists going to bed
   Bizzare night habits   Comes to parents' bed
   Enuresis
Particular fears
Nervous habits
Tics
Ritualistic activities

Table 10-2. (continued)

Behavioral History (continued)

Parents' description of child's "worst habit"
Discipline problems at home or at school
Evidences of poor self-concept

Nutritional history

Evaluation of diet (get 24-hour diet history)
Food likes and dislikes
Pica (e.g., wall plaster, dirt)
Food allergies
Diet modifications tried (food additives, megavitamins, hypoglycemic diets)

From the University of Tennessee Center for the Health Sciences, Department of Pediatrics, Section of Developmental and Behavioral Pediatrics. Reprinted by permission.

When possible, the parents should cite the actual age at which the various milestones were attained. Documentation from notes in a "Baby Book" is an ideal method of tracing the developmental history. Often parents will give a history of "normal" early development that, when carefully explored, is actually markedly abnormal. In the older child the history of development is extended to include a range of more specialized adapative behaviors involving social, motor, and language skills and their integration in performing more difficult tasks. It is important to trace the child's progress in playing with other children, use of language, creativity, and other more complex skills.

A family and social history is particularly important in assessing developmental, behavioral, and learning problems. Exploration of family psychodynamics and relationships may provide significant diagnostic clues relating to the child's interaction at home and at school. A significant number of behavioral difficulties are direct responses to situations of emotional stress at home or school. Virtually all developmental problems affect the interpersonal relationships of family members to some degree. The physician should attempt to obtain an accurate and detailed impression of the child's home situation. An appreciation of family relationships is necessary in the diagnostic process as well as in counseling family members as to the nature of the child's problems. The family's level of concern, degree of acceptance, and ability to comprehend are vital factors in determining the success

Table 10-3. Overview of the Major Sequences in Development.

Age	Gross Motor	Fine Motor	Adaptive	Language	Personal–Social
4 weeks	Tonic neck reflex position. Head sags forward in sitting position. Holds chin up when prone.	Fists held clenched. Hands clench on contact.	Focuses on objects put in line of vision. Follows to midline. Drops objects almost immediately.	Small throaty noises. Cries when uncomfortable.	Stares at surroundings for long periods.
8 weeks	Holds chest up when prone.	Hands may be held open.	Eyes follow moving objects.	Cooing sounds.	Regards objects and persons with diminished activity.
16 weeks	Head steady in a sitting position. Pushes with feet if held erect. Lifts head to 90° when prone on forearms.	Can seize objects held in front of him. Hands to scratch and clutch.	Follows moving object with eyes. Moves arms at sight of toy. Puts hands in mouth. Inspects own hands in play.	Laughs aloud.	Opens mouth for feedings. Smiles spontaneously.
28 weeks	Sits alone and leans forward on hands. Bounces actively when held erect. Attempts supporting weight in standing.	Palmar grasp to pick up small object. Rakes at object with entire hand.	Bangs objects on table. Transfers objects from one hand to the other. Reaches for objects. Beginning prehension.	Vocalizes "m-m-m" when crying. Babbles at toys.	Knows strangers. Enjoys mirror and pats mirror image. Puts feet to mouth when supine.

40 weeks	Sits alone indefinitely. Pulls to standing position. Crawls, creeps and may cruise.	Holds own bottle. Good approximation of thumb and index finger (prehension).	Index finger aproach. Points with index finger. Matches two objects in hand.	"Mama" and "dada" with meaning. One or more other words.	Plays peekaboo. Waves "bye-bye." Feeds self a cracker. Turns head when called.
52 weeks	Walks with support. Stands alone.	Good pincer grasp. Drops objects into bottle.	Holds cup to drink. Tries to build a 2-cube tower. Serial play with objects.	Knows 2 words besides "mama" and "dada." Obeys "no-no." Gives toy on request.	Cooperates in dressing. Feeds self in a fashion.
15 months	Walks alone. Toddles independently. Crawls up stairs.	Good pincer grasp to put pellet in bottle.	Builds a 2-cube tower. Marks with a crayon or pencil.	Jargon. Says 4 to 5 words with meaning. May name familiar objects.	Indicates wants by pointing or vocalizing. May indicate wet pants.

Table 10-3. (continued)

Age	Gross Motor	Fine Motor	Adaptive	Language	Personal–Social
18 months	Walks well. Runs. Seats self in a child's chair. Throws a ball.	Turns pages in a book, many at one time.	Stacks a 3–4 cube tower. Scribbles with pencil or crayon. Imitates a stroke. Inverts bottle to dump pellet.	About a 10-word vocabulary. Can identify some body parts. Verbalizes "hello" and "thank you."	Partially feeds self. Plays with pull-toy. Hugs doll.
24 months	Runs without falling. Climbs up and down stairs. Kicks a ball.	Turns pages singly. Cuts with scissors.	Stacks a 6–7 cube tower. Lines up cubes to imitate a train. Can draw a line.	Constructs a 3-word sentence. No longer uses jargon. Can follow a 4-part simple direction. Uses pronouns and verbs.	Dresses self with simple garments. Verbalizes toilet needs. Feeds self.
36 months	Alternates feet in climbing stairs. Jumps. Pedals a tricycle.	Holds crayon well. Copies a circle. Imitates a cross.	Stacks a 9–10 cube tower. Constructs a 3 cube bridge.	Gives full name and sex. Repeats 3 digits. Sings a few songs. Names 3 objects in a picture.	Dresses self and puts on shoes. Feeds self well. Unbuttons clothes. Comprehends "taking turns."

4 years	Alternates feet in descending stairs. Can broad jump. Throws ball overhand.	Copies a square.	Counts 4 pennies. Imitate a 5-cube gate. Draws man with at least 2 parts.	Comprehends "on," "under," "in back," "in front," "beside."	Partially dresses self. Enjoys simple group activities. Washes and dries face and hands. Learning to lace shoes. Goes on simple errands outside of home.
5 years	Skips. Stands on 1 foot for 8 or more seconds.	Copies a square and attempts a triangle.	Draws a recognizable figure with body parts. Identifies 4 colors. Counts 10 objects.	Names coins. Knows age. Carries out 3 commissions.	Dresses and undresses. Laces shoes. Asks questions.
6 years	Throws a ball well. Can stand on each foot alternately.	Copies a triangle. Attempts to copy numbers and letters. Attempts to copy a diamond.	Draws a human figure with details (neck, hands, clothes). Knows right from left. Counts 13 pennies.	Remember 3 or 4 directions. Repeats 4 digits in sequence.	Differentiates between morning and afternoon. May count to 30.

Adapted from the University of Tennessee Center for the Health Sciences, Department of Pediatrics, Section of Ambulatory Pediatrics.

of a treatment plan constructed by the interdisciplinary team. An outline of family psychodynamics apears in Table 10–4 and a differential diagnosis of disturbed educational development in Table 10–5.

Physical and Neurological Examinations

A thorough physical examination, with emphasis on the neurological evaluation must be performed on any child with a developmental or learning problem. An outline of the physical examination and neurological screening appears in Table 10–6. It is the

Table 10-4. Family Psychodynamics.

Type of Relationship	Parental Interactions	Effects on Child
Confused	Parents are concerned but unsure of how to cope with child's difficulty. Usually parents have tried unsuccessfully to work with child; frustrated. Parents have a sense of failure, guilt. Ambivalence may interfere with seeking professional intervention.	The child appears anxious; always testing limits. Child's self-concept reflects parents' confusion and frustration.
Inconsistent	Parents use varying means to control child, no pattern. Parents transmit two opposite messages at the same time.	The child is confused. Child may withdraw, or may become anxious and rebel.
Denial	Parents minimize or do not admit to child's difficulty. Parents' goals, expectancies, dreams for child have been thwarted. Parents usually first react by feeling child will outgrow problem.	The child is confused and frustrated because of dichotomy between reality and parents' denial. This confusion may bring withdrawal or acting out. Feeling of insecurity may occur. Self-confidence is shaky.

Table 10-4. (continued)

Type of Relationship	Parental Interactions	Effects on Child
Vicarious	Parents live through the child. Child is to realize aspirations parents could not achieve. Child's handicap destroys the parents' dreams for the child.	The child may be pressured to achieve despite handicap. Child may be pushed to overcome handicap. Child may have poor self-concept.
Symbiotic	Abnormally close tie exists between one parent and child. Parent begins to devote his/her life to this child. Situation may reflect deep-seated emotional problems in the parent.	Child does not develop an independent personality. Child lacks independence; infantile reactions, fear of separation.
Overprotective	Parents try to shield child from ordinary hazards of life, exaggerated with a child with a handicap. Parents' concerns are limitless. Parents may reflect guilt feelings.	Child may become fearful; self-confidence and esteem are low. Handicap becomes exaggerated and out of proportion to reality.
Overpermissive	Parents permit a wider range of behavior than normal. Parents cannot set limits. Parents may be ineffectual. Parents may be responding to guilt feelings.	Child with handicap may be given free rein because of misconceptions, pity, etc. Child may not conform socially. Child may become overly dependent.
Rigid	Parents set very high standards. Parents may be perfectionists.	Child may be disappointment to parents because of handicap. Child may also strive for perfection.

Table 10-4. (continued)

Type of Relationship	Parental Interactions	Effects on Child
Rigid *(continued)*	Parents are organizers, compulsive at times.	Child may rebel actively or passively.
	Parents apply these standards and rules for child; expectations higher than child's capability.	Child may withdraw and regress.
Disinterested	This relationship is often seen in multiproblem or disorganized households.	Child is usually withdrawn or passive; loner.
	Child's problems secondary to more pressing problems/conflicts family faces each day.	Later, child is likely to act out; run away, delinquent.
		Child is more likely not to conform socially.
Neglectful	Parents exhibit lack of responsibility for child.	There is a wide range of neglect, including physical and emotional needs of child.
	Child's handicap may create negative feelings in parents.	Child feels unwanted and unloved.
	Parents have ambivalent feelings toward child.	Child may focus on handicap as cause.
Fragmented	Parental discord of pathological degree.	Child may see handicap as cause of parental problems.
	Parental separation usual result.	Child has feelings of insecurity and rejection.
Rejecting	Parents may actually reject child; may be precipitated by handicap.	Child feels unwanted and unloved.
	Something about child may cause negative feeling.	Child may blame handicap for feeling of rejection.
		Poor self-concept results; child is apprehensive about all peers and adults.

Adapted from J. L. Schulman, *Management of Emotional Disorders in Pediatric Practice.* (Chicago: Year Book Medical Publishers, 1969), and from E. Webster, *Professional Approaches with Parents of Handicapped Children* (Springfield, Ill.: Thomas, 1976).

Table 10-5. Differential Diagnosis of Disturbed Educational Development.

Cause	Characteristics often Reported by	
	Parent	Teacher
Specific Learning Disability	Usually no problems except for school difficulty. Plays well with friends. Often uneventful preschool experiences.	Puzzling, child may perform well in some academic and social areas. May have superimposed behavior problem.
Mental Retardation	May be undetected, depending on severity. Possibly delayed maturation. Plays with younger children.	Child unable to compete at grade level or with children of same age.
Organic Handicap (e.g. hearing loss)	Functions well in uninvolved areas. Organic deficit usually recognized at onset.	Functions well academically in uninvolved areas. Peer rapport good.
Somatic Illness	No difficulty except for illness. Behavioral changes may occur with illness.	Change in performance related to onset of illness.
Psychosis	Disturbed parent relationship; affects relationships with sibs and peers (social relationships are poor).	Bizarre responses. May be withdrawn and unresponsive.
Behavioral Disorders	Better on 1:1. Occasionally disturbed parent–child relationship.	Attention-seeking behaviors. May annoy classmates. Acting-out behaviors are disruptive.
Socioeconomic Deprivation	Functions well in own cultural environment. Friends with similar circumstances.	May be characterized as poorly motivated. Superimposed problems in health, nutrition, etc.

Adapted from E. Webster, *Professional Approaches with Parents of Handicapped Children* (Springfield, Ill.: Thomas, 1976).

Table 10-6. Physical Examination and Neurological Screening Form.

Name
Date of examination

General Pediatric Examination

Vital signs: Head circ. ——, Chest circ. ——, Height ——,
             Weight ——, Span ——, BP ——, P ——, R ——.
  General
  Obvious anomalies
  Head
  Facies
  Eyes
  Ears
  Nose
  Teeth
  Palate
  Neck
  Throat
  Heart
  Lungs
  Abdomen
  Extremities
  Spine
  Vascular system
  Genitalia
  Skin, hair, nails
  Lymph nodes
  Muscular-skeletal system

Vision Acuity
  OD   OS
  OD (glasses)   OS (glasses)

Auditory Sensitivity
  Audiometer screening
  Impedance testing
  Tuning forks

Neurological Screening
  Activity (1 to 4 +)
  Attention span
  Cranial nerves
  Motor system
  Sensory system
  Deep tendon reflexes

Table 10-6. (continued)

Neurological Screening *(continued)*

Abnormal reflexes
Handedness
Footedness
Dominant eye
Muscle tone
Gait
Heel walking
Toe walking
Tandem gait
Pincer grasp
Rapid finger tapping
Alternate rapid hand movements
Romberg
Past pointing
Two-point discrimination
Proprioception
Stereognosis
Tremors or abnormal movements
Sense of laterality (self and crossed)
Synkinesis (mirror movements)
2-point touch
Finger-nose Test
Graphesthesia
Follow multiple directions
Digits (repeated forward)
Digits (repeated backward)
Articulation disorders

From the University of Tennessee Center for the Health Sciences, Department of Pediatrics, Section of Developmental and Behavioral Pediatrics. Reprinted by permission.

physician's unique responsibility to identify medically treatable deterrents to full developmental or educational performance. Poor vision and impaired hearing are among the more obvious conditions to be detected and treated. In addition, detection and therapy is necessary for acute and chronic diseases, such as seizure disorders, poor nutrition, anemia, and a variety of other treatable conditions which may contribute to a child's academic underachievement.

The medical assessment of the learning-disabled requires a thorough neurological evaluation. The integrity of the central nervous system is investigated as it relates to cognitive and behavioral adaptation (Silver, 1971a, b; Schain, 1972; Stine, Saratsiotis, & Mosser, 1975). As part of the complete neurologic evaluation, an effort should be made to elicit the "soft" neurologic signs (Table 10–7) which have been presumed to be associated with disorders of learning (Adams, Kocsis, & Estes, 1974; Barlow, 1974; Hart, Rennick, Klinge, & Schwartz, 1974). Fine motor coordination, perception of laterality, and other neurological signs can be evaluated in preschool children by having the child button a garment, identify right and left, and perform other simple gamelike tasks. Electroencephalographic (EEG) findings are probably of limited value in the diagnostic evaluation. The interpretation of EEG findings has not been resolved and pathognomonic signs are not established (Capute, Niedermeyer, & Richardson, 1968; Meier, 1971; Satterfield, Cartwell, Saul, & Usin, 1974).

Table 10-7. "Soft" Neurologic Signs.

Transient strabismus

Dysdiadochokinesis

Excessive synkinesis (mirror movements)

Poor coordination of fingers

General awkwardness (clumsiness)

Confused laterality

Inability to perform tandem gait

Involuntary minor movements

Increased deep tendon reflexes

Articulation defects

Graphesthesia disturbances

Stereognosis impaired

Poor fine motor coordination

Mild apraxias

Developmental and Behavioral Assessment

In addition to the techniques of interview and phsyical examination, which are regarded as "traditional" medical responsibilities, office screening procedures can be a part of the general examination to evaluate the child's psychomotor, perceptual, and academic abilities. In 1977 Benfield and her associates analyzed the screening inventories for preschool children, such as the Denver Developmental Screening Test, the Washington Guide to Promoting Development in the Young

Child, the Physician's Developmental Quick Screen for Speech Disorders, and the Slosson Drawing Coordination Test. The screening process does *not* provide a definitive diagnosis, nor is it intended to replace a complete psychometric testing. Developmental screening inventories serve to identify delays or weaknesses in a child's development and to determine the selection of professionals for additional consultations.

Two examinations, which are easily and quickly administered are the Denver Developmental Screening Test (DDST) and the Slosson Drawing Coordination Test. DDST (and similarly designed inventories) is an easily administered method of assessing the psychomotor development of children, between birth and 6 years of age. It is also valuable in estimating older children whose abilities fall in the preschool range. The DDST is based upon the standardized plotting of developmental sequences in four skill areas: (1) personal-social, (2) fine motor adaptive, (3) language, and (4) gross motor. By using the parents' history and the child's performance of simple tasks, a skill profile may be graphed which may help to identify the developmentally delayed youngster. The DDST can be administered quickly by office personnel. It is important to realize that it is in no sense a test of intelligence and should never be used by a physician or interpreted to the parents as such.

The Slosson Drawing Coordination Test, which consists of a series of geometrical figures of increasing complexity to be copied by the child, can be used to screen the child's visual motor coordination and perception. The Slosson can be quantitatively scored, but this is not necessary for its use as an age-correlated screen of visual perception and motor integration.

The screening of the older, school-age child is concerned with a broader range of learned, academic skills than is the assessment of the more developmentally programmed skills of the preschooler. An enlargement of the concept of academic screening, alluded to in the technique of the initial interview, can be used to obtain some overall impression of the child's academic level. A general developmental, perceptual, and academic potpourri, such as the screening test for school-age children developed at the University of Tennessee Center for the Health Sciences, Clinic for Exceptional Children, examples of which are shown in the Appendix to this chapter, utilize both verbal and performance tasks freely adaptable to various ages and developmental levels. This approach may be expanded or abbreviated according to the needs of the particular child. One must keep in mind that its purpose is *not* to provide a quantitative estimate of intelligence (or specific diagnosis) but to allow the physician to become better acquainted with the patient and his abilities. The screening is an aid in determining the need for further psychological and achievement testing.

Counseling and Coordination

The pediatrician's comprehensive history, physical examination, and screening evaluation may reveal no abnormalities or cause for concern, thereby sparing the need for a more comprehensive interdisciplinary effort. Many children, however, will show sufficient evidence of difficulties to warrant further consultation and diagnostic studies. Based on the initial evaluation, the physician should be able to design and coordinate an appropriate plan of diagnostic referrals for the child. Since the child's personal physician is a relative constant in the annually changing system of schools and teachers and has a prior and ongoing relationship with the child and family, the physician is also in a favored position to serve as counselor, coordinator, and monitor (Todd & Gottlieb, 1976).

The evaluation for the developmentally delayed or learning handicapped child most often requires an interdisciplinary effort (Lerner, 1976). Therefore, physicians must be familiar with the terminology, methods, and expertise of a variety of disciplines, including: child psychiatry, clinical psychology, general and special education, audiology and speech pathology. A list of some tests administered by these disciplines is shown in Table 10–8. (See Chapters 13 and 14 for a more detailed evaluation of many of those listed.) The physician must be familiar with resources which are available in his community and how to secure these services for his patient. For example, near a university center one can usually contact the university department of pediatrics, for a complete multidisicplinary examination. Under less ideal circumstances the physician may need to arrange for each consultation on an individual basis. In either case, the child's primary physician contributes to the interdisciplinary dialogue, arranging for the best diagnostic and therapeutic program.

Therapeutic Intervention

The most complete and expert evaluation is of little value for the child unless its recommendations can be used to arrange the best program of therapy *actually available to the patient*. As the child's advocate, and as a representative of the interdisciplinary team, it is the

Table 10-8. Test Instruments for Children with Learning Disorders.

Intelligence and Readiness Tests

Stanford-Binet Intelligence Scale
Wechsler Intelligence Scale for Children-Revised (WISC-R)
Peabody Picture Vocabulary Test (PPVT)
Vineland Social Maturity Scale
First-Grade Screening Test

Perceptual Development

Slosson Drawing Coordination Test
Bender Visual Motor Gestalt Test
Illinois Test of Psycholinguistic Abilities (ITPA)
Wepman Auditory Discrimination Test
Frostig Developmental Test of Visual Perception
Benton Visual Retention Test
Sentence Memory Test and Digit Memory Test
McCarthy Scales of Children's Abilities

Speech and Language

Goldman-Fristoe Test of Articulation
McDonald Deep Screening Articulation Test
Conversation Sample
Peabody Picture Vocabulary Test (PPVT)
Illinois Test of Psycholinguistic Abilities (ITPA)
Wepman Auditory Discrimination Test
Porch Index of Communicative Ability in Children
Northwest Syntax Screening Test
Roswell-Chall Auditory Blending Test
Assessment of Children's Language Comprehension

Achievement Tests

Wide Range Achievement Test (WRAT)
Metropolitan Achievement Test
Gray Oral Reading Test
Peabody Individual Achievement Test
Diagnostic Reading Scales

Emotional Development

Children's Apperception Test (CAT)
Thematic Apperception Test (TAT)
Draw-a-Person Test
Play Therapy Observation
Sentence Completion Test

physician's responsibility to help minimize "the red tape" so often limiting full implementation of a child's individual therapeutic program. Since the major responsiblity for treatment of learning disabilities rests with special educators, a dialogue between physician and teacher is necessary. The physician does *not* write the educational prescription, nor does he dictate educational policies or techniques (Cruickshank, 1977). The physician, however, should communicate to those responsible for the child's academic supervision those factors—physical, neurological, intellectual, perceptual, or emotional—that might contribute to the child's educational handicaps.

At some time during the course of the supervision of the child, the phsyician may be asked for medication in an attempt to solve the child's difficulties, particularly if disruptive behavior is a part of the problem. It is common to have children referred for medical supervision with a note from a harried teacher reading "Hyperactive—please medicate!" Only when behavior is viewed as the final common pathway for a variety of organic, developmental, situational, environmental, and emotional factors can the problem be approached meaningfully. "Hyperactivity" is a description of behavior; as such, it is a symptom rather than a primary disease. Hyperactive behavior may be associated with brain damage (often associated with seizures, marked intellectual impairment, and motor disabilities), minimal brain dysfunction syndrome, stressful or anxiety-provoking situations, developmental factors, or emotional problems. The four major categories of psychotropic drugs and the generic names of those drugs in each category are listed in Table 10–9. Several basic principles concerning medication must be emphasized: (1) The majority of children referred by parents or teachers as "hyperactive" suffer behavioral reactions rather than organically initiated forms of hyperkinetic behavior. (2) Medication is not uniformly successful, even in selected cases. In fact, there is considerable difference of opinion concerning the validity of positive responses to drugs. (3) Drugs should not be expected to work educational miracles. A successful trial of medication should be interpreted as having better enabled the child to attend to specific stimuli. A sound program of special or remedial education is the crucial factor for enhancing academic progress. And (4) the administration of medications is recommended for selected cases, following a thorough medical, psychological, and educational evaluation (Ambrosino & DeFonte, 1973; American Academy of Pediatrics, Committee on Drugs, 1970; Arnold, 1973; Baldwin, 1973; Gottlieb, 1975). In the final analysis, psychoactive drugs (methyl-

Table 10-9. Four Major Categories of Psychotropic Drugs.

Generic Name	Trade Name
Cerebral Stimulants	
Dextroamphetamine sulface	Dexedrine
Methylphenidate hydrochloride	Ritalin
Pemoline	Cylert
Sedatives and Tranquilizers	
Barbiturates	Phenobarbital
Phenothiazines	Thorazine
Chlorpromazine	Mellaril
Thioridazine	Valium
Diazepam	Benadryl
Diphenhydramine	Librium
Clordiazepoxide	Equanil
Meprobamate	Miltown
Antidepressants	
Imipramine	Tofranil
Amitryptyline	Elavil
Anticonvulsants	
Barbiturates	Phenobarital
Diphenylhydantoin	Dilantin

phenidate, dextroamphetamine, pemoline) have limited place in the comprehensive management of children with learning disabilities.

Effective therapy for the child in educational jeopardy demands constant reassessment of the therapeutic program and continual communication between the professionals sharing responsibility for the child's development. In no aspect of pediatric medicine is the physician's responsibility as a guardian of potentials more necessary or more rewarding.

SUMMARY

The role of the physician in assisting the learning-disabled child is multifaceted: (1) diagnostic intervention (history, physical examination, and developmental screening), (2) selection and referral to appropriate professionals, (3) coordination of an interdisciplinary team,

(4) counseling of parents, child, and professional, (5) monitoring the progress of diagnostic and therapeutic programs, and (6) acting as an advocate for the learning-disabled child in community efforts. The effectiveness of the physician in fulfilling this medical responsibility in part will be a reflection of (1) the concern and understanding of the nature of learning disabilities, (2) the ability to communicate with and appreciate interdisciplinary professional interaction, (3) the awareness of available community resources, and (4) the willingness to help secure needed resources.

The problems encountered by learning-disabled children and their families are measured in terms of academic underachievement and associated emotional trauma. The devastating complications of lack of self-esteem (self-concept), disturbed family relationships, and loss of potentials are a challenge to physicians dedicated to comprehensive health care for children. Medical intervention is essential in safeguarding the learning-disabled child from a lifetime of disturbed family and peer relationships, confused feelings of confidence and worth, educational jeopardy, and social disaster. The vicious cycle of learning disability, academic underachievement, and poor self-concept is often manifested during adolescence as antisocial attitudes and juvenile delinquency (Zinkus & Gottlieb, 1978a, b).

The physician is uniquely responsible for active intervention in serving the learning-disabled child. The physician is usually the first professional to see the learning-disabled child, and thus may be the first to identify him as a child at risk. The physician is likely also to be the first to be consulted by anxious parents or concerned teachers. While he may treat some of the organic and behavioral impediments to learning, the child's doctor may also serve as his advocate in helping to shape family, educational, and community priorities. The physician has no less a responsibility for the learning-disabled child than for a patient with meningitis, appendicitis, pneumonia—or any other "traditional" pediatric problem. The child in educational jeopardy faces emotional and social disaster. The complications of learning disabilities are lifelong. The physician's involvement is mandatory!

Robert G. Thompson, Jr.,
Marvin I. Gottlieb

REFERENCES

Adams, R. M., Kocsis, J. J., & Estes, R. E. Soft neurological signs in learning-disabled children and controls. *American Journal of Diseases of Children,* 1974, *128,* 614–618.

Ambrosino, S. V., DeFonte, J. M. A psycho-educational study of the hyperkinetic syndrome. *Psychosomatics,* 1973, *14,* 207–213.

American Academy of Pediatrics, Committee on Drugs (1970): An evaluation of the pharmacological approaches to learning impediments. *Pediatrics,* 1970, *46,* 142–144.

American Academy, Council on Child Health. Statement: Children with learning disabilities. Evanston, Ill.: the Academy, 1973. (a)

American Academy, Council on Child Health. Statement: Early identification of children with learning disabilities. The preschool child. Evanston, Ill.: the Academy, 1973. (b)

Arnold, L. E. The art of medicating hyperkinetic children. A number of practical suggestions. *Clinical Pediatrics,* 1973 *12,* 35–41.

Baldwin, R. W. The treatment of behavior disorders with medication. In S. G. Sapir, & A. C. Nitzburg, (Eds.), *Children with learning problems.* New York: Brunner / Mazel

Barlow, C. F. "Soft signs" in children with learning disorders. *American Journal of Diseases of Children,* 1974, *128,* 605–606.

Bax, M. C. O. The assessment of the child at school entry. *Pediatrics,* 1976, *58,* 403–407.

Benfield, R. M., Bendersky, A. M., & Thompson, A. Early identification of children with learning disabilities: Hearing, vision, and developmental screening of the preschool child. *Learning Disabilities: An Audio Journal for Continuing Education,* 1977, *1,*(8).

Boder, E. School failure—Evaluation and treatment. *Pediatrics,* 1976, *58,* 398–403.

Capute, A., Niedermeyer, E., Richardson, F. The electroencephalogram of children with minimal brain dysfunction. *Pediatrics,* 1968, *41,* 1104–1114.

Cruickshank, W. M. Myths and realities in learning disabilities. *Journal of Learning Disabilities,* 1977, *10,* 51–58.

Francis-Williams, J. Early identification of children likely to have specific learning difficulties: Report of a follow-up. *Developmental Medicine and Child Neurology,* 1976, *18,* 71–77.

Gottlieb, M. I. Pills: Pros and cons or medications for school problems. *Acta Symbolica,* 1975, *6,* 35–64.

Gottlieb, M. I. A model medical student curriculum on the needs of exceptional children. In *The needs of exceptional children.* Baltimore: University Park Press (in press).

Hart, Z., Rennick, P. M., Klinge, V., & Schwartz, M. L.: A pediatric neurologist's contribution to evaluations of school underachievers. *American Journal of Diseases of Children,* 1974, *128,* 319–323.

Jabbour, J. T., Duenas, D. A., Gilmartin, R. C., Gottlieb, M. T. *Pediatric neurology handbook* (2nd ed). Flushing, N.Y.: Medical Exam Publishing, 1976.

Kappelman, M., Roberts, P., Rinaldi, R., & Cornblath, M. The school health team and school health physician. *American Journal of Diseases of Children,* 1975, *129,* 191–195.

Lerner, J. W. (Ed.). *Children with learning disabilities: Theories, diagnosis and teaching strategies,* (2nd ed.). Boston: Houghton Mifflin, 1976.

Meier, J. H. Prevalence and characteristics of learning disabilities found in second-grade children. *Journal of Learning Disabilities,* 1971, *4,* 1–16.

Olson, M. E. Minimal cerebral dysfunction: The child referred for school-related problems. *Pediatric Annals,* 1975, *4,* 69–92.

Satterfield, J. H., Cantwell, D. P., Saul, R. E., & Usin, A. Intelligence, academic achievement, and EEG abnormalities in hyperactive children. *American Journal of Psychiatry,* 1974, *131,* 391–395.

Schain, R. J. *Neurology of child disorders.* Baltimore: Williams & Wilkins, 1972.

Schulman, J. L. *Management of emotional disorders in pediatric practice.* Chicago: Year Book Medical Publishers, 1969.

Silver, L. B. A proposed view on the etiology of the neurological learning disability syndrome. *Journal of Learning Disabilities,* 1971, *4,* 123–133. (a)

Silver, L. B. Familial patterns in children with neurologically based learning disabilities. *Journal of Learning Disabilities,* 1971, *4,* 349–358. (b)

Stine, O. C., Saratsiotis, J. B., & Mosser, R. S. Relationship between neurological findings and classroom behavior. *American Journal of Diseases of Children,* 1975, *129,* 1036–1040.

Thompson, R. G., & Gottlieb, M. I. Educational Jeopardy, an interdisciplinary problem: The physician's contribution. *Acta Symbolica,* 1973, *4,* 47–72.

Todd, M., & Gottlieb, M. I. Interdisciplinary counseling in a medical setting. In E. J. Webster (Ed.), *Professional approaches with parents of handicapped children.* Springfield, Ill.: Thomas, 1976, pp. 191–216.

Webster, E. *Professional approaches with parents of handicapped children.* Springfield, Ill.: Thomas, 1976.

Zinkus, P. W., & Gottlieb, M. I.: Educational jeopardy and juvenile delinquency. *Learning disabilities: An Audio Journal for Continuing Education,* 1978, *2*(4). (a)

Zinkus, P. W., & Gottlieb, M. I.: Learning disabilities and juvenile delinquency. *Clinical Pediatrics,* 1978, *17,* 775–780.

APPENDIX
GENERAL ABILITIES SCREENING INVENTORY
Directions for General Abilities Screening

The following is a general screening examination. It is *not* a standardized evaluation. It is designed to give you some general impressions about a child's abilities. This is *NOT* a test of intellectual or academic function. The screening should be used only in the context of providing you with some *general* insights about the child's school readiness. The screening can be used in conjunction with other testing procedures to help formulate a child's developmental profile.

The following screening inventory is designed to assess basic learning and perceptual skills. The value of this screening is to help determine minimum skills in

1. General information/academic achievement
2. Auditory processing
   a. auditory closure
   b. auditory discrimination
   c. auditory blending
   d. auditory spatial and temporal relationships
   e. auditory sequential memory
   f. auditory short term memory (nonvisually clued and visually clued).
3. Visual processing
   a. visual closure
   b. visual spatial orientation
   c. visual discrimination
   d. visual short-term memory
   e. visual sequential memory
   f. visual motor coordination
4. Auditory-visual integration

From the University of Tennessee Center for the Health Sciences, Department of Pediatrics, Clinic for Exceptional Children. Reprinted by permission.

Fig. 10-1. To test visual motor coordination, ask the child to draw a line connecting the dots to get the bee into the hive and to draw a line in the middle of the highway from car to stop-sign, without touching the sides.

Fig. 10-2. To test visual closure and visual motor coordination, ask the child to complete the drawings.

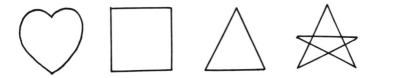

Fig. 10-3. To test auditory memory of visually-clued patterns, give the child multiple directions, e.g., put a dot in the heart, a circle inside the square, a circle around the triangle, etc. Note the number of correct responses.

11

EARLY IDENTIFICATION OF LEARNING DISORDERS

NORMAL CHILD DEVELOPMENT

The basic drive to be normal, healthy, and happy is manifest throughout the human life span. The desire to create normal offspring is equaled only by the fear that "something may be wrong with the baby." It can be predicted, almost with certainty, that the first question asked by the new mother will be, "Is my baby all right?" Parents usually seek reassurances, either directly or indirectly, that they have produced and are rearing a normal, healthy child. To do otherwise is to feel the bitter barbs of guilt and disappointment and to experience agonies of grief over a "less than perfect child." Almost from the moment of conception, the maturational sequence of the child is carefully scrutinized by conscientious parents and pediatricians. Even the vaguest indication of atypical development triggers a protective biological alarm, which prompts attention by physician and other allied health specialists.

Descriptions of "normal" child development have varied over the centuries (Biehler, 1976). In the 1700s Jonathan Edwards described children as being inherently wicked, while Rousseau characterized them as basically good. Locke philosophized that all children were as "blank slates" ready to be inscribed by their first postnatal experiences. In the 1920s, John B. Watson was so convinced of the power of the environment to determine developmental skills that he bargained to produce "doctor, lawyer, merchant, thief . . ." if given normal, healthy children at birth. Conversely, Gesell stressed the importance of genetic input, the built-in maturational timetable. The sequence of

297

development was envisioned as an "unfolding from within" of this maturational timetable, with environmental effects of minor significance.

The controversy persists concerning the relative influence of heredity vs. environment on the child's development. Skinner (1953), a recognized authority of the behaviorist-associationist-environmentalist philosophy, stressed that the environment determines individual development, and, in this sense, we are products of our environmental conditioning. As the leading spokesman of humanistic psychology, Maslow (1968) suggested that individuals are, to a considerable extent, self-made. Consequently, the significance of laying the foundation for wise choices is Maslow's prescription for creating individuals who are ultimately self-disciplined and self-motivated. Critics of behavior modification fear a growing dependency on external rewards and/or the consequences of "brain-washing" techniques.

No American has introduced a concept of child development that approximates the scope of theories proposed by Freud, Erikson, and Piaget (Biehler, 1976). Freud and Erikson emphasized psychosexual and psychosocial development. The ideal goal according to Erikson is a sense of integrity. Freud's theory focuses on the ability to love well and work well. According to Piaget's theory of cognitive development, thinking logically about abstract ideas is the ultimate goal in individual development.

The significance of early developmental experiences has received increasing attention over the years. Freud more than any other scholar is responsible for having formulated accepted concepts that *all* behavior is caused (none is random or meaningless), and to appreciate later behavior, it is necessary to understand development in infancy and early childhood (Jones, 1953).

Freud's identification of the importance of oral activities during infancy coincides with Erikson's emphasis on developing a sense of trust, both initial stages are concerned with the feeding experience. Simply meeting the nutritional needs of the infant is not sufficient. A "positive infant–caregiver" interaction appears to be essential for guiding normal development. Although institutionalized infants' nutritional and medical needs are being met, these children may fail to thrive if emotional and social needs are being denied. The need for love is apparently innate, while the ability to love is learned.

The process of attachment to significant adults is dramatically illustrated in the latter part of the first year of the infant's life. As a consequence of attachment, the infant typically becomes fearful of separation and fearful of strangers. The development of these two fears is seen almost universally and is one parameter of the infant's emotional, social development.

The process of attachment and its related fears may also be seen as a significant reflection of the child's cognitive development. Piaget's research with infants reveals their lack of "object permanence." The young infant responds (or fails to respond) to the disappearance of an object from his sight. He does not search for the missing object; it is as though the object ceased to exist. During the latter part of the first year of life the child exhibits evidence of an awareness that objects continue to exist although they are out of sight. Perhaps "knowing" that mother continues to exist and will return is part of the young child's adjustment to the fear of separation and strangers.

The development of object permanence is seen as a major developmental milestone during the sensorimotor period. According to Piaget, the infant comes to know himself and his world primarily through sensory experiences and his own motoric activities (Ginsberg & Opper, 1969). White and Watts (1973) correlated the quality of adult–child interaction during the 10- to 18-month period with the level of competence the child demonstrates at age 3 years. The child who at 3 years of age is competent in the nursery classroom and on the playground (who "has it together") has typically experienced a competent caregiver as an infant and toddler. The competent caregiver encourages the child's natural curiosity and exploratory behavior, is sensitive to the need for physical contact, and possesses the ability to soothe an irritable baby. White's research suggested that the competent caregiver delights in the young child's accomplishments. The caregiver is described as a "consultant" and is available to respond to verbalization attempts. Middle-class caregivers have been described as more likely to be verbal rather than physical in relating to children.

Opportunities for firsthand sensory-motor experiences appear to lay the foundation for later abstract concept development. As the child progresses through the sensory-motor period, he develops a new tool that will become very significant in cognitive development. The development of language during the second year of life opens additional avenues for learning. By 4 years of age most normal children in most cultures have acquired language. The universality of language acquisition supports the theory that language primarily evolves as a result of man's unique, innate, biological predisposition for the development of meaningful speech (Chomsky, 1968). Children vary in the rate that they acquire grammatical form, but there is amazing uniformity in the order in which they emerge. Factors that influence the child's language development include the socioeconomic level of the family, the ordinal position, sex, and intelligence. Recently, attention has focused on the significance of the child's auditory perception.

Erikson's (1963) theory of development emphasizes the importance of a sense of autonomy and initiative during the early years. Many psychologists and educators are convinced of the value of "freedom within limits" that Erikson espouses. Defining limits, establishing what is acceptable and what will not be tolerated, is reassuring for the child. In most circumstances the limits should be clearly delineated and consistently maintained. Freedom to choose, within limits, seems essential to the development of an autonomous, self-governing individual. A very significant component of a healthy self-concept is the child's feeling of control or power over his own life. Opportunities to choose within appropriate boundaries enhances confidence in "self." A favorable as well as a realistic self-concept, in turn, helps the child to choose wisely.

During the latter part of the preschool years children typically begin to identify with the parent of the same sex. Freud and Erikson agree that this is one of the most significant events during the first years of life. Two major consequences of the process of identification are sex typing and the development of conscience.

"Sex typing" may be defined as the process by which individuals acquire the behavior and attitudes regarded by their culture as characteristically masculine or feminine. The development of masculinity and femininity has taken on new dimensions within the past few years. Whether the child is born a boy or girl has been described as the single most important determinant of personality characteristics. The sex of the child influences emotional, social, moral, language, intellectual, and creative development as well as self-concept. Traditional interpretations of masculinity and femininity have been criticized as limiting the development of the individual. Yet, nontraditional interpretations remain controversial within society at large. Are boys normally (or biologically) more physical and aggressive than girls? Are girls more verbal than boys because of inherent differences between the sexes? Some authorities feel that as much as 90 percent of the differences in the sexes is due to the socialization process. Others feel the biological "rock-bottom" differences may be more pervasive than is generally acknowledged (Papalia & Olds, 1975).

The development of conscience theoretically comes about as a result of the child's identification with significant adults in his life. Identification is described as the process whereby the individual begins to think, feel, and behave as though the characteristics of the adult models and peer models are all currently being studied.

Kohlberg's theory of moral development suggests that preschool and early elementary children's moral development is directly related to their cognitive development (Kohlberg & Turiel, 1972). Their basic motivation for moral judgments seems dependent on rewards for acceptable behavior and/or punishment for unacceptable behavior. Kohlberg and Piaget agree that the later stages of moral development are dependent on the older child's cognitive ability to take into consideration another point of view. The young child is normally egocentric. He does not share because he can not begin to imagine how much another child wants some of his candy or a ride on his tricycle. Indeed, Kohlberg suggests that most of the trouble in the world today is the "inability to imagine the innerness of other lives."

Factors Influencing Normal Development

Throughout the discussion thus far factors influencing normal child development have been implied. Variations in development appear to be primarily due to genetic components, prenatal factors, early experiences and/or childhood diseases. Genetic counseling has become more widely available to meet the needs of parents with reason to be concerned about specific hereditary factors. Although the majority of American babies proceed from conception to delivery without obvious difficulty, various factors may significantly influence prenatal development. The lifetime dietary habits of the mother as well as her nutritional status during pregnancy are receiving increasing attention. The specific influence of drugs, alcohol, smoking, and radiation is being studied. Maternal illnesses, age, and emotions as well as the number and spacing of pregnancies may affect the developing child. Prematurity is the greatest single cause of neonatal deaths. A poor, inadequately nourished, nonwhite teenager who has received little or no prenatal care is most likely to deliver a premature infant with high risk for developmental problems.

Children's early experiences have multiple effects as well as long-term consequences. Recent research suggests an overriding significance of the general home environment as reflected by social class (Jencks, 1972). Low-achieving school children typically come from homes headed by parents with limited education, few occupational skills, and low incomes. A recent report from the Carnegie Council on Children recommends a guaranteed minimum income to all families with children (Keniston, 1977). Single parents would be given the option of caring for their young children full time. Some psychologists reason that improving child-care techniques used in the home environment will improve the intellectual functioning of children. Others suggest the need for quality infant day care with the fastest growing proportion of job-holding mothers being those with babies under 2 years of age. White believes that most parents would willingly adjust their lives to their babies' needs in the crucial first 3 years if they were convinced of the importance of their task in producing competent children (White, 1973).

Developmental Milestones

To study the whole child may seem to be a simplistic approach to understanding child development. Yet, medical and educational specialists need to be sensitive to the whole child as he interacts with the significant people in his life to produce unique variations in his development. The following developmental milestones are broad, general characteristics of young children's normal development (Quick & Campbell, 1976).

Infancy. The newborn may be viewed as a bundle of reflexes with primarily physiological needs to be met. Other interpretations view the neonate as a more complex being whose psychological development must be taken into account. Responding promptly and positively to his earliest forms of communication seem essential to his development of a sense of trust. His early smile may indeed be a survival reflex; certainly it influences the warmth of the caretaker's reaction to the infant. During the first year he reaches for and wants to be held by familiar persons. Toward the latter part of the first year he is likely to exhibit fear of strangers and fear of separation from those to whom he has become attached.

Gross motor control proceeds from the head downward. By 6 months of age the infant sits unsupported and moves about by rolling, creeping, or scooting. Pulling himself upright to a standing position and standing alone for a few moments are cause for celebrating the first birthday. His fine motor skill has progressed to drinking from a cup or glass with assistance, placing food into his mouth with his hand, and grasping small objects with his thumb and index finger.

Responsiveness to the voice of the caretaker may be seen throughout infancy. Initially the infant smiles, coos, and babbles. At 9 months of age he responds to "bye bye" and may begin to imitate adult sounds such as "da da" or "ma ma."

Toddler. Once the child is walking without assistance, he begins to explore more of his immediate surroundings. Although his safety and health are of utmost importance, he does need the freedom of physical movement as well as opportunities for various sensory experiences. "Child-proofing" at least part of the home allows parents to enjoy their toddler's natural curiosity and drive to explore.

The toddler begins to follow simple instructions and is responsive to "no" if the caretaker is not unduly restrictive. The toddler's verbal development proceeds from one-word utterances to two-word phrases—"Mommy gone," "Want milk," or "Coffee hot." Elaboration by the adult, such as "Yes the coffee is hot," will not be immediately duplicated by the toddler, but it does reinforce his attempts at communication. It becomes apparent that the toddler understands much more language than he can produce.

The child's interest in pictures is to be encouraged as he points to familiar objects named by the adult. Pointing to his eyes, ears, nose, etc., is a fun game which promotes his language and cognitive development as well as social relationships. Socially, he plays near other children with limited interaction or cooperation.

Weaning usually occurs near the end of the first year. The toddler's lower consumption of milk after weaning is not a reason for concern if he is learning to eat a wide variety of meats, vegetables, and fruits. He enjoys feeding himself with a spoon.

2-year-olds. The degree of mobility displayed by the 2-year-old child is evident as he runs, jumps, climbs stairs, and learns to pedal his own tricycle. The significance of fine motor skill development is demonstrated in the 2-year-old's ability to string 1-inch beads, build a tower of blocks, complete a three-shape formboard, scribble with crayons, and experiment with the use of scissors.

The 2-year-old is generally capable of naming familiar objects and persons, including his own name. His sense of ownership seems exaggerated at times with strong proclamations of "me" and "mine." On occasion, "no" appears to be his favorite word. Freedom within clearly understood limits helps him through this negative phase. Three-word sentences, including plurals, are typical of his progress in language acquisition.

The 2-year-old child moves toward mastery over his own body in toilet training, self-dressing, and self-feeding. Toilet training is usually achieved without stress if children are maturationally ready to begin training, reinforced when they are successful and when failure is minimized. Removal of coat or sweater precedes putting on one's coat. Buttoning awaits a later stage of development.

Eating with a fork as well as a spoon is possible for most 2-year-olds, and they can suck from a plastic straw. Their appetites are not likely to be as good as they were during the first year of life. Limiting between-meal snacks and encouraging vigorous outdoor play will promote healthy attitudes toward eating. Finger foods and small servings of a new food served alongside favorite foods help the young child to enjoy mealtime. His imitation of adult models may be reflected in his food likes and dislikes.

3-year-olds.   During the third year of life a child manages walking up stairs, one foot per step without using the rail. His perceptuocognitive skills include stringing one-half-inch beads, copying a circle, and building or putting small toys together. Awareness of various colors and shapes helps him in working a three- or four-piece puzzle and in simple sorting and matching games according to color. He is able to match geometric shapes, count three objects, and build a bridge with three blocks.

Fairly complete, four-word sentences become apparent, and he is able to listen to short stories. He can name most familiar objects in his immediate environment. Relating simple experiences that he has had recently can be a delightful opportunity for sharing ideas, promoting warm relationships, and enhancing communication skills. His enjoyment of simple songs and / or nursery rhymes is to be encouraged.

His interest in other children promotes cooperative play as well as sharing upon request. For many 3-year-olds a regular play period with other children is welcomed, although they may resist leaving mothers until they are convinced that parents can be counted on to return for them.

Often 3-year-olds are pleased to help with simple household tasks. They may in turn imitate adults' behavior in their own dramatic play. Opportunities to "play like Mommy and Daddy" seem to contribute to their imaginative creative development as well as the process of identification with significant adults.

Later preschool years.   During the latter part of the preschool years, additional gross motor feats are accomplished, such as skipping, galloping, and catching a large ball. Fine motor skills are displayed as the 4- to 5-year-old uses scissors, draws a three-part man, works a twelve-piece puzzle, and copies a cross or square from an example. The level of comprehension includes explaining the function or use of familiar objects, relating appropriate activities for day and night, meaningfully counting several objects, and naming common coins.

The child averages five-word sentences with an attempt to use new words spontaneously. His speech is 90 percent intelligible with little or no infantile speech present.

Separation from mother for regularly scheduled activities is generally easy for the 4- or 5-year-old child. Peers begin to influence his behavior, and he generally plays with others with minimal friction. Disagreements are often intense but usually short-lived. The child is beginning to assume some responsibilities in picking up toys after playing.

Except for tying shoes, he is fairly independent in dressing and undressing. Washing face and hands, brushing teeth, and taking a bath are routinely managed with little adult assistance.

Readiness for reading and other academic pursuits are observed in the child's recognition of familiar words from television commercials, cereal boxes, and road signs. The child's attention span lengthens and an interest in "reading" picture books may be noted. As he relates personal experiences, the child may take into account what happened "first, next, and last." The ability to follow simple directions is another indication of readiness for the next stages in development.

It is in terms of this baseline that growth and development during the critical preschool years are measured. This is not to say that deviations are necessarily negative. They are indications of our uniqueness—sometimes positive, sometimes negative—always challenging. It is the task of those in care-giving roles to determine their significance to the learning process.

EARLY IDENTIFICATION OF LEARNING DISABILITIES

A wealth of research and information is now available in the area of learning disabilities. Within the last 40 years contributions have come from specialized areas within medicine, psychology, and education. There is an increased awareness of learning disabilities and their ramifications on the part of involved professionals as well as the general public.

Differential diagnoses are now possible for less obvious learning disabilities and at increasingly earlier ages. Ironically, these capabilities make the problem of appropriate utilization of the diagnoses more complex. In the past the population of children identified as the learning-disabled generally had handicapping conditions that relegated them to special classes. Their teachers usually had specific training in working with gross handicaps.

The current state of knowledge allows identification of more subtle and circumscribed learning problems. While these disabilities are significant in the learning process, they are less obvious and do not necessarily indicate the need for special-class placement. In fact, the trend toward mainstreaming implies that fewer children will be placed in special classes. It also means that teachers not trained in specific learning disorders are required to design and administer specialized learning experiences within the regular classroom. Depending on the size and resources of the school system, psychological services and resource programs might or might not be available.

Diagnosis of learning disabilities at increasingly earlier ages also brings with it a particular set of problems. Preschool teachers are no more likely to be trained in the area of learning disabilities than are public school teachers. Preschool programs are also less likely to have specialized support services available. Another problem is the more centralized role of parents in working with preschool children with special needs. Both teachers and parents require understanding, knowledge, and specific directions in order to maximize the learning opportunities for exceptional children. Neither teachers nor parents can be expected to have the requisite skills to do this.

Maximum intervention calls for rather precise information on each learning-disabled child: precise diagnosis and precise plans for remediation. It is incumbent on and increasingly challenging for professionals to make a differential diagnosis, translate it to specific educational prescriptions, and communicate these to other professionals as well as untrained persons in a way that positively affects the learning capabilities of each child.

There is convincing evidence to show that providing an "enriched" environment that is appropriate to the interest and developmental abilities of the child does not make up for past deficits. This implies that the educational program should be based on the needs of each child rather than on a formal curriculum. Continual diagnosis, both formal and informal, is required for the teacher to determine each child's readiness for a particular activity (Bereiter & Englemann, 1966; Lerner, 1971; Taba & Elkins, 1966).

Increased use of diagnostic instruments should also add to the existing knowledge of specific disabilities and their relation to the learning process. In addition, their use should be helpful in determining how particular experiences contribute to the development of specific developmental processes (Simeonsson & Wiegerink, 1975; Zigler, 1970). Diagnostic measurements, from this perspective, become a tool to use in constructing environments appropriate to the child's needs rather than a procedure for assessing the child's capacity.

Developmental assessment as a basis for curriculum design has been studied in several preschool programs. The Ceremerel Language and Thinking: New Directions Program is a hierarchical skills-oriented approach with assessment procedures as an integral component. Significant treatment effects have been found with the use of this model (Willis, 1972).

Another study of an early intervention program utilized a prescriptive program for each child designed on the basis of differential diagnosis. It was found to be superior to a traditional preschool curriculum. The emphasis on the continual assessment of each child's learning systems was also identified as a positive addition to the educational component. In addition, longitudinal data indicated that the children maintained their developmental gains in auditory and visual perception through grade two (D'Annunzio & Steg, 1972).

Another early identification and intervention strategy being employed combines existing diagnostic tools. Appropriate referrals for individual children are made on the basis of the child and family history, both physical and social; psychological, speech, hearing, vision, motor and developmental screening; and medical and dental examinations. The use of this type of interdisciplinary program implies a team approach not only to the diagnostic process, but also to the remediation process (McDonald & Soeffing, 1971; Thompson, Garrett, & Striffler, 1976).

Improved classroom performance of disadvantaged preschoolers can be shown with the use of one diagnostic procedure in curriculum design. As a result of classroom assignment of kindergarteners on the basis of readiness scores, it was found that experiences for the different classes could be more easily planned to maximize the development of each (Lee, 1970). Although this is a relatively unsophisticated use of the concept of developmental assessment, it does indicate more than a theoretical commitment to meeting individual needs.

Diagnostic screening batteries are also being developed for use by persons working with young children who have had no experience or formal training in evaluation procedures. In one such project children in three different types of preschool programs made significant improvement, when compared to a control group, after being involved in a diagnostic/intervention program designed and implemented by volunteers (Caldwell, 1971). The Early Identification and Programming Guide developed by Webb (1973) is another type of strategy being used to assist teachers in the diagnosis and programming of children with borderline disabilities.

Even a cursory perusal of the literature indicates that the most defensible basis for intervention is an ongoing assessment of each child. Because no one teaching strategy can meet each individual's needs, the choice should be based on an analysis of each child's specific difficulty. The alternative is a trial-and-error approach or reliance on one remedial procedure (Frostig, 1967).

The derivation of achievement scores, mental ages, language age equivalent, perceptual age levels, and similar scores has been a terminal goal in many cases. If those who are responsible for mediating learning disabilities are to make a significant impact, this type of information needs to be utilized in order to implement a diagnostic/treatment pattern of education rather than a diagnostic / labeling one. The role of assessment should then fall into proper perspective (Langley, 1976; Reger, 1970).

On the basis of what is known regarding education for learning-disabled children, the diagnostic / prescriptive approach appears to be a fruitful area for development. It encourages a more eclectic view of educational programs based on a tremendously increased body of information on each child. Most importantly, it gives the child a more central position in his own educational process.

The MEMPHIS Model

One example of a specific prescriptive program that has been utilized is the MEMPHIS model. It is an individualized system of preschool program planning and evaluation based on a developmental assessment of each child. The traditional program with which it was compared was a curriculum-centered nonprescriptive approach. In attempting to determine the relative value of both types of learning experiences in mediating the developmental delays of disadvantaged preschool children, a contrast group composed of children with no organized preschool experience was used as a baseline for both approaches (Nunn, 1974). In order to meet the goals of effective and early remediation, an educational system was designed for early childhood programs for exceptional children. Entitled the MEMPHIS Model of Individual Program Planning and Evaluation: A System of Developmental-Educational Evaluation and Educational Program Planning for Preschool Age Handicapped Children, the model does not require the use of the other program components (Quick, Little & Campbell, 1974).

The MEMPHIS model is a three-part diagnostic/prescriptive/reassessment system—a continuous method of ascertaining, implementing, and evaluating an intervention program. The five developmental skill areas involved in this process are personal-social, gross motor, fine motor, language, and perceptuocognitive. The three components of the system are:

1. Developmental evaluation
2. Individual education program planning
3. Educational evaluation

Developmental evaluation is done with the use of the Memphis Comprehensive Developmental Scale. This scale includes 260 developmental tasks that have been identified as significant for later school success. In addition, the chronological norms for appearance of these skills are arranged in the developmental sequence in which they most often appear. Composed of five scales, one for each of the developmental skill areas, this instrument was specifically designed for teacher use.

The model provides for individual educational program planning. As a result of developmental evaluation on each child, the teacher can identify each child's educational needs in terms of the next skills on the developmental scale which the child has not mastered. These skills then become the basis for each child's educational program, and are listed on the Developmental Skill Assignment Record. Several lesson plans for possible teacher use as well as suggestions for material and equipment are included in the model.

The model has been expanded to include lesson plans for the developmental tasks that are part of the Memphis Comprehensive Development Scale. They were developed after the completion of this study (Quick et al., 1973).

The Continuous Record for Educational-Developmental Gain is used on a daily basis for ongoing assessment of each child's progress relative to skill assignments. Dates and ratings of performance relative to skill mastery are included to provide a continuous record of each child's progress from the beginning to the end of the treatment period. At the end of this period the total number of skills mastered is entered on the Completion Record. From this precise record of each child's developmental progress the teacher is able to determine the needs of the child as well as the program. Thus, the educational evaluation becomes an important component of the recycling process.

At the end of a designated amount of time, usually 3 to 6 months, each child is reassessed on the Memphis Comprehensive Developmental Scale. At this point a new cycle of individual program planning based on the developmental assessment begins.

The MEMPHIS model is thus a systematized and continuous diagnostic / prescriptive approach to preschool education for children between the developmental ages of birth and 5 years. It is applicable for any of the developmental skill areas. Not tied to any one curriculum model or teaching style, it can be used in any type program.

The diagnostic / prescriptive approach of the model was shown to have a significant positive influence in remediating developmental delays in preschool children. In comparison to the traditional approach, the data indicate a difference in the amount of gain and the areas of emphasis. The experimental group gained from 7 to 10 months in all areas of the developmental assessment during the 4-month period. The control group gained 4 months only in gross motor and personal-social skills. These results illustrate the need for rather specific experiences developed on the basis of individually identified needs (Nunn, 1974).

More diagnostic / prescriptive approaches should be developed as the capabilities of differential diagnosis and prescriptive program planning increase. The MEMPHIS study, as well as others, very emphatically demonstrates the efficacy of diagnosis and teaching as an integrated approach to meeting the needs of each learning-disabled child.

Inventories for Remediation of Identified Weaknesses

The need for early identification and remediation of learning disabilities has been clearly shown. The rationale for diagnosis rests in understanding and remediating learning disabilities. In the following discussion several available inventories that have either formal prescriptive programs or implications for specific experiences that address remediation of identified weaknesses are detailed. Their appropriateness in terms of population, assessment area covered, resources, personal training, etc. should be noted.

Information on these assessments, and others, can be found in Chapters 13 and 14 of this volume as well as the *Sixth Mental Measurements Yearbook* (Buros, 1958) and the manual accompanying each assessment.

Denver Developmental Screening Test, *ages 2 weeks–6 years, 15–20 minutes administration time.*

This general screening instrument assesses developmental levels in the gross motor, fine motor-adaptive, language, and personal-social areas. It is easily and quickly administered. Its "strength" is its ability to highlight specific developmental areas for further study. It should be noted, however, that the Denver is not specific and sensitive enough to direct intervention strategies on its own.

Basic Concept Inventory (BCI), *preschool and kindergarten, 15–20 minutes administration time.*

The BCI is a prototype of an assessment designed to evaluate specific skills in which the child has had experiences. It is a checklist of basic concepts in three areas: basic concepts, statement repetition and comprehension, and pattern awareness. The scores are designed to be utilized to form instructional groups. The BCI includes specific educational strategies for helping children master specific concepts.

Cognitive Skills Assessment Battery for Pre-Kindergarten and Kindergarten (CSAB), *preschool and kindergarten, 30–40 minutes administration time.*

Like the BCI the CSAB is designed to assess specific skill competencies identified as basic to school success. The efficacy of this assessment is, therefore, in terms of the validity of these competencies. The areas included are orientation to environment coordination, visual and auditory discrimination, visual and auditory memory, and comprehension and concept formation. The specific competency base nature of the CSAB makes it conducive to small-group or individual prescriptive program planning.

Handbook in Diagnostic Teaching: A Learning Disabilities Approach, *preschool and elementary, variable administration time.*

The *Handbook in Diagnostic Teaching* includes easily administered and interpreted diagnostic instruments in spelling, reading, and general development. There are specific task curriculum suggestions as well as a format for the development of other diagnostic / prescriptive aids.

In addition, support materials are supplied on the theoretical basis of the approach and other sources of materials are noted.

Learning Abilities: Diagnostic and Instructional Procedures for Specific Early Learning Disabilities (Threshold).

This program contains informal diagnostic assessments and observation checklists in the areas of learning disabilities, emotional disturbance, mental retardation, physical handicaps, visual impairment, hearing impairment, and language delay. The emphasis is on prescriptive programming rather than on diagnostics. For each area there are instructional ideas for small groups or individuals along with progress record forms. The strengths and weakness of each child are highlighted.

Frostig Developmental Test of Visual Perception (DTVP), *ages 3–8 years, 30–45 administration time, specific training required to administer.*

The DTVP is concerned with visual perceptual skills assessment and makes no attempt to look at the total child. It consists of five subtests: eye-motor coordination, figure-ground discrimination, form consistency, position in space, and spatial relations. Suggestions for specific training activities accompany the battery. It should be noted that minority group children are expected to score below the norm.

Experienced and trained persons are required to administer the DTVP. In general, the Frostig test is considered an adequate overall assessment of visual perceptual skills.

Vineland Social Maturity Scale, *ages birth–adult, 20–30 minutes administration time.*

The Vineland attempts to assess the areas of self-help, self-direction, locomotion, occupation, communication, and social relations. In dealing with young children, its strength lies in the insights it provides in understanding the child and his environment. The specificity of the scale allows for prescriptive program planning in specific areas of weakness.

SUMMARY

It is incumbent on those who attempt to understand and maximize a child's development to address the central issues of what is known and the direction it implies. The process of becoming a unique inidividual is fascinating, complex, and never ending. It is also unique to each individual—partially due to genetic factors, partially as a function of the environment. The ways in which genetic and environmental factors interact to make each one of us a singular individual are infinite.

It is only through knowledge of normal development that developmental disorders can be identified and mediated. This chapter is an attempt to summarize parameters of development and strategies for individual diagnostic / prescriptive programs of early intervention for learning disorders.

Virginia I. Nunn
Dixie R. Crase

REFERENCES

Bereiter, C., & Englemann, S. *Teaching disadvantaged children in the preschool.* Englewood Cliffs, N.J.: Prentice-Hall, 1966.

Biehler, R. F. *Psychology applied to teaching* (2nd ed.). Boston: Houghton Mifflin.

Biehler, R. F. *Child development: An introduction.* Boston: Houghton Mifflin, 1976.

Buros, O. K. *The sixth mental measurements yearbook* (6th ed.). Highland Park, N.J.: Gryphon, 1958.

Caldwell, J. A preschool screening program. *Dissertation Abstracts International,* 1971, *31,* 5229A.

Chomsky, N. *Language and the mind.* New York: Harcourt Brace Jovanovich, 1968.

D'Anntanzio, A., & Steg, D. E. *Helping problem learners during the early years.* Bethesda, Md.: ERIC Document Service, Ed 063038, 1972.

Erikson, E. H. *Childhood and society* (2nd ed.). New York, Norton, 1963.

Frostig, M. Testing as a basis for educational therapy. *Journal of Special Education,* 1967, *2,* 15–25.

Ginsburg, H., & Opper, S. *Piaget's theory of intellectual development: An introduction.* Englewood Cliffs, N.J.: Prentice-Hall, 1969.

Jencks, C. S. *Inequality: A reassessment of the effect of family and schooling in America.* New York: Basic Books, 1972.

Jones, E. *The life and work of Sigmund Freud.* Vol. 1: *The formative years and the great discoveries.* New York: Basic Books, 1953.

Keniston, K. *All our children: The American family under pressure.* New York: Harcourt Brace Jovanovich, 1977.

Kohlberg, L., & Turiel, E. *Recent research in moral development.* New York: Holt, Rinehart, and Winston, 1972.

Langley, B. Translation of assessment data into practical classroom procedures. Paper presented at the International Conference on Exceptional Children, 1976.

Lee, R. E. Preschool grouping of kindergarten children. *Illinois School Research*, 1970, *7*, 19–21.

Lerner, J. W. *Children with learning disabilities: Theories, diagnosis, and teaching strategies.* Boston: Houghton Mifflin, 1971.

Maslow, A. H. *Toward a psychology of being* (2nd ed.). Princeton, N.J.: Van Nostrand, 1968.

McDonald, P. L., & Soeffing, M. Prevention of learning problems: Capsule summaries of research studies in early childhood education. *Exceptional Children*, 1971, *37*, 681–686.

Nunn, V. I. *A comparative study of the effect of a traditional model and the MEMPHIS model on developmental gains of disadvantaged preschool children.* Memphis, Memphis State University Press, 1974.

Papalia, D. E., & Olds, S. W. *A child's world.* New York: McGraw-Hill, 1975.

Quick, A. D., & Campbell, A. A. *Lesson plans for enhancing preschool developmental progress.* Dubuque, Iowa: Kendale / Hunt, 1976.

Quick, A. D., Little, T. L., & Campbell, A. A. *The training of exceptional foster children and their foster parents: Enhancing developmental progress and parent effectiveness.* Memphis, Tenn.: Memphis State University Press, 1973.

Quick, A. D., Little, T. I., & Campbell, A. A. *Project MEMPHIS: Enhancing developmental progress in preschool exceptional children.* Belmont, Calif.: Fearon, 1974.

Reger, R. *Preschool programming of children with learning disabilities.* Springfield, Ill.: Thomas, 1970.

Simeonsson, R. J., & Wiegerink, R. Accountability: A dilemma in infant intervention. *Exceptional children*, 1975, *41*, 474–481.

Skinner, B. F. *Science and human behavior.* New York: Macmillan, 1953.

Taba, I. I., & Elkins, D. *Teaching strategies for the culturally disadvantaged.* Chicago: Rand McNally, 1966.

Thompson, R. J., Garrett, D. J., & Striffler, N. A model interdisciplinary diagnostic and treatment nursery. *Child psychology and human development,* 1976, *6*, 224–232.

Webb, J. R. Early identification and programming guide for young children with mild or borderline disabilities. *Dissertation Abstracts International,* 1973, *33*, 4992A.

Willis, H. D. *CEMEREL's language and thinking program: Some preliminary preschool findings.* ERIC Document Reproduction Service, Ed. 063024, 1972.

White, B. L. *Today's child,* January, 1977.

White, B. L., & Watts, J. C. *Experience and Environment: Major influences on the development of the young child* (Vol. 1). Englewood Cliffs, N.J.: Prentice-Hall, 1973.

Zigler, E. The environmental mistique: Training the intellect versus development of the child. *Childhood Education,* 1970, *46*, 402–412.

12

SCREENING TECHNIQUES FOR EARLY INTERVENTION

A textbook that focused on learning disorders of children would be of limited value if it did not also emphasize normal development. Current trends in pediatric practice require that physicians have increased sophistication in understanding and assessing developmental processes in normal children. In the past, the major concern of child health care has simply been growth and physicial assessment. Today the developmental evaluation of children is becoming an integral component of improved care. Hopefully, this chapter will assist health professionals in identifying verbal and nonverbal indicators of normal and abnormal development in children. The emphasis will be on the child from 2 to 6 years of age since this age period is critical for all parameters of development. In addition, it represents a time when intervention can be optimally effective.

Data obtained from a child's comprehensive medical history or medical examination may suggest delayed development. Unfortunately, in some cases the attending physician may overlook the data, underestimate their significance, or take a "wait-and-see" attitude. If a physician does suspect that a problem exists, he or she should clearly define the problem before requesting a psychometric evaluation or further diagnostic consultation. Without the ability to assess developmental problems adequately, the health care provider is not able to evaluate a most critical area of the patient's health. Delay in the therapeutic intervention for developmental disabilities may have disasterous consequences on the future quality of a child's life.

This chapter considers behavioral indicators that allow a physician to identify significant variation in a child's development.

Development delays may be confirmed by psychometric measurements or other evaluation data (Zinkus, 1977). The Stanford-Binet Intelligence Scale (Terman, 1960) or the Wechsler Intelligence Scale for Children-Revised (Wechsler, 1974) are two of the more objective measures in evaluating development. Diagnostic tools must be used judiciously as the physician coordinates an evaluation plan to resolve his diagnostic suspicions.

The administration and interpretation of standardized psychological examinations require skilled and well-trained professionals. Pediatricians and other child care professionals have devised "screening" instruments which can provide a developmental skill profile. Although these inventories are not widely standardized, they are sufficiently accurate to identify incipient or gross developmental delays (Thorpe & Werner, 1974). Two widely used screening tests are the Denver Developmental Screening Test (Frankenburg, Dodds, & Fandal, 1970) and the Thorpe Developmental Inventory (Thorpe, 1973). Through years of use these inventories have become better standardized (and more complex to administer). They offer an overall picture of the child's developmental progress. Screening instruments should *not* be used for predicting future potential. They can, however, establish a profile which may suggest and guide further evaluation.

Various developmental problems reflect genetic and neurological abnormalities that are well known to most physicians. Several of these disorders, such as Down's syndrome or cerebral palsy, are identifiable at birth or shortly thereafter. Traditionally, training in the prevention, diagnosis, and management of disorders of this type is part of a medical school curriculum. There are, however, a host of developmental disabilities that may not become manifest until many months after birth and then only in very subtle ways. These disorders, related to the development of intelligence, speech and language, perceptual and learning abilities, are often less obvious both to parents and health care professionals. Thus, they remain undetected for longer periods. Since the physician is usually the first professional to encounter these developmental disabilities, it is really his responsibility for early detection. Although early intervention may not be necessary for every child with suspected developmental delays, thorough and careful monitoring of the child's progress is almost always indicated. In addition to routine immunizations, assessment of physical growth and developmental and nutritional evaluations, the concerned physician must add a variety of developmental screening instruments to his evaluation routine.

The major focus of this chapter is to review general guidelines for the evaluation of normal and abnormal development in children. Emphasis is placed on intellectual, speech, language, motor, and social skills development. Subtle problems in development will be illustrated and discussed. The course of normal development will be reviewed and used as a baseline. Sophistication in developmental testing will eventually result in the early diagnosis of the child with developmental delays.

DIAGNOSTIC CLASSIFICATIONS OF DEVELOPMENTAL PROBLEMS

Intelligence

There is still considerable debate over the nature of intelligence, and no single concept of intelligence has ever enjoyed universal or lasting acceptance. Intelligence is not a definite entity that exists in concrete form; rather, it is a hypothetical construct that is utilized to describe and predict adaptive behavior. The increasing complexity of the central nervous system (CNS) in the developing child increases the sophistication and range of adaptive behaviors. Injuries to the CNS in the pre-, peri-, or postnatal periods may significantly influence its growth and affect adaptive behavior. The resultant damage may retard the development and organization of brain tissue, thereby decreasing the potential for a normal rate of adaptive learning.

It is important to note that IQ and intelligence are not synonymous. The results of an "intelligence" test reflect a measurement of observable behaviors, and from these behaviors a level of intelligence is inferred. Comparisons of intelligence among individuals is essentially the comparison of behaviors of individuals under standard situations.

While initial evaluation may indicate subnormal intelligence, reevaluations may indicate substantial change as development increases. Mental retardation refers to significantly subaverage general intellectual functioning existing concurrently with deficits in adaptive behavior and manifested during the developmental period. The term "subaverage" refers to performance on standardized tests of general intellectual functioning that is two or more standard deviations below the population mean of the age group involved. The level of general intellectual functioning may be assessed by performance on one or more of the various objective tests which have been developed for this purpose, for example, the Wechsler Intelligence Scale for Children—Revised or the Stanford-Binet. The upper age limit of the developmental period is generally regarded to be 18 years.

The definition of mental retardation specifies that the subaverage intellectual functioning must be reflected by impairment in adaptive behavior. "Adaptive behavior" refers primarily to the effectiveness of the individual in adjusting to the natural and social demands of his environment. Impaired adaptive behavior may be reflected in many ways:

1. During infancy and early childhood
   a. Sensory-motor skill development
   b. Communication skills
   c. Self-help skills
   d. Socialization
2. During childhood and adolescence
   a. Application of basic academic skills in daily life activites
   b. Application of appropriate reasoning and judgment in mastery of the environment
   c. Social skills
3. During late adolescence and adult life
   a. Social responsibilities and performances
   b. Vocational responsibilities and performances

"Rate of maturation" refers to the timetable of sequential development of self-help skills (e.g., sitting, crawling, standing, walking, talking, etc.). "Learning ability" refers to the facility with which knowledge is acquired as a function of experience. Learning difficulties are usually manifested in the academic situation; thus if mild in degree, they may not become apparent until the child enters school. Social adjustment at the adult level is judged in terms of the degree to which the individual is able to function independently in the community, achieves success in gainful employment, and is able to meet and conform to other personal and social standards and responsibilities set by the community.

The definition of mental retardation emphasizes the current functional status of the individual with respect to intellectual ability and adaptive behavior. Intellectual function may change, with levels of ability determined by comparing the individual's performance to the behavioral standards of norms for the individual's chronological group. The definition differs from traditional concepts about mental retardation in the following ways:

1. It is specifically developmental in approach.
2. It is a description of present behavior (it discourages the consideration of potential intelligence), implying that a person may legitimately be called retarded at one time and not at another.
3. It is couched in terms of many measurements.
4. It treats mental retardation as a symptom which might be the result of many interacting influences, both physical and social.

The classification of mental retardation on the basis of IQ scores is outlined in Table 12-1.

Table 12-1. Classification of Mental Retardation by IQ.

Borderline	−1.01 to −2.00 SD below the population mean (IQ: 85–70)
Mild retardation	−2.01 to −3.00 SD (IQ: 69–55)
Moderate retardation	−3.01 to −4.00 SD (IQ: 54–40)
Severe retardation	−4.01 to −5.01 SD (IQ: Below 40)
Profound retardation	Greater than −5.00 SD

SD—standard deviation

Using the traditional incidence of about 3 percent for estimating the occurrence of mental retardation, approximately 6.5 million persons would be classified as retarded. If the "borderline" range (not to be labeled mental retardation) were included, the percentage would increase to about 16 percent. A very significant number of children exhibit delays in intellectual development. Children with suspected intellectual problems should receive a thorough multidisciplinary evaluation, including medical, neurological, psychological, speech language, and other assessments. Periodic evaluations, in combination with early stimulation experiences in a preschool setting, are strongly urged.

Speech and Language

Language represents the mechanism by which the child is able to convey ideas of varying complexity and to respond to others in his environment. Delayed speech and language development presents a significant diagnostic challenge for the physician. Much of the assessment of intellectual ability in the early childhood years relies on language capability. However, in some cases speech and language skills may be delayed while intellectual function is essentially normal.

Delays in the acquisition of speech and language are associated with a variety of etiologies. Neurological injuries can severely disrupt the normal maturational sequence of speech and language development. Congenital or acquired dysphasias arise from injury of the central nervous system. Other types of language delays may arise from subtle types of neurological insults or delayed neurological maturation (Geschwind, 1965). For many children the only manifestation of neurological abnormality may be the delayed speech itself although delay of speech development may indicate serious intellectual deficiencies such as mental retardation.

The most immediate concern in evaluating the child with speech and language deficits is auditory sensitivity, and the assessment of auditory acuity is the first step in any language evaluation. Problems in auditory acuity often manifest themselves as delayed speech and language. Recent evidence suggests that recurrent otitis media during the language formative years (birth to 3 years) significantly influences language development (Holm & Kunze, 1969). Transient hearing losses, as well as considerable distortion of speech sounds, appear to have a significant influence on the development of speech and language. In a study of children with severe chronic otitis media during the first 3 years of life, language delays were manifested in early childhood and there were severe auditory processing deficits during the early school years (Zinkus & Gottlieb, 1978a). Although language in the form of single words was within normal limits for these children, the development of three or more word phrases was delayed up to the age of 36 months.

There are numerous other causes for speech delays. The deaf child encounters significant and obvious obstacles to the development of adequate language skills. Other conditions, such as emotional disabilities, may manifest some symptomatology in the language area. It is not unusual for autistic children to evidence severe disruption of speech and language skills.

In some family situations language skills may not be adequately developed because of environmental circumstances. Some children are allowed to gesture for their needs. They communicate by pointing or using sign language. In other situations environmental deprivation may account for delay in language development due to lack of stimulation. On the whole, if the problem is identified and treated at an early age, language delay arising from environmental causes may be reversed, with an excellent prognosis.

More obscure etiologies for speech and language problems exist. In many cases thorough neurological evaluations may not define the etiology for the delays. Mild language delays can be early indicators of subsequent developmental problems and the physician should be alert for signs of poor progress in other areas.

The prognosis for normal speech and language development is greater if therapy is begun early. Some speech and language programs treat children with language delays as early as 18 months to 2 years of age. Regardless of age, the child with language delays can profit greatly from therapy.

Various other speech and language problems may develop later in childhood, such as articulation difficulties which are a common source of concern for parents. The norms for articulation development are often misunderstood. Speech sounds develop within a certain range of time and are closely tied to neurological maturation. Understanding the pattern of articulation is necessary for the proper evaluation of speech and language skills. Problems with speech dysfluencies may be related to different age ranges. The child with uncomplicated stuttering at age 3 will resolve the difficulty spontaneously. However, secondary stuttering, which occurs at an older age represents a pathological condition. A differentiation of speech and language problems requires a thorough understanding by the physician of the normal development of speech and articulation skills. Diagnostic criteria for the assessment of speech and language in the pediatric patient are presented later in this chapter. The major emphasis for the physician is accurate diagnosis and early intervention. With early intervention the prognosis for normal patterns of speech and language in later childhood is greatly improved.

Learning Disabilities

In recent years health care professionals have been increasingly concerned about the learning-disabled child. Numerous physical, psychological, and social difficulties have been acknowledged as complications of the learning-disability syndrome (Todd & Gottlieb, 1976). The terminology, as well as etiology, are usually complex and often contradictory. Again, a basic understanding of the many facets of the syndrome—with its obvious and subtle manifestations in a child—is necessary for the practicing pediatrician.

Learning disabilities represent a heterogeneous mixture of deficits related to perceptual processing, reading disabilities, and problems in attention. The most direct manifestation of a child's difficulty in learning is the inability to function normally in the classroom. The term "learning disability" may imply to some professionals that the syndrome can only be diagnosed when the child is in the school situation. This approach is much too narrow since early intervention, prior to entering school, could prevent many of the frustrations and emotional disabilities that the child will eventually encounter in a school setting (Zinkus & Gottlieb, 1978b). Perceptual abnormalities do not occur immediately upon entering school; in fact, they may have been developing over a long period. It is, therefore, incumbent on the pediatrician, as well as other health care professionals, to become knowledgeable of the early warning signals that create a high-risk profile for potential educational jeopardy (Gottlieb & Zinkus, 1979).

Learning disabilities appear to have many etiologies. Neurological dysfunction has frequently been hypothesized as the underlying cause (Johnson & Myklebust, 1967). From this viewpoint, children with learning disabilities have psychoneurological problems. A dysfunctioning central nervous system results in selected deficits and *not* a generalized incapacity to learn. The definition of a learning disability proposed by the United States Office of Education and the National Advisory Committee on Handicapped Children reflects this viewpoint and is the definition incorporated into the Children with Specific Learning Disabilities Act of 1969:

> Children with specific learning disabilities exhibit a disorder in one or more of the basic psychological processes involved in understanding or using spoken or written language. These may be manifested in disorders of listening, thinking, talking, reading, writing, spelling or arithmetic. They include conditions which have been referred to as perceptual handicaps, brain injury, minimal brain dysfunction, dyslexia, developmental aphasia, etc. They do not include learning problems which are due primarily to visual, hearing, or motor handicaps, to mental retardation, emotional disturbance or to environmental disadvantage.

The definition suggests that the development of a learning disability has origins in the pre- or perinatal periods and, therefore, can potentially be identified by careful analysis of the development of the child. Perceptual development occurs over a protracted period. For example, the perceptual development of the child of 5 years is significantly advanced over that of the same child at 3 years of age because the child's neurological system is at a more advanced stage of development. In addition, the central nervous system of a child 5 years of age has a greater capacity to process information, and its increasing maturation and sophistication allows for more comprehensive and complex types of language skills such as reading, listening, and cognitive development (Geschwind 1965).

Various perceptual deficits have been detected in the learning-disabled child. *Visual perception* involves spatial orientation, laterality orientation, visual motor coordination, and figure-ground perception. These skills are necessary in order to develop consistent abilities in overall academic performace. Problems in visual perception may be noted in the preschool period. It is not uncommon for a child of 3 or 4 years of age to reverse geometric designs, letters, and other types of figures. Perpetuation of these skill deficits later in the child's development, however, must be dealt with quickly and effectively before incorrect learning habits are ingrained. The child with motor incoordination early in development, including clumsiness and awkwardness, may be displaying the first indications of faulty perceptual development. When first identifying the awkward child, the physician may not immediately initiate therapeutic intervention (Thompson & Gottlieb, 1973). He should, however, monitor the child's development over the course of several years. With the use of various screening instruments, the pediatrician may periodically be able to assess the child's overall development in visual perception and motor coordination.

Auditory perception (Rampp & Plummer, 1977; Willeford, 1978) involves the processing of auditory information. It includes auditory sequential memory, auditory discrimination, and the development of sound-blending skills. Much of what is taught in reading is phonetically oriented, and a heavy premium is therefore placed on auditory skills. Following directions in a classroom is essential to learning and requires intact auditory perception. Often a delay in language development may indicate impending or underlying auditory perceptual difficulties. The child who has difficulty following multiple directions, in the home as well as in the school, is often misdiagnosed as having a poor attention span or "not listening." On closer scrutiny it may be determined that the child is acting inappropriately because of an auditory perceptual deficit. When presented with three or four directions at one time, the child may become confused and performs in an awkward manner. The physician can screen for this type of problem by giving the child three or four directions without visual cues, e.g., "put a pencil on a chair, touch the door, pick up the ball," without pointing to the objects. Confusion in this type of skill, by the age of 4 years, may indicate auditory perceptual difficulties. Further evaluation may be required by a speech and language specialist in order to determine the exact nature and severity of the problem.

Dyslexia is a diagnostic classification applied to many disorders of reading (Critchley, 1970). In many cases, however, the problem originates from underlying perceptual deficits, which in the strictest sense cannot be classified as dyslexia. Critchley (1970) has defined dyslexia as "a disorder manifested by difficulty in learning to read despite conventional instruction, adequate intelligence, and sociocultural opportunity. It is dependent upon fundamental cognitive disabilities which frequently have constitutional origin." The etiology appears to lie in neurological abnormalities, many of which remain obscure.

Dyslexia cannot be diagnosed until the child has received sufficient instruction in reading. It is difficult to ascertain whether early diagnosis is actually possible with this type of disorder. Reading difficulties often occur as a result of perceptual disturbances, whereas the classical dyslexic disturbance involves an isolated deficit in reading. A demonstrable lesion in the temporal-parietal area of the dominant hemisphere may be expected. Considerable emphasis must be placed on early diagnosis and treatment of the child in kindergarten or first grade who is beginning reading instruction. Difficulty in remembering letters of the alphabet (and correctly identifying them) may be the first indication of underlying severe reading deficits. Early intervention is the best treatment. The physician must listen carefully to parental complaints that their child is not reading well. Complete evaluation of reading disorders may involve a multidisciplinary team with neurological, psychological, speech and language, and educational expertise.

Minimal brain dysfunction (MBD) (Clemments, 1966) has been assigned as a diagnostic label to numerous disorders. MBD has been used synonymously with learning disabilities, since the two are often found in the same child. There are numerous symptom complexes associated with minimal brain dysfunction, many of which have been pointed out in other chapters. As noted, the chief manifestatons of MBD are hyperactivity, short attention span, distractibility, motor incoordination problems, perceptual deficits, and other types of "soft" neurological signs (Thompson & Gottlieb, 1973). The overly active child must be carefully assessed on the basis of his age. In many cases there are multiple etiologies contributing to the child's hyperactivity. Administration of medication should be attempted only after the factors of emotion, physical, perceptual, and psychosocial development have been assessed. Behavior management techniques may be used in conjuction with medication if the problem is due to psychosocial or parental origins. The physician must carefully evaluate all possible etiologies, as well as combinations of etiologies, for the disorder. Often a neurological evaluation is helpful in providing an explanation for the overactivity and distractibility. An evaluation of speech, language, and motor development is very important before final diagnosis is made. Hearing disorders, as well as problems in communication, may cause anxieties and frustration which promote "hyperactive" behavior. Resolution of the developmental problems may resolve many of the behavioral difficulties.

STAGES OF NORMAL DEVELOPMENT

The text to follow arranges chronologically the significant skills expected to be present in a given age group. They are categorized into *verbal* (expressive and receptive) and *nonverbal* (gross motor and fine motor perceptual) skills. In addition, an index of school readiness and of first-grade achievement is supplied. The data presented are specifically limited to ages 2 through 5 because delayed development during this period is most critical for medical intervention. We emphasize again that it is the physician more than any other professional who has frequent or sole contact with this younger age group. Anxious parents frequently question a physician about physical and mental development. Early intervention can prevent a lifelong reduction in the child's potential and alleviate the debilitating effects of parental anxiety.

During the first 2 years of life, assessment of sequential motor abilities, language development, socialization, and self-help skills is an important index of neurological maturation. Comprehensive screening of cognitive and precognitive function is possible after age 2 years when language, social, motor, and perceptual abilities are becoming more sophisticated. It is possible to challenge the child with a variety of skill tasks and to compare responses with those obtained from peers of the same age. In general, screening or testing results obtained before age 2 years correlate poorly with the child's subsequent level of intellectual function. Psychometric evaluation in older children is a more reliable measure of later mental abilities. Almost all meaningful testing and screening procedures require that the child perform standardized tasks, scaled to the mean performance level of his age peers. The child is then compared with peers and ranked accordingly. Despite a highly structured and professional testing situation, however, the assessment of a child's performace is very much a "clinical skill" of the examiner. This critical variable underscores the fact that the experience of the physician (or other examiner) is an important element in the evaluation. Similarly, the physician's success in evaluating the development status of a child may be dependent upon the variables of his expertise, interest, and selection of appropriate screening inventories (Hartlage & Lucas, 1973).

A few of the more significant verbal and nonverbal skills have been selected for review. These skills can be readily assessed during the course of a routine pediatric examination, with only a minimal increase in patient contact time. The more serious student of developmental pediatrics will recognize that many specific skills and characteristics of the preschool child are not included in the screening inventories. The materials presented are meant to be utilized as a triage mechanism.

The following items are recommended for performing a developmental assessment:

1. Twelve multicolored blocks (1-in. x 1 1/2-in. cubes)
2. White paper (8 1/2 in. x 11 in.)
3. Large crayons and pencils
4. Geometic designs to be copied
5. Two balls (one small enough to grip in one hand, one large)
6. Mirror
7. Assorted children's books
8. Shoe with shoestring
9. Coins
10. Knife, fork, spoon, cup or glass (preferably made of plastic)
11. Child's safety scissors

In the discussion to follow a developmental assay will be constructed that provides profiles of the child within a chronological age grouping. It should be emphasized that no two children are exactly alike, and a range of biological and psychological variation is to be anticipated.

The 24-month-old Child

Receptive verbal skills of a 2-year-old child can be evaluated by presenting items for identification. The child of 2 years recognizes three or four prominent parts of the body, such as the mouth, eyes, arms, legs, and tummy. The child should also be able to identify clearly line drawings of such common items as a chair, car, shoe, ball, cup, door, and shirt. The 2-year-old can usually identify his own image in the mirror.

Expressive verbal skills can be assessed quickly since most 2-year-olds can formulate simple phrases consisting of two to four words, or more. Phrases such as "all gone," "want that," "open door" are more characteristic of the 18-month-old, whereas the 2-year-old reveals more sophisticated word structures, such as "I want some more," "I see daddy," "Milk is all gone," "Shut the door," and "I don't want to go to bed." The child who can communicate effectively with three- or four-word phrases, may not, however, cooperate in the physician's office. A reliable history may be the only indication that the child has good expressive verbal skills. Single- or two-word responses to the command, "Can you say 'nice doggy,' 'kitty,' 'big girl'" are often successful in eliciting speech.

Some children are able to pronounce words clearly and distinctly from the time they first speak late in the first year, whereas others are almost unintelligible to nonfamily members until a much later age. In the 2-year-old there is a wide variation in clarity of speech. Articulation errors are not considered a serious problem at this age. By ages 3 to 3 1/2 years, articulation should be adequate for conversational speech. Gross articulation errors should bring prompt referral to a speech pathologist. By age 3 years about 93 percent of a child's speech will be articulated clearly, and by age 4 almost 100 percent is clearly articulated. Dysfluency, or the tendency to have difficulty with the flow of speech (primary stuttering), is normally present in some children under 3 years of age. If significant dysfluency persists after age 5 years referral for speech evaluation is advisable to prevent the development of pathological or secondary stuttering.

The average 2-year-old can perform a variety of nonverbal tasks: throw a ball overhand, build a tower of at least three or four cubes, walk backward for several steps, remove a coat or other garments, and slip off a shirt without assistance. In addition, the toddler can initiate vertical and circular strokes in a random-type scribbling with a large crayon and can turn the pages of a child's picture book one by one.

The 30-month-old Child

The 30-month-old child is increasing his use of language and is better able to perform tasks requiring eye-hand coordination. The child is much more aware of himself as a person and recognizes many more parts of the body. He can follow simple commands, such as "Hand me your coat," "Go over to the chair." At least four or five blocks can be stacked, and by this age hand preference may be established. Receptive language skills are significantly developed, allowing the identification of objects and their function. When presented with a series of objects, (e.g., coins, cup, pencil, picture book), the child can respond correctly to questions such as "Which one do you read?" or "Which one is used for writing?" Gross motor skills are much better developed as evidenced by the ability to stand briefly on one foot and to kick a ball placed on the floor.

The 36-month-old Child

With increasing ego identity, the 3-year-old actually is more of an individual than the 2-year-old. A 3-year-old child is very aware of himself as a person, and his desire to please is usually apparent to the examiner during evaluation. Socialization is more apparent, and the child is usually able to identify his own sex as boy or girl. At this age speech is well defined, and communication is accomplished by complete sentences. The child can recognize a wider variety of common objects, such as bird, horse, cat, or dog. Many children of this age can identify more unfamiliar and uncommon animals such as snake, duck, elephant, lion, or tiger. Among families where picture books and special experience trips, such as visits to the zoo, are not part of the milieu, one must interpret accordingly. The 3-year-old can usually provide the correct verb to such simple question as "What do fish do?" "What do airplanes do?" "What does a kitty cat say?" Nouns can be properly supplied for such questions as "What do you wear on your feet?" Similarly, the child can recognize actions such as swimming, drinking, carrying, and cooking.

Motor skills can be demonstrated by permitting the child to use scissors to cut paper. The developmental history should reveal an ability to ride a tricycle (if one is available for the child). The child can touch the tip of his nose with his forefinger on request. He can catch a large ball by grasping it to his body with arms extended, once out of three or four short throws.

The 42-month-old Child

On a developmental clock, at the younger ages, 6-month intervals are relatively long periods of time, and changes continue at a rapid rate. Social independence is increasing rapidly, and language skills are accelerating. At 42 months the child usually knows both his first and last name. He can distinguish between two objects on the basis of size ("Which is bigger?"). Circles are drawn more accurately, and many children can make a cross mark. The child can build a bridge from blocks after demonstration. He can balance briefly on one foot. The child can repeat three digits from memory, even though it may take two or three trials.

Self-help skills include the ability to wash and dry his own hands and face, and the 42-month-old is more readily separated from his mother. Cooperative play behavior is observed with one or several other children.

The 48-month-old Child

At 48 months the child is less anxious in the examining situation. The child usually separates readily from the mother with minimal reassurance. Verbal skills have increased greatly, and the child is frequently outspoken and assertive. Improved verbal quality may prompt the examiner to credit the child with unwarranted precosity. The child is generally talkative, using the pronoun "I" with great frequency. He is able to dress and undress himself with ease, brush his teeth, and lace shoes. The child of this age, however, usually is not able to tie his shoelaces.

Gross motor skills have advanced considerably. Cephalocaudal maturation produces more stable and capable total body abilities. The 4-year-old can broad jump, extending the 3-year-old-s skill of vertical up-and-down leaps to combine the vertical and horizontal dimensions. Standing on one leg is considerably prolonged, often lasting more than 5 seconds. The child can now successfully tandem walk, one foot in front of the other over a 5- or 6-foot distance with fairly good equilibrium. The 4-year-old may be unable to hop well on one foot, but this skill is usually developed by approximately 4½ years. Fine motor skills become more sophisticated, and the child can button clothes, draw a more rounded and closed circle, draw a cross, and begin a rudimentary drawing of a person. This child can also fold a piece of paper diagonally as well as copy an oblique or diagonal line with a pencil or crayon. He should also be able to catch a large ball from a 5-foot distance, in about one out of two or three tries. The child will catch the ball with his arms flexed at the elbows. Verbal skills are of sufficient caliber to allow correct answers to questions involving opposite analogies and numbers concepts. Repetition of seven- to eight-word sentences or number combinations is possible. The child demonstrates competency with how, why, and what concepts.

The 60-month-old Child

At 5 years of age the child is characteristically more independent than previously noted. The child is also more self-controlled by his knowledge of social propriety than he was at 4 years. The 5-year-old is more agile, has better balance, and has developed many fine motor, perceptual, and social skills necessary for the beginning educational process. Cognitive and language skills are expanded and include a knowledge of the common colors and names of familiar objects, which can be explained in terms of function. Number concepts, through at least the number 10, are demonstrated. Verbal abstractions are elicited from pictured events. The 5-year-old can comprehend arguing, fighting, saluting, and other more complex activities. Cause-and-effect relationships are understood and proper responses are obtained from such questions as "What do you do if you fall down and hurt your knee?" The 60-month-old child knows his own age, understands a few concepts of social responsibility, and comprehends what is fair and just for himself and others.

Gross motor development has progressed to the point where the child can skip smoothy and execute tandem walking. Standing on one foot is significantly improved. Improved fine motor skills are reflected in more refined use of a comb, tooth brush, tools, writing and coloring materials. The child's ability to draw is markedly improved, revealing good control of circular, downward vertical, left to right horizontal and downward oblique maneuvers. Now the child can correctly copy a square and a triangle. The diagonal lines in a diamond, however, may cause difficulty.

The 66- to 72-month-old Child

Between 5 and 6 years of age the child is usually involved in some type of school program. Frequently, parents will seek professional assistance if the child is felt to be "immature" or if verbal or motor behavior is not up to par. The problem is usually first presented to the pediatrician or primary care physician.

In this age group it is now time to consider the indices of developmental maturity, specifically the verbal and motor skills, that are necessary for first-grade academic success. Gesell and Ilg (1940) have outlined 11 general areas of maturity necessary for adequate first-grade performance:

1. Normal (or corrected) vision
2. Normal hearing
3. General mental level of 6 to 6½ years
4. Good motor coordination, particularly manual control as evidenced in drawing
5. Relatively mature personality
6. Normal use and comprehension of language
7. Articulation not more than "slightly immature"
8. Relatively even development in the various fields of behavior
9. Interest and ability to follow stories of moderate length
10. Ability to control attention on set tasks
11. Ability to adjust to the requirements of a classroom routine

Children who were in good kindergarten programs probably were tested academically during the last month of that school year. "Readiness examinations," such as The Metropolitan Readiness Tests, a series of standardized tests, can be used. Progress through the first-grade program and beyond correlates fairly well with scores on such tests. Motor skills are important for developing first-grade reading, writing, and number-concept skills. Fine motor perceptual abilities are necessary to recognize and reproduce shapes of letters and to arrange those shapes into the meaningful patterns of words. A knowledge of and an ability to recognize letters of the alphabet, to count, and to understand numbers (to at least 10) are importanat preschool skills. The reproduction of geometric patterns with curved, straight, horizontal, perpendicular, and diagonal components is necessary in order to perceive and to copy those numerical and alphabet symbols perequisite for arithmatic and reading.

Verbal skills in the "readiness" category include more sophisticated word meaning and listening skills. For example, while viewing

Category A—Superior

Essential Characteristics

In addition to characteristics required for B, C, and D below, most of the following:

    Clothing non-transparent.
    Lines firm and meeting at proper points.
    Such details as neck, hands, shoulders, correct number of fingers,
       waistline.

Category B—Above Average

Essential Characteristics

In addition to characteristics required for C and D, most of the following:

    Arms and legs in *two* dimensions.
    Better proportions (length of trunk greater than breadth).
    Clothing clearly indicated.

Figure 12-1. Reproduced from the *Metropolitan Readiness Tests* by permission. Copyright © 1965 by Harcourt Brace Jovanovich, Inc. All rights reserved.

pictures of three dogs—a bulldog, Pekinese, and a collie—the child of 5 years 9 months to 6 years of age can point out the collie. He can discriminate between similar objects of animals. While viewing pictures such as a bear, rabbit, and an owl, the child can correctly respond to statements such as "He is busy in the summer, but he sleeps in a den all winter." Auditory memory proves to be more important in the learning process than heretofore realized.

    The mature child, aged 5 years, 9 months to 6 years, can view a series of pictures of increasing complexity and should be able to respond to questions which are picture-related. The child's responses are typically well-constructed sentences expressing complete thoughts. Adverbs, adjectives, and abstract ability are easily demonstrated.

    Drawings constructed by children of people or of themselves (or objects) are very useful measurements of maturity. Standardized tests, such as the Goodenough-Harris Drawing Test (Harris, 1963), allow

Category C—Average

Essential Characteristics

In addition to characteristics required for D, most of the following:

Fingers (any number) ears, and nostrils
Better proportions among parts than in D

Category D—Below Average

Essential Characteristics

Most of the following features:

Arms and legs (may be one-dimensional).
Trunk, head, mouth, nose, hair.

Category E—Immature

Figure not recognizable as a human being.
Parts of body (such as arms, legs, trunk, head) if given, are not connected.

Figure 12-1. (continued)

more than subjective interpretation since approximately 72 details may be analyzed and the drawings compared with norms. The drawings, quite apart from their use as indices of mental development, are often revealing in other important ways. Artistic skills, motor abilities, and manual dexterity can be evaluated (see Figure 12–1). These factors may influence success in school writing or drawing. The drawings are a vehicle for expressing ideas and subconscious feelings and desires. The more subtle implications require expert interpretation when distorted or bizarre drawings are produced.

The following 3 case histories are included to illustrate the physician's approach to selected developmental problems seen in practice. Although these reports represent children with developmental and learning problems less severe than the mental retardation (M.R.) group, one would be able to diagnose the M.R. child with a similiar workup.

CASE HISTORIES

A Question of Mental Development

JR, a white male, age 5½ years, came from a nearby rural community to visit the pediatrician's office for evaluation of a chief complaint of "lumps in the neck." The lumps, according to his mother, had been noticed about 1 year previously, but they seemed to have enlarged in recent weeks. The masses were nontender and not visible to the eye. The medical history indicated that the child had a bad cold 3 weeks prior to the examination but had recovered without complications.

The patient was in the third month of his kindergarten year. He was not doing well, in spite of the mother's offhand comment that "the teacher was pleased with his progress." The family lived on the outskirts of a small town, 40 miles distant. The family consisted of mother, father, and two siblings older than JR. The 15-year-old sister had not "taken to school good," had been in special-education classes for a while, and was currently enrolled in a vocational education program. A brother, age 9½ years, had developed normally and was a fourth-grade student, progressing satisfactorily in school. The father, 36 years old, a truck driver, was reportedly in good health. He had not completed high school, dropping out in the eleventh grade to start working. The mother, age 34, was in good health except for being "nervous." She had completed high school. Additional family history revealed a paternal uncle who was said to have had a "birth injury" and who never attended school.

The obstetrical history revealed that the mother was 28 years old at conception. She was gravida III, para II and the pregnancy was uneventful. She was followed by a local physician and received adequate prenatal care. No high-risk prenatal factors were reported. She did not smoke and consumed alcohol modestly. Delivery was at term, with an uncomplicated labor lasting approximately 4 hours. JR's birth weight was 6 lbs 8½ oz. The mother knew of no perinatal problems.

The infant was discharged with his mother on the third postpartum day. Growth and development were good during the first 6 months of life. General health history revealed no significant illness or injury. No convulsive episodes had occurred.

Developmental history revealed that JR sat up independently from a prone position at about 8 months, began creeping at 10 to 11 months, was pulling up at 12 months, and began taking independent steps at 14 months. Meaningful use of two or three single words was established by 26 to 30 months with use of multiword phrases at 36 to 40 months. Articulation was poor, and speech was difficult to understand, except for the family, until about age 4 to 4½. JR was toilet trained at 3 1/2 years but occasionally still wets the bed at night. Behavior has been a problem. His mother describes him as "always into everything, stubborn, hard-headed, and hard to discipline." He has always been rather awkward and clumsy and was unable to ride his tricycle until almost 5 years of age. JR runs into things without looking and falls frequently. His attention span is short, except when watching certain TV programs that he likes.

The physical examination revealed a normal but somewhat "immature" youngster for 5½ years of age. Speech, when elicited, showed poor articulation with frequent substitutions.

There were no phenotypic abnormalities observed, and the child's vital signs were normal. Height was at the twenty-fifth percentile for chronological age, and weight was at the tenth percentile. Head circumference was at the seventy-fifth percentile. Positive finding on examination included a few small, nontender anterior and posterior cervical lymph nodes.

The physical examination revealed several significant neurological and developmental observations. The child had difficulty separating from the mother, was fearful, was uncooperative, and cried during the initial part of the examination. He had difficulty balancing on one foot more than 1 second and was unable effectively to tandem walk or take backward steps. He could not draw a good circle, cross mark, or square, and he was unable to complete a triangle, doing poorly on the diagonal. His drawing of a person (see Figure 12–2) was compatible with that of an average 4-year-old. He was unable to color pictures or stay within lines. He showed right-hand, -foot, and -eye preference. His auditory memory was poor with successful repetition of only an occasional double or triple digit. JR could show his age on his five fingers, but he

Figure 12-2. JR's Draw-a-Person.

could not respond to the question, "How many years is that?" He was unable to say more than three or four letters of the alphabet and could not reproduce any of these with paper and pencil.

The remainder of the neurological examination was within normal limits. Vision and hearing screenings were also within normal limits.

In reviewing this case, the attending physician obtained critical information in the evaluation. The family had driven a considerable distance for consultation about a chief complaint—"lumps in the neck," which on evaluation proved insignificant (and obviously not the family's real concern about the child). After suggesting to the mother that the examiner thought she had other reasons for concern and naming the developmental difficulties that were apparent, the mother revealed that JR's development was one of great anxiety. The family feared that JR was going to be "slow" like his sister and suffer many of the same social problems. Further probing disclosed that the kindergarten teacher had relayed her concern that JR "wasn't really ready for the kindergarten program at the present time." The family history revealed a developmental disability in the paternal uncle and the older sister. There were no other prenatal, perinatal, or postnatal high-risk factors in the history. The history further indicated that the developmental milestones were consistently delayed in the neuromotor, language, and self-help areas.

Examination confirmed the impression of "immaturity," which had been suspected on initial observation. Gross motor function analysis revealed a child whose skills were more compatible with that of a 42- to 48-month-old child: balancing, tandem walking, and standing on one foot. Visual motor and visual perceptual skills were poor. JR's ability to reproduce geometric shapes was more consistent with the ability of an average 4-year-old. Language showed an articulation defect, and screening of receptive cognitive skills also revealed delayed maturation. The examiner tentatively concluded that this child showed significant developmental delays in the areas of gross motor, fine motor perceptual, language, self-help, and socialization skills. In effect, JR showed a rather general deficit in overall development. The estimate of at least a 12- to 18-month deficit for this 66-month-old boy suggested an overall developmental function at 48 to 54 months. The following additional studies were completed:

1. Routine CBC and urinalysis were normal.
2. Urinary screening for abnormal amino acids was normal.
3. Genetic consultation (with chromosomal analysis) revealed no apparent abnormality. (This study was done because of the positive family history despite failure to observe phenotypic abnormalities.)

4. Psychological evaluation: the Wechsler Intelligence Scale for Children revealed overall verbal and nonverbal skills at just over 47 months with little scatter among the subtest groups. The IQ score was in the borderline area
5. Language evaluation revealed overall language function at 52 months for receptive skills and at 45 months for expressive ability. An articulation defect was present.

From this information the clinical impression is confirmed that the child's IQ, at about 75, was low borderline. Although the criteria for a diagnosis of mental retardation was not justified, there was an immediate challenge to place the child in an appropriate school program. Future educational difficulties could be anticipated without special-education assistance.

JR was subsequently placed in a preschool program that provided special emphasis in gross and fine motor training and language stimulation. In addition, the program was aimed at promoting acceleration of self-help and socialization skills. Future school placement will depend upon progress and future revaluation as the child progresses through the first year of this placement.

This case illustrates the type of historical and objective data needed to recommend referral for further standardized testing. At the completion of the pediatric evaluation, the findings dictated the need for additional evaluation of numerous skills. Testing by a qualified clinical psychologist, using standardized testing instruments, was indicated. Evaluation by speech and language specialist (and educational experts) was similarly indicated. From these data, the physician was able to effect many of the required therapeutic programs. Periodic office evaluations, as well as communication with teachers at school, was programmed.

The Learning-disabled Child

TF had a chronic history of developmental problems. Difficulties were first noted in the area of speech and language development. These delays were not gross in nature: single words were not apparent until approximately 15 months of age, and development of sentences did not occur until approximately 36 months. On the other hand, motor skills developed adequately, and the child first walked without assistance at approximately 11 months. The pregnancy was uncomplicated. Perinatal as well as postnatal history was within normal limits. Other than slow speech and language development, the child appeared to be "normal" in every way. Two older siblings did not show problems in speech and language.

TF's family, from an upper-middle-class socioeconomic background, were educationally-oriented. Both parents were college graduates and fairly successful in their separate careers. There were no unusual traumas in the home situation. TF's early history was characterized by an enriched environment. TF began nursery school at age 4 years. The teacher noted, on several occasions, that he had "difficulty in remembering colors and some letters of the alphabet." Figure drawings were poor and resembled those of a much younger child. The teacher called these observations to the parents' attention. In consultation with the teacher the parents requested assistance from their pediatrician.

Physical examination was within normal limits. There were no obvious abnormalities on either physical or neurological screening. On developmental and behavioral assessment, however, various difficulties readily became apparent. When given three directions to perform in sequence, the child experienced considerable difficulty. He responded inappropriately to questions. When asked the question "What must you do to make water boil?" he responded, "Eggs." In addition, although the child was now in kindergarten, he could not correctly identify letters of the alphabet. Reversals and rotation of letters were common in his attempts to write. The child had considerable difficulty spelling his name, and the final production did not remotely resemble the correct spelling. Figure drawings were unimaginative and primitive, indicative of a much younger child in their lack of sophistication. Simple tasks, such as drawing a circle, (which is easily within the ability of a 3-year-old) and a square (which can be expected from a normal 5-year-old child), proved to be exceedingly difficult for TF. Hearing and vision examinations were within normal limits. Based on the findings from the history and examination, the physician determined that a thorough multidisciplinary evaluation was necessary.

Psychological evaluation, using the Stanford-Binet Intelligence Scale, indicated a full-scale IQ of 98. Because the Stanford-Binet Test is a verbally oriented examination, it was felt that the overall intellectual potential was considerably higher. The child consistently misinterpreted verbal items at the 3½- and 4-year levels of the test. On the other hand, many of the items related to concept formation were passed at the 5- and 6-year level, indicating much higher levels of intellectual potential. It appeared that brief auditory input was handled in a highly competent manner by the child. When the auditory input became more complex, however, the child was unable to respond correctly. Speech and language evaluation confirmed the presence of auditory perceptual deficits. A neurological consultation was performed, and mild abnormalities were found on the electroencephalogram. The pattern was difficult to interpret, but the generalized diffuse slowing observed on the EEG appeared to be characteristic of an "immature" central nervous system. Although the EEG was not diagnostic of any specific condition, it provided some evidence of organicity.

Early special-education intervention was prescribed. The child was placed in an educational program designed to assist with the improvement of perceptual difficulties. As time progressed, reading and spelling skills improved, although at a very slow initial rate. An important therapeutic consideration throughout the entire evaluation was the need for counseling with the parents. This was their youngest child, and the parents had never encountered this type of problem before. They were aware of the concept of learning disabilities, through the popular media, but when confronted with this problem in their own family, a considerable period of shock and anxiety developed. Reassurance by the pediatrician was helpful in allaying these anxieties and enabling TF to begin a normal type of school career. Eventually TF was able to function in a regular classroom with resource assistance. The child attended a regular classroom, but for approximately an hour a day he was given special-education instruction in reading.

TF's case history is similar to that of thousands of children with learning disabilities. A myriad of symptomatologies are exhibited which appear abnormal for a child at any particular age. The symptoms are certainly disruptive for basic learning tasks. In isolation any one of the symptoms may be of minor significance, but in combination they represent a formidable roadblock to effective learning. It must be stressed that even though TF had special-education techniques available, it was the parental counseling that became the most important therapeutic factor. Parental anxiety and concerns may often be disruptive to a child's progress and may increase the tension and frustration of the child. With periodic counseling of the parents and medical monitoring of the child's progress, as in this case, it is possible to allay many anxieties within the family. Periodic revaluation also gives the physician necessary data to monitor effectively the program set up.

The Hyperactive Child

The parents of CB, a 4-year-old boy, were concerned that their child was "different" from his siblings. CB was precocious in walking and talking, and, according to the parents, "he entered the "terrible twos" at approximately 15 months of age." From that point in time, his behavior became almost impossible to control. CB appeared to have endless stores of energy. He would often channel this excess energy toward various kinds of disruptive activities. The child was unable to sit still for any lengthy period, including TV viewing. Direct parental attention failed to stop the fidgeting and endless movement. The parents often disagreed on discipline. In addition, it seemed to them that nothing worked consistently in controlling the child's behavior. Numerous approaches, involving physical punishment, deprivation, and reasoning with the child, proved to be of little value. CB had difficulty with peer relationships. His play with other children often ended with a "wounded child" (CB did not hesitate throwing toys at playmates).

The pediatrician offered some counseling regarding behavioral management techniques. The impatience of the parents, however, often led to their discontinuing the techniques advised. At the age of 4 years a consensus was reached that a more thorough evaluation of CB was needed.

In the physician's office the child's behavior was characterized by random, chaotic activity. Attention span was very short, and the child was very easily distracted. Various control methods were attempted during the examination (including stern words from the pediatrician), but all proved to be of little value in holding the child's attention, even for brief periods of time. A multidisciplinary evaluation was initiated by the physician.

Psychological evaluation revealed that the child had a Stanford-Binet IQ of 142. Although testing was extremely difficult, it was obvious that the child was very advanced intellectually. Neurological examination indicated subtle abnormalities, but they were mainly centered around the child's extremely high activity level, short attention span, and distractibility. Speech and language evaluation was within normal limits. The physician suggested that a combination of behavior modification techniques and medication was in order. Behavior management techniques proved to be extremely effective in combination with medication and served effectively to allay much of the parents' anxiety.

This child represented a diagnostic dilemma. In many cases the etiology of hyperactivity is complex and the use of medication may treat only one cause of the hyperkinesis. The hyperactive child is often inconsistently managed, resulting in exaggeration of the behavioral problems. Reduction in hyperactivity and improvement in attention span represent a major step in preventing subsequent problems in learning. Continuous monitoring is necessary because the learning capabilities of this child may also be affected. It is advisable for psychologists and educators to continue the periodic assessment at least through the second or third grade of school. Overall multidisciplinary assistance is extremely valuable in this case, and an excellent prognosis can be anticipated.

SUMMARY

A complex of primary and secondary problems are associated with the child exhibiting developmental delays. The physician is in the unique situation of observing the child over a considerable period of time during which intellectual, perceptual, speech, motor, and social skills are developing. Understanding normal development is the first step in evaluating the many subtle and diverse symptoms of developmental delays. Early medical intervention improves the prognosis to a very significant degree. The physician's careful analysis of each patient's potential for developmental problems may prevent unnecessary delay in diagnosis and treatment. It must be remembered that, quite apart from the disability itself, the emotional sequelae of undiagnosed and untreated learning disabilities further undermine the basic foundations of each human's potential (Williams, 1976) as well as that of society as a whole (Zinkus & Gottlieb, 1978b).

James S. Brown
Peter W. Zinkus

REFERENCES

Clements, S. D. Minimal brain dysfunction in children: Terminology and identification. NINDB Monograph No. 3. Washington, D.C.: U.S. Department of Health, Education, and Welfare, 1966.

Critchley, E. M. R. *The dyslexic child.* London: 1970.

Frankenburg, W. K., Dodds, J. B., & Fandal, A. *The revised Denver developmental screening test manual.* Denver: University of Colorado Press, 1970.

Geschwind, N. Disconnexion syndromes in animals and man. *Brain,* 1965, *88*(3): 585–644.

Gesell, A., & Ilg, F. L. *The first five years of life.* New York: Harper & Row, 1940.

Gottlieb, M. I., & Zinkus, P. W. Educational health and development, in the learning-disabled child. In J. Hughes (Ed.), *Synopsis of pediatrics* (5th ed.). New York: Mosby, 1979.

Harris, D. B. *Goodenough-Harris drawing test manual.* New York: Harcourt Brace Jovanovich, 1963.

Hartlage, L. C., & Lucas, D. G. *Mental development evaluation of the pediatric patient.* Springfield, Ill.: Thomas, 1973.

Hildreth, G. H., Griffiths, N. L., & McGauvran, M. E. *Metropolitan readiness test.* New York: Harcourt Brace Jovanovich, 1965.

Holm, V., & Kunze, L. Effects of chronic otitis media on language and speech development. *Pediatrics,* 1969, *43*:833–839.

Johnson, D., & Myklebust, H. *Learning Disabilities: Educational principles and practices.* New York: Grune & Stratton, 1967.

Rampp, D. L., & Plummer, B. A. Auditory processing dysfunctions and impaired learning. *Learning Disabilities: An Audio Journal for Continuing Education,* 1977, *1*(7).

Terman, L. M., & Merrill, M. A. *The Stanford-Binet intelligence scale.* Boston: Houghton Mifflin, 1960.

Thompson, R. G., & Gottlieb, M. I. Educational jeopardy, an interdisciplinary problem: The physician's contribution. *Acta Symbolica,* 1973, *4*(2):46–72.

Thorpe, H. S. *The Thorpe developmental inventory: Ages three to six years* (2nd ed.). Davis, Calif.: Office of Medical Education, University of California School of Medicine, 1973.

Thorpe, H. S., & Werner, E. E. Developmental screening of preschool children: A critical review of inventories used in health and education programs. *Pediatrics,* 1974, *53*(3):362–370.

Todd, M., & Gottlieb, M. I. Interdisciplinary counseling in a medical setting. In E. Webster (Ed.), *Professional approaches with parents of handicapped children.* Springfield, Ill.: Thomas, 1976, 191–216.

Wechsler, D. *The Wechsler intelligence scale for children–Revised.* New York: Psychological Corporation, 1974.

Willeford, J. Evaluation of central auditory dysfunction in learning-disabled children. *Learning Disabilities: An Audio Journal for Continuing Education,* 1978, *2*(2).

Williams, J. Learning disabilities: A multifaceted health problem. *Journal of School Health,* 1976, *46,* 515–521.

Zinkus, P. W. Understanding psychological evaluations. *Learning Disabilities: An Audio Journal for Continuing Education,* 1977, *1*(7).

Zinkus, P. W., & Gottlieb, M. I. Chronic otitis media and auditory processing deficits: A preventable learning disability, *Ohio Journal of Speech and Hearing,* 1978, *13*(2):86–92. (a)

Zinkus, P. W., & Gottlieb, M. I. Learning disabilities and delinquent youth: *Journal for Continuing Education,* 1978, *2*(4). (b)

Zinkus, P. W., & Gottlieb, M. I. Developmental and psychoeducational sequelae of chronic otitis media. *American Journal of Diseases of Children,* 1978, *132,* 1100–1104. (c)

13

PSYCHOLOGICAL EVALUATION OF THE LEARNING-DISABLED CHILD

The major deficits among learning-disabled children are related to their difficulty with *information processing*. Basically, information processing deals with the reception, coding, retrieval, and expression of information. Developmentally, children learn through one modality (auditory, visual, or tactile) before they begin to integrate information through several modalities (i.e., visual-motor integration). Some children may be deficient in the use of a perceptual modality, and thus that pathway is unproductive in the learning process (Wepman, 1968). Diagnostic materials are available for evaluating specific components of information processing, and specific remedial intervention can be designed.

Five major areas of information processing are recognized: (1) auditory processing, (2) visual processing, (3) motor processing, (4) haptic processing, and (5) cross-modal information processing. *Auditory processing* requires adequate auditory sensitivity, good attention, ability to discriminate, and the ability to remember and ascribe meaning to sounds. It encompasses skills in auditory discrimination, auditory memory, auditory sequencing, and auditory blending. *Visual processing* pertains to the ability to receive, code, remember, and express information through visual channels. Both visual and auditory processing disturbances are considered only after adequate visual acuity and auditory sensitivity have been established. Similarly, intellectual retardation must be ruled out. Visual processing includes skills in visual discrimination, visual spatial relationships, figure-ground discrimination, visual closure, and object recognition. Barrett (1965) suggested that object recognition in kindergarten children may be a good predictor of future reading abilities. *Motor processing* includes skills in fine motor (handwriting) and gross motor (throwing a ball). Gross motor deficits may interfere with peer activities, whereas fine motor deficits may create problems with self-help skills. *Haptic processing* refers to the acquisition of information through tactile (sense through touch) and kinesthetic (sense through motion and muscle feeling) modalities. Writing and spelling are probably in part dependent on haptic processing skills. Wedel (1973) associated spelling difficulties and haptic defects; the child receives feedback regarding the correctness of the spelled word partly from the sensations that result from writing the letters. *Cross-modal information processing* implies that information is obtained and expressed through an integration of modalities. Reading, for example, represents a complex combination of both visual and auditory processing. Children learn to read (and perform other academic tasks) by seeing material, hearing material, and combining materials. Ayers (1968) postulated that reading is dependent on the integration of visual, tactile, and kinesthetic perception.

During the discussion in this chapter references will be made to the various components of information processing.

PSYCHOLOGICAL EVALUATION

The initial identification of a learning-disabled child is seldom made by the psychologist. In most instances it is the parent, teacher, or pediatrician who first suspects a learning or developmental problem and refers the child to the psychologist for further diagnosis and remediation. It is imperative, therefore, that the parent, teacher, and pediatrician be aware of "signs" that may indicate a problem and the need for further investigation. They must also know how to interpret the psychologist's report and understand the remedial suggestions since their understanding and support is necessary for the implementation of remediation. The special skills of the psychologist are evaluating and treating problems related to the intellectual, academic, emotional, and social strengths and weaknesses of the individual. Which of the numerous methods of evaluation the psychologist uses depends ultimately upon the child's special needs as well as questions to be answered regarding the child's problem.

In answering the basic questions posed by parents, teachers, and pediatricians—"What is wrong with the child?" and "What can we do?"—the psychologist provides several inputs. The first is one of pinpointing the problem, that is *diagnosis*. The psychologist begins the diagnosis by performing a psychological evaluation, assessing intellectual level, academic performance, developmental progress, and psychosocial status. To do this, the psychologist has at his disposal a variety of assessment inventories and diagnostic instruments. The findings are integrated with those of other professionals, and the psychologist assists in planning a program of *intervention*. The final input is one of *follow-up*, in which the psychologist reassesses the child periodically to determine progress and to modify the intervention procedures as necessary.

To gain the information needed for a psychological evaluation, there are three basic procedures: (1) obtaining a comprehensive history of past events and behavior, (2) direct observation of behavior, and (3) the use of standardized tests to measure behavior.

HISTORICAL INFORMATION

Throughout this volume it is stressed that a complete understanding of the past and present behavior of the child is mandatory for an effective evaluation. The purpose of a comprehensive history is to assess further the presenting problems, investigate evidence of other problem areas, and begin the search for the etiology of the behavior. The information required in obtaining a history will vary according to the needs of the child and the reason for referral. Some basic information, however, is usually necessary. The pediatrician or family physician should be contacted for data on medical and developmental histories to supplement that obtained from the parent and thus provide a complete dossier on the child's background.

Developmental history. Information regarding the child's rate of attainment of developmental milestones provides insight into the integrity of the central nervous system. The parents may not recall the details of the child's developmental history. Contacting the pediatrician may be useful in obtaining this information.

Medical history. Several factors such as the age of the mother at conception and the presence of infections such as rubella or birth trauma have been associated with brain damage in the newborn (Kawi & Pasamanick, 1959). Other factors such as prematurity, low birth weight, toxicity in the pregnant mother, accidents to the pregnant mother, and trauma to the child before and after birth could result in disturbances of the central nervous system and a subsequent learning disorder (Graham, Matarazzo, & Caldwell, 1956).

Family medical history. Genetic studies have shown the possiblity of genetic linkage with learning disabilities (Bakwin, 1973; Scott & Thomas, 1973). Family history of neurological disorders, learning disabilities or developmental disorders should be thoroughly investigated.

Diet. Studies have suggested the possibility of faulty fetal development due to maternal malnourishment (Fort, 1972). The reduction of intellectual potential resulting from poor nutrition during infancy and childhood has been supported in the literature (Schain, Watanabe, Harel, et al., 1973). It is evident, as well, that the child with poor eating habits will not perform up to his potential in the school setting.

Past and present sleeping habits. The child with faulty sleep habits generally will not be alert in school and will be unable to perform at his best potential. The evidence of poor sleep habits may also be a symptom of other problems deserving of medical attention (e.g., seizure activity).

Family stability and parental expectations. If family problems exist at home, the child's attention and motivation in school will likely suffer. If there have been emotionally traumatic events (such as a move to a new school, death in the family, divorce of parents), school performance may also be affected. In the same vein, high parental expectations placed upon the child produce anxiety-provoking situations in the school setting and at home.

Parent's interpretation of the child's problem behavior. The parent's perception of the child's problem is very important. Many times a child is referred for evaluation by another professional, and the parent is not in agreement as to the presence or importance of the presenting problem. It is imperative, therefore, first to see if the problem does actually exist and, second, to determine whether the parents are motivated to help in the process of diagnosis and treatment. Investigation of this area may take more than one visit, since some parents may not actually recognize the problem and others, while recognizing the problem, are reluctant to acknowledge that it exists.

EDUCATIONAL INFORMATION

The parents can frequently provide valuable insights into previous educational problems as well as those that exist currently. Research has indicated that children ultimately diagnosed as learning-disabled exhibited signs of difficulty as preschoolers (Owen, Adams, Forrest, et al., 1971). An interview with the teacher, of course, is essential. Since the teacher, sees the child for concentrated periods of time, views him in various settings, and is able to make comparisons with peers, he or she is the primary source for information regarding academic functioning, peer relations, and the child's attitude in school. The teacher may also provide samples of the child's work, some of which may be of diagnostic significance.

MEDICAL EVALUATION

The physician is an invaluable resource to the psychologist in the evaluation and subsequent treatment of learning disorders. As was previously mentioned, the family physician or pediatrician may provide the developmental and medical history of the child. In addition, the psychologist will depend upon the physician to give the child a thorough physical examination so that the child's current medical status is detailed. The purpose of a general physical examination is to assess the organ systems and rule out medical reasons for lowered functioning, including school-related performance. A vision and hearing examination is particularly important when a learning disability is suspected. It may also be necessary to have a speech pathologist or audiologist further investigate speech and hearing problems. Presence of disease, anemia, poor nutrition, and inadequate dental care are just a few phsyical components that may affect school performance.

Neurological evaluation is an inherent facet of a complete evaluation of the central nervous system. The physician may perform a neurological screening to determine the presence of "soft" signs indicating possible neurological dysfunction. He may also recommend further neurological examinations and laboratory tests for the complete evaluation and delineation of strengths and weaknesses of the central nervous system.

DIRECT OBSERVATION OF BEHAVIOR

In some instances the psychologist will want to observe the child's behavior directly. This should be done in several settings in order to obtain a sample of behaviors in response to different situations. Observations should be made of appearance, movement, interpersonal relations, attention, and other behavioral aspects pertinent to the presenting problem.

The psychologist may also have the parent and / or teacher observe and record the child's behavior. He may create a behavior rating scale for the observation of specific behavior, or he may provide standardized behavioral scales, such as the Devereux Elementary School Behavior Rating Scale or the Devereux Child Behavior Rating Scale.

The Devereux scales are used by the teacher to compare the child with his peers regarding classroom behavior. In the Devereux Elementary School Behavior Rating Scale the child is rated on such variables as classroom disturbance, impatience, disrespect, external blame, achievement anxiety, external reliance, comprehension, inattention, irrelevant responses, creativity, and need for closeness. The Devereux Child Behavior Rating Scale is similarly divided into areas which may affect school performance, such as distractibility, body coordination, emotional and social status, anxiety, and inappropriate behaviors. It can be used by both parents and teachers.

STANDARDIZED TESTS

Characteristics and Procedures

"A psychological test is essentially an objective and standardized measure of a sample of behavior" (Anastasi, 1968). No psychological test can do more than measure behavior. Whether such behavior may serve as an indicator or predictor of other behavior may only be determined by further study. A psychological test score, therefore, is not a measure of capacity but rather an indicator of present functioning.

The purpose of obtaining a sample of behavior is to enable a comparison of a specific child with other children, thus determining if the behavior deviates from the average or normative range and by how much. Measures of this sort in the hands of an experienced examiner also enable a study of individual differences or differences in a child's pattern of strengths and weaknesses. The latter is important because it is necessary for the construction of a remediation program, which is the major purpose of standardized testing.

For a test to be a useful behavioral sample, it must be standardized, reliable, and valid. By "standardized" we mean that the test is always given under similar conditions with the same instructions and scored by the same method. In order to provide comparison, the test must initially be given to a representative sample of the type of subjects for whom the test is designed. Thus a set of norms for the test is established. Such norms not only indicate average performance, but also the varying degrees of deviation above and below the mean. This enables the evaluation of different degrees of strength and deficit.

Reliability refers to the consistency of the test. To be useful, a test must be reliable or produce relatively similar results, whether given at different times or by different examiners. By "validity" we mean that the test measures what it has been designed to measure. For example, if a test is designed to measure arithmetic abilities, it must include a representative sample of arithmetic problems appropriate for the various age groups being tested.

When a psychologist tests a child, he attempts to obtain the child's best possible performance without jumping the boundaries of standardized procedures. To do this, he must spend time building rapport with the child. If the child is uncomfortable during the testing, the examiner may not obtain the best performance, and the validity of the results becomes questionable.

The examiner must also be aware of the historical factors previously obtained from the mother, teacher, and pediatrician that might reflect on the child's performance. For example, if the child needs glasses, the examiner should be certain he is wearing them during the testing. If the child is receiving medication, the examiner must ascertain that the child is feeling his best and is appropriately alert during testing. Before a child is tested, all medical intervention should be taken care of, not only for health reasons, but also to insure the validity of the results.

Observations obtained during testing are invaluable. For example, the examiner must be able to ascertain, through observation, that the child is attentive, cooperative, and motivated to do his best.

Otherwise, the results may be invalid. Evidence of poor attitude, hyperactivity, or impulsivity is also significant because these may be typical behaviors displayed in the classroom. The results will, therefore, reflect how the child functions in the classroom, but they may not reflect the performance of which he is potentially capable. The psychologist's impressions as to the validity of the test results will assist others in interpreting the findings.

The choice of a test battery is dependent upon (1) the information required to plan an intervention program and (2) the extent to which the test is useful for the particular child. For example, the Stanford-Binet Intelligence Scale is a highly verbal test and would not adequately reflect the total functioning of a language-impaired individual. In general, more than one test is usually required in order to obtain an adequate sample of behavior and contribute to intervention planning.

There are numerous types of psychological tests available. Table 13–1 lists the most widely used tests by their major subtypes. These measures will be briefly described as to their utility in understanding the learning-disabled child.

Individual Intelligence Tests

A psychologist will frequently begin his testing program with a test of general intellectual functioning. General IQ tests serve as a basis for determining both intra- and interindividual differences and can direct the choice of further assessment measures. Some of the more widely used intelligence measures are the Wechsler intelligence scales (see Table 13-1), The Wechsler Intelligence Scale for Children—Revised (WISC-R), a major revision of the original WISC, is designed for persons 6 through 16 years of age.

The WISC-R is probably the most widely used measure of intellectual functioning. Its 12 subtests are divided into two categories, verbal and performance. In addition to verbal and performance IQs, the measure provides an overall IQ. These intelligence quotients indicate the amount by which a person deviates from the average performance of his age group. An intraindividual comparison may also be made by comparing the verbal and performance subtests for different aspects of auditory and visual processing skills. Wide discrepancies in verbal and performance areas may reflect substantial subtest variation indicative of perceptual deficits or other types of learning disorders. Table 13-2 gives the classification and ranges of the IQ scores obtained on the WISC-R. One must keep in mind, however, that the presence of an information processing dysfunction or learning prob-

Table 13-1. Psychological Tests.

Type of Test	Age Range	Description of Test
General Intelligence Tests		
Wechsler Preschool and Primary Scale of Intelligence (WPPSI) (Psychological Corporation, 1967)	4-0 to 6-6	Individually administered, providing a general IQ score, verbal, and performance IQs, and separate subtest scores enabling the comparison of skills.
Wechsler Intelligence Scale for Children (WISC), (Psychological Corporation, 1949)	5-0 to 15-0	Similar to WPPSI but for older children.
Wechsler Intelligence Scale for Children—Revised (WISC-R) (Psychological Corporation, 1974)	6-0 to 16-11	A revised version of the WISC.
Wechsler Adult Intelligence Scale (WAIS) (Psychological Corporation, 1955)	16 to 75	Upward extension of the WISC.
Stanford-Binet Intelligence Scale for Children—Revised (Houghton, Mifflin, 1960)	2-0 to 18-0	Individually administered, providing a mental age (MA) score and IQ score. Due to the heavy verbal emphasis, used most extensively with children 2-0 to 6-0 years.
Group Intelligence Tests		
Lorge-Thorndike (Houghton Mifflin, 1964)	kindergarten to twelfth grade	Usually administered by school personnel. Less reliable than individual intelligence tests.
Otis-Lenon (Harcourt Brace, Jovanovich, 1968)	kindergarten to twelfth grade	Basically same as above.
Kuhlmann-Anderson (Personnel Press, 1963)	kindergarten to twelfth grade	Basically same as above.
Intelligence Tests for the Handicapped		
Leiter International Performance Scale (C. H. Stoelting, 1948)	2-0 to 12-0	Individually administered for deaf or speech handicapped.

Table 13-1. (continued)

Type of Test	Age Range	Description of Test
Intelligence Tests for the Handicapped (continued)		
Arthur Point Performance (Form II) (Psychological Corporation, 1947)	5-0 to 15-0	Individually administered test for the language and/or hearing impaired.
Hiskey-Nebraska Test of Learning Aptitude (Marshall S. Hiskey, 1966)	3-0 to 16-0	Basically same as above.
Wechsler Intelligence Scale for Children (verbal sub-tests) (Psychological Corporation, 1949)	5-0 to 15-0	Individually administered test for the visually handicapped.
Hayes Adaptation of the Stanford-Binet (Houghton Mifflin, 1960)	2-0 to 18-0	Adaptation of Stanford-Binet for the visually impaired.
Peabody Picture Vocabulary Test (PPVT) (American Guidance Service, 1959)	2-3 to 18-5	Individually administered screening device. Can be used with language-impaired children.
Individual Achievement Tests		
Wide Range Achievement Test (Psychological Corporation, 1965)	kindergarten to college	Individually administered test of oral word reading, arithmetic, and spelling
Peabody Individual Achievement Test (PIAT) (American Guidance Service, 1970)	5-3 to 18-3	Individually administered, testing math, spelling, reading, and general information skills.
Group Achievement Tests		
California Achievement Test (California Test Bureau, 1963)	first grade to fourteenth grade	Usually administered by school personnel for screening of academic skills.
Stanford Achievement Test, (Harcourt Brace Jovanovich, 1964)	first grade to twelfth grade	Basically same as above.
Metropolitan Achievement Test, (Harcourt Brace Jovanovich, 1964)	first grade to twelfth grade	Basically same as above.

Table 13-1. (continued)

Type of Test	Age Range	Description of Test
Perceptual Tests		
IllinoisTest of Psycholinguistic Abilities (University of Illinois Press, 1968)	2-4 to 10-3	Individually administered device, assessing receptive, associative, and expressive processes.
Southern California Sensory Integration Tests (Ayers) (Western Psychological Services, 1972)	4-0 to 10-0	Individually administered, used to assess visual, tactile, and kinesthetic functioning.
Auditory Perceptual Tests		
Wepman Auditory Discrimination Test (Language Research Associates, 1958)	5-0 to 8-0	Individually administered auditory discrimination test. Requires the concept of same and different.
Goldman-Fristoe-Woodcock Test of Auditory Discrimination (American Guidance Service, 1970)	4 and over	Individually administered test of discrimination of speech sounds.
Test for Auditory Comprehension of Language (Carrow) (Learning Concepts, 1973)	3-0 to 6-11	Individually administered, used to assess auditory comprehension.
Visual Perceptual Tests		
Bender Visual Motor Gestalt Test for Children (Western Psychological Services, 1962)	5-0 to 11-0	Individually administered, test of figure copying which may also indicate organic involvement.
Developmental Test of Visual-Motor Integration (Follet Publishing, 1967)	2-0 to 15-11	Individually administered, geometric form copying.
Frostig Developmental Test of Visual Perception (Consulting Psychologist Press, 1961)	3-0 to 9-0	Individually administered, used to assess visual perception in various forms.
Slosson Drawing Coordination Test (Slosson Educational Publications, 1973)	1-0 to 12-0	Individually administered, form copying.

353

Table 13-1. (continued)

Type of Test	Age Range	Description of Test
Personality Tests		
California Test of Personality (California Test Bureau, 1953)	kindergarten to adults	Self-report inventory assessing areas such as self-reliance, sense of personal worth and social, family, and school relations.
Early School Personality Questionnaire (ESPQ) (Institute for Personality and Ability Testing, 1974)	6-0 to 8-0	Group or individually administered. Self-report measurement.
Children's Personality Questionnaire (Institute for Personality and Ability Testing, 1963)	8-0 to 12-0	Basically same as above.
Rorschach Inkblot Test (Grune & Stratton, 1960)	3 and over	Individually administered projective test, utilizing 10 ink-blot designs.
Thematic Apperception Test (TAT) (Psychological Corporation 1943)	4-0 to adult	Individually administered projective test, child responds to pictures, story construction
Children's Apperception Test (CAT) (C.P.S., 1961)	3-0 to 10-0	Similar to TAT. A series of animal or human cards available for story construction.
Symond's Picture Story Test, (Teacher's College Press, 1975)	adolescent	Personality inventory for adolescents.
Draw-A-Person (DAP), (Western Psychological Services, 1963)	5 and over	Individually administered, providing insight to self-concept. May be used as an IQ screening device.
House-Tree-Person Projective Technique (HTP) (Western Psychological Services, 1964)	3 and over	Individually administered, providing insight to self-concept and the child's perception of his environment.

Table 13-1. (continued)

Type of Test	Age Range	Descrption of Test
Developmental Scales		
Bayley Scales of Infant Development (Psychological Corporation, 1969)	0-2 to 2-6	Individually administered, providing a separate mental and psychomotor score.
Cattell Infant Intelligence Scale (Psychological Corporation, 1940)	0-2 to 2-6	Individually administered extension of the Stanford-Binet.
Gesell Developmental Schedules (Psychological Corporation, 1949)	4 weeks to 6-0	Individuall administered test of early development.
Denver Developmental Screening Test (DDST) (LADOCA Project and Publishing, 1969)	birth to 6-0	Individually administered screening measure of early development.
Vineland Social Maturity Scale (Psychological Corporation, 1953)	all ages	Administered to child or guardian, assessing competence for daily living.
Behavioral Rating Scales		
Devereux Child Behavior Rating Scale (Devereux Foundation, 1966)	preschool	Administered to parent or teacher, assesing child's self-help, social and emotional behavior.
Devereux Elementary School Behavior Rating Scale (Devereux Foundation, 1967)	school-age children	Administered to parent or teacher, assessing child's school-related behavior.
Neuropsychological Tests		
Reitan-Indiana Neuropsychological Test Battery, (Neuropsychology Laboratory, 1955)	5-0 to adult	Individually administered, used to assess the presence of brain dysfunction and various perceptual and cognitive abilities.

Table 13-2. Intelligence Classifications for the WISC-R.

I.Q.	Classification
130 and above	Very Superior
120–129	Superior
110–119	High Average
90–109	Average
80–89	Low Average
70–79	Borderline
69 and below	Mentally Deficient

lem may lower the overall IQ score, and this score will not adequately reflect the child's total functioning.

A further study of intraindividual differences may be made by examining the pattern of subtest scores. Table 13–3 lists the subtest, a brief description of each, and a list of factors delineated by Wechsler (1958) associated with each subtest.

Several means of regrouping the WISC-R subtests to assess differential functioning have been offered. Waugh and Bush (1971) have combined Bannatyne's (1968) and Money's (1962) systems in an effort to categorize the measure into various areas of functioning (see Table 13–4).

Many of the individual items within each subtest may prove helpful in evaluating learning-disabled children. For example, one subtest item asks, "What should you do when you cut your finger?" If a child responds "knife" this may be a clue or "sign" supporting the possibility of an auditory processing problem. In this case, the child may be picking up key words in the question and responding without processing the entire auditory message. Sometimes a child may need to have an item repeated frequently or may confuse one word for another.

Table 13-3. WISC Subtests – Description and Wechsler's Factors.

Subtests	Description of Subtests	Wechsler's Factors
Information	Questions are presented which may be answered by a simple stated fact.	Wealth of available information and verbal comprehension.
Comprehension	Questions deal with interpersonal relations and societal activities.	Judgment, understanding, and verbal comprehension.

Table 13-3. (continued)

Subtests	Description of Subtests	Wechsler's Factors
Arithmetic	Questions are given that require the use of arithmetical operations.	Concentration, memory, arithmetical reasoning.
Similarities	Questions require simple analogies and the concept of same.	Verbal comprehension concept formation, abstract thinking.
Vocabulary	The child is asked to define words.	Verbal comprehension and word meaning.
Digit Span (Supplementary)	The child is asked to repeat number series ranging from three to nine digits (forward and backward).	Memory and attention.
Picture Completion	The child is asked to discover the important missing part of the picture.	Visual discrimination of essential and nonessential parts.
Picture Arrangement	The child changes the position of pictures to tell a story.	Social knowledge, anticipating, planning, sequencing, and synthesizing.
Block Design	The child is asked to reproduce a design using colored blocks.	Reproduction of Abstract design, perception, synthesis and analysis.
Object Assembly	The child puts puzzle pieces together to form a recognizable object.	Visual motor coordination, perception, spatial relations, synthesis of parts.
Coding	The child matches and reproduces associated marks with appropriate shape or number.	Eye-hand coordination, speed, and manipulation of a pencil.
Mazes (Supplementary)	The child uses a pencil to draw his way through a maze.	Visual motor coordination and planning ability.

Adapted, in part, from J. M. Sattler, *Assessment of Children's Intelligence* (Philadelphia: Saunders, 1974) and K. Waugh and W. Bush, *Diagnosing Learning Disorders* (Columbus, Ohio: Merrill, 1971).

Table 13-4. A Proposed System for Categorizing the WISC Subtests.

Skill	Measured by:
Spatial	Picture completion, block design, and object assembly
Conceptual	Comprehension, similarities, and vocabulary
Perceptual organization	Block design and object assembly
Verbal comprehension	Information, comprehension, similarities, and vocabulary
Concentration	Arithmetic and digit span

Adapted from K. Waugh and W. Bush, *Diagnosing Learning Disorders* (Columbus, Ohio: Merrill, 1971).

These are all useful observations that contribute to the diagnostic evaluation.

Another widely used test of general intelligence is the Stanford-Binet Intelligence Scale for those 2 to 18 years of age. Originated in 1916, it has gone through several revisions—the latest in 1960. Some of the test items are dated; however, the scale is probably the most preferred test for ages 2 to 6 years. The Stanford-Binet is divided into age levels, with 6-month intervals for ages 2 to 5 and 1-year intervals thereafter. Each interval contains age-appropriate verbal and performance tasks. Scores obtained on the Stanford-Binet may be expressed as a mental age level (MA). This score is compared with the child's chronological age (CA), and an IQ is derived. This IQ score is interpreted in terms of levels of intellectual functioning according to a distribution similar to the one in Table 13–2. The scale is limited because of its emphasis on verbal tasks. In addition, the subtests are not classified according to various areas of functioning. An experienced examiner, however, will be able to use the Stanford-Binet profitably to analyze strengths and weaknesses.

Group Intelligence Tests

In an attempt to gain information on large groups of people quickly and economically, the group intelligence test was devised. Because these tests are not individually administered, several diagnostic features are forfeited, such as observation of the individual's motivation and attention during testing. Group intelligence tests are usually administered by school personnel and may be used to plan teaching strategies. While these tests are useful screening measures, one must recognize their limitations resulting from, as we have noted, the inability to observe the child's behavior on a one-to-one basis and the decreased reliability of the test (approximately .70 compared to .90 on the Wechsler and Binet scales). A low score on a group intelligence test indicates a need for further individual assessment and should not be viewed as an end in itself. Often, subtle learning deficits are present which contribute to IQ scores not representative of the child's true ability. The most commonly administered group intelligence tests are the Lorge-Thorndike, the Otis-Lennon, and the Kuhlmann-Anderson. Age ranges of these measures may be found in Table 13–1.

Intelligence Tests for the Handicapped

Some intelligence tests are specially designed for handicapped individuals. The Leiter International Performance Scale may be used with hearing- or language-impaired individuals. The directions are pantomimed, and the child performs the tasks nonverbally. Both the Arthur Point Performance and Hiskey-Nebraska Test of Learning Aptitude do not require speech or hearing on the part of the child. In testing blind children, the verbal scale of the Wechsler and / or the Hayes Adaptation of the Stanford-Binet may be given. The Peabody Picture Vocabulary Test is useful when testing language-deficient and physically impaired children.

Individual Achievement Tests

Individual achievement tests are utilized in determining a child's academic standing. In addition, they indicate the type of errors that occur on reading and spelling tasks. Perhaps the two most widely used measures are the Wide Range Achievement Test (WRAT) and the Peabody Individual Achievement Test (PIAT). These tests provide evaluation of math, spelling, and reading knowledge as well as give insight into information processing skills. With the WRAT, fine motor skills may be assessed through samples of handwriting. Visual and auditory processing abilities are observed through the child's performance on tests of spelling words and word pronunciation. Grade equivalents are obtained from each academic area and for the total test, thus enabling investigation of academic strengths and weaknesses. It is also possible to compare achievement scores with intellectual test performance, and thus the evaluator can attempt to assess whether the child's academic functioning is commensurate with his assessed intellectual abilities.

Group Achievement Tests

Almost all school children encounter group achievement tests several times during their academic career. The same limitations that apply to group intelligence testing are found here: inability to observe motivational factors, lowered reliability, and the need to follow a poor performance with an individual achievement measure The same positive factors apply also: time and money are saved by their use, and they provide input for directing prescriptive teaching. Group achievement tests are also a vehicle for determining the child's progress and enable the school staff to assess strengths and weaknesses in the instructional program. The California Achievement Test, the Stanford Achievement Test, and the Metropolitan Achievement Test are widely used by school districts throughout the United States.

Tests of Perceptual Skills

After evaluating the scores of the individual intelligence and achievement tests given to a particular child, the psychologist may decide that an information processing deficit may exist. To substantiate the tentative analysis, a measure explicitly designed to assess specific information processing skills can be administered.

The Illinois Test of Psycholinguistic Ability (ITPA), enables the psychologist to observe and compare several perceptual modalities. This test is designed for ages 2.4 to 10.3 years. Its scale is divided into 12 subtests. A composite of the subtest scores may be obtained in the form of a psycholinguistic composite age (PLA). The PLA is similar to the MA score on the Stanford-Binet. The PLA may also be transformed into a psycholinguistic quotient (PLQ), which is comparable in nature to an IQ score. A psycholinguistic age is obtained on each subtest as well, thus enabling an investigation of differential performance.

The subjects include auditory and visual reception, memory, and association; visual and grammatic closure; and verbal and manual expression with supplementary tests of auditory closure and sound blending. The pattern of results may be analyzed by comparing each scaled score with the mean overall performance of the child. If a difference of 10 or greater is obtained in a positive or negative direction, the subtest is considered to be significantly discrepant.

Relatively new in the field of perceptual diagnostics are the Southern California Sensory Integration Tests (Ayers, 1972), which assess sensory integration within the visual, tactile, and kinesthetic modalities. Standardized data exist on approximately 1,000 subjects with norms provided for ages 4 to 10. Ayers provides remedial suggestions with this measure. She does not maintain that her therapeutic suggestions eliminate the underlying dysfunction; rather she contends that, as a supplement to educational intervention, they help to reduce the severity of the child's perceptual deficits.

Tests of Auditory Perceptual Skills

Several measures evaluate auditory processing skills. The Wepman Auditory Discrimination Screening Test has been used with children 5 to 8 years of age to assess discrimination between 30 word pairs, different in a single phoneme (e.g., tub and tab, led and lad, etc.). The child is not able to see the examiner as these pairs are read aloud. The scores are based on the number of errors committed. Limitations of the measure include the possibility of errors due to dialectical differences and lowered reliability due to the variation of the stimulus materials resulting from the utilization of different examiners.

A measure that does not have these limitations is the Goldman-Fristoe-Woodcock Test of Auditory Discrimination, which can be used for children 4 years of age and older. A standardized prerecorded tape provides speech sounds under quiet and noisy conditions. The Carrow Test for Auditory Comprehension of language is designed to assess auditory comprehension of various linguistic categories. It is used with children of age 3 to 6.11 years and yields scores that can be expressed as age equivalents.

Tests of Visual Perceptual Skills

One of the most popular measures for assessing visual processing skills is the Bender Visual Motor Gestalt Test, which is suitable for ages 5 to 11 years. The Bender-Gestalt has wide application, ranging from personality appraisal to assessing the presence of brain damage. The test consists of geometric designs that the child copies. Errors such as rotation, distortion of design, perseveration, and poor integration of parts have diagnostic significance for the experienced clinician.

Norms are available for scoring the child's performance in terms of a visual motor age equivalent. A measure similar to the Bender-Gestalt that is applicable for ages 2 to almost 16 years is the Developmental Test of Visual Motor Integration. It measures five areas of performance: visual motor integration, visual perception, tracing, tactual kinesthetic skills, and motor skills. The results are expressed as a developmental quotient, which is reported in years and months. This instrument may be administered by the classroom teacher.

The Frostig Developmental Test of Visual Perception, appropriate for ages 3 to 9 years, may also be administered by the classroom teacher. The subtests include eye-motor coordination, figure-ground, constancy of shape, position in space, and spatial relationships and are summarized by a Perceptual Age Equivalent indicative of the child's overall processing ability. The Slosson Drawing Coordination Test, another widely used visual motor screening device, can be administered to children ages 1 to 12 years. It consists of a series of designs that the child copies in triplicate. A standard score may be obtained on this measure.

Personality and Projective Tests

Other important diagnostic scources are personality and projective tests. These tests are designed to measure behavioral and personality traits and to indicate the presence of emotional difficulties. There are two categories of personality measures—structured inventories and projective measures.

Widely used personality inventories for children include the California Test of Personality, the Early School Personality Questionnaire and the Children's Personality Questionnaire. These instruments form a profile used to analyze behavioral and personality dimensions.

Projective tests are less structured than personality tests. They are designed to allow the "projection" of the individual's attitudes, values, and perceptions into verbal responses. There is an associative measure such as the Rorschach Inkblot Test in which the child responds to an ambiguous stimulus in a manner indicative of his personality integration. Several popular constructive tests are the Thematic Apperception Test (TAT), the Children's Apperception Test (CAT), and the Symond's Picture Story Test. These measures require the child to construct a story in response to a picture. The CAT is for children 3 to 10 years of age, the TAT for children 8 and older and the Symond's for adolescents. The pictures are designed to elicit stories concerned with parental relationships, family relations, school problems, and peer interaction difficulties. Other personality measures include the Draw-A-Person and House-Tree-Person (HTP) drawing tests. The child is required to draw a human figure in both evaluations. In the HTP the child is also asked to draw a house, respresenting his home situation, and a tree, symbolizing his perceived identity and role. As with all personality measures, an interview with the child is conducted to explore the findings on these measures and to investigate problem areas.

Developmental Scales

Prevention rather than remediation is the ultimate goal of all professionals concerned with the area of learning disabilities. Therefore, the need for early detection cannot be overemphasized. There are several measures available to assess developmental progress from birth. These scales may be used to discover areas of uneven development and to monitor developmental progress. At this point in time, however, we are only able to assess current functioning. The presence of specific learning disabilities cannot be predicted from these measures. The Bayley Scales of Infant Development are appropriate for the assessment of mental and motor functioning in infants from birth to 2½ years of age. The instrument is well standardized and has adequate coverage of verbal and reasoning areas. The Bayley Scale is most useful in planning stimulation activities and allows the means of monitoring developmental progress. The Cattell Infant Intelligence Scale is applicable from 2 to 30 months and is a downward extension of the Stanford-Binet. The large number of items within each age interval and small intervals between the age levels are strong points of the test. The Gesell Developmental Schedules are used with children within the age span of 4 weeks to 6 years. The scale is divided into four major areas: motor skills, language or communication skills, adaptive behaviors, and personal-social skills.

There are several developmental screening measures that may be administered by professionals, thus providing economical use of time as well as helping to provide direction for further testing. These instruments should not be misconstrued as tests of intelligence; they are a means of recording behavior. One such measure is the Denver Developmental Screening Test (DDST), which is given to children ranging from birth to 6 years of age. Various developmental skills are assessed that fall into four categories: personal-social, fine motor, language, and gross motor. The DDST provides an indication of whether developmental delays exist and furnishes evidence of differential developmental functioning. The score may be expressed by age equivalents in each category and developmental progress assessed in relation to the child's chronological age.

The Vineland Social Maturity Scale is a developmental screening instrument appropriate for individuals from birth upward. The data may be obtained in an interview with the individual, parents, or any reliable informant having knowledge of the person's development. The scale covers eight areas of functioning: general self-help, self-help eating, self-help dressing, self-direction, occupation, communication, locomotion, and socialization. A total score or Social Quotient is obtained on this measure, and a comparison of interindividual functioning may be made with this test and the DDST.

Neuropsychological Tests

A neuropsychological evaluation assesses the presence of brain dysfunction through the observation of behavioral correlates. Most theoretical explanations of learning disabilities promote the assumption that cerebral dysfunction exists, hence the need to diagnose this defect and explore areas of intervention.

The investigations of Ward into the behavior of individuals who had suffered from brain lesions led to the development of the Reitan-Indiana Neuropsychological Battery. The primary function of the tests is not to assess knowledge but rather to discover how well the child is able to solve various problems. The subtests of the Reitan-Indiana assess concept formation, sensory-perceptual functions (tactile, auditory, and visual), which are investigated bilaterally, and tactile processing (fingertip writing perception and the recognition of forms through feeling alone).

The results of neuropsychological measures, along with IQ and academic tests, help the neuropsychologist in pinpointing or diagnosing a child's problem and the strengths and weaknesses in several functional areas. The latter will be valuable in formulating remedial techniques to alleviate the problem.

DATA INTERPRETATION

It is not a simple task to interpret psychological data, integrate the findings, and formulate tentative diagnoses. The data gathered from contributing professionals (pediatrician, speech pathologist, teacher, etc.), the parent interview, observations, and standardized tests may be analyzed by using a framework similar to the one illustrated by Zinkus (1977). Zinkus suggests a framework for the analysis of test data which includes comparing the child against a normative sample, searching for clues which suggest a particular diagnosis, and analyzing test score patterns. An analysis of the child in comparison to others in regard to his level of performance is useful in defining whether the child deviates from the norm and the degree of deviation. This information helps to determine the need for a remediation program. For example, a low math score on an achievement test indicates the need for help in this area. However, simply knowing a problem exists does not provide enough information for an adequate remediation program. Further data analysis is, therefore, required.

The pathognomonic-sign approach in data interpretation consists essentially of searching for clues or "signs" in the child's history of behavior that might help in the diagnosis of the underlying problem. For example, a teacher's complaint that "the child does not seem to remember what he is told" and "occasionally answers orally presented questions inappropriately" may be pathognomonic signs of an auditory processing dysfunction. These same behaviors may also indicate poor auditory acuity or possibly an emotional problem. While these signs provide information, as does a knowledge of the child's performance level, the data is still insufficient for the determination of a diagnosis and treatment plan.

An analysis of the test score patterns must take overall performance into account as well as the differences within and among tests. For example, a difference of 15 points or more between the verbal and performance IQs on the WISC-R, reveals strengths and weaknesses in several areas. An analysis of differences between tests is useful as well. For example, if a child cannot copy the geometric figures on the Slosson Drawing Coordination Test and yet is able to match these identical figures on the Discrimination of Forms subtest of the Stanford-Binet, this may be one indication of a visual motor integration problem or a fine motor problem rather than of a visual discrimination problem.

Despite the careful analysis of the test material by various professionals, there may still be inadequate data or a lack of agreement for the formation of a diagnosis. Due to our limited understanding of learning disabilities and assessment methods, it may be necessary at times to form diagnostic impressions rather than unequivocal diagnoses. These impressions may then lead to directions for further assessment.

REMEDIATION

The most extensive evaluation is useless if it does not lead to positive action. It is necessary, therefore, to review the resources available for the treatment of a learning-disabled child so that some type of remediation program, based on the comprehensive test results, may be initiated.

Community Resources

There are numerous resources within the community or nearby to which the evaluation team may turn for aid in providing useful information and facilities for treatment programs. Almost all state health departments sponsor clinics which offer medical, mental health, speech, hearing, and other services. Numerous private national associations can be invaluable in various ways. The United Cerebral Palsy Association, for example, provides centers for the diagnosis and treatment of cerebral-palsied children. The American Academy of Pediatrics maintains lists of health services available in various locales, as does the Association for Children with Learning Disabilities. A review of these services and of other local organizations may prove fruitful in finding the right resource for the learning-disabled child.

Preschool Programs

A preschool experience can be very worthwhile for a potential learning-disabled child. Many communities have several preschools that offer specific help in such areas as delayed development, speech and hearing problems, social/behavioral problems, and physicial handicaps. The evaluating team (or single professional) should be familiar with the services, fees, and requirements of these programs and direct their client to the one best suited to deal with his disability. In addition, the referring professional should work with the school personnel in providing the best possible remediation program for the child.

Public Schools

Recent national legislation has ruled that each state must provide appropriate education for all children, the handicapped—regardless of the type of handicap—as well as the normal child. Many professionals, however, do not agree as to what constitutes "appropriate education." Many educational theorists contend that severely handicapped children (trainable mentally retarded, blind, deaf, or suffering from other incapacitating deficits) should be assigned to small separate classes known as "self-contained" classrooms or enrolled in the special schools available for such children. However, there are numerous arguments on the question of whether the more mildly impaired child, such as the learning-disabled child, should be taught in a small, self-contained class or a regular classroom. Proponents of the self-contained placement assert that these children need the help of a specially trained teacher, more individual attention, and protection against the frustration of having to compete with normal children. Those who support keeping these children in the regular classroom, that is, "mainstreaming" the child, argue that these children suffer from being labeled and possibly teased by other children when placed in special classes. They also argue that the children in special classes will eventually become members of a competitive society and they will not have learned how to deal with the frustrations of that society. If the impaired children do remain in the regular classroom, remedial help must be available and a specific program constructed. Here the psychologist should be an active participant and help the regular classroom teacher with the formation of a remediation program.

All school districts maintain homebound programs for children with special problems. The child receiving this service may be severely handicapped, a child who is absent for long periods of time due to illness, or, in some cases, a child with severe behavioral, social, or emotional problems.

THE PSYCHOLOGIST'S ROLE

The classroom or special-education teacher accepts major responsibility for the educational treatment of a learning-disabled child. In those districts where the services of a psychologist is available to school personnel, the psychologist should provide input, first, by explaining the test results and diagnoses and, second, by offering specific suggestions for remediation.

Just as it is difficult to diagnose unequivocally a learning-disabled child, it is equally difficult to know which remediation procedures would best benefit the child. It is sometimes necessary to work from a trial-and-error approach. There are many formal and informal remediation programs available and just as many controversies sur-

368 / MARY J. SANDERS

rounding their usage. At this point, there are no universal remediation procedures which have been proven effective each time and in each case for every child. There are various procedures, however, that are behaviorally oriented and directed toward the treatment of the assessed disability. The psychologist, from his knowledge of these remediation procedures, is able to offer expertise in designing aspects of a remedial program. Consequently, the teacher and psychologist are continually able to assess the usefulness of the program and to design modifications that are deemed necessary. Follow-up of the child's progress may be the most important stage of a psychological assessment. If the child does not receive appropriate help, the psychological evaluation is really no more than an exercise in futility.

SUMMARY

The psychologist provides vital information in the evaluation, diagnosis, and treatment of the learning-disabled child. However, the psychologist is a generalist in many aspects. He must rely on other professionals, such as the pediatrician, the speech pathologist, and teacher, for input and assistance at all stages of the evaluation. Parental support, as well, is imperative for a thorough understanding of the child and for the success of any treatment plan.

The purpose of this chapter has been to provide an overview to the parent, teacher, and pediatrician regarding assessment procedures, interpretation methods, and resources available for remedial help. A definition and a brief explanation of terms commonly used to describe the functioning of a learning-disabled child have been offered. The complexity of the assessment measures have also been explored. Most importantly, the need both for close follow-up and continual evaluation of the remediation program is emphasized.

Mary J. Sanders

REFERENCES

Anastasi, A. *Psychological testing* (3rd ed.). New York: Macmillan, 1968.

Ayers, A. J. Reading—A product of sensory integrative process. In H. K. Smith (Ed.), *Perception and reading.* Newark, N.J.: International Reading Association, 1968, pp 77–83.

Ayers, A. J. *Southern California sensory integration tests.* Los Angeles: Western Psychological Service, 1972.

Bakwin, H. Reading disability in twins. *Journal of Learning Disabilities,* 1973, *6,* 439–440.

Bannatyne, A. Diagnosing learning disabilities and writing remedial prescriptions. *Journal of Learning Disabilities,* 1968, *4,* 242–249.

Barrett, T. C. Visual discrimination tasks as predictors of first-grade reading achievement. *Reading Teacher,* 1965, *18,:* 276–282.

Bryan, T. H., & Bryan, J. H. *Understanding learning disabilities.* Port Washington, N.Y.: Alfred, 1975.

Carrow, E. *Test for auditory comprehension of language.* Austin, Texas: Learning Concepts, 1973.

Fort, A. T. Mental subnormality: The result of prenatal famine. In *Contiguity and continuity in general and special education.* Boulder, Col.: Western Interstate Commission for Higher Education, 1972.

Gearheart, B. R. *Learning disabilities: Educational strategies* (2nd ed.). St. Louis: Mosby, 1977.

Graham, F. K., Matarazzo, R. G., & Caldwell, B. M. Behavioral differences between normal and traumatized newborns: II, Standardization, reliability, and validity. *Psychological Monography,* 1956, *70:* 17–33.

Hallahan, D. P., & Kaufman, J. M. *Introduction to learning disabilities— A psycho-behavioral approach.* Englewood Cliffs, N.J.: Prentice-Hall, 1976.

Johnston, R. B., & Magrab, P. R. *Developmental disorders: Assessment, treatment, education.* Baltimore: University Park Press, 1976.

Kawi A., & Pasamanick, B. Prenatal and paranatal factors in development of childhood disorders. *Monographs of the Society of Research in Child Development,* 1959, *24.*

Kenney, T. J., & Clemmons, R. L. *Behavioral pediatric and child development: A clinical handbook.* Baltimore: Williams & Wilkins, 1975.

Lerner, J. W. *Children with learning disabilities: An interdisciplinary field.* Boston: Houghton Mifflin, 1971.

Money, J. *Reading disability: Progress and research needs in dyslexia.* Baltimore: Johns Hopkins Press, 1962.

Owen, R. W., Adams, P. A., Forrest, T., et al. Learning disorders in children: Sibling studies. *Monographs of the Society for Research in Child Development,* 1971, *36.*

Reitan, R. M. Assessment of brain-behavior relationships. In P. McReynolds (Ed.), *Advances in psychological assessment* (Vol. III). San Francisco: Jossey-Bass, 1975, pp. 186–242.

Sattler, J. M. *Assessment of children's intelligence.* Philadelphia: Saunders, 1974.

Schain, R. J., Watanabe, K. Harel, S. et al. Brief postnatal fasting and brain development. *Pediatrics,* 1973, *51,* 240–250.

Scott, C. I., Jr., & Thomas, G. H. Genetic disorders associated with mental retardation: Clinic aspects. *Pediatric Clinics of North America,* 1973, *20,* 121.

Thompson, R. G., & Gottlieb, M. I. Educational jeopardy, an interdisciplinary problem: The physician's contribution. *Acta Symbolica,* 1973, *4,* 47–72.

Waugh, K., & Bush, W. *Diagnosing learning disorders.* Columbus, Ohio: Merrill, 1971.

Wechsler, D. *The measurement and appraisal of adult intelligence.* Baltimore, Williams & Wilkins.

Wechsler, D. *Wechsler intelligence scale for children—Revised: Manual.* New York: Psychological Corporation, 1974.

Wedell, K. *Learning and perceptuo-motor disabilities in children.* New York, Wiley, 1973.

Wepman, J. The modality concept. In H. K. Smith (Ed.), *Perception and reading.* Newark, N.J.: International Reading Association, 1968, pp. 1–6.

Zinkus, P. W. Understanding psychological evaluation. *Learning Disabilities: An Audio Journal for Continuing Education,* 1977, *1*(3).

TEST PUBLISHERS

American Guidance Services, Inc., Publisher's Building, Circle Pines, Minnesota 55014

California Test Bureau, Del Monte Research Park, Monterey, California 93940

C. H. Stoelting Company, 424 N. Homan Ave., Chicago, Illinois 60624

Consulting Psychologists Press, 577 College Ave., Palo Alto, California 94306

C. P. S. Inc., P.O. Box 83, Larchmont, New York 10538

Devereux Foundation, Devon Pennsylvania 19333

Follett Educational Corporation, Box 5705, Chicago, Illinois 60680

Grune & Stratton, Inc., 111 Fifth Ave., New York, New York 10003

Harcourt Brace Jovanavich, Inc., 757 Third Ave., New York, New York 10017

Houghton Mifflin Company, 2 Park St., Boston, Massachusetts 02107

Institute for Personality and Ability Testing, 1602 Coronado Drive, Champaign, Illinois 61822

LADOCA Project and Publishing Company, Denver, Colorado 80216

Language Research Associates, Box 95, Chicago, Illinois 60637

Learning Concepts, 2501 N. Lamar, Austin, Texas 78705

Marshall S. Hiskey, 5640 Baldwin, Lincoln, Nebraska 68507

Neuropsychology Laboratory, 7708 89th Place, S.E., Mercer Island, Washington 98040

Personnel Press, Inc., 20 Nassau St., Princeton, New Jersey 08540

Psychological Corporation, 316 E. 45th St., New York, New York 10017

Slosson Educational Publications, 140 Pine St., East Aurora, New York 14052

Teachers College Press, 1234 Amsterdam Ave., New York, New York 10027

University of Illinois Press, Urbana, Illinois 61801

Western Psychological Services, Dept. E, 12031 Wilshire Blvd., Los Angeles, California 90025

14

SPEECH AND LANGUAGE EVALUATION OF THE LEARNING-DISABLED CHILD

Communication is one of the most vital facets of a child's total development. Learning to communicate adequately is "essential" in our verbally oriented society. A child should have intact speech, language, and hearing abilities; a deficit in any one of these areas can contribute to a communication disorder. Language reflects the amalgamation of biological, psychological, and environmental factors and is vulnerable to the myriad of associated high-risk influences.

Speech, language, and hearing skills are fundamental processes in the acquisition of learning and communication. Lerner (1971) described language as "one of the few starting points in the educative process." The National Advisory Committee on Dyslexia and Related Reading Disorders (1969), in a reading report sponsored by the U.S. Department of Health, Education and Welfare, stresses the importance of mastering basic language prior to enrollment in an academic setting. The report emphatically states that "The child must know the language he expects to read." The rapidly increasing number of referrals of learning-disabled children from schools to speech/language pathologists for evaluation and therapy attests to the paramount importance of language in learning.

Many disciplines have contributed to a more comprehensive understanding of disorders of communication, but speech pathology is

373

in the forefront. It is the responsibility of the speech pathologist, (1) to identify and classify the problems that affect oral communication and (2) to determine the effect of language disorders on the total child. The speech / language pathologist must be knowledgeable concerning normal development and performance, cognitive processes as they relate to language, anatomical and physiological parameters, and dialectal and environmental influences on speech and language development. In addition, it is necessary to have an understanding of the various handicapping conditions that contribute to delayed development of communication skills. The speech/language pathologist who in the past functioned in isolation today must work cooperatively with other professionals in coordinating programs and comprehensive services for handicapped children.

THE EVALUATION

The diagnostic speech and language evaluation assesses the severity of the problem, attempts to determine its etiology, and recommends appropriate treatment programs. Ongoing evaluations are performed in order to determine the effectiveness of the treatment plan. The necessary diagnostic information is gathered from three sources: the case history and/or interview, clinical observations, and standardized as well as informal tests.

The Case History

The evaluation of a child to determine speech and language abilities requires comprehensive biographical and historical documentation. Case history information, as noted throughout this volume, usually includes an analysis of the chief complaint or reason for attempting to secure assistance, a chronological description of the problem, and specific data concerning general development, past medical history, behavioral, educational, and social history, and family background. Information can be obtained from the parents by direct questioning or completion of a detailed questionnaire form.

The history should be reviewed by the examiner prior to the examination of the child. With this information the examiner can more effectively analyze the child's problem and the associated contributing factors. The case history serves as a guideline for future interviews with the parents. The history, in part, helps the examiner in the selection of test instruments and additional information-collecting guides. The examiner may elect to expand on the case history by administering the Vineland Social Maturity Scale (Doll, 1946), the Verbal Language Development Scale (Mecham, 1958), and / or the Receptive-Expressive Emergent Language Scale (Bzoch & League, 1971). Additional data and insights may be obtained from others concerned about the child's development and performance, such as teachers, physicians, guidance counselors, relatives, or friends. Regardless of the methods employed in accumulating information, the case history should provide a comprehensive picture of the child to be evaluated.

Observations and Test Procedures

Speech/language pathologists have available a variety of standardized and informal assessment tools, useful in assessing the severity of a communication disorder (see Table 14–1). Formal tests sample performance in a specific area of function. During their administration the child participates in tasks presented by the examiner, and his performance is compared to the standardized norms of the instrument. The reliability and validity of the examinations are supported by statistical data. Unfortunately many behaviors are not adequately identified by these formal tests. A structured test situation may actually interfere with the spontaneity of the client. For this reason speech/language pathologists frequently depend on direct observation of the child and performance on informal test measures. This approach permits the collection of more descriptive data about the child's communicative behaviors and also corroborates or refutes findings of more formal test measures.

LANGUAGE SYSTEMS AND ASSESSMENTS

Communication is necessary for the exchange of ideas between people and may be accomplished either by verbal or nonverbal systems. It requires a "give-and-take" relationship. Language, the modality that we most commonly employ to communicate, necessitates competence in both receptive and expressive abilities. A complete study or description of a child's language abilities is based on information about certain language systems.

Phonology focuses on the sound system of language, of which a *phoneme* is the smallest unit. Phoneme utilization is important in performing written as well as oral language. The recognition, analysis,

Table 14-1. Tests for Assessing Language Behavior.

Area	Test	Age Range
Language		
Reception		
Vocabulary	Peabody Picture Vocabulary Test	2-3 to 18-5
	Full-Range Picture Vocabulary Test	2-0 to adult
Grammar/Syntax	Test for Auditory Comprehension of Language	3-0 to 7-11
	Assessment of Children's Language Comprehension	3-0 to 6-5
Expression		
Vocabulary	Vocabulary Usage Test	2-10 to 5-3
Grammar/Syntax	Carrow Elicited Language Inventory	3-0 to 6-11
Conversation	Mean Length of Utterance (MLU)	1-6 to 2-0
	Mean Length of Five Longest Responses (M5L)	1-6 to 2-0
	Number of Single Words (N1W)	1-6 to 2-0
	Developmental Sentence Score (DSS)	2-0 to 6-11
	Developmental Sentence Type (DST)	2-0 to 2-11
	Structural Complexity Score (SCS)	3-0
Reception/Expression	Illinois Test of Psycholinguistic Abilities	2-4 to 10-3
	Northwestern Syntax Screening Test	3-0 to 8-0
	Porch Index of Communicative Abilities in Children	preschool to 12-0
	Receptive-Expressive Emergent Language Scale	birth to 3-0
Developmental Scales of Language	Verbal Language Development Scale	birth to 16-0
	Utah Test of Language Development	1-6 to 14-5
	Houston Test of Language Development	birth to 3-0 (Part I)
		3 to 6 (Part II)

Category	Test	Age Range
Articulation	Goldman-Fristoe Test of Articulation	2-0 to adult
	Templin-Darley Tests of Articulation	3-0 to 8-0
	McDonald Screening Deep Test of Articulation	school age to adult
	Fisher-Logeman Test of Articulation Proficiency	all inclusive birth to adult
Oral Mechanism	Through examination of speech musculature	birth to adult
General Development	Lexington Development Scale	birth to 6-0
	Denver Developmental Screening Test	birth to 6-0
	Communicative Evaluation Chart	0-3 to 5-0
	Vineland Social Maturity Scale	birth to adult
Auditory Processing		
Discrimination	Goldman-Fristoe-Woodcock Test of Discrimination	4-0 to adult
	Wepman Auditory Discrimination Test	5-0 to 8-0
Blending	Roswell-Chall Auditory Blending Test	6-0 to 10-0
	Sound Blending Subtest (ITPA)	2-4 to 8-7
Memory/Sequencing	Digit Span subtest—WISC-R	2-0 to adult
	Stanford-Binet Intelligence Scale	2-6 to 7-0
	Repeating Digits	
	Repeating Digits Reversed	
	Memory for Sentences	
	Auditory Memory Span Test	5-0 to 8-0
	Auditory Sequential Memory Test	5-0 to 8-0
	Spatial-temporal tasks	5-0 to 8-0

Table 14-1. (continued)

Area	Test	Age Range
Auditory Acuity		
History of Hearing Acuity	Hearing Questionnaire	birth to 0-6 months
Behavioral Response to Speech	Play Audiometry, Sound Field Audiometry	birth to preschool
Threshold Measure	Pure-Tone Audiometry	2-0 to adult
Integrity of Middle Ear	Impedance Audiometry	2-0 to adult
Reading		
	Durrell Analysis of Reading Difficulty	Grades 1 to 6
	Gray Oral Reading Test	Grades 1 to 8
	Reading Recognition Subtest—PIAT	kindergarten to adult
	Reading Comprehension Subtest—PIAT	

and synthesis of phonemic elements is known as *phonics*. The verbalization of "tat" for "cat" represents a phonological (articulation) error.

The smallest meaningful unit sound is called a *morpheme*. The construction or synthesis of words from morphemes is the definition of *morphology*. Failure to use plurals, and "ungrammatical" sentences ("I goed to the circus." "I fighted with him.") suggest morphological errors.

The aspect of grammar that is concerned with the arrangement of words into meaningful sequences is called *syntax*. This subset of rules includes phrase and sentence structure and features of word order. Word inversions ("What you are eating?") are an indication of a syntactical error. The term *semantics* reflects the meaning of words, phrases, and sentences. Children exhibiting semantic errors have difficulty relating groups of words to meaningful association.

The speech/language pathologist assesses communicative abilities in order to determine the individual's development of language competence and performance. *Competence* reflects the speaker's knowledge of language and is the basis for defining a language disorder. Linguistic competence cannot be measured directly; it is estimated or inferred from the child's performance. A detailed analysis of language usage, in all areas of its development, is necessary in order to determine the severity of the disorder.

Performance is defined as the outward manifestation of competence, i.e., the actual use of language. Performance must be observed directly and is subject to variance with the situation. Variables may affect language performance to the degree that usage may *not* adequately reflect knowledge or competence. Judgments about an individual's level of competence should be withheld until expressive and receptive performance have been thoroughly and carefully investigated.

AREAS OF ASSESSMENT

Receptive Language

Language reception is a prerequisite for language expression; that is, the ability to comprehend speech is necessary before speech can be produced. One method commonly employed in measuring language maturity is to estimate the child's knowledge of word meaning, i.e., the child's vocabulary. Several formal measures assess receptive vocabulary, including the Peabody Picture Vocabulary Test

(PPVT) (Dunn, 1965) and the Full-Range Picture Vocabulary Test (Ammons & Ammons, 1958). The PPVT, appropriate for ages 2 years, 3 months to 18 years, 5 months provides an estimate of the child's single-word receptive vocabulary. A test word is verbalized by the examiner, and the subject indicates which one of four pictures best represents the stimulus word. The raw score obtained on the examination is converted to a mental age, a percentile, or an intelligence quotient. The test is limited to measuring vocabulary and is a quick method of identifying possible language problems. The Full-Range Picture Vocabulary Test essentially measures the same skills as the PPVT, evaluating receptive vocabulary in subjects 2 years of age through adulthood.

Although these examinations furnish valuable information about a child's ability to understand individual words, vocabulary assessment should include more specific tests of comprehension: What is the child's ability to understand words in connected speech or in language sequences? An evaluation answering the shortcomings of pure vocabulary tests is the Assessment of Children's Language Comprehension (ACLC) (Foster, Gidden, & Stark, 1972). This four-part examination evaluates a child's ability to process and interpret verbal sequences as well as single vocabulary words. As with the vocabulary measures, the child is asked to identify a picture that best represents the verbally presented items. The ACLC was designed for children aged 3 to 6½ years. The analysis of error patterns can provide guidelines for remediation. This test has been reported by Semmell and Wiig (1975) to be helpful in identifying language deficits in learning-disabled children. Carrow (1973) developed an inventory for assessing receptive language by the use of pictured stimuli, the Test for Auditory Comprehension of Language. Specifically, this index measures auditory comprehension of a variety of linguistic categories in children ranging from 3 to 7 years, 11 months. The raw score can be computed to yield an age equivalent and a percentile rank.

Expressive Language

Speech/language pathologists can identify some general stages and characteristics in a child's language acquisiton (Table 14–2). Language learning is hierarchial, and seems, to some extent, to follow a regular schedule. There is, however, a great deal of individual difference in the rate of acquisition of language: not all children at a particular age will be performing at the same level. Menyuk (1971) and Byrne and Shervanian (1977) are among those authors who have writ-

Table 14-2. The Acquisition of Language.

Age	General Characteristics	Vocabulary	Mean Length of Utterance	Comprehension
6 to 9 months	Syllables present, intonation	Jargon	—	Responds to speech by smiling and vocalizing
9 to 12 months	Echolalia—repetition of sounds made by self and others	First words	—	Some receptive ability, will wave "bye-bye"
12 to 18 months	Intentional use—beginning of true speech	From 1 to 20 words	1 word	Responds to simple commands, one-word phrases
18 to 24 months	Meaningful speech	Up to 300 words	2-word sentences	Comprehension exceeds production
2 to 3 years	More intelligible speech; some normal dysfluencies appear	Up to 900 words	3 to 4 words	Understands tense, basic number concepts, but does not consistently produce them.
3 to 4 years	Increased in complexity; language becoming more refined	Up to 1,500 words; increase in use of various parts of speech	4 to 8 words	Comprehends most adult language structure, more number concepts
4 to 5 years	More complete language form and structure, more abstract	Up to 2,500 words	7 + words	Knows opposites, defines words, uses "how" and "why" Questions.
5 to 6 years	Continued refinement of developing language	2500 + words	Averages 4.5 words	Displayers inner logic, abstracting, categorizing
6 to 7 years	Language more symbolic; begins to read and write	Words increase in size and complexity	Averages 6.5 words	Defines, explains, understands time, seasons, laterality
7 + years	Fluent usage	Likes to use bigger, more complex words		Understands causes/effect relationships

Adapted from N. R. Bartel, in D. Hammill and N. R. Bartel, *Teaching Children with Learning and Behavior Problems* (Boston: Allyn & Bacon, 1975).

ten about the sequence of language development. Their information has been modified and organized in tabular form (Table 14–3). Specific types of verbal production have been investigated, and measurements of a child's verbal output can be determined.

In early studies a sample of the child's spontaneous speech was the basis for evaluation of language development in the child. One of the most widely used diagnostic procedures requires analysis of a language sample, obtained during the presentation of object or pictorial stimuli. Fifty utterances are transcribed precisely as verbalized by the child, and from this a number of useful measures of verbal output can be analyzed. Darley and Moll (1960) suggested that adequate sample size varies with the language measure and that the 50 samples, though adequate for mean length of utterance (MLU), may not be sufficient for other language measures, such as the mean of five longest responses (M5L), number of single-word responses (N1W), structural complexity score (SCS), and type token ratio (TTR).

Mean length of utterance (MLU), probably the most frequently used measure of language development, has been described by Dale (1972) as possibly "the best single indicator of language development . . . at least for children of age 5 and under." Shriner and Sherman (1967) concluded from their research that "if a single measure is to be used for assessment of language development, this one would appear to be most useful among those studied." The analysis of MLU requires counting the number of words in each utterance, totaling the numbers, and dividing the number of words in the sample by 50. Brown (1973) has recently reported normative data for MLU based on the results of previous studies.

Table 14-3. Sequence of Language Development.

Average Age	Stage	Description
birth to 6 months	Infant Period	Child produces such vocalizations as coos, cries, grunts, and gasps.
6 to 9 months	Babbling Period	Child produces utterances that are acoustically similar to adult utterances and vary from one situation to another.
9 months	Jargon Period	Stress and intonation patterns begin to emerge, as well as some imitation of language-like patterns.

Table 14-3. (continued)

Average Age	Stage	Description
9 to 12 months	Quiet Period	This period marked by a decrease in vocalization. Because a transition occurs from the use of jargon to the use of whole words, changes in language habits are not immediately obvious.
1 to 2 years	Holophrastic Stage	Single words are used to represent whole phrases and the beginning of the child's vocabulary. Receptively, the child understands much of what is said to him and responds to speech by pointing or following a command. During this period the child's vocabulary grows from approximately 20 words to 200 words.
2 years	Growth in Vocabulary Development	The child now produces 2 and 3 word phrases and sentences characterized by pivot-open structure. Vocabulary increases in number from 300 words at 2 years to 1,000 words at 3 years. Phrases marked by intonational patterns.
3 years	Sentence Period	Sentences now contain grammatical features that approximate adult syntax and clearly express an idea.
3 to 5 years		The child employs varied sentence structure: functionally complete but grammatically incomplete simple sentences, compound and complex sentences.
5 years to maturity		There is now an increase in sentence length as well as in the variety of types of sentences used. Mastery of phonemes usually occurs by 8 years of age.

Davis (1937) suggested using the mean length of the five longest responses (M5L) as an indication of the child's maximum linguistic skill. This measure is computed by totaling the words in the five longest utterances and dividing by five.

For additional information regarding linguistic maturity, Davis (1937) and Templin (1957) calculated the number of one-word responses (N1W). Templin's normative data for this index reveals that the number of single-word responses decreases with age, indicating increasing language development in children.

Additional measures of expressive language functioning have been designed, including the number of different words (NDW), Templin's structural complexity score (SCS), and the type-token ratio (TTR). The Developmental Sentence Scoring (DDS) (Lee & Canter, 1971) may also be used to analyze language samples that contain at least 50 utterances. Each grammatical form is scored independently, using a weighted scoring system. Scores range from 1 (lowest) to 8 (most complex) for most of the 8 grammatical forms. Sentence scores are totaled and divided by 50 (utterances) to yield the DDS. Lee's Developmental Sentence Types (DST) (1966) is employed with children of 2 to 3 years of age to classify presentence structures according to length and form.

In addition to these informal means of assessing a child's expressive vocabulary, a variety of standardized tests are available for quantifying verbal output. Standardized evaluations include the Verbal Expression subtest of the ITPA (Kirk, McCarthy & Kirk, 1968), the Vocabulary Usage Test (Nation, 1972) and the Carrow Elicited Language Inventory (CELI) (Carrow, 1974). Nation's test, based on the Peabody Picture Vocabulary Test, may be used with children between 2 years, 10 months and 5 years, 3 months of age. This examination requires that the child name a picture presented by the examiner. The CELI utilizes sentence repetition to diagnose deficits in linguistic production.

Developmental Language

Language rating scales are useful in evaluating overall language abilities of a child. These scales enable the examiner to keep a chronological account of the onset and progressive development of a number of language milestones.

The Utah Test of Language Development (Mecham, Jex, & Jones, 1963) is a checklist which permits the examiner to chart the language development of a child in age-graded tasks. This standardized test combines the information obtained from the parent interview with information gained from direct observation of the child. Another overall measure of receptive and expressive language skills is Mecham's Verbal Language Development Scale (1958). This inventory uses the interview technique and is reported in a language-age equivalent. Crabtree (1958) developed the Houston Test of Language Development for children from birth to 6 years of age. Part One of this scale is an instrument for observing linguistic behavior characteristic of children 3 years of age and younger. Part Two, for children ranging from 3 to 6 years, assesses various abilities, such as vocabulary and sentence length. Both sections are summarized by a language-age equivalent score.

Receptive and Expressive Language

Several authors have effectively developed techniques for evaluating both receptive and expressive language abilities with a single diagnostic instrument, such as the Illinois Test of Psycholinguistic Abilities (ITPA) (Kirk, McCarthy, & Kirk, 1968). The ITPA provides information about the interactions of the auditory, visual, and motor modalities. Areas of strength and weakness can be determined following the administration of 10 subtests and 2 supplementary tests. The diagnostic profile which results may be helpful as a model for programming instruction. Details of these subtests will be described in other sections of the chapter.

Lee's Northwestern Syntax Screening Test (1969) is an effective screening instrument for receptive and expressive abilities. The test is useful for measuring the ability of children, from 3 to 8 years of age, to process, interpret, and recall syntactic structures. Bzoch and League (1971) developed an instrument for rating expressive and receptive vocabulary in youngsters from birth to age 3 years. Based on information obtained from both the parent interview and direct observation of the child, the Receptive-Expressive Emergent Language Scale (REEL) yields language quotients. Kleffner (1973) describes this evaluation as "one of the most useful language scales for children up to 3 years of age."

The Porch Index of Communicative Abilities in Children (Porch, 1974) is an assessment which may add to the understanding of global language problems. The test has gained respect as a reliable index of general communication abilities (gestural, verbal, and graphic) and describes associated behavior as well as language reception and production. The examiner is required to have 40 hours of training for valid administration of the PICAC. The examination is useful in defining the differential diagnosis, suggesting a prognosis, and providing direction for a therapeutic approach.

General Development

Defective speech, or delayed language development, may be associated with a generalized developmental or maturational lag or may appear in isolation. The recognition of a single area of maturational delay should alert the clinician to examine all areas of development. Numerous scales and checklists are available which provide "norms" of development of early motor, language, socialization, and cognitive skills. Frankenburg and Dodds (1967) standardized a developmental screening method, The Denver Developmental Screening Test (DDST), to assist in the early identification of delayed maturation in children from birth to 6 years of age. The DDST covers four functions: gross motor, language, fine motor adaptive, and personal-social skills.

Additional information about general development may be obtained from the Communicative Evaluation Chart (Anderson, Miles, & Matheny, 1953). The language items on this scale rate the integrity of the speech musculature, development of auditory acuity and perception, acquisition of vowels and consonants, and receptive and expressive language abilities. The performance tasks evaluate physical well-being, normal growth and development, motor coordination, and gross visual-motor-perceptual skills. This scale can be administered in a play situation to chidren, ages 3 months to 5 years. A language and performance age may be obtained by computing point values at each age level.

The Vineland Social Maturity Scale (Doll, 1946) is a developmental instrument which employs parental interview in order to assess six categories of maturity: self-help skills, locomotion, occupation, communication, self-direction, and socialization. The examination may be biased in that it is a parent's subjective appraisal of the child's development. The Lexington Development Scale (United Cerebral Palsy of the Bluegrass, 1974) is valuable in estimating the child's language, motor, cognitive, and personal-social abilities. The Short Form is appropriate for use with children from birth to 6 years of age. Items on the Short Form are taken directly from the more comprehensive Long Form, which may be administered to subjects ranging from birth to 6 years of age.

Articulation

Disorders of articulation (the production of speech sounds in words) most often accounts for the largest proportion of the speech clinician's case load (Weston & Leonard, 1976). Several synonyms have been used to describe this disorder: baby talk, infantile speech, lisping, delayed speech, and lalling. Each of these terms refers to the individual who is unable to produce accurately certain sounds in words. Phoneme errors can be categorized in several groups: *omissions* (a sound is completely omitted), *substitutions* (one sound used for another), and *distortions* (using unacceptable approximation of the sound). Errors of substitution and distortion are generally considered to be less severe than omission errors. A variety of examinations are available for assessing articulatory proficiency.

Normative data are often used by speech-language pathologists in the evaluation of articulation behavior. Table 14–4 summarizes the data from three research studies that show the sequence of phonome development. By reviewing these figures, one can obtain a general idea of which sounds are mastered early and which are mastered later. The primary difference between these studies is the finding of earlier ages for correct phoneme production by Prather et al., whose study is the most recent of the three cited.

The Goldman-Fristoe Test of Articulation (Goldman & Fristoe, 1969) can adequately and accurately sample the subject's speech production under several conditions, ranging from imitative (Sounds-in-Words Subtest) to conversational speech (Sounds-in-Sentences Subtest). The third subtest, (Stimulability Subtest) is designed to assess phonemes misarticulated on the previous subtests. The examination is generally used in evaluating a population from 2 years of age and older. McDonald's Screening Deep Test of Articulation (1964) permits quick observation and evaluation of the child's ability to articulate nine consonants in a variety of contexts. The test was designed to assess the effect of phonetic environment (other sounds in sequence) on the manner in which a sound is produced. Recording the errors encountered provides a phonetic profile for the child.

One of the most versatile and widely used means for measuring articulation proficiency is the Templin-Darley Tests of Articulation (Templin & Darley, 1969). This diagnostic battery uses pictures to evoke single-word productions. Also included in this 141-item inventory is the Iowa Pressure Articulation Test to assess velopharyngeal sufficiency. A Sentence Articulation Test for use with older subjects and A Screening Articulation Test are also included. The Templin-

Table 14-4. Comparison of ages at which children correctly produce specific consonant phonemes in three studies.

Phoneme	Templin* (1957)	Sander† (1972)	SICD‡ (Prather et al., 1975)
m	3	before 2	2
n	3	before 2	2
ŋ	3	2	2
p	3	before 2	2
f	3	3	2–4
h	3	before 2	2
w	3	before 2	2 to 8
j	3½	4	2 to 4
b	4	before 2	2 to 8
d	4	2	2 to 4
k	4	2	2 to 4
g	4	2	3
r	4	3	3 to 4
s	4½	3	3
ʃ	4½	4	3 to 8
tʃ	4½	4	3 to 8
t	6	2	2 to 8
l	6	3	3 to 4
v	6	4	4 +
θ	6	5	4 +
ð	7	5	4
z	7	4	4 +
ʒ	7	6	4
dʒ	7	4	4 +

*Age at which 75% of children used sound correctly in word initial, medial, final position.
†Age at which 51% of children used sound correctly in two of the three word positions.
‡Age at which 75% of children used sound correctly in two of the three word positions.

Darley Tests of Articulation is one of the few articulation batteries that supplies norms for comparison of a child's performance with a normal population.

A widely-used articulation test has been devised, the Fisher-Logemann Test of Articulation Competence (Fisher & Logemann, 1971). This examination includes linguistic components and focuses on sound production in syllables rather than positional words.

A child is usually recommended for articulation therapy on the basis of intelligibility of connected speech. Therefore, it is important to obtain a sample of "free" conversation from which the examiner can judge intelligibility under "natural" conditions. In addition, "free" conversation assists in rating the conspicuousness of a defect. In the event that a conversational sample is difficult to elicit, the examiner should listen to the child as he talks to his parents or siblings or when he is unaware that he is being observed.

Voice

In order to produce speech with all of the features of our sound system, voice is required. Communication may be compromised by any insult to the voice mechanism. Obviously, assessment of voice integrity is an important diagnostic consideration. It is the responsibility of the speech/language pathologist to recognize any deviant voice quality and provide the appropriate assessment for determining the severity of that disorder.

It has been estimated that 5 to 10 percent of the speech-handicapped have voice-related problems. Chronic hoarseness is the most common voice disorder of childhood. Results of a recent survey by Silverman and Zimmer (1975) indicate that a large percentage of school-age children exhibit chronic hoarseness.

Voice problems can be categorized into disorders of pitch, quality, and/or loudness. Organic voice disorders are characterized by a physical alteration of the laryngeal mechanism and warrant examination by a physician. Functional voice disorders occur in the absence of organic deviations.

Fluency

Stuttering is traditionally regarded as an impairment of speech fluency by interruptions. In addition to interruptions in rhythm, there may be an impairment in the rate, ptich, articulation, and facial expression of the speaker (Bloodstein, 1969). Characteristics such as repetitions, blocks, and prolongations are generally common to stutterers. Stuttering behaviors, however, may vary in affected children. In order to evaluate a disorder of stuttering, attention must be given to the stutterer's speech behavior, his own feelings about his speech, and the reaction and attitudes of listeners to his mode of speaking. Formal measures are available for use in the assessment of fluency; however, most clinicians prefer to evaluate through informal measures such as observation, description, and judgment. It can be said, therefore, that the examination should include (1) a history of the individual's problem; (2) a description of the symptoms; and (3) investigation of the person's attitudes and reactions toward the problem.

Oral Peripheral Examination

Examination of the speech mechanism is included in all diagnostic evaluations, especially when the child presents with voice and articulation disorders. Any abnormality of the oral mechanism may cause deficits in speech development. Standard inspection requires a light source, mirror, and tongue depressor. Assessment should include inspection and estimation of function of the tongue, lips, teeth, jaws, hard and soft palates. The organs of the oral cavity are examined while the child is at rest and also during articulatory maneuvers. Observations are recorded of the client's use of the articulators and their physical growth as well as oral diadochokinesia and the integrity of the velopharyngeal mechanism.

Auditory Processing

Orton (1937) was one of the first to suggest a relationship between developmental communication disorders and perceptual disturbances, emphasizing the prevalence of memory and sequencing disabilities in language-impaired children. Language disabilities frequently occur in association with auditory processing disturbances. Similarly, the child with a language disability has a high probability of manifesting an auditory perceptual disturbance. Numerous surveys (e.g., Aram & Nation, 1975; Stitt & Huntington, 1969) stress the importance of assessing auditory processing skills (attention, blending, discrimination, memory, and sequencing) in resolving the differential diagnosis of a language disability.

Learning-disabled children generally present deviant patterns of attention and experience difficulty in selecting relevant auditory stimuli. Dykman and his co-workers (1971) reported that disorders of learning may result from disorders of attention rather than from faulty perception. If the deficit is severe enough to interfere with a particular program of instruction, then training in attention may be required as the initial step in remediation. During the course of the diagnostic evaluation an assessment of attention span can be made. The examiner estimates the length of time a child can sustain attention under varying conditions of the test situation.

Sound blending refers to the ability of the child to synthesize phonemes into words. Auditory synthesis is a critical skill necessary to accomplish reading. When reading, it is sometimes necessary to "sound out" a word before it can be fully understood or integrated. A child who is deficient in phonetic skills experiences considerable difficulty in learning to hear isolated sounds and perceive them as a whole. The Roswell-Chall Auditory Blending Test (Roswell & Chall, 1963) contains 30 items and assesses the subject's ability to blend sounds into words. The Sound Blending Subtest of the ITPA more specifically measures auditory blending of phoneme sequences into meaningful and nonmeaningful units.

The ability to differentiate between various types of auditory signals is believed to be essential for normal speech and language development. Disturbances in *auditory discrimination* are manifested by difficulty in phoneme discrimination as well as discrimination of environmental sounds. Intact auditory discrimination skills are required for adequate performances with word "attack" skills and reading (Zigmond, 1969), as well as with spelling and tests of psychological ability (Rechner & Wilson, 1967). The Wepman Auditory Discrimination Test (Wepman, 1958) is one method of determining a child's ability to recognize the fine differences that exist between phonemes in the initial, medial, and final positions. The child is asked to perform a "same-different" judgement of 40 paired words. During the testing the examiner sits behind the subject so that visual cues are not given. Normative data are provided for children 5 to 8 years of age. The ability to discriminate phonemes against a quiet and noisy background can be assessed by the Goldman-Fristoe-Woodcock Test of Auditory Discrimination (Goldman, Fristoe, & Woodcock, 1970). In this picture-type test monosyllabic words are presented under controlled listening situations, and compose the Quiet and Noise subtests. While the test is designed for use with children as young as four years of age, it can also be used with adults.

Two additional auditory processing skills should be evaluated: *auditory sequencing* (the ability to recall the order of verbally presented material) and *auditory memory* (the ability to receive, store, and retrieve what is heard). Memory is all-encompassing and is critically involved in almost all mental functions. It is not surprising that deficits in auditory sequencing and serial memory are often reported in children with delayed language development and/or reading skills. To assess auditory memory, the child is challenged with a variety of nonsense syllables, individual phonemes, sentences of varying length and digits. Digit span is probably the most common method for determining a child's memory span. Children should generally be able to recall as many digits as they are years, up to 6 or 7 years of age. Formal measures for evaluating short-term digit memory include the Auditory Sequential Memory Subtest of the ITPA the Digit Span Subtest of the Stanford-Binet (Terman & Merrill, 1960) and the Auditory Sequential Memory Test (Wepman & Morency, 1973). The Stanford-Binet requires the child to repeat digits forward as well as in reversed order.

The recall of unrelated words is thought to be more closely related to language functioning than is memory for digits. Wepman and Morency (1973) recently developed a test of word recall—the Auditory Memory Span test—which is suitable for administration to children from 5 to 8 years of age. Verbatim repetition of oral sentences is required on sentence memory tests, such as the Memory for Sentences Subtest of the Stanford-Binet. Menyuk (1971) and Rodd and Braine (1971) have reported a high correlation between performance in sentence repetition and linguistic competence. Caution, however, should be exercised regarding the use of sentence repetition tasks with language-disordered children. Kleffner (1973) has reported that these language-disordered children always perform less well than "normals" on sentence repetition. An additional evaluation of recall and comprehension can be made by observation of the child's ability to store, retrieve, and perform multiple directions. The child is asked to complete a series of verbal requests in proper sequence so that both memory and sequential ordering are measured.

Auditory processing assessments also include the evaluation of performance on auditory spatial and temporal tasks. Tests analyzing the ability of these children to perceive sequential events and to reproduce temporal orders may help to explain more precisely the deficit in auditory functioning that may be impeding the learning process. Spatial and temporal abilities are measured by requiring a specific order for item recall, e.g., days of the week, months of the year, alphabet, multiplication tables, and the like.

READING

A final step in the assessment of a child's auditory processing skills is the evaluation of reading readiness. Reading proficiency requires adequate functioning in each of the auditory processing abilities. Reading is the ability to acquire meaning from the printed word. It has been described by Kavanaugh (1968) as being "parasitic" on language, that is, reading is normally learned in relationship to the auditory experiences of language. In a review of the literature concerning speech and reading difficulties, Artley (1948) commented on the existence of a relationship between speech difficulties and reading disabilities. Although investigations have not been productive in identifying the underlying variable which accounts for both adequate speech and reading, a close relationship between the two has been correlated.

Two tests which are widely used for evaluating reading achievement are the Gray Oral Reading Test (Gray, 1963) and the Durrell Analysis of Reading Difficulty (Durrell, 1937). Gray's test consists of a series of standardized reading paragraphs for individual administration. Paragraphs are scored for speed, accuracy, and comprehension. The Durrell is an individually administered measure that yields a detailed analysis of six phases of reading difficulty, including silent and oral reading, listening comprehension, word analysis, faulty pronunciation, writing, and spelling. The Peabody Individual Achievement Test (PIAT) (Dunn & Marquardt, 1970) is a comprehensive educational screening instrument and includes subtests for reading recognition and reading comprehension.

AUDITORY SCREENING

It is vital to a child's early language, cognitive, and social development to have "normal" hearing acuity during the early years of life. Studies indicate that even mild losses can have an irreversible effect on normal speech and language development and document the fact that defective auditory skills can and do contribute to educational difficulties (Ling, 1972).

To obtain information on hearing status for subjects between the ages of birth and 6 months, diagnosticians rely on parental interview, direct observation of the child, infant audiometric screening, or a combination of these methods. The purpose of a questionnaire is to determine if auditory behavior is within normal limits and if there is a need to refer for a more comprehensive evaluation. A suitable questionnaire was published by Northern and Downs in 1974.

Preschool children may require assessment by play audiometry, a procedure which involves conditioning the child to make a motor response to an audiotry stimulus.

With school-age children and adults, audiometric screening procedures commonly utilize pure tones as a gross test of hearing acuity. Downs and Northern (1974) recommend a hearing screening level of 25 decibels at frequencies of 500 to 6000 Hz. Failure of this procedure results in referral for a more comprehensive audiological evaluation, including air and bone testing at additional frequencies, assessment of speech reception and discrimination, and tympanometry.

SUMMARY

An overview has been presented of basic diagnostic processes and identification procedures used by the speech-language pathologist in the description of language behavior. The evaluation which includes case histories, interviews, and formal and informal tests measures— should provide an in-depth look at the client's problem, and identify the set of problem behaviors to be modified. On the basis of the evaluation, attempts can be made to design the most efficacious therapeutic program; such programs provided by speech-language pathologists form an important part of the comprehensive therapy for learning-disabled children.

Anne Thompson

REFERENCES

Ammons, R., & Ammons, H. *The full-range picture vocabulary test*. Missoula, Mont.: Psychological Test Specialists, 1958.

Anderson, R., Miles, M., & Matheny, P. *The communicative evaluation chart*. Cambridge, Mass.: Educational Publication Service, 1963.

Aram, D. M., & Nation, J. E. Patterns of language behavior in children with developmental language disorders. *Journal of Speech and Hearing Research*, 1975, *18*, 229–241.

Artley, A. S. A study of certain factors presumed to be associated with reading and speech difficulties. *Journal of Speech and Hearing Disorders*, 1948, *13*, 351–360.

Bartel, N. R. Assessing and remediating problems in language development. In D. Hammill & N. R. Bartel (Eds.), *Teaching children with learning and behavior problems*. Boston: Allyn & Bacon, 1975, pp. 155–201.

Bloodstein, O. *A handbook of stuttering*. Chicago: National Easter Seal Society for Crippled Children and Adults, 1969.

Brown, R. W. *A first language*. Cambridge: Harvard University Press, 1973.

Byrne, M. C., & Shervanian, C. C. *Introduction to communicative disorders*. New York: Harper and Row, 1977.

Bzoch, R., & League, R. *The receptive-expressive emergent language scale*. Gainesville, Fla.: Treepof-Life Press, 1971.

Carrow, E. *Test for auditory comprehension of language*. Austin, Texas: Learning Concepts, 1973.

Carrow, E. *Carrow elicited language inventory*. Austin Texas: Learning Concepts, 1974.

Crabtree, M. *Houston test for language development*. Houston: The Houston Texas Co., 1963.

Dale, P. S. *Language development, structure and function*. Hinsdale, Ill.: Dryden, 1972.

Darley, F. L., & Moll, K. L. Reliability of language measures and size of sample. *Journal of Speech and Hearing Disorders*, 1960, *3*, 166–173.

Davis, E. A. The development of linguistic skills in twins, singletons with siblings, and only children from age five to ten years. *Child Welfare Monograph*, 1937, *14*.

Doll, E. *The Vineland social maturity scale*. Circle Pines, Minn.: American Guidance Service, 1946.

Dunn, L. *Peabody picture vocabulary test*. Circle Pines, Minn.: American Guidance Service, 1965.

Durrell, D. D. *Durrell analysis of reading difficulty*. New York: Harcourt Brace Jovanovich, 1937.

Dykman, R. A., Ackerman, P. T., Clements, S. D., & Peters, J. E. Specific learning disabilities: An attentional deficit syndrome. In Myklebust, (Ed.), *Progress in Learning Disabilities* (Vol. II). New York: Grune & Stratton, 1971, pp. 56–93.

Fisher, H. A., & Logemann, J. A. *The Fisher-Logemann test of articulation competence*. Boston: Houghton Mifflin, 1971.

Foster, C. R., Gidden, J. J., & Stark, J. *Assessment of children's language comprehension*. Palo Alto, Calif.: Consulting Psychologist Press, 1972.

Frankenburg, W. K., & Dodds, J. B. *The Denver developmental screening test*. Denver: University of Colorado Medical Center, 1967.

Goldman, R., & Fristoe, M. *The Goldman-Fristoe test of articulation*. Circle Pines, Minn.: American Guidance Service, 1969.

Goldman, R., Fristoe, M., & Woodcock, R. W. *Goldman-Fristoe-Woodcock test of auditory discrimination*. Circle Pines, Minn.: American Guidance Service, 1970.

Gray, W. S. *The Gray oral reading test*. Indianapolis: Bobbs-Merrill, 1963.

Johnson, W., & Ammons, R. Studies in the psychology of stuttering: XVIII. The construction and application of a test of attitude toward stuttering. *Journal of Speech Disorders*, 1944, *9*, 39–49.

Kavanaugh, J. F. *Communicating by language: The reading process*. Bethesda, Md.: National Institute of Child Health and Human Development, 1968.

Kirk, S. A., McCarthy, J. J., & Kirk, W. D. *Illinois test of psycholinguistic abilities*. Urbana: University of Illinois Press, 1968.

Kleffner, F. R. *Language disorders in children.* New York, Bobbs-Merrill, 1973.

Kleffner, F. R. The direct teaching approach for children with auditory processing disabilities. *Acta Symbolica,* 1975, *6* (Part 2), 65–93.

Lee, L. Developmental sentence types: A method for comparing normal and deviant syntactic development. *Journal of Speech and Hearing Disorders,* 1966, *31,* 311–330.

Lee, L. *The Northwestern syntax screening test.* Evanston, Ill.: Northwestern University Press, 1969.

Lee. L. L., & Canter, S. Developmental sentence scoring: A clinical procedure for estimating syntactic development in children's spontaneous speech. *Journal of Speech and Hearing Disorders,* 1971, *36,* 315–337.

Lerner, J. W. *Children with learning disabilities: Theories, diagnosis, and teaching strategies.* Boston: Houghton Mifflin, 1971.

Ling, D. *Rehabilitation of cases of deafness secondary to otitis media.* In A. Glorig, K. S. Gerwin (Eds), Otitis media. Springfield, Ill.: Thomas, 1972, pp. 249–253.

McDonald, E. T. *A screening deep test of articulation.* Pittsburgh, Penn.: Stanwix, 1964.

Mecham, M. *Verbal language development scale.* Los Angeles: Western Psychological Services, 1958.

Mecham, M., Jex, J., & Jones, J. *Utah test of language development* (rev. ed.). Salt Lake City: Communication Research Association, 1967.

Menyuk, P. *The acquisition and development of language.* Englewood Cliffs, N.J.: Prentice-Hall, 1971.

Nation, J. A vocabulary usage test. *Psycholinguistic Research,* 1972, *1,* 22–31.

National Advisory Committee on Dyslexia and Related Reading Disorders. *Reading disorders in the United States.* Chicago: Developmental Learning Materials, 1969.

Northern, J. L., & Downs, M. P. *Hearing in children.* Baltimore: Williams & Wilkins, 1974.

Orton, S. T. *Reading, writing, and speech problems in children.* New York: Norton, 1937.

Porch, B. E. *Porch index of communicative abilities in children.* Palo Alto, Calif.: Consulting Psychologist Press, 1974.

Prather, E. M., Hendrick, D. L., and Kern, C. A., Articulation development in children aged two to four years. *Journal of Speech and Hearing Disorders,* 1975, *40:* 179–191.

Rechner, J., & Wilson, B. A. Relationship of speech sound discrimination and selected language skills. *Journal of Communication Disorders,* 1967, *1,* 26–30.

Riley, G. D. A stuttering severity instrument for children and adults. *Journal of Speech and Hearing Disorders,* 1972, *7,* 14–22.

Rodd, L., & Braine, M. Children's imitations of syntactic constructions as a measure of linguistic competence. *Journal of Learning and Verbal Behavior,* 1971, *10,* 430–443.

Roswell, F. G., & Chall, J. S. *Roswell-Chall auditory blending test.* New York: Essay Press, 1963.

Sander, E. When are speech sounds learned? *Journal of Speech and Hearing Disorders,* 1972, *37,* 55–63.

Semmel, E. M., & Wiig, E. H. Comparison of syntactic structures and critical verbal elements by children with learning disabilities. *Journal of Learning Disabilities,* 1975, *8,* 53–58.

Shriner, T. H., & Sherman, D. An equation for assessing language development. *Journal of Speech and Hearing Research,* 1967, *10,* 41–48.

Silverman, E., & Zimmer, C. H. Incidence of chronic hoarseness among school-age children. *Journal of Speech and Hearing Disorders,* 1975, *40,* 211–215.

Stitt, C. L., & Huntington, D. A. Some relationships among articulation, auditory abilities, and certain other variables. *Journal of Speech and Hearing Research,* 1969, *12,* 576–593.

Templin, M. *Certain language skills in children.* Minneapolis: University of Minnesota Press, 1957.

Templin, M., Darley, F. *Templin-Darley tests of articulation* (2nd ed.). Iowa City: University of Iowa Bureau of Educational Research and Service, 1969.

Terman, L. M., & Merrill, M. A. *Stanford-Binet intelligence scale.* Boston: Houghton Mifflin, 1960.

United Cerebral Palsy of the Bluegrass. *Lexington development scale.* Lexington, Ky.: Child Development Centers, 1974.

Wechsler, D. *Wechsler intelligence scale for children—Revised.* New York: Psychological Corporation, 1949.

Wepman, J. *Auditory discrimination test.* Chicago: University of Chicago, 1958.

Wepman, J., & Morency, A. *Auditory memory span test.* Los Angeles: Western Psychological Services, 1973. (a)

Wepman, J., & Morency, A. *Auditory sequential memory test.* Los Angeles: Western Psychological Services, 1973. (b)

Weston, A. J., & Leonard, L. B. *Articulation disorders; Methods of evaluation and therapy.* Lincoln, Neb.: Cliff Notes, 1976.

Wiig, E. H., & Semmel, E. M. *Language disabilities in children and adults.* Columbus, Ohio: Merrill, 1976.

Zigmond, N. K. Auditory processes in children with learning disabilities. In L. Tarnopol (Ed.), *Learning disabilities: Introduction to education and medical management.* Springfield, Ill.: Thomas, 1969, pp. 196–216.

15

EDUCATIONAL EVALUATION OF THE LEARNING-DISABLED CHILD

Special education is primarily a twentieth-century phenomenon. The area that has grown most rapidly during the past decade has been the field of learning disabilities. Educators have struggled with terminology to describe conditions that are educational in nature but may be medical in origin. It is interesting to note that Kirk's book, *Educating Exceptional Children* (1962), at one time considered to be *the* introductory book for students majoring in special education, mentions learning disabilities under the general heading of cerebral palsy.

The term "learning disabilities" developed from a medical model closely associated with emotional disturbances and mental retardation (Hallahan & Kaufman, 1976). Most early writings generally considered learning disabilities to be a product either of cerebral dysfunction or a previous experience, such as emotional disturbance (Hewitt, 1977). As has been noted throughout this volume, confusion resulted because numerous terms were used interchangeably to describe the learning-disabled child. Exceptional children were variously categorized as having "minimal brain injury," "specific learning disabilities," "psychoneurological learning disabilities," "perceptual disabilities," "reading disabilities," to cite just a few of the more than two dozen terms used by professionals in an attempt to pigeonhole children into neat categorical definitions (Hallahan & Kaufman, 1976). Each definition, however, overlooked the basic fact that some children cannot adequately read, write, or perform arithmetic.

The indiscriminate application of specific labels has probably resulted in a significant number of children being misdiagnosed and misplaced (Hammill & Bartel, 1978).

It would be well to compare Kirk's (1962) early definition of learning disability:

> A learning disability refers to a retardation, disorders, or delayed development in one or more of the processes of speech, language, reading, spelling, writing, or arithmetic resulting from a possible cerebral dysfunction and/or emotional or behavioral disturbance and not from mental retardation, sensory deprivation, or cultural or instructional factors.

with a more recent definition proposed by the National Advisory Committee on Handicapped Children and adopted by the Ninety-first Congress:

> Children with special learning disabilities exhibit a disorder in one or more of the basic psychological processes involved in understanding or in using spoken or written language. These may be manifested in disorders of listening, thinking, talking, reading, writing, spelling or arithmetic. They include conditions which have been referred to as perceptual handicaps, brain injury, minimal brain dysfunction, dyslexia, developmental aphasia, etc. They do not include learning problems which are due primarily to visual, hearing, or motor handicaps, to mental retardation, emotional disturbance, or to environmental disadvantage.

There are at least six major premises common to most definitions used today when referring to the learning-disabled (Hallahan & Kaufman, 1976):

1. Academic retardation.
2. Uneven pattern of development.
3. Central nervous system dysfunction may or may not exist.
4. Learning problems are not due to environmental disadvantage.
5. Learning problems are not due to mental retardation.
6. Learning problems are not due to emotional disturbance.

We suggest the following as a more workable educational definition:

Specific learning disability, as defined here, refers to those children of any age who demonstrate a substantial deficiency in a particular aspect of academic achievement because of perceptual or perceptual-motor handicaps, regardless of etiology or other contributing factors. The term "perceptual" as used here relates to those mental (neurological) processes through which the child acquires his basic alphabets of sounds and forms (Wepman, Cruickshank, Deutsch, et al., 1975).

This definition appears educationally sound because (1) it is noncategorical, (2) etiology is not critical, and (3) perception is used to imply that the ability to organize and interpret is important (Hallahan & Kaufman, 1976).

After reviewing possible definitions, the education specialist in the field of learning disabilities faces a basic challenge: How is a learning-disabled child to be educated? The remainder of this chapter relates to this issue. Specific suggestions for educational diagnosis are discussed.

Historically, medicine, psychology, and social work, have dominated the focus diagnosis of children with suspected learning problems. The inclusion of educational diagnostics in most clinical settings is a rather recent occurrence. The "bottom line" for the majority of referrals is the serious question of appropriate educational placement and diagnostic-prescriptive teaching. The educational specialist is a critical member of the diagnostic team. The need for professional competence is increasing as programs for the handicapped continue to grow. Significant growth in the 1980s is expected in response to state and federal mandates and through new laws and continued litigation on behalf of handicapped individuals. The rights of parents, due process proceedings, equal protection under the law are additional factors affecting the provision of comprehensive evaluation for all suspected handicapped children.

THE INTERDISCIPLINARY TEAM

Distinction must be made regarding the difference between an *inter*disciplinary team and a *multi*disciplinary team in evaluating learning-disabled children. Many groups claiming to be interdisciplinary are often a group of professionals from various fields, housed together in the same facility, each doing their "own thing." A truly interdisciplinary team, on the other hand, is comprised of several professionals who may individually communicate their individual findings, but together they arrive at recommendations which focus on the total child and his environment. Prerequisites for effectiveness are *flexibility* and the *ability to listen*. Working in this way, the team can provide continuous stimulation and a learning experience for the staff as well as multifaceted observation of the child. The educational diagnostician as a member of this team often provides working answers at the end of the evaluation process. The evaluation generally centers around several basic questions: What is the child's problem? Why and / or how did this happen? and What can be done for the child to achieve maximum potential? The nature of the questions by necessity involves some type of school or training plan. Here the educational diagnostician serves as a participant and guide.

THE EDUCATIONAL DIAGNOSTICIAN

There are certain qualifications that an educational diagnostician who will function as part of an interdisciplinary team should have: at least a master's degree in special education (preferably in a generic type program); an in-depth knowledge of developmental disabilities, mental retardation, learning disabilities, behavioral disorders, behavior modifications, and a knowledge of current legislation related to exceptional children; and teaching experience in special education, with various types of children. The specialist should be experienced in performing a wide range of educational evaluations and possess the ability to communicate these findings and recommendations in written form. Last but not least, the diagnostician should be able to work with parents.

To interact effectively with other professionals (sometimes as many as 15 in one facility) requires a broad background. It would be unrealistic to assume that the educational diagnostician can become an expert in each field (he or she would be no more expected to detect a congenital heart disorder than the physician would be expected to teach reading). The educational diagnostician, however, must be familiar with the terminology commonly used by professionals working in the areas of mental retardation and learning disabilities and have a clear understanding of their findings and recommendations. A familiarity with standardized tests used by other disciplines, and the results they yield, is imperative for meaningful communication with co-workers.

When the educational diagnostician provides information at team staff meetings concerning the educational evaluation, it should be more concise than that included in a written evaluation. It is important to report grade-level performances, areas of strength and weakness, and educational placement plans. It is not necessary to spend long hours "entertaining" fellow staff members with the phonic sounds Johnny missed and the words he could *not* spell. It is sufficient to report, for example, that the child reads on a certain level, cannot decode, has difficulty copying from book to paper, and performs written arithmetic on a particular grade level. In addition to grade levels, strengths and weaknesses in various learning modalities should be noted. Staff members who are particularly interested will often ask questions concerning more specific areas, such as reading comprehension, listening skills, ability to follow oral directions, etc.

It is essential, as already noted, to have an understanding of the findings and recommendations of all involved professions since the educational diagnostician may be one of the team members interpreting the data for the parents. Information, per se, can only be useful if it is conveyed to the appropriate people in a clear, factual, and meaningful manner.

Before the diagnostic process can begin, some expectations should be established in terms of the final goals and objectives. A realistic and practical approach: for the specialist would be to ask himself/herself "What information is necessary in order for me to make an educational appraisal of this child?" If the specialist conducts classes for exceptional children, the question to be asked is "What information is necessary in order for me to begin teaching him the first day that he enters my class?" The answer is fairly clear. The specialist must know the child's reading level (which involves both word recognition and commensurate comprehension), specific phonic skills, listening comprehension, spelling grade level, written and oral arithmetic skills, and handwriting abilities. Then an assessment must be made of the child's strengths and weaknesses in learning modalities. It is advisable for the specialist to maintain a written record of these details in order to set goals and objectives for the child and check the child's progress.

TESTING PROCEDURES

Testing is the primary vehicle by which the necessary data are collected. In education, as in other fields, there is disagreement concerning tests: which to use, which are more effective, etc. Administration of any examination is fairly simple, with enough practice. Most individuals could be taught to administer such diagnostic tests as the Gray Oral Reading Test, the Gates-McKillop Test, and the Peabody Individual Achievement test in a reasonably short period of time. (See Table 15–1 for a description of the educational tests described in this sec-

Table 15-1. Tests Used in the Diagnostic Evaluation of Educational Problems.

Tests	Abilities Measured	Publisher
Bender Visual Motor Gestalt Test (Ages 5–11)	Copying geometric figures Score: Mental age	Western Psychological Service
Daniel's Word Recognition List (Grades 1 to 8)	Word recognition in isolation Score: Percentage correct	
Detroit Tests of Learning Aptitutde (Ages 3 to 18)	Pictorial and verbal absurdities Pictorial and verbal opposites Motor Speed Auditory attention span for unrelated words Oral commissions Oral directions Social adjustment Visual attention span for objects and letters Number ability Disarranged pictures Likenesses and differences Designs Free association Score: Mental age both composite and individualized by test	Bobbs Merrill Publishing Company
Diagnostic Reading Scales (Grades 1 to 8)	Word recognition in isolation Oral and silent reading Listening comprehension Eight phonic subtests	McGraw-Hill Book Company

Test	Description	Publisher
	Auditory discrimination Score: Grade levels	Garrard Press
Dolch Basic Sight Word Test (Preprimer to Third grade)	Word recognition in isolation High-utility words with lists for each level (PP-3rd) Score: Percentage correct	
Durrell Analysis of Reading Difficulty (Grades 1 to 6)	Word recognition in isolation—both flash and analysis Oral and silent reading Listening comprehension Visual memory (two levels) Hearing sounds in words Phonic spelling Spelling test Copying from book to paper Score: Grade levels	Psychological Corporation
Gates-MacGinitie Reading Test: Readiness Skills (Grades kindergarten to 1)	Listening comprehension Auditory discrimination Visual discrimination Following oral directions Letter Recognition Visual motor coordination Auditory Blending Optional word recognition test Score: Stanine and weighted score for each subtest readiness standard score, readiness percentile score	Teachers College Press

405

Table 15-1. (continued)

Test	Abilities Measured	Publisher
Gates-MacGinitie Reading Tests (Grades 1 to 12)	Vocabulary and comprehension—(grades 1 to 3) Vocabulary, comprehension, speed—(grades 4 to 12) Score: Standard score, percentile score, grade-level score	Teachers College Press
Gates-McKillop Reading Diagnostic Test (Grades 1 to 7)	Vocabulary Oral reading Word attack Spelling Auditory discrimination Scores: Grade levels	Teachers College Press
Gray Oral Reading Test (Grades 1 to 12)	Oral reading Score: Grade Levels	Bobbs-Merrill Company, Inc.
Keymath Diagnostic Arithmetic Test (Grades 0.5 to 9.5)	14 subtests in the content application and operation areas with both auditory and visual presentation No reading required Samples of oral and written ability Score: Total grade score	American Guidance Service, Inc.
Peabody Individual Achievement Test (Grades kindergarten to 12)	5 subtests: Spelling, mathematics and reading comprehension-multiple choice	American Guidance Service, Inc.

Test	Description	Publisher
San Diego Quick Assessment List (Grades preschool to 11)	Word recognition and general information require verbal responses Score: Grade and age equivalents percentile rank, standard score	Psychological Corporation
Wide Range Achievement Test (Grades kindergarten to 12)	Word recognition in isolation using graded sight word lists Score: 80% accuracy Word recognition Arithmetic computation Spelling (in written form) Score: Standard score grade level	
Woodcock Reading Mastery Tests (Grades kindergarten to 12)	5 subtests: Letter identification Word identification in isolation Word attack Word comprehension Passage comprehension Score: Easy reading level, reading grade score, failure reading level	American Guidance Service, Inc.

407

tion.) However, test *administration* is not the name of the game! The key word is *interpretation!* A test is only as good as the person who interprets and integrates the results into a learning plan. The evaluator requires a detailed knowledge of assessing (1) oral reading errors, (2) patterns of phonic and spelling errors, and (3) particular weaknesses in arithmetic techniques. Of necessity the pragmatic approach often dictates the use of a test battery instead of an individual program tailored for the particular child. It may be comfortable and secure to give the same test to each child, regardless of age, learning ability, or degree of retardation. A competent tester has good instincts and the ability to interpret the child's strengths and weaknesses while testing. These skills are necessary in order to direct the testing session and to investigate various problems which may occur. A tester's skill in part includes enough experience with children to anticipate their moods, fears, or, perhaps, malingering. An unusually low performance in one area may indicate the need to proceed to another task, then to came back to the original problem area using an alternative test to evaluate the same skill.

To test reading, a sample of oral and silent reading is necessary, along with listening comprehension, which is considered to be an indication of reading potential (or reading expectancy level). Any one of the following batteries are satisfactory examinations, scored in the standard manner, with 75 percent comprehension required—Durrell Analysis of Reading Difficulty, Diagnostic Reading Scales, Gates-McKillop Reading Diagnostic Test, or Gray's Oral Reading Test. Each of these tests assess oral and silent reading and may be used for listening comprehension.

In addition, an evaluation of the child's ability to recognize words in isolation is necessary, not only to arrive at a grade level, but also to observe the ability to attack words. The Durrell and Diagnostic scales include a word-recognition list. Other popular word tests are the San Diego Quick Assessment List, Dolch Basic Sight Word Test, and Daniel's Word Recognition List. Unless otherwise specified 75 percent accuracy is considered competency by most educators. Word attack skills should be thoroughly examined for future teaching purposes. In this area a standardized test is *not* necessarily required, as it is far more important to learn specific skills than to obtain a grade level.

Regardless of the testing tool utilized, the required information should be obtained in this progression: ability to reproduce consonants (in isolation), consonant blends, short vowels, and digraphs. Then evaluate whether the child can blend sounds into words, beginning with consonant short vowel-consonant and progressing to blends and digraphs, application of vowel rules, and, finally, multisyllable words. Both the Woodcock Reading Mastery Test and the Gates-McKillop Diagnostic Reading Test include subtests of blending phonically regular nonsense words. Other information necessary is visual memory or words, auditory discrimination, ability to hear sounds in words, and reading rate.

The examiner should then look for patterns, strengths, inconsistencies, and weaknesses. For older children the Woodcock Reading Mastery Tests paired with the Gates-MacGinitie Reading Tests at the appropriate grade level will provide an adequate picture of word recognition, word attack, ability to give word analogies, and silent reading comprehension using the multiple-choice format.

The Detroit Tests of Learning Aptitude have been informally called the "poor man's IQ test." The subtests examine learning modalities, with tests designed for specific age levels. After testing reading and reading-related skills, the Detroit subtests dealing with auditory sequential memory, ability to follow oral directions, visual sequential memory, and verbal opposites will help complete the picture of basic learning potentials. Results are expressed in terms of mental age and, again, interpretation is of utmost importance. For example, to relate that "Sally follows oral directions at a 6-year 8-month level" is too global. To report that she can complete two-part directions for pencil-and-paper tasks within a specified time period but is unable to recall three-part directions provides the teacher with a starting point for instruction.

To assess spelling, either the Durrell Spelling List (primary or intermediate) or the Spelling Subtest of the Wide Range Achievement Test determine a grade level of functioning. Interpretation aids in instructional planning based on error pattern. Along with a handwriting sample from the spelling test, ability to copy should be assessed. The Durrell test gives norms for copying based on number of letters per minute using their reading material. Along with speed, omissions, reversals, deletions, and substitutions should be duly recorded and considered in the remedial program. It is also useful to compare these findings with results of the Bender-Gestalt test for practical purposes.

The Keymath Diagnostic Arithmetic Tests give a thorough picture of mathematical skills in the content, operation, and application areas. Consisting of fourteen subtests, the Keymath (1) evaluates the child's abilities to compute in oral and written form, (2) the method of deriving answers, and (3) the ability to apply basic techniques in situational or abstract settings. Ancillary skills assessed include usage of money making measurements, and telling time. Two advantages of this test are the elimination of a time limit and the elimination of reading for test performance.

Throughout the testing sessions the diagnostician should be aware of problems that require evaluation by other disciplines, such as speech pathology, audiology, occupational therapy, or neurology. Generally a psychological evaluation should be completed before the education evaluation. In many cases, the educational referral has come from the psychologist.

For young retarded children, the Gates-MacGinitie Reading Test, Readiness Level, gives an in-depth assessment of learning modalities. Paired with Keymath or the Numbers Subtest on the Detroit Tests of Learning Aptitude (plus some informal phonic and alphabet testing), this battery will usually be sufficient for planning a program.

PLAN OF INSTRUCTION

After information has been collected, the task is to formulate a plan for instruction. Comprehensive assessment includes talking to the parents (to determine where the child has been in school), what special instruction if any he has been receiving, and the parents perception of the child's strengths and weaknesses. If any behavioral or medical problems are known, this information can be useful in planning recommendations. Don't forget the child! Question the child about school. If he is old enough, ask, "Why are you here?" The responses will be far from standard or dull. Resist the temptation of telling results to the parents until all team members have seen the child. Avoid the embarrassment of telling the parents the child is inattentive and uncooperative only to discover the following day from the audiologist that the child has a moderate bilateral conductive hearing loss.

Test data, regardless of how detailed, are of little value unless they are analyzed and interpreted concisely and clearly in a written appraisal. Proceed to explain what the child can and cannot do. By using the behavioral approach, information will be conveyed in a meaningful and useful manner. The report should include educational history, examinations employed and scores, description of test performances, observations of strengths and weaknesses in various areas, behavioral observations, and, finally, academic recommendations regarding placement. If you stop there, the teacher reading the report will be perfectly justified in saying, "So what!" In order for the report to be useful, it must offer suggestions for remediation. List specific methods, materials, and resources for the teacher to employ in remediating specific areas. A task-oriented approach is more practical at this level rather than a process-oriented one. The diagnostician is responsible for suggesting a reading series and even a game (a useful technique for helping the child improve in areas of weaknesses) using the child's strengths to implement success. In addition, recommendations should include behavioral techniques, methods for the regular education teacher to deal with the child (if mainstreaming is involved), and ways of providing success experiences for the child. For example, consider a learning-disabled 12-year-old, reading on the second-grade level, with listening comprehension on the seventh-grade level, and receiving 2 hours of resource assistance each day. His reading problems prevent him from success in all subject areas, but if, for example, the social studies lessons are tape-recorded, enabling him to listen to the material, and tests are given orally, he will be evaluated on his knowledge of social studies, not on his inability to read. Suggestions such as this are useful along with specific remedial techniques.

After the recommendations have been formulated and the procedures reviewed with other members of the evaluating team, the parents should again be contacted. When talking with parents, it is important to remember that problems are far easier to accept if solutions are included. Relate as much specific educational information as they desire. Some parents are content with grade levels while others may want to know specific problem areas and remedial techniques. Recommendations should be as specific as possible and geared to the facilities available. If resource-room teaching is recommended, try as realistically as possible to estimate how many hours the child should remain in this setting. For a child attending a school with no remedial facilities, provide the parent with the names of two or three tutors whose work you, the specialist, are familiar with and respect. When recommending a specific special school, determine beforehand if openings are available and if the child is eligible for the school. Then provide the parents with the name and telephone number of the person in charge. The diagnostician has a professional obligation to inform the parents of their child's right to an appropriate education, as provided in Public Law 94-142.

A referral to local parents groups whose concerns are exceptional children is especially helpful for the parents who may be hearing for the first time that their child has a specific problem. These groups provide information and strength in helping cope with problems. Often at informing interviews, parents are assaulted with such a multitude of facts that it is impossible for them to assimilate all of the information at one sitting. Additional meetings should be scheduled, if possible. It is helpful to suggest that parents call if they have further questions or problems. At a stressful time, it is comforting for parents to know that someone is available to help solve problems, to provide clarification, and to lend support.

Communication with the school involved in the remediation plan (be it a child's regular school or a special one suggested by the team) depends on many factors: the parents willingness, the school's receptiveness to intervention by the team, and the schedule of the diagnostician. Ideally, the diagnostician would like to follow each child in his school, help set up his program, and in many cases teach the child. Since this is neither diplomatic nor feasible an alternate plan must be devised. Communication with the school prior to the evaluation may set the stage for follow-up. If this is not practical, the diagnostician should offer to contact the school. The parents may, in turn, relay this offer to the school. The teacher, after reading the report, has the option to contact the diagnostician. If contact is made, it will probably be because the teacher is receptive to suggestions.

Particular attention to the assessment of handicapped children has become critical in recent years because of the new laws and recent court decisions. Clearly, all professionals charged with the diagnosis and evaluation of the handicapped must realize their responsibilities to parents, teachers, community, and, above all, to the child.

Amy P. Dietrich
Wilson L. Dietrich

REFERENCES

Hallahan, D. P., & Kaufman, J. M. *Introduction to learning disabilities: A psycho-behavioral approach.* Englewood Cliffs, N.J.: Prentice-Hall, 1976.

Hammill, D. P., & Bartell, M. R. *Teaching children with learning and behavior problems.* Boston: Allyn and Bacon, Inc., 1978.

Hewett, E. M., & Forness, S. R. *Education of exceptional learners.* Boston: Allyn and Bacon, Inc., 1977.

Kirk, S. A. *Educating exceptional children.* Boston: Houghton Mifflin, 1962.

National Advisory Committee on Handicapped Children. Special Education for Handicapped Children: First Annual Report, Washington, D.C.: U.S. Department of Health, Education and Welfare, 1968.

Wepman, J. M., Cruickshank, W. M., Deutsch, C. P., et al. Learning disabilities. In N. Hobbs (Ed.), *Issues in the classification of children* (Vol. 1). San Francisco: Jossey-Bass, 1975, pp. 300–317.

APPENDIX

NAME: SMITH, CAROL
BD: 12-15-63
School: West View
Grade: Eighth
Date: 11-28-77

EDUCATIONAL EVALUATION

I RELEVANT EDUCATIONAL INFORMATION

Carol was referred for educational testing by Dr. William Jones. Past educational history reveals difficulty in school since fourth grade. She failed fourth grade but was promoted on the basis of achievement test scores. Academic performance has become progressively worse each year. At present, Carol is enrolled in eighth grade at West View. Mrs. Smith reports that Carol is failing all academic subjects. In addition to regular class instruction, she receives tutoring in order to increase her attention span. Short attention span and poor academic performance were reported as her primary difficulties.

II EDUCATIONAL TEST RESULTS

Detroit Tests of Learning Aptitude

Test	*Mental Age Score*
Verbal Opposites	14-0

413

Durrell Analysis of Reading Difficulty

Test	*Grade Level*
Word Recognition	middle sixth grade
Oral Reading Comprehension	fifth grade
Silent Reading Comprehension	fifth grade
Visual Memory	above sixth grade

Gates-MacGinitie Reading Tests, Survey E, Form I

	Speed and Accuracy		Vocabulary	Comprehension
	No. Attempted	No. Correct	No. Correct	No. Correct
Raw Score	14	11	17	21
Grade Score	7.0	6.2	5.9	4.1

Wide Range Achievement Test

Test	*Grade Score*
Spelling	7.0

KeyMath Diagnostic Arithmetic Test

Subtest	*Raw Score*	*Grade Score*	*Possible Score*
Content			
A. Numeration	19	6.1	24
B. Fractions	6	5.3	11
C. Geometry & Symbols	18	6.8	20
Operations			
D. Addition	13	6.6	15
E. Subtraction	9	4.9	14
F. Multiplication	8	6.2	11
G. Division	7	6.8	10
H. Mental Computation	8	6.1	10
I. Numerical Reasoning	6	3.4	12
Applications			
J. Word Problems	11	6.8	14
K. Missing Elements	5	4.4	7
L. Money	9	4.9	15
M. Measurement	20	5.6	27
N. Time	17	6.8	19
			209

Total Raw Score: _____ 156 _____

Grade Equivalent: _____ 5.6 _____

III INTERPRETATION OF EDUCATIONAL TEST RESULTS

A. Behavioral Observations

Carol is a delightful, cooperative young lady who worked diligently during the two-and-one half hour testing session. She attempted all tasks presented without complaint, and responded immediately to questions. Rapport was established quite easily and Carol conversed with the examiner throughout the evaluation. She discussed her academic problems in a matter of fact manner. Although she reportedly has an extremely short attention span in the regular classroom and during tutoring sessions, this was not observed during the evaluation. Carol worked for over two hours without a break. Her attention was excellent at all times. Attention difficulties in the classroom may be due to the fact that Carol is working at frustration level in eighth grade (due to her deficits in reading comprehension and basic arithmetic computation). She is also reportedly deaf in her right ear. Unless classroom seating has been arranged with her left ear nearest auditory instruction, Carol will miss a great deal of oral instruction in the classroom. Preferential seating is essential.

B. Reading and Spelling

Selected subtests appropriate for Carol's age were administered from the Durrell Analysis of Reading Difficulty and Gates-MacGinitie Reading Tests to assess reading and reading related abilities. Carol recognized words in isolation on middle sixth grade level, and decoded multisyllable words she did not immediately recognize. When she read in context, her word recognition was higher. Carol read the fifth through seventh grade oral reading selections at sixth grade speed without error. Her comprehension of material read was below this level. Carol achieved competency of 75% for the fifth grade selection but was unable to answer most questions dealing with the sixth or seventh grade passages. Free recall of material read silently was also on fifth grade level. Following the same pattern observed in oral reading, Carol had adequate understanding of the fifth grade passage but related only four facts from the sixth grade selection. In a timed silent reading test where answers were selected on a multiple choice basis, comprehension was essentially the same. Comprehension of one word, written vocabulary was commensurate. The final test given involved comprehension of material read silently with fifty-two questions. Because of Carol's intellectual level and present grade placement, the test for grades seven through nine was administered. She completed the test in twelve minutes, scoring at fourth grade level. Based on performance for several other tests, this score did not appear to be an accurate assessment of her abilities. Instructional reading level was overall on fifth grade level. This was directly related to the comprehension factor since word recognition was higher.

Tests in reading-related areas revealed good phonic skills. Carol decoded easily in context and isolation. Visual memory was assessed by allowing the student to view a series of fifteen nonsense words, one at a time, for a three second period each. After each viewing the student was required to write the word from memory. Carol performed above the ceiling score of sixth grade, making only two errors. Written spelling performance was on seventh grade level with most errors due to phonetic spelling. A screening test of expressive vocabulary was administered from the Detroit Tests of Learning Aptitude. Carol supplied antonyms for words dictated by the examiner at a fourteenyear mental age level. This was commensurate with her chronological age at the time of testing.

C. Arithmetic

The Key Math Diagnostic Arithmetic Test was administered to determine abilities in the content, operation and application of mathematics. Tests included ten oral and written subtests. Individual subtest scores ranged from middle third grade to high sixth grade and are described below by grade level.

Sixth Grade

Number sequence, rank in order, Roman numerals, decimal values, rounding off numbers.

Identification of Mathematical abbreviations and computational signs.

Written addition computation including regrouping, column addition, decimals and fractions with common denominators.

Written multiplication computation with single and double digit multipliers.

Written division computation with single digit divisors. Carol was unsure of the long division process, attempting it unsuccessfully. She correctly computed $3/8 \div 1/2$ but failed to reduce the answer to lowest terms.

Fifth Grade

Knowledge of fractional parts of the whole. This did not involve written computation.

Measurement concepts and equivalents. Carol did not know the number of inches in a yard, how to read the setting on an oven or the temperature of a healthy person.

Fourth Grade

Written subtraction computation. Carol demonstrated understanding of the renaming process but made errors when "double borrowing" or zeros were involved. An example of her errors: $62.07 - 7.9 = 55.17$.

Determining missing information in situational settings with accompanying visual clues

Money. Carol identified coins with corresponding equivalent and totaled coins but was unable to compute change.

Third Grade

Finding double missing numbers in paired equations, i.e. $2 - \Delta = 1$, $3 - \Delta = \square$. Carol successfully computed the first missing number but did not transfer that answer to determine the final answer.

Total grade score was 5.6, middle fifth grade. Computational skills in all areas except subtraction were above fifth grade level. Carol did not solve addition, subtraction or multiplication problems involving mixed numbers due to her inability to find the common denominator.

IV EDUCATIONAL SUMMARY AND RECOMMENDATIONS

Carol, a fourteen year-one month-old girl functioning within the average intellectual range, is currently enrolled in eighth grade at West View. In addition to the regular classroom instruction, she receives tutoring to increase her attention span. Results of the educational evaluation indicated academic achievement levels to be fifth grade in reading and arithmetic, seventh grade in spelling. Recommendation is made to initiate academically based tutoring in the following areas:

1. Reading comprehension and study skills.
2. Arithmetic computation including renaming in subtraction, finding common denominators, review of basic multiplica-

tion facts, division with double digit divisors, and counting change.

3. Preferential seating in the classroom with left ear nearest oral instruction.

Reading instruction is needed to raise comprehension level. Carol recognizes words in isolation on sixth grade level and higher when reading in context. Instruction in comprehension and study skills should be as pragmatic as possible. A sample of Carol's oral word recognition may be taken using one of her eighth grade texts. If she scores 90% or above, counting errors in the standard manner for an IRI, the text may be used to improve comprehension. In this way, comprehension instruction is provided along with reinforcement of material presented in the regular classroom setting. The SQ3R Method (Francis Robinson) or The Manzo Method would be applicable for improvement of study skills. A Xerox copy of these methods is included with the report. In addition, some routine comprehension exercises would be helpful on a bi-weekly basis using such commercial materials as *Using the Context,* E; *Getting the Facts,* E; and *Getting the Main Idea,* E; in the Specific Skills Series (Barnell-Loft); and *Reading for Concepts,* E (Webster Division, McGraw-Hill); *Standard Test Lessons in Reading,* E (McCrae & Crabb). This reinforcement activity should be at sixth grade level, to enable Carol to achieve success while perfecting her skills in reading for meaning. Outlining would also be useful to reinforce relevant facts. If the classroom textbooks prove too difficult, drop down one grade level using the same study skill methods. Carol's phonic skills and good visual memory should be utilized in presentation and reinforcement of new words. Vocabulary words should be presented first in context, later in isolation if that type of reinforcement is necessary.

Arithmetic instruction should be developmental and remedial in nature. Multiplication facts may be improved by daily completion of facts sheets, beginning with multipliers of six. Competency requirement of fifty correct responses per minute should be required before moving to the sevens. Subtraction with triple digit numbers will probably need only a review, talking out the problem, and marking out numbers for double borrowing. When Carol can verbalize the process for a one week period, written reinforcement for a brief period will be necessary. The majority of time should be spent on division with double digit divisors, then finding common denominators. Be sure to remain with the first concept until Carol consistently computes problems correctly. Then require completion of one problem each day on the blackboard before resuming instruction in common denominators. Either the Houghton-Mifflin *Modern School Mathematics* Series V or the Ginn *Essential Modern Mathematics* D would be applicable for instruction. While counting change is not a skill assessed in school at this point, Carol will need this ability to function in everyday life. *The DLM Moving Up In Money* series may be used on a short-term daily basis. If this is not available, practical experience is suggested. This may include management of her own money through an allowance and assuming purchasing responsibilities for her parents (initially under their supervision).

Carol's attention should improve when instruction moves from frustration to functioning level. If this remains a problem for the tutor, a systematic behavior approach should be taken. Baseline should be recorded for a week to determine an average length of attending. Carol should subsequently be rewarded before frustration is reached by either a check mark or token, to be redeemed later for a tangible reward of her choice. Attention may be graphed to record improvement. As attention improves, the required time span for reward will be increased. This should be included in an academically based tutoring period. Incorporation of academic instruction with increasing attention span will make the task relevant to Carol and shorten time needed to complete tasks while focusing on academic improvement in problem areas.

INDEX